FLETCHER, BEAUMONT

& Company

FLETCHER, BEAUMONT

& Company

Entertainers to the Jacobean Gentry

LAWRENCE B. WALLIS

1968
OCTAGON BOOKS, INC.
New York

Reprinted 1968
by special arrangement with Mrs. Lawrence B. Wallis

OCTAGON BOOKS, INC.
175 FIFTH AVENUE
NEW YORK, N. Y. 10010

LIBRARY OF CONGRESS CATALOG CARD NUMBER: 68-22292

Printed in U.S.A. by
NOBLE OFFSET PRINTERS, INC.
NEW YORK 3, N. Y.

To

OSCAR JAMES CAMPBELL

MARIANNE BROCK

LOUISE WOTHERSPOON WALLIS

Preface

THIS book has evolved from the idea of re-examining Stuart tragi-comedy. Since the body of plays popularly known as "The Works of Beaumont and Fletcher" is at the center of such a study, it was clear from the beginning that a careful perusal of the tragicomedies in this corpus—and of the tragedies as well—came first. Then, as I read through the whole body of the plays, studying at the same time much of the twentieth century criticism of Fletcher, Beaumont and Massinger, I was slowly deflected from my original purpose. A point of irritation had been set up in my mind by the differences between my own reactions to the plays I was reading and certain opinions about them which I found in recent criticism.

The suspicion that these opinions might be conventional reflections of earlier attitudes set me to tracing back through the centuries the reputation of "Beaumont and Fletcher." As I amassed all the critical materials which I could locate, the projected book on Stuart tragicomedy gradually yielded place to a study of Fletcher, Beaumont and Company, with the growth of whose reputation I was becoming familiar.

In a number of instances my suspicion about modern opinions of these playwrights proved to be justified. I therefore came to believe that there existed a need for a re-interpretation of "Beaumont and Fletcher" which would be solidly based upon a widely representative and, at the same time, critical survey of their reputation from Stuart times to the present. It seemed probable that such a history of the attitudes towards these play-wrights would reveal the weaknesses in certain present day opinions about them which derive from the past, and would thus, at various points, clarify or even make valid, this re-interpretation. At the same time the survey might well fill an existing gap in the history of the repu-tations of the Elizabethan-Stuart playwrights—and thus have an addi-tional usefulness for readers of Jacobean drama.

Several years before I began this study, when trying to make clear to college classes why *Hamlet* is actually superior to *The Maid's Tragedy*, I had learned that modern young readers might still succumb to the deft craftsmanship of Beaumont and Fletcher. So I had analyzed with them certain portions of the latter play in order to bring out what I have since named its "emotional patterning." In doing so, I had found that I could make students understand the means by which the drama's plausible smoothness and artistry had deceived them. More recently, while making an analysis of the Commendatory Verses printed in the First Folio of 1647, I became aware that certain of the authors of these eulogies appreciated the emotional intent of the "Beaumont and Fletcher" plays— and that they had obviously seen them performed by the King's Men. Here, then, appeared to be a clue to the actual dramatic aims and methods of these playwrights.

By the time a leave of absence from my teaching duties finally permitted me to settle down to the writing of this book, I had acquired the further conviction that a modern tendency to under-estimate and even to villify Fletcher decidedly needed to be offset, and his importance among the collaborators insisted upon. I had come to believe that he was the innovating master craftsman of this group of dramatists, however great the abilities of the sometimes over-praised Beaumont. Furthermore, I had concluded that the most valuable approach to these playwrights would be to look at them as the practical men of the theatre that they were rather than as great dramatic poets—even if that led to understressing their indubitable poetic gifts. These opinions and convictions have only been strengthened during nearly a year of writing.

This book has, accordingly, developed into two complementary sections, which depend upon each other for completion. The four chapters of Part One attempt to give a full-bodied, critical, and yet not unwieldy history of the reputation of "Beaumont and Fletcher" from Stuart times until nearly the present day. Although the survey aims to be balanced and just—and, I hope, in due measure entertaining—certain issues of special importance to the re-interpretation receive particular attention, and a critical approach that will later be more explicitly developed can be detected. At points in the first chapter of Part One, a brief bird's-eye view of the career of the plays on the seventeenth century stage has been included; and an account of their decline on the boards since 1700 forms the substance of the Appendix. For this career, especially in its earliest phases, had a definite influence upon the development of the "Beaumont and Fletcher" reputation.

The three chapters of Part Two re-interpret the playwrights in terms of their social, educational and theatrical milieu, their early experiences in playwriting, their manner of collaboration, and the basic elements of their dramatic method. These chapters take for granted the background supplied by Part One, and frequently rely upon the reader's knowledge of it to give ballast to the matters now under discussion. Recent criticism notably significant for the re-appraisal is woven into these chapters. A reader who expects to be particularly interested in a new interpretation of Fletcher, Beaumont and Company may, if he so chooses, read Part Two first. In that case, however, he may well judge that the house of criticism was erected, in part, on a shaky foundation—unless he is willing to accept on faith the assumption that firm underpinnings were set in place in Part One.

The unorthodox double structure of the book thus has a double purpose: (1) that of scraping away some of the barnacles of more than three centuries of criticism, so that (2) the work of Fletcher and Beaumont (and other collaborators) can more convincingly be shown to be the natural product of their milieu, dramatic aims and craftsmanship. The criticism of past ages sometimes illuminates but as often obscures this approach, and the obscurity needs to be dissipated, that the light may shine more clearly.

The thesis of the book is that Fletcher, Beaumont and Company can be most wisely understood, and appreciated, if regarded above all as entertainers to the gentry of their day. It takes exception to the long-continued tendency—traced in Part One—to adjudge their theatrical methods and attainments as though their dramas gave primary emphasis to action characterization and poetry. Instead, it finds the structure and treatment of their plays to be controlled by "emotional form,"—a phrase whose meaning should become fully clear in the final chapter.

When "Beaumont and Fletcher" criticism, the milieu of the playwrights, their response to it, and the plays themselves, have been linked together, it becomes evident that Fletcher, Beaumont and Company had no other significant aim than entertainment. They had no serious philosophy of life to offer; no profound interpretation of human nature to give; no deep political, social or poetic insight to reveal. They sought to devise plays which would grip, move, startle, surprise and amuse the audience for whom they wrote, and they developed their theatrecraft to this end. Seen in this light, their craftsmanship not only has a measure of originality but is, in its kind, also admirably skilful and artistic. As Professor Krutch has pointed out to me, these playwrights might be regarded as remote Jacobean ancestors of those nineteenth century dramatists who developed the "well-made play."

When the dramatic method of Fletcher and his collaborators is understood, much of the moral reprobation that their plays have had to endure will be seen to be irrelevant. For it is a misunderstanding of the nature of these plays, quite as much as a puritanic tendency in criticism of the past two hundred years, which has underlain most of the charges of pandering to audiences and of immorality. There is, therefore, an element of confused thinking in the practice of blaming Fletcher and, in lesser degree, Beaumont for the decline of Stuart drama—often stigmatized as "decadence."

Although these playwrights, responding to theatrical demand, simply reflected the standards of speech and behavior current among gentlefolk of their day, they were by no means the first writers for the playhouses to do so. The causes of the Jacobean decline did not originate with Fletcher and Company but must be sought partly earlier and partly in different areas. An important one was the failure of other dramatic geniuses approaching Shakespeare's stature to emerge. Other causes will be suggested later.

One mistake that has done much harm to the reputation of Fletcher, Beaumont and Company has been the tendency to measure the theatrical methods and attainments of these expert craftsmen by the supreme dramatic genius of Shakespeare. Doubtless this tendency was inevitable, since our playwrights appear to have been held in higher esteem than England's greatest dramatist for more than a generation, or, roughly, from the 1630's to the 1670's. But their plays are not fabricated in exactly the same ways as Shakespeare's and, in my opinion, should not be judged as though they were, or should have been. In their own lesser kind, they often have high aesthetic quality. The spell of the Coleridgean tradition in the criticism of "Beaumont and Fletcher" should, in this as in other respects, be broken.

Some readers may feel that the following pages do not do full justice to Beaumont. I harbor, however, neither open or concealed dislike for this brilliant colleague and attractive comrade of Fletcher; I have simply been concerned to right the balance, as I have conceived it, between the two men. Massinger has figured less largely in this book than I had originally intended. But the minor attention given him in criticism of "Beaumont and Fletcher" has come to seem not altogether unfair. Fletcher was the master, Massinger the pupil—or perhaps better, the junior partner—and, later, the reviser. In joint work, he tended to reflect his master's theatre-craft, in a somewhat less lively way. The dramas written by him alone did not come within the scope of this book, nor did a full separate study of his achievement in collaboration, however interesting that might prove. As for the other helpers in Fletcher's "studio," their contributions were of miniscule importance to the purpose of the book.

My task of re-interpretation has been considerably lightened by the able recent work of such critics as Miss U. M. Ellis-Fermor, Professors

Oscar James Campbell and Arthur Mizener, and Dr. Eugene M. Waith. It was, for instance, encouraging to discover that Professor Mizener and I, independently, had reached very similar conclusions about the emotional form of the Fletcher, Beaumont and Company plays. The points of view which these four critics have, in different connections, expressed, have been particularly stimulating and confirming. I have endeavored to indicate, in the body of the book, my indebtedness to their writings.

It is a pleasure to acknowledge indebtedness, even though words are inadequate to express one's gratitude for help received. I wish to thank the staffs of the Columbia University and Mount Holyoke College libraries—and especially my friend and former graduate student, Mrs. Marion Marsh Randall—for many courtesies and much assistance; those various other libraries to which, through inter-library loans, I have been a ghostly visitant; and Mount Holyoke College, through the kind offices of President Roswell G. Ham, whereby a leave of absence and other aid made the writing of this book possible.

My friend, Mr. James E. Elson, tactfully assisted at the inception of the book during many a pleasant dinner in New York, several years ago. My colleague, Professor Dorothy Foster, who painstakingly proof-read the chapters after they were drafted, has contributed, with characteristically cordial interest, from her abundant knowledge of Shakespeare and other Elizabethan dramatists. Professor Charlotte D'Evelyn has not only considerately removed practical obstacles to the carrying out of this project but has also generously given me, in the reading of proof, the benefit of her accurate and scholarly knowledge. The pertinent criticisms of Professor Joseph Wood Krutch and Dr. Henry E. Wells on the manuscript have been signally helpful in revealing weaknesses, and in suggesting improvements, in the various chapters.

There are three individuals to whom I gladly acknowledge special indebtedness. Professor Oscar James Campbell deepened my interest in Shakespeare and aroused it in "comicall satyre." He has followed every phase of this book's progress with gracious encouragement, wise and inspiriting counsel, shrewd criticism, and a comprehending skill in saying the right word at the right time. My colleague, Professor Marianne Brock, herself the able editor of *The Knight of Malta* (her Bryn Mawr College doctoral dissertation), has shared my enthusiasm for a re-examination of Fletcher, Beaumont and Company, and has been a ready help in moments of difficulty. I have first tested out many of my ideas with her; and some of her own, I feel certain, have now made their unacknowledged way into the book. My wife, Louise W. Wallis, Director of the Laboratory Theatre at Mount Holyoke College, needs no recounting of what the book owes to her staunch support over the years; words utterly fail at this point.

To these three, who have practised the Renaissance virtue of friendship so abundantly, this book is dedicated. Be its imperfections on my own head!

South Hadley, Massachusetts

Contents

PART 1

Decline of a Reputation

CHAPTER ONE

One of the Triumvirate

IN the opinion of the Stuart world of the mid-seventeenth century, "Beaumont and Fletcher" were the twin stars, the Castor and Pollux,[1] in the shining galaxy of English playwrights. Their only rivals were Shakespeare and Jonson. The latter was normally considered the leading English playwright,[2] but there were those who held that even the twins outshone Shakespeare.[3] Gentlemen by birth, and writing with both eyes on their Blackfriars Theatre audience, they cared mainly about holding their spectators by whatever theatrical means and formulas they found effective. Expert and light-handed play carpenters, they succeeded brilliantly in entertaining the Stuart gentry. Verily, they had their reward, in commercial success and in Cavalier esteem.

Today their lustre has tarnished, and their glory largely departed. Towards the end of the Restoration era, Shakespeare began to forge ahead of them. The decline of their reputation passed through various stages, reflecting the apathy or interest, critical prepossessions and knowledge of successive ages; but the end result has been a sharp downward revision, in which Beaumont usually fares rather better than Fletcher and the latter's other collaborators.

It is easy to assume that the Stuart enthusiasts for the Beaumont and Fletcher corpus of plays were writing with their tongues somewhat in their cheeks, were incompetent critics, or lacked perspective. No doubt these assumptions have varying degrees of truth in them. But it may equally be that the critical viewpoint of the Stuarts, so different from the modern, offers some corrective to our own, especially if we are to envision the achievement of this group of collaborators as practical playwrights, writing in a definite milieu with high technical competence for a definite theatre and audience. And likewise, through considering the decline of the critical reputation of these plays, the past may be found to throw useful light on present day critical attitudes, and to give points of departure for a revaluation of Fletcher, Beaumont and Company. This

chapter and the three which follow will therefore examine, selectively
rather than exhaustively, the reputation of this body of plays as it has
unfolded during the past three centuries.

I

One of the oddities in the history of Beaumont and Fletcher criticism
is the long-standing confusion about the actual authorship of many of
the dramas. It arose almost at once, and has lingered on, like a dense
cloud, nearly to our own day. Nor is critical opinion even yet in entire
agreement on the authorship of some of the plays, to say nothing of individual scenes. For the purposes of this book, however, problems in authorship have been sufficiently clarified, and will chiefly concern us as an
historical phenomenon.

How soon the confusion arose is demonstrated by John Earle, who
penned his verse tribute to Beaumont shortly after that playwright's
death in 1616. Earle distinguished as Beaumont's three dramas, including
A King and No King, without recognizing Fletcher's shares in them. Referring back to Plautus and Aristophanes, he said:

> Alas, what flegme are they, compared to thee,
> In thy *Philaster*, and *Maids-Tragedy*?
> Where's such an humour as thy Bessus?[4]

The confusion was worse confounded by the time the First Folio of
1647, containing 34 plays and Beaumont's masque,[5] was published. Even
the "Beaumont and Fletcher" of the book's title, conventional thereafter,
demonstrates this. Of the 34 plays, none of which had been printed before, Fletcher is now generally conceded to be sole or part author of all
but two; and it is not completely certain that he had nothing to do even
with these twain. Massinger collaborated with Fletcher on a round
dozen,[6] and may have done so on at least two more.[7] Harbage[8] also lists
The Laws of Candy as by Massinger, assigns to him *Love's Cure, or The
Martial Maid*—with Webster and Dekker as possible co-writers—and indicates that both plays may have been revised Beaumont and Fletcher origi-
nals. Oliphant[9] concludes that Ford is the author of the former, though
he finds traces of Fletcher; he hesitantly assigns the latter to Beaumont,
Massinger and Jonson—a curious partnership if true.

Beaumont is much less often present in these 34 dramas. Harbage lists
him as certainly a collaborator in only two: *The Coxcomb* and *Four
Plays in One;* but Oliphant disagrees about the latter play, assigning it
solely to Fletcher and Field.[10] Harbage lists Beaumont's questionable

hand in only three other dramas,[11] while Oliphant considers him co-author in four further plays,[12] including *Love's Cure,* mentioned above. Thus Beaumont, in addition to a share in *The Coxcomb,* with more or less dubiousness may have collaborated, at most, in eight other of these pieces. Even Nathan Field, a minor co-author, arouses less disagreement; he is thought, with much assurance, to have had a hand in four of the 34.[13]

Surely a more descriptive title for the First Folio would have been "Fletcher, Massinger and Company." So far as mere quantity goes, Massinger out-collaborated Beaumont, even when the remaining plays of the "Beaumont and Fletcher" canon are added. Yet he managed to get well obscured in the authorship fog until rescued by modern researchers engaged in untwisting the knotty skeins of collaboration by various well chosen methods. The one truth to which the Beaumont and Fletcher attribution does point is the superiority of Beaumont over Massinger as co-author with Fletcher. But this can scarcely be demonstrated from the First Folio plays.

How uncertainty as to authorship arose is clear enough. Practices of the Jacobean theatre, now well understood, account for much of it. A play ceased to be the author's private property as soon as purchased by an acting company. It existed for the theatre, not the arm chair. It could be revised at intervals, with or without the author's consent and labor; original authorship might, in fact, become blurred. Sometimes plays, when thoroughly made over, were presented in the name of the reviser—as appears to have been the case with Shakespeare's *Hamlet.* For reasons of money need by the playwrights or pressing demands for quick work on new plays from the players, collaboration was frequent. Perhaps for both reasons, Fletcher was a perennial collaborator—remarkably so for a playwright of his prominence. Oliphant and Harbage agree that only 16 of the Beaumont and Fletcher corpus are pure Fletcher;[14] he seems to have worked with others on a generous two thirds of the pieces in which he can be detected. Hence, when at last a play came to be printed, as some did when "pirated" or no longer important in a repertory, mistakes in attribution might easily be made. And a playwright not so much concerned as was Ben Jonson about printing his "Works" might not bother about correcting such mistakes. Sufficient the plaudits of the theatre.

In the instance of the plays of the 1647 Folio, there were special circumstances as well. The first "smash hits" of our group of playwrights were the joint work of Beaumont and Fletcher. As Earle's lines suggest, Beaumont established a high reputation for himself during the few years he was writing for the stage. Then, in 1613, he married and, apparently, retired to his country estate. Fletcher, however, continued to turn out

plays, chiefly for the King's Men—wholly for them after 1616[15]—until his
death by plague in 1625. His success in entertaining the Jacobean gentry
resulted in his being the more vividly remembered of the two in Caroline
days, as the preponderance of tributes to him among the First Folio
Commendatory Verses shows.[16] But the linking of Beaumont's name with
his, strikingly established in the years 1609 to 1613, also persisted.

Curiously, Massinger drops out. It is easy to see why Field and other
minor helpers were not remembered, but Massinger's plight is, perhaps,
more puzzling. That his relationship with Fletcher had been close and
friendly is clear from the epitaph which Sir Aston Cockaine wrote on
them, to this effect:

> In the same grave Fletcher was buried here
> Lies the State Poet Philip Massinger;
> Plays they did write together, were great friends
> And now one grave includes them in their ends:
> So whom on earth nothing did part beneath
> Here in their fames they lie in spight of death.[17]

Had either playwright been living in 1646, the injustice to Massinger
might not, perhaps, have occurred.

Massinger left the King's Men in 1623, but after Fletcher's death he
returned to them, and wrote for them until his own demise in 1640. The
King's Men must have known about the jointly-written plays; yet they
never mentioned Massinger. Obviously, to these actors as to the Stuart
audiences, Fletcher's was the name to conjure with. His social standing
was higher, and his plays more popular. Perhaps the actors looked upon
Massinger as a skilful but pedestrian, run-of-the-mill playwright—one
who had been called in when the Master, under pressure, wanted help. In
any case, most of these previously unprinted plays had been written long
ago; they had been the property of the King's Men for 21 years or more
when Humphrey Moseley, the stationer, bargained for them in 1646.[18]
Certainly, "The Epistle Dedicatorie" of the 1647 Folio, signed by ten
leading members of the now defunct King's Men's Company,[19] does not
suggest any reluctance to having these plays published as by the "twin
stars" in contemporary fame.

Some light might have been thrown on authorship, had Moseley carried out an earlier project. In "The Stationer to the Reader," prefixed to
the First Folio, he writes: "It was once in my thoughts to have Printed
Mr. Fletcher's workes by themselves, because single & alone he would
make a Just Volume: But since never parted while they lived, I conceived
it not equitable to seperate [sic] their ashes."[20] It is doubtful, however, if
this cogitated volume would have been greatly helpful; Moseley gives no

sign of recognizing Massinger and others in some of the plays, though he "had the Originalls from such as received them from the Authours themselves."[21]

Moseley's sentiment about leaving ashes undisturbed appears to have been generally acceptable. There were, to be sure, dissenters. Abraham Cowley in 1656 lifted his voice in general protest against the printing of "counterfeit pieces" (as well as of inferior though true "coyn"), suggesting two reasons for this, and referring directly to "Fletcher":

. . . whether this proceed from the indiscretion of their Friends, who think a vast heap of Stones or Rubbish a better Monument, then a little Tomb of Marble, or by the unworthy avarice of some Stationers, who are content to diminish the value of the Author, so they may encrease the price of the Book. . . . This has been the case with Shakespear, Fletcher, Johnson, and many others. . . .[22]

There is, too, Cockaine, represented in the 1647 Folio by a tribute to Fletcher.[23] Some time later, in one poem to his cousin, Robert Cotton, and in another to Moseley and Robinson, he berated them for not making clear what shares the respective dramatists had in the plays of the Folio. He wondered that Cotton would permit "so great an injury to Fletcher's wit," since he had been the playwright's friend and companion, and pointed out to the printers that "Beaumont writ in few and Massinger in other few," while the "main" were Fletcher's sole work.[24] Though he was Massinger's friend and patron, he apparently lacked exact knowledge himself, and wanted these others to supply it. But they never did.

The result was that when Gerard Langbaine, in 1691, attempted to assign the plays of the Beaumont and Fletcher corpus as to authorship, he was obliged to confess to his readers:

I wish I were able to give the Reader a more perfect Account what Plays He [Fletcher] writ alone: in what Plays he was assisted by the Judicious Beaumont, and which were the Plays in which Old Phil. Massinger had a hand: but Mr. Charles Cotton being dead, I know none but Sir Aston Cockain (if he be yet alive) that can satisfy the World in this particular:[25]

There was an opinion among some Stuart playgoers that Beaumont excelled in tragedy, Fletcher in comedy—a distinction likewise often made today. According to J. Berkenhead:

> Some thinke Your Witts of Two Complexions fram'd,
> That One the Sock, th'other the Buskin claim'd,
> That should the Stage embattaile all it's Force,
> Fletcher would lead the Foot, Beaumont the Horse.[26]

But Berkenhead disagrees. "Each piece is wholly Two, yet never splits," he asserts. And no doubt most readers were content to think of the two playwrights as indivisible, as does Jasper Maine:

> Great paire of Authors, whom one equall Starre
> Begot so like in Genius, that you are
> In Fame, as well as Writings, both so knit,
> That no man knowes where to divide your wit,
> Much lesse your praise; you, who had equall fire,
> And did each other mutually inspire; . . .
> Where e're your parts betweene your selves lay, we
> In all things which you did but one thred see,
> So evenly drawne out, so gently spunne,
> That Art with Nature nere did smoother run.[27]

Henceforth, for two centuries and a half, critics sometimes spoke of Fletcher, sometimes of Beaumont and Fletcher. Lack of certainty was present even when they tried to distinguish between them; some refused to do so. That Massinger was known to be a collaborator added to the confusion, though not all critics took cognizance of him. Only since Fleay and others, from 1874 on, began to apply carefully selected tests to the problems of co-authorship have the shares of the co-workers on a given play been gradually disentangled with something like reasonably accurate results. "Beaumont and Fletcher" criticism has, through the generations, necessarily been colored by these facts. The "twins" have emerged clearly as individual playwrights of differing abilities only in recent days.[28]

II

Formal criticism of English drama was sparse until the Restoration era. Thomas Rymer, casting an eye backward in 1674, sees nothing at all except one burly figure:

At this time with us many great Wits flourished, But Ben Jonson, I think, had all the Critical learning to himself; and till of late years England was free from Criticks as it was from Wolves.[29]

Rymer, saluting a fellow classicist across the wasteland and ignoring Sidney,[30] had especially in mind writings which developed dramatic theory from the neo-classical point of view, or which applied neo-classical principles to the works of English dramatists, as he himself did.[31] But his estimate of scarcity in formal dramatic criticism was sound. Even such Puritan diatribes against stage plays as Prynne's,[32] which might have been expected to contain at least negative criticism of playwrights and dramas, do not get down to cases. They confine themselves to vituperation against the ribaldry, "prophanenesse," lewdness, lasciviousness and unlawfulness of stage plays in general.

Nonetheless, there are two satisfactory means by which the high repute of Fletcher, Beaumont and Company in Jacobean and Caroline days can be estimated: records of performances, and tributes in verse. The fact that their plays were frequently seen until the closing of the theatres in 1642, and surreptitiously thereafter, helped build, as well as demonstrates, their reputation. From the tributes some grist of critical attitudes can be extracted.

Dryden reports of Beaumont that "the first play that brought Fletcher and him in esteem was their *Philaster:* for before that, they had written two or three unsuccessfully."[33] Their contemporary fame thus begins in or about 1609. The first recorded performance at King James I's court of a Beaumont and Fletcher play occurs two years later: *A King and No King* on December 26, 1611.[34] The records of plays given at court performances, however, are very incomplete; so this may not be the actual first.

The years 1612 and 1613 show the King's Men as presenting at Court *Philaster, The Maid's Tragedy, A King and No King, Love Lies a-Bleeding* (can this be, as some suppose, an original version, by Fletcher alone, of *Philaster?*), *Cardenna* (lost play by Shakespeare and Fletcher?), and *The Captain.*[35] In the same years the second Queen's Revels Company, with child actors, performed at Court *Cupid's Revenge* three times and *The Coxcomb* twice.[36] Beaumont and Fletcher had "arrived" as dramatists.

Perhaps the most convincing evidence of continuing popularity on the stage may be found in Bentley's table of "King's Men's Plays at Court" from the winter season of 1615-16 to 1642.[37] Of the 114 performances of dramas new and old named by title, the Beaumont and Fletcher corpus is far in the lead with 41; only 15 are by Shakespeare and seven by Ben Jonson. Concerning the 20 evenings of plays given at the Court playhouse, the Cockpit, in the winter of 1630-31, Bentley remarks: "That ten of the twenty evenings . . . should have witnessed performances of Beaumont and Fletcher plays, half of them fifteen years old, speaks eloquently of the advantage which ownership of these plays gave the King's Men."[38]

No wonder Rhys comments that in Herrick's time the pieces of our ensemble were "more to the taste of the town than Shakespeare's. They were gentlemen," he adds, "and fine and fashionable gentlemen, so far as their dramatic function went. . . ."[39] It is significant, too, in the troublous months before the outbreak of civil war and the closing of the theatres, to find Prince Charles amusing himself at one of their plays. "On Twelfe Night, 1641," that is, January 6, 1642, "the prince had a play called *The Scornful Lady,* at the Cockpitt," notes Sir Henry Herbert, Master of the Revels, "but the kinge and queene were not there; and it was the only play acted at courte in the whole Christmas."[40]

Glapthorne, looking backward in this fateful year, says with some nostalgia, in his elegiac poem, *White-Hall:*

> Then those two thunderbolts of lively wit,
> Beaumont and Fletcher gloriously did sit
> Ruling the Theatre, and with their cleane
> Conceptions beautifying the Comick Scene.[41]

During the lean years of Puritanism that followed, the actors often managed to give more or less surreptitious performances, as best they could, in the old playhouses. Hotson remarks that "Surprising as it may appear, even during the height of the war, plays were given with remarkable frequency at the regular playhouses in London."[42] Rummaging around in old pamphlets, letters, ordinances, news-letters and other documents, he added to the items of Wright[43] and Rollins[44] many new details. The five instances that concern us here are from the years 1647 to 1654.

It is noteworthy that on the three occasions when the authorities halted the performance of a play specifically named in the account of the occurrence, the piece is a "Beaumont and Fletcher" one. On October 6, 1647, the sheriffs of London and their officers broke up the presentation of *A King and No King* at Salisbury Court.[45] In the winter of 1648, after several undisturbed performances, the actors playing *The Bloody Brother* at the Cockpit were "surprized . . . about the middle of the Play," and carried off to prison in their costumes.[46] It was *Wit Without Money* that was routed, on December 30, 1654, by a raid of soldiers on the Red Bull.[47] In the summer of 1647, moreover, the House of Commons was indignant to learn that one of several pieces currently being performed was *The Scornful Lady,* and sent an Alderman to suppress the players. It is not clear, however, that he did so while the play was in progress.[48] We also learn that to advertise another performance of *Wit Without Money* at the Red Bull on February 3, 1648, handbills were thrown into the coaches of gentlemen.[49] It would seem that bootleg "Beaumont and Fletcher" was in special demand during the years of prohibition.

Another indication of the exceptional popularity of these plays is the extent to which, in the decade preceding the Restoration, they were turned into "drolls." These can best be described as dramatic miniatures. Of the 38 extant drolls, 24 or nearly two-thirds are brief abridgements of five act plays almost entirely consisting of comic scenes; but the rest are of such other natures as farces, jigs, masque-like pastorals and non-comic playlets in verse.[50] These could be combined with dancing, easily staged anywhere, and produced inexpensively. They were an acceptable substitute, when it proved too difficult to produce full length plays.

In 1662 Henry Marsh collected 27 of these drolls and published them under the title of *The Wits, or Sport Upon Sport*.[51] Of these, a majority of 14 are from the pens of Fletcher and his co-workers, while Shakespeare and Shirley are represented by only two each, Jonson by one.[52]

When we turn from this record of stage popularity with Stuart and Commonwealth playgoers to the tributes of critical applause in verse (more rarely, in prose), appearing before the Folio of 1647, we find other evidence of esteem. One of the unsuccessful plays preceding *Philaster* to which Dryden may have been referring was Fletcher's *The Faithful Shepherdess*, known to have failed on the stage. When, shortly afterwards, it was published in 1609 or 1610, there were prefaced to it verse tributes by Jonson, Chapman and Beaumont, vigorously deploring the bad taste of the audience, and commending the play.

Jonson, deriding the "many-headed bench, that sits Upon the life and death of plays," assures Fletcher that

> Thy murder'd poem. . . shall rise
> A glorified work to time, when fire,
> Or moths, shall eat what all these fools admire.[53]

Chapman tells his "good friend" that his dramatic poem

> Renews the Golden Age, and holds through all
> The holy laws of homely Pastoral,

and cannot be properly appreciated by "this Iron Age."[54] Thus speak two literary scholars, who feel that the sound merits of this pastoral tragicomedy have been unduly slighted. And Fletcher's close friend, Beaumont, scoffing at the audience, thinks that the printed play may stir the conscience of readers

> to see the thing they scorned
> To be with so much wit and art adorned.[55]

Defensive praise, if you will, as much as criticism—but in point of time, the first. And the first notice, also, of Fletcher's "wit."

That Beaumont and Fletcher were well thought of by another contemporary dramatist appears in John Webster's preface to his tragedy, *The White Devil*, printed in 1612. After phrases of praise bestowed upon

Chapman and Jonson, Webster singles out "the no lesse worthy compo-
sures of both worthily excellent Maister Beaumont, & Maister Fletcher,"
and then lumps together "lastly (without wrong last to be named)"
Shakespeare, Dekker and Heywood for their "right happy and copious
industry."[56] And to the "copious" Heywood, also, his fellow-dramatists
were praiseworthy. Looking backward in 1634, he includes in his muster-
role

> Excellent Bewmont, in the foremost rank
> Of the rarest wits . . .
> Fletcher and Webster, of that learned packe
> None of the mean'st. . . . [57]

Such bestowal of an epithet or two by Webster and by Heywood is
typical of many of the verse and prose tributes written by nonprofes-
sionals. True, there is much praise, but it adds up simply to high regard
for our playwrights. Often they divide brief acclaim with Shakespeare
and Jonson, occasionally with Chapman, more rarely with Heywood and
Massinger and, as time goes on, with Shirley.

What does come clear is that Beaumont and Fletcher (and in that order in time) emerge into equal prominence with Shakespeare and Jonson.
In Caroline days the "triumvirate" is well established; Jonson's *Works*
(1616) and Shakespeare's *First Folio* (1623) are offset, until the Folio of
1647 comes out, by the greater popularity of our playwrights' dramas on
the stage.

So Owen Felltham, the essayist, writing in 1638 to the memory of Ben
Jonson, indicates that the main jewels in the crown of the drama of "our
halcyon days" now past are "Shakespeare, Beaumont, Jonson, these
three."[58] So, too, an anonymous gentleman, penning an effusion not later
than 1640, launches into hyperbole about

> Shakespeare and Beamond, Swannes to whom the Spheares
> Listen, while they call back the former yeares. . . .

and lauds only Jonson else of the moderns, along with a number of the
ancients.[59] Two years later James Shirley, entertainer to the Caroline
gentry, and more disciple to Fletcher than to any other playwright,[60]
similarly praises the triumvirate in the prologue to his own play, *The
Sisters*. In a vein that suggests the remarks he will make in *To the Reader*
in the 1647 Folio, he speaks of

> Fletcher, the Muses' darling, and choice love
> Of Phoebus, the delight of every grove;
> Upon whose head the laurel grew, whose wit
> Was the times wonder, and example, yet. . . . [61]

Only one other tribute published earlier than the First Folio need detain us further. In 1616, the year of Beaumont's death, Robert Anton, acclaiming certain poets as well as dramatists, states that

> Among which most massive metals I admire
> The most iudicious Beaumont and his fire. . . . [62]

It was to become traditional that Beaumont had better judgment than Fletcher, and exercised the shaping hand in their joint efforts, pruning Fletcher's luxuriance. Later he was often to be thought merely the corrector of Fletcher.[63] Some of Anton's other epithets, such as "Morrall Daniell" and "the labor'd Muse of Iohnson," were already conventional enough. This arouses the suspicion that the "judicious," as applied to Beaumont, was likewise an epithet accepted by his contemporaries. If so, this affords some grounds for the view that Fletcher may have profited in dramatic technique from his collaboration with this partner.

III

The First Folio of 1647 marks the flood-tide in the reputation of "Beaumont and Fletcher." At last Cavalier gentlemen, who for five years had been able to see their plays only in illegal performances, or to read those few which had come out earlier, and singly, in quartos, could peruse and appreciate all their available works. Moseley, with much "Care & Pains," and an expense so considerable that he had to associate Robinson with him in the enterprise, succeeded in rounding up all but one of the then known unpublished plays. This one, as he frankly explained to his readers, was Fletcher's comedy, *The Wild-Goose Chase*. When it later turned up, in 1652, he published it separately, in part as a benefit to the impoverished actors, Lowin and Taylor, of the former King's Company. Of the 34 plays in the Folio, Moseley apparently purchased the rights to all but ten from this group of actors who, knowing well the value of their wares, obviously asked a good price. Nor could it have been easy to gather the other scattered pieces. In the collecting, as in the printing, the book was a major publishing venture.[64]

Nor was this the only evidence that the publication of the Folio, as Bald remarks, "was regarded as a literary event of the first importance."[65] An exceptionally large number of "Commendatory Verses," 36 in all, was secured. Their authors comprise something like a muster-role of Cavalier writers of verse. Suckling and Carew, not present, were dead; but Herrick, Lovelace, Denham, Waller, Habington, Stanley, Cartwright and many another poet, scholar or literary gentleman are there; even Ben Jonson is represented by his early lines praising his friend, Beaumont.

These tributes, moreover, have an impressive framing-in: a dedication by ten leading members of the disbanded King's Men's Company to their former noble benefactor; addresses to the reader by James Shirley, "son" of Fletcher, and by Humphrey Moseley, the publisher; a poem "To the Stationer" lauding the project; and, bringing up the rear of the commendatory poems, verses from the labored pen of Moseley himself by way of epilogue.[66] The players urge that the plays of Beaumont and Fletcher are "all the Treasure we had contracted in the whole Age of Poesie," and that they are "the most justly admir'd, and belov'd Pieces of Witt and the World."[67] And Shirley enthusiastically asserts that but to mention Beaumont and Fletcher

is to throw a cloude upon all former names and benight Posterity; This Book being, without flattery, the greatest Monument of the Scene that Time and Humanity have produced, and must Live, not only the Crowne and sole Reputation of our owne, but the stayne of all other Nations and Languages. . . .[68]

A grave political situation lies behind the appearance of the Folio at just this time. When Moseley and Robinson entered 30 of these plays in the Stationers' Register on September 4, 1646, the First Civil War was over, and the royalist cause at ebb. King Charles the First had put himself into the hands of the Scotch on May 5, Oxford had yielded seven weeks later, and Raglan Castle had surrendered on August 19. Only at Harlech on the far Welsh coast was the king's flag still flying. In London a Presbyterian parliament, hostile to stage-plays, was in the ascendancy. To the players, the prospect of a legal reopening of the theatres must have seemed more hopeless than ever.[69]

The appearance of the Folio during the time when King Charles was negotiating with Parliament and with the Independent army, has a tinge of royalist literary manifesto. Some of the writers of commendatory verses do not overlook this significance. Two think that the "Great tutelary Spirit of the Stage" should not have appeared "now, in the worst scaene of Time," as William Habington puts it, but should have waited until "men might bee Taught how to reade, and then, how to reade thee."[70] For, as Roger L'Estrange explains,

> The Palate of this age gusts nothing High;
> That has not Custard in't or Bawdery.
> Folly and Madnesse fill the Stage; The Scaene
> Is Athens; where, the Guilty and the Meane,
> The Foole 'scapes well enough; Learned and Great
> Suffer an Ostracisme; stand Exulate.

But L'Estrange then proceeds to reverse himself, bringing out into the open a point which must have been in the minds of many: that the Folio might prove an aid to the royalist cause. He considers the volume to be "Balsame" and "Hellebore," which must purge

> Our Crazy Stupor to a just quick Sence
> Both of Ingratitude and Providence. . . .
>   Fletcher sets the world cleare
> Of all disorder and reformes us here.[71]

Thomas Peyton also emphasizes the political challenge of the Folio, with his flings at Parliament (word omitted, but rhyming with "discontent",) and at the "Roundhead" army:

> . . . whether to commend thy Worke will stand
> Both with the Lawes of Verse and of the Land,
> Were to put doubts might raise a discontent
> Between the Muses and the————. . . .
> For he that gives the Bayes to thee, must then
> First take it from the Militarie Men;
> He must untriumph conquests, bid 'em stand,
> Question the strength of their victorious hand.[72]

Peyton thus suggests that the Puritans may not like this publication, implying in so doing that it constitutes a measure of propaganda for the royalists, and then goes on to describe the good he thinks the book may do pious (and Puritan?) ladies, soldiers and others.

Henry Mody, Baronet, asserts that, in the midst of "the Worlds mad zeale and ignorance," it is "kind providence" which has "locked some of this treasure up"

> For a reserve untill these sullen daies:
> When scorn, and want, and danger, are the Baies
> That Crown the head of merit.[73]

Stanley, at this gloomy time for Cavaliers, sings of Fletcher:

> Dispaire our joy hath doubled, he is come,
> Thrice welcome in this Post-liminium.[74]

And Lovelace rejoices, in the midst of his war activities in the King's cause,

> That Fate should be so mercifull to me,
> To let me live t'have said I have read thee.[75]

Three of the poems link the Folio and its publication at this time directly with the royal family. Richard Brome points out the following parallels:

> In the first yeare, our famous Fletcher fell,
> Of good King Charles who grac'd these Poems well,
> Being then in life of Action: But they dyed
> Since the Kings absence;. . .
>   Now at the Report
> Of the Kings second comming to his Court,
> The Bookes creepe from the Presse to Life, . . .[76]

Robert Gardiner, referring in the second line to Queen Henrietta and her entourage, puns upon play titles, but with a wish nonetheless serious:

> Oh, could his *Prophetesse* but tell one *Chance,*
> When that the *Pilgrimes* shall returne from France.
> And once more make this Kingdome, as of late,
> *The Island Princesse,* and we celebrate
> A *Double Marriage;* every one to bring
> To Fletcher's memory his offering.[77]

And Shirley, in the concluding verse tribute, says:

>   let me prophesie,
> As I goe Swan-like out, Our Peace is nigh;
> A Balme unto the wounded Age I sing,
> And nothing now is wanting but the King.[78]

It will not do, then, to underestimate the literary importance to royalist readers of the First Folio, nor the genuineness of the critical estimates embedded in its commendatory verses. When all deductions are made for hyperbole, conventional flattery, and overstatement, it should still be clear that the Cavalier party did consider their favorite playwrights a "Balme" and a rallying point. And in their tributes a core of reasons can be found for their high regard for this body of plays.

To modern ears their plaudits may have, it is true, a hollow ring. Fletcher, sole recipient—for reasons already made clear—of 25 of the 36 tributes, is hailed as "King of Poets!" "Best Poet of thy times," "sole Monarch . . . In Wits great Empire," "The Joy! The Life! The Light of this tempestuous Age," in whose works "Art, Language, Wit sit ruling in one Spheare," "whose Fame no Age can ever wast; Envy of Ours and glory of the last," "Witnesse thy Comedies, Pieces of such Worth, All Ages still shall like but ne're bring forth."[79] We are told that "the whole World to reverence will flock" to his plays, that "the least our age can say now thou art gone, Is that there never will be such a one," and that "Tis vaine to praise . . . For he that names but Fletcher must needs be

Found guilty of a loud hyperbole."[80] Indeed, Edmund Waller would have us think that "Fletcher's" character, Aspatia (now assigned to Beaumont's hand), and his "Comick stile" in *The Scornful Lady*, deter him from writing tragedy and mock his toil at comedies:

> Thus has thy Muse, at once, improv'd and marr'd
> Our Sport in Playes, by rendring it too hard.[81]

But most difficult of all for modern readers to digest is the opinion, implied or expressed by several writers, that Fletcher excels Shakespeare. The poet Denham, recalling the time when Fletcher, Jonson, and Shakespeare "sway'd in the Triumvirate of Wit," believes that Fletcher succeeded in combining Jonson's art and Shakespeare's naturalness:

> Yet what from Johnsons oyle and sweat did flow,
> Or what more easie nature did bestow
> On Shakespeares gentler Muse, in thee full growne
> Their Graces both appeare, yet so, that none
> Can say here Nature ends, and Art begins
> But mix't like th'Elements, . . .[82]

In the first of his two commendatory poems, Cartwright—university teacher, poet and playwright—agrees with Denham, finding that Fletcher so steered " 'Twixt Johnsons grave and Shakespeares lighter sound" that

> Something still was found
> Nor this, nor that, nor both, but so his owne
> That 'twas his marke, and he by it was knowne.
> Hence did he take true judgements, . . .[83]

In other words, Fletcher found the Aristotelean "golden mean" between Jonson and Shakespeare. Berkenhead considers Fletcher a more consistently fine playwright than Shakespeare:

> Brave Shakespeare flow'd, yet had his ebbings too,
> Often above Himselfe, sometimes below;
> Thou Always Best; . . .[84]

Absurd? But more startling passages follow. About the team of "Beaumont and Fletcher," Berkenhead takes what may well be a more or less characteristic royalist point of view, when he says:

> Shakespeare was early up, and went so drest
> As for those dawning houres he knew was best;
> But when the Sun shone forth, You Two thought fit
> To weare just Robes; and leave off Trunk-hose Wit.

It was not the playwright of the dawn, nor yet old Ben Jonson, but the
later meridian Twins who perfected the English drama:

> Now, now 'twas Perfect; None must looke for New,
> Manners and Scenes may alter, but not You;
> For Yours are not meere Humours, gilded straines;
> The Fashion lost, Your massy Sence remains.[85]

Cartwright similarly, but still more decidedly, says of Fletcher:

> Shakespeare to thee was dull, whose best jest lyes
> I'th ladies questions, and the Fooles replyes.
> Old fashion'd wit, which walkt from town to town
> In turn'd Hose, which our fathers call'd the Clown; . . .

And not only that; Shakespeare's

> . . . Wit our nice times would obsceannesse call,
> And which made Bawdry pass for Comicall:
> Nature was all his Art, . . .

By contrast, Fletcher's

> veine was free
> As his, but without his scurrility;
> From whom mirth came unforc'd, no jest perplext,
> But without labour cleane, chast, and unvext.[86]

In the light of later critical opinion, all this may seem topsyturvy. Are
these royalists weak in critical insight and perspective? Do they lack the
judgment of a Milton, who includes Shakespeare's and Jonson's comedies
in the pleasures of *L'Allegro,* but never mentions Beaumont and
Fletcher? No doubt; but there is something more to be said, even after
discounting party spirit.

One clue to understanding this royalist point of view lies in Berkenhead's placing of Shakespeare in the dawning hours of the Elizabethan
drama against Beaumont and Fletcher in the full sun, and in Cartwright's
adjective, "old fashion'd." Shakespeare, once at the height of popular
esteem, had been eclipsed in fashionable circles by these younger, newer
men who had written so much more definitely for the sheer entertainment of Jacobean gentlemen—and who still delighted royalists.

Frequent indeed in literary history is the partial or total eclipse of an
author one or two generations after his success: witness the attitude
towards the Victorians of the decades now liquidated by World War II.
This tendency, being a facet in the psychological revolt of the sons
against the fathers, is an oft-recurring pattern of behavior, and an im-

portant factor in this instance. It is natural enough that the more up-to-date playwrights should seem the better ones. It is an easily tested truism that perspective comes with distance; near to, hills may seem to overtop mountains.

As for wit, and humor as well, fashions often change. Nothing is more lively and apposite than today's; nothing more dead than yesteryear's. By many playgoers, clowns and their buffoonery had long since been deemed a crude element in drama; indeed, there are moderns who do not consider Shakespeare's clowns one of his strongest attractions. His punning and word-play were obviously "dated" to our critics, his slang not the current lingo of gentlemen.

That Beaumont and Fletcher were still, in 1647, admired as the "Gemini of Wit"[87] is, perhaps, already somewhat evident. An examination of the commendatory poems would show that nearly all at least glance at this quality; Shirley, in *To the Reader*, calls it "the best wit ever trod our English Stage."[88] And it should be borne in mind that wit, in the seventeenth century, connoted nimbleness of mind and fancy, as well as the clever intellectual perception of incongruities, pointedly phrased.

In those dark days for the theatres, one of the attractions of the Folio is, as Lovelace rejoices, that reading it "We . . . glory in thy Wit, and feast each other with remembring it."[89] John Webb carries this point even further:

> The Presse shall give to ev'ry man his part,
> And we will all be Actors; learne by heart
> Those Tragick Scenes and Comicke Straines you writ,
> Un-imitable both for Art and Wit; . . . [90]

To Robert Stapylton, Knight, the volume may even have an educational value:

> The Native may learne English from his lines,
> And th'Alien if he can but construe it,
> May here be made free Denison of wit.[91]

But the ecstatic lines of Hills best sum up the general enthusiasm:

> Monarch of Wit! great Magazine of wealth!
> From whose rich Banke, by a Promethean-stealth,
> Our lesser flames doe blaze! His the true fire,
> When they like Glo-worms, being touch'd, expire.[92]

On the issue of moral cleanness, Cartwright may sound extreme in his contrasting of Shakespeare's "obsceannesse" with Fletcher's freedom from "scurrility"; but as regards our playwrights, at least, he is in numerous company. He is not intentionally writing balderdash; his viewpoint, seen in terms of change of taste, is understandable. Shakespeare's coarseness, being of an elder fashion, was easily perceptible; that of Fletcher, hard to discern because still à la mode.

Certainly, on no point is the testimony of the tributes in the Folio more direct than on this one of sound morality. And on no point is it more at variance with much criticism of later generations. There is a paradox here which, in due time, needs examination. Neither the chance that these writers were intentionally countering the hostile Puritan attitude about the immorality of stage-plays, nor the slur that their own moral sense left something to be desired, is wholly satisfactory in explanation. At this point, however, some passages showing characteristic attitudes must suffice.[93]

Stapylton, possibly influenced by Donne into using a geographic image, sees the exalting of virtue and exposing of vice as Fletcher's dramatic aim:

> . . . his maine end does drooping Vertue raise,
> And crownes her beauty with eternall Bayes;
> In Scaenes where she inflames the frozen soule,
> While Vice (her paint washt off) appeares so foule;
> She must this Blessed Isle and Europe leave,
> And some new Quadrant of the Globe deceive:[94]

Grandison asserts that their moral aim is achieved by Beaumont and Fletcher:

> Desert has here reward in one good line
> For all it lost, for all it might repine:
> Vile and ignobler things are open laid,
> The truth of their false colours are displayed:
> You'l say the Poet's both best Judge and Priest,
> No guilty soule abides so sharp a test,
> As their smooth Pen;[95]

It would be indeed difficult to prove a charge of moral squint-sightedness against the poet Habington. Yet he calls upon Fletcher to "revive" in order to teach morality. Oddly enough, this pious man who was proud of his own chastity, and married the Castara of his lyric devotions, does not find that our playwright's maidens, technically virtuous, have bawdy minds, as do some later critics; instead, he emphasizes the plays' healthy moral effect:

> Instruct the Envious, with how chast a flame
> Thou warmst the Lover; how severely just
> Thou wert to punish, if he burnt to lust.

> With what a blush thou didst the Maid adorne,
> But tempted, with how innocent a scorne.
> How Epidemick errors by thy Play
> Were laught out of esteeme, so purg'd away.
> How to each sence thou so didst vertue fit,
> That all grew virtuous to be thought t'have wit.[96]

Even the thoughts and language of these plays were considered "pure." Berkenhead says of Fletcher's thoughts that they were "cleare" and "Innocent," and adds that "thy Phancy gave no unswept Language vent."[97] J. M. (Jasper Maine?) points to his "Safe Mirth, full language" throughout the plays, "All Innocence and Wit, pleasant and clear."[98] Lisle, kinsman of Beaumont, praises his "Plot, Sence, Language, All's so pure and fit," and Earle his "Wit untainted with obscenity," "All in a language purely flowing drest."[99]

But the most surprising passage comes from Richard Lovelace, gallant embodiment of the Cavalier Spirit. Apparently annoyed by the vile language of "foule speakers, that pronounce the Air of Stewes," he calls upon them to read *The Custom of the Country,* in which a male house of prostitution is portrayed, in order "to cloathe aright your wanton wit":

> View here a loose thought said with such a grace,
> Minerva might have spoke in Venus face;
> So well disguis'd, that 'twas conceiv'd by none
> But Cupid had Diana's linnen on: . . .

He adds that if other playwrights had observed Fletcher's "grace" and modesty, "The Stage (as this work) might have liv'd and Lov'd."[100] Now this is the play which Dryden chose as a shining example of bawdiness, when stung by Jeremy Collier's witty attack, in 1698, on the immorality of Restoration comedies, including his own. Curiously, Collier had been kinder to Beaumont and Fletcher than to Shakespeare. He had found *The Faithful Shepherdess* "remarkably Moral, and a sort of Exhortation to Chastity."[101] Quoting from the prefaces to *The Woman-Hater* and *The Knight of the Burning Pestle,* he had extolled the good intentions of our playwrights. If they had not always been steady in carrying these intentions out, that might have been Beaumont's fault, since the later plays of Fletcher "are the most inoffensive."[102] While discussing Dryden's defense of *The Mock-Astrologer,* whose title character remained unpunished at the end of the play, Collier had also remarked that he could give some instances from Fletcher's comedies of just punishment inflicted on the immoral.[103]

In rebuttal the vexed Dryden exclaimed, with understandable exaggeration, "Neither has he judged impartially betwixt the former age and us. There is more bawdry in one play of Fletcher's, called *The Custom of the Country*, than in all ours together."[104] And others have since quoted him in agreement about this play, though Swinburne was to enter a protest, in recent days, against Dryden's opinion.

The truth, no doubt, lies somewhere between Lovelace and Dryden. The former believed that the play was cleaner in its language and moral tone than were those of the actual haunters of brothels in his time, and he was in a position to know. He evidently accepted the portrayal of a stew as a legitimate target of comedy. Whether or not Stuart theatregoers were less squeamish about moral matters than many modern critics since Schlegel and Coleridge, they obviously agreed that in actual performance of these plays, the moral tone was not decadent but healthy; and this we shall have to reckon with. Certainly, they were no more shocked at plays by Fletcher and Company than sophisticated modern playgoers are at a Noel Coward comedy.

The emotional impact of our plays on Stuart spectators and readers alike was one of the secrets of their appeal. However theatrical they may seem to us, they had been so concocted that they moved these royalists' "passions." Robert Herrick, whose own gay lyrics to Julia and other ladies of his imagination have delighted generations of poetry lovers, characteristically stresses this point:

> Here melting numbers, words of power to move
> Young men to swoone, and Maides to dye for love.
> Love lies a bleeding here, Evadne there
> Swells with brave rage, yet comely every where
> Here's a *mad lover*, there that high designe
> Of *King and no King* (and the rare Plot thine)
> So that when 'ere wee circumvolve our Eyes,
> Such rich, such fresh, such sweet varietyes,
> Ravish our spirits, that entranc'd we see
> None writes lov's passion in the world, like Thee.[105]

Shades of *Romeo and Juliet!*

To Henry Harington the plays actually affected the conduct of ladies and gentlemen, in ways of which he approves:

> Thy Language so insinuates, each one
> Of thy spectators has thy passion.
> Men seeing, valiant; Ladies amorous prove:
> Thus owe to thee their valour and their love:
> Scenes! chaste yet satisfying! . . .[106]

In his prefatory blurb, James Shirley fancifully assures the reader that if he is melancholy, one comedy will cure him; he will find his "exalted fancie in Elizium." If "sick of this cure," he will find many "a soft purling passion or spring of sorrow so powerfully wrought high by the teares of innocence, and wronged Lovers" that he will be moved to weep.[107] John Webb finds that "A Soul-affecting Musick" is one of the causes of this emotional impact, "ravishing both Eare and Intellect." He then speaks of the "rare Invention" and "Conflicts that beget New strange delight,"[108] thereby pointing to the capacity of Fletcher and Company to sustain tension by new turns to situations, frequent surprises and reversals, and moving displays of wit and feeling. Comments on the actual emotional effect of the plays on spectators, to be considered later,[109] sustain these opinions.

Cartwright who, despite his views on Shakespeare, sometimes shows a playwright's acuteness, detects the ability of our dramatists to "keep 'em guessing." He says that no one can foresee what they are up to

> At the first opening; all stand wondring how
> The thing will be untill it is; which thence
> With fresh delight still cheats, still takes the sence;
> The whole designe, the shadowes, the lights such
> That none can say he shewes or hides too much: . . .
> Nought later than it should, nought comes before, . . . [110]

Evidently, then, many of the plays had a bit of the appeal that a movie "Whodunit" has today.

Fletcher's "sweet fluent veine" is much commended in the tributes; it "did like Rivers flow." We are given to understand that he felt no "pangs" of effort such as others did, worked up no "sweat"; what was "toyle" to others was "play" to him, though possibly, as an alternative, "his file and care" may have had something to do with his "smoothnesse." He was not "loud and cloudy"; he did not "render harsh" some "gloomy sense"; he was not "swoln nor flat," nor did one have to construe his sentences "to untye a knot Hid in a line." Here was no "stiff-affected Scene," nothing "all unlac'd, nor City-startched and pinn'd," no "long-long-winded sentences."[111]

Instead, as Powell sees it, the style is easy to grasp and natural:

> so obvious to sence, so plaine,
> You'd scarcely think't ally'd unto the braine:
> So sweete, it gain'd more ground upon the Stage
> Then Johnson with his selfe-admiring rage
> Ere Lost: and then so naturally fell
> That fooles would think, that they could doe as well.[112]

According to Alexander Brome, it was sprightly, too:

> a Magazine of sence
> Cloathed in the newest Garbe of Eloquence.
> Scaenes that are quick and sprightly, in whose veines
> Bubbles the quintessence of sweet-high straines.[113]

So Palmer of Christ Church, Oxford, tells us that ladies, their pages, and serious students can equally enjoy them:

> thy Playes
> To ev'ry understanding still appeare,
> As if thou only meant'st to take that Eare;
> The Phrase so terse and free of a just Poise,
> Where ev'ry word ha's weight and yet no Noise, . . .
> Thy Poems (sacred Spring) did from thee flow,
> With as much pleasure, as we reade them now.[114]

The far richer poetical quality of Shakespeare's lines and his ranging imagery put more strain on the attention of playgoers than the easy, "flowing" speeches of Fletcher and Company. Doubtless this was another reason for the greater popularity of the latter in Stuart times.[115]

One more strong element of appeal these plays had to royalist lovers of drama: they were, from their viewpoint, politically sound. The authors were not enemies of the Stuart monarchy and the Anglican church, like the Puritans. "Nor Church nor Lawes were ever Libel'd here," says J. M.,[116] and on the same note Berkenhead remarks of Fletcher, a bishop's son, that (thou)

> Slaunderst not Lawes, prophan'st no holy Page,
> (As if thy Father's Crosier aw'd the Stage:)
> High crimes were still arraign'd, though they made shift
> To prosper out foure Acts, were plagu'd i'th Fift:
> All's safe, and wise.[117]

Harris, also, perhaps thinking of the all too numerous Puritan pamphleteers, finds him politically safe:

> Not like those Meteor-wits which wildly flye
> In storm and thunder through th'amazed skie;
> Speaking but th'Ills and Villanies in a State,
> Which fooles admire, and wise men tremble at, . . .[118]

Nor was "Fletcher" considered a mere lickspittle to the divine right of Kings. Habington, a good royalist himself, makes it clear that, in his opinion, these plays were not kind to tyranny:

> Thou didst frame governments, give Kings their part,
> Teach them how neere to God, while just they be;
> But how dissolv'd, stretch'd forth to Tyrannie.[119]

Indeed, Harris even maintains that Fletcher, knowing "all dark turnings in the Labyrinth of policie," walked uninfected by this knowledge as "the great Genius of Government":

> Thou couldst unfold darke Plots, and shew that Path
> By which Ambition climb'd to Greatnesse hath.
> Thou couldst the rises, turnes, and falls of States,
> How neare they were their Periods and Dates:
> Couldst mad the subject into popular rage,
> And the grown seas of that great storme asswage,
> Dethrone usurping Tyrants, and place there
> The Lawfull Prince and true Inheriter; . . . [120]

These opinions, it is true, may be partisan; they may reflect the "Cavalier Psyche"; but are they necessarily more partisan than the modern view that Beaumont and Fletcher were contemptibly servile monarchists? At any rate, it should now be possible to understand why Powell thinks that Fletcher, better than Jonson, Shakespeare, or Chapman, could have dealt, in drama, with the civil tragedy that had come upon the eagle, England:

> Yet none like high-wing'd Fletcher had bin found
> This Eagles tragick-destiny to sound,
> Rare Fletcher's quill had soar'd up to the sky,
> And drawn down Gods to see the tragedy: . . . [121]

Thus, the authors of these "Commendatory Verses" did indeed have a core of reasons for their high critical esteem for the Fletcher, Beaumont, Massinger and Company plays. Published at a time when they could serve as a "balme" and an unfurled standard to rally royalists, they combined Jonson's art with Shakespeare's naturalness, and overflowed with wit and humor less old-fashioned and "chaster" than Shakespeare's—the "best" of the English stage. They were healthy and of good effect in moral tone, had a stirring impact on emotions (especially when dealing with "lov's passion" and valor), kept audiences and readers in suspense as to what would happen next, were written in a manner that was fluent, easy to understand and sprightly, and were sound in political insight.

Never again, after this generation died out during the Restoration years, would "Beaumont and Fletcher" be so intimately appreciated and so highly regarded.

IV

When one and then two theatrical companies began playing after the restoration of the Stuart line to the throne in 1660, the popularity of our body of plays was at first still at its peak. We have seen that they had been exceptionally popular during Civil War and Commonwealth days, whether performed at full length or in miniature versions as drolls. As we are aware, Charles II and many of his older courtiers had known and loved these plays of the past. Besides, the commercial stage is normally conservative, often preferring the tried and tested old to the hazardous new; in 1660 it picked up where it left off in 1642. The older plays had to fill the gap until sufficient new playwrights should develop.

The facts of performance confirm Wilson's remark that "Of all the old plays, those of Beaumont and Fletcher loomed largest on the dramatic horizon."[122] Witness the list of the Red Bull stock-plays for 1660-1662 and a part of 1663, which included nine of the Fletcher canon to three by Shakespeare, one by Jonson, and seven scattering. The list of performances by the King's Company, 1660-1662, including 72 in all, tells the same story: 26 performances of our authors' plays, as against three each of dramas by Shakespeare and Jonson.[123] Wilson informs us that during the dramatic season of 1661-1662 "there were at least nine performances of eight plays by Shakespeare, forty-one of twenty-one by Beaumont and Fletcher, and ten of three by Jonson."[124] Of revivals of plays by other old dramatists, only 28 presentations of 19 plays are recorded.

These figures accord with Dryden's often quoted remark, set down in 1668, that "Their plays are now the most pleasant and frequent entertainments of the stage; two of theirs being acted through the year for one of Shakespeare's or Johnson's." He adds: "the reason is, because there is a certain gaiety in their comedies, and pathos in their serious plays, which suits generally with all men's humours."[125]

According to his diary, Samuel Pepys, Restoration devotee of the theatre and its actresses, saw 69 performances of these plays during this decade of the 1660's.[126] As Miss McAfee points out, Pepys was an individualist rather than "a professed literary critic or a typical Restoration playgoer."[127] But since he belonged to the younger generation, he struck a new note; he was free from memories of Caroline playgoing, and from worshipping at old shrines. Not notably an admirer of Shakespeare, he expressed strongest enthusiasm for Jonson's popular major comedies: *The Alchemist, Volpone, The Silent Woman.*

Pepys really liked well only a minority of the 26 Fletcher and Company plays which he saw. He enjoyed *The Chances, Monsieur Thomas* and *The Woman's Prize,* found *The Island Princess* (in an altered version) pretty good and then excellent, and commended *The Night Walker* as "a very merry and pretty play." All these are Fletcher's, the last revised by Shirley. Of the Beaumont and Fletcher collaborations, he thought *The*

Maid's Tragedy "too sad and melancholy" on seeing only its final scenes, but later considered it a good play; and when he first saw a woman in the name role of *The Scornful Lady*, the piece rose in his esteem. This particular comedy was our dramatists' most popular play on the Restoration stage.[128] Pepys' evident preference for lighter vehicles checks with Sprague, whose records suggest "a predilection on the part of Restoration audiences for our authors' comedies, as against their tragedies and tragicomedies."[129]

The remainder ranged from fairly good to the worst Pepys had ever seen: *The Custom of the Country*. It is true that he liked *The Mad Lover* when he read it, but he did not show any enthusiasm for two performances of it. He was greatly disappointed when he saw *Philaster* on the stage, and scorned *The Coxcomb*, *The Faithful Shepherdess* and *The Humorous Lieutenant* as silly. Neither did he like at all some others, including *Rule a Wife and Have a Wife*, long to be a stage favorite, *Wit Without Money* and *The Wild-Goose Chase*. As for *The Sea Voyage*, he agreed with modern opinion that it was a "mean" piece compared to Shakespeare's *The Tempest*.

Pepys must have been a less than average admirer of our playwrights' work during these years of the diary. Sprague tells us that during the twenty years, 1663-1682, 38 of these plays, the largest part of the corpus, were produced—many of them frequently.[130] Perhaps Pepys is more symptomatic of the decline in popularity which may have had its onset during the later 1670's, and which was certainly under way in the next decade.

It is odd that the publication of the Second Folio in 1679 should, roughly, mark the turn of the tide. Unlike the First Folio, this one is not particularly notable, except that it includes the remaining 16 plays then known to belong to the corpus. This brings the total from 34 to 50 dramas, plus Beaumont's masque. There has also crept in one drama now assigned to James Shirley: *The Coronation*. On the other hand, *A Very Woman*, the recently discovered *Barnavelt*, and the probable Shakespeare collaborations, *Henry VIII* and *The Two Noble Kinsmen*, are missing. The commendatory poems have been trimmed down to eleven.[131] Despite the greatly reduced chorus of praise that thus accompanies the Second Folio, it seems probable that this first inclusive edition had little effect on stage popularity, though it made readily available some plays previously hard to come by.

That the tragicomedies written by Beaumont and Fletcher still moved spectators when well acted is attested by an anonymous poem, "An Elegy on that Worthy and Famous Actor, Mr. Charles Hart, Who departed this

Life Thursday August the 18th, 1683." Appearing in *The Maid's Tragedy* and *A King and No King*,

> Such Pow'r He had o'r the Spectators gain'd,
> As forc'd a Real Passion from a Feign'd.
> For when they saw Amintor bleed, strait all
> The House, for every Drop, a Tear let fall;
> And when Arbaces wept by sympathy,
> A flowing Tide of Wo gush'd from each Eye.[132]

The waning of stage popularity is very evident in the years 1682 to 1695 when, according to Sprague, only 18 of the plays were given by the one acting company of this period, and more frequent use was made of revised editions.[133] As new Restoration playwrights rose to fame, our authors were losing some of their appeal, especially when not revised to please new tastes. From 1695 to 1706, two companies were acting instead of one, as had also been the case before the union of the King's and the Duke's companies in 1682. Yet only 21 plays of our corpus were produced during these eleven years, and about half of that number were acted in altered versions.[134] This indicates a marked falling off in stage popularity since the 1660's, though some of the pieces still held the boards successfully. By now "Beaumont and Fletcher" were no longer the chief idols of the theatre-goer.

Such influence as Fletcher and Company had on the plays of the Restoration dramatists is another indication of their popularity in this age. But it has often been exaggerated, just as has the impact of French neoclassical tragedy and comedy. While French drama did influence the Restoration theory and practice of play construction, suggested plot materials and characters, and often was plundered or adapted, it did not supply the modes of Restoration drama. These came from English antecedents; but our corpus of plays was, in the main, only an indirect source for these modes.

Harbage[135] has supplied the missing link in the evolution of the heroic play: the sprawling, amateurish pieces written by Cavaliers for the special delectation of Queen Henrietta. This sprightly and socially gracious French noblewoman not only enjoyed acting in private court theatricals but had imbibed the French précieuse taste for such romances as her favorite, D'Urfé's *Astrée*. The plays which she inspired Suckling, Cockaine, Carlell, the Killigrews and others to write have, for the first time, the grandiloquent tone, the atmosphere of court etiquette, the heroic and strained sentiment, the love and honour emphasis, that we find in the much abler heroic plays of Dryden.

True, Fletcher, like the Cavaliers, drew on Sidney's *Arcadia* and seventeenth century offspring of the late Greek romances, including D'Urfé's *Astrée*, for plot material. Such similarities as there are between the plays of our corpus and those of Caroline courtiers may largely derive from this fact, which also helps to explain why our playwrights were so popular with Caroline and Restoration audiences. But Fletcher made use of these sources in the workaday manner of a practical playwright, with little or no interest in précieuse attitudinizing, the refinements of platonic love, and exotic, fine-spun doctrines and dilemmas.[136] It was from the Cavalier drama that the inflated strain of these romances passed to the Restoration writers of heroic plays. So Richard Flecknoe, in saying that "Beaumont and Fletcher first writ in the Heroick way, upon whom Sucklin and others endeavor'd to refine agen,"[137] gave too much honor to our playwrights, who merely and somewhat dimly showed the way. But in pointing to the Cavalier dramatists as the direct source of the heroic mode, this victim of Dryden's ridicule in *MacFlecknoe* was more accurate than his satirizer, who held that the qualities of this species of play first saw the light in D'Avenant's *The Siege of Rhodes* (1656).[138]

So it is with the social mode of Restoration comedy. Miss Lynch,[139] in tracing the gradual evolution of this mode in seventeenth century drama, finds the précieuse or Cavalier tradition in comedy the most immediate influence on Restoration playwrights. She points out that very few Fletcher pieces could be termed "comedies of manners," and even these few, while showing a nascent "taste for social portraiture," are only spasmodically of this quality. She concludes that Fletcher's "persons of fashion still have an incurable zest for random adventure and farcical intrigue"; the playwright did not have "more than passing sympathy with the conventionalized attitudes of fashionable society." The contemporary Middleton, still more the later Brome, and most of all Shirley in *Hyde Park* and *The Lady of Pleasure,* anticipate the social mode of Restoration comedy better than Fletcher.

A stronger case for influence can be made out, from another angle, for such Fletcher plays as *The Wild-Goose Chase, Wit Without Money* and *The Woman's Prize.* It may well be that these infected Restoration playwrights with that hardy perennial among comedy themes: woman hunts man—object, matrimony. Here, as in the frequently revived *The Scornful Lady,* the relation between the sexes is unsentimental; as Lewis remarks, the women not only bend the men to their will, but "are outspoken and determined in behalf of the interests of their sex."[140] One thinks immediately of Congreve's Millamant, with her provisos, and her concession that she may by degrees dwindle into a wife.[141] Moreover, since the Restoration particularly admired the wit and ingenuity of Fletcher, it is not a difficult feat to demonstrate that his flair for rapid-fire farce and for nimble, occasionally coarse repartee, in these and other plays, were well studied by writers of comedy.

Influence on tragedy is also revealed by Nathanial Lee's statement in

"The Epistle Dedicatory" to *Mithradates* (1678) that "I have endeavour'd in this Tragedy, to mix Shakespear with Fletcher: The Thought of the former . . . and the Softness and passionate Expressions of the latter." Lee thus reflects a popular view that Fletcher excelled in love scenes. But we should be a bit wary, for only a few lines later he adds, "I hope, the World will do me Justice to think, I have disguis'd it into another Fashion more suitable to the Age we live in, . . ."[142] Here we have the spirit in which adaptations were made by Restoration playwrights. There is a strong family resemblance between Lee's remark and Nahum Tate's assertion, in the "Epistle Dedicatory" to his alteration of *The Island Princess,* that "Those Defects in Manners, that were too palpable throughout the Work, must be imputed to the Age in which they wrote; but still there are so many and transcending Beauties in all their Writings, that I judg'd it safest to Rob the Treasure"[143] by trimming and patching an earlier adaptation of this melodrama.

Shakespeare had begun to suffer from this habit of alteration even earlier than Fletcher and his collaborators. Nicoll considers this growing frequency of adaptation of the older playwrights as due to the "infinite self-confidence" of the age. "It was not truly creative," he explains, "but it craved for art; and it had no scruples about making up for its lack of creative power by filching and altering dramatic glories of the past."[144]

There were, too, other "disguisings" than those of Lee and Tate, not so openly avowed. These took the form of character types, repartee, situations, scenes and plots snatched from Fletcher and Company plays not recently on the boards. Sprague informs us that our authors were liked "as very practical playwrights indeed, as expert purveyors of varied and full-bodied entertainment."[145] Hence, in Wilson's words, "they were made use of as excellent models for would-be successful playwrights."[146]

Since, then, the plays came down from a less polished age, they had palpable defects but were, for all that, well worth altering and plundering. Even the neo-classical John Sheffield, Earl of Musgrave, expressed the mood of Restoration theatre-lovers when, after characteristically giving the palm for dialogue to Plato and Lucian in *An Essay Upon Poetry* (1682), he admits that in justice we must allow that

> Shakespear and Fletcher are the wonders now:
> Consider them, and read them o're and o're,
> Go see them play'd, then read them as before.
> For though in many things they grossly fail,
> Over our Passions still they so prevail
> That our own grief by theirs is rockt asleep,
> The dull are forc'd to feel, the wise to weep.

But unfortunately these earlier playwrights had not observed the supposed rules of Aristotle; so he concludes: "Their Beauties imitate, avoid their faults."[147]

V

The neo-classical spectacles behind which one could view the faults of the older dramatists were not yet firmly adjusted to the noses of critics in the first Restoration years. Meanwhile, the wealth of tributes and allusions in verse and prose attests to the overwhelming supremacy of Jonson, Fletcher and Shakespeare over other playwrights of the past.

The dramas of the triumvirate were, of course, easily accessible in collected editions. But this was more a result than a cause of their popularity and high repute. While mention of any one of the triumvirs almost automatically brought up the names of one and usually both of the other two, only rarely was a further dramatist added to the list. Even then, later authors like Cowley and Davenant or the contemporary Dryden were aptest to appear. Most readers would have agreed with Sir John Denham, writing in 1667, that it was "By Shakespear's, Johnson's, Fletcher's lines" that "Our Stages lustre Rome's outshines"[148]—unless they preferred the ancients to the moderns.

Even Langbaine, trying in 1691 to deal justly with each earlier playwright in his biographical and critical accounts of the English dramatists, reflects this comparative obscuration of others than the accepted three. For instance, he thinks the better of Middleton because of his associations; for he

was Contemporary with those Famous Poets Johnson, Fletcher, Massinger and Rowley, in whose Friendships he had a large Share; and tho' he came short of the two former in parts, yet like the Ivy by the assistance of the Oak (being joyn'd with them in several Plays) he clim'd up to some considerable height of Reputation. He joyn'd with Fletcher and Johnson, in a Play called *The Widow*, . . . and certainly most Men will allow, That he that was thought fit to be receiv'd into a Triumvirate, by two such Great Men, was no common Poet.[149]

As for Rowley, Langbaine is careful to tell us that he was "beloved by those Great Men, Shakespear, Fletcher, and Johnson," but that in the main "he joyn'd in writing with Poets of the second Magnitude, as Heywood, Middleton, Day and Webster."[150]

Richard Flecknoe, comparing the triumvirate in 1664, made briefly the distinctions which were to be rephrased and repeated by others in a kind of formula: "Shakespeare excelled in a natural vein, Fletcher in Wit, and Johnson in Gravity and ponderousness of Style; . . ."[151] Eleven years later, Edward Phillips, Milton's nephew, elaborated this "symmetry of perfection," as he called it, saying specifically of Fletcher that he "excelled . . . in a courtly Elegance, and gentle familiarity of style, and withal a wit and invention so overflowing, that the luxuriant branches thereof were frequently thought convenient to be lopt off by his almost inseparable companion Francis Beaumont."[152] William Winstanley simply copied Phillips' statement in 1687, as did T. P. Blount in 1694; and so it went.[153] Such critics as the last two, not bent on being original, saved themselves whatever labor they could.

Flecknoe, continuing his discourse, made criticisms of Beaumont and Fletcher which henceforth were to gain ground in some quarters. By raising the standard of decorum, he shows himself touched by a neo-classical shibboleth. He declared that our authors "often err'd against Decorum" by "seldom representing a valiant man without something of the Braggadoccio, nor an honorable woman without somewhat of Dol Common in her." Flecknoe was possibly the first dramatic critic thus to detect something unorthodox in our playwrights' methods of characterization. Moreover, moral cleanness was beginning to be called into question here, as in the erroneous statement that "Fletcher was the first who introduc't . . . witty obscenity in his Playes." And surprisingly enough, considering the modern bias about our authors' servility to the divine right of kings, Flecknoe rebuked "their irreverent representing Kings persons on the Stage, who shu'd never be represented, but by Reverence."[154] Fletcher, it seems, was no longer "the genius of government." These critical abatements may be indicative of why Flecknoe gave definite preference to Shakespeare when, six years later, he wrote:

> So hard 'tis now for any one to write
> With Johnson's fire, or Fletcher's flame & sprite:
> Much less inimitable Shakespears way,
> Promethian-like to animate a Play.[155]

Two critics call for fuller attention than any of the others: Thomas Rymer and John Dryden. It so happens that Rymer's challenging book, *The Tragedies of the last Age Consider'd*, (1678), which criticized certain tragedies and tragicomedies of Shakespeare and Fletcher from the standpoint of classical tragedy, was answered by Dryden in his *Heads of an Answer to Rymer's Remarks on the Tragedies of the Last Age*.[156] Here is one skirmish, deeply significant for our playwrights, in the quarrel of the ancients and moderns which, as Noyes remarks, "exhausted no small degree of literary energy for seventy-five years after the Restoration."[157]

As Flecknoe's qualified praise would indicate, Rymer was not the first to express derogatory opinions about the early playwrights. Another instance is William Arrowsmith's comedy, *The Reformation*, (1673), wherein a glancing blow had been struck by one of the characters. Speaking first of three Italian playwrights, he pontificated:

> There are many pretenders but you see how few succeed; and bating two or three of this nation as Tasso, Ariosto and Guarini, that write indifferently well, the rest must not be named for Poesy: we have some three or four, as Fletcher, Johnson, Shakespeare, Davenant, that have scribbled themselves into the bulk of follies and are admired too, but ne're knew the laws of heroick or dramatick poesy, nor faith to write the English neither.[158]

Different indeed is this sneering character's comment from Edward Howard's, who dared "averre, that the Ingenuities of Johnson, Beaumont, and Fletcher, with some other of our former Poets, left our language more improved, as it expressed their thoughts, then if the best of Italian, Spanish, and French Wit, had been translated by the greatest of Pens."[159]

Rymer it was, however, who first developed a full-panoplied onslaught on representative older plays from a sternly neo-classical point of view. Though he did not spare Shakespeare's *Othello* any more than he did *The Bloody Brother, A King and No King*, or *The Maid's Tragedy*, the three latter plays bore the brunt of the attack. To Rymer it was Jonson's *Catiline* which, in spite of flaws, had "more of Poetry and of good thought, more of Nature and of Tragedy, then peradventure can be scrapt together from all these other plays."[160] In this carping treatise we shall see how astigmatic could be the vision of one who rigidly adhered to the touchstone of the pseudo-Aristotelean rules.

What obviously irritated Rymer is indicated by his "opinion, that the English want neither genius nor language for so great a work." They had simply lacked the good judgment to imitate the Greeks: "Had our authors began with Tragedy, as Sophocles and Euripedes left it; had they built either upon the same foundation, or after their model; we might e're this day have seen Poetry in greater perfection, and boasted such monuments as Greece or Rome never knew in all their glory."[161] Here was the rub!

As so often happens, it was the premises of the author himself which were at fault. If these are granted his critique, though rigid and malicious, makes a good deal of sense, and his argument carries much logical force.

What Rymer and others of his neo-classical persuasion did not realize was that Aristotle, in his *Poetics*, was not laying down dramatic laws for all time. The Stagirite's results were arrived at by looking at a specific drama, the Greek, at a specific point of time, the fifth and fourth centuries, B. C. Acutely analyzing the actual practice of this drama, and basing his theories thereon, Aristotle did hit upon some fundamentals of dramatic technique; but not all the things he said would hold true of all kinds of drama everywhere.

Renaissance critics, understanding little of the actual conditions of staging and performance in the Greek theatre, erected Aristotle into an absolute authority. They confirmed him from the Greek plays, whose practical structural necessities they but dimly comprehended, and from Seneca's recital-pieces. Their own worshipful ingenuities in compiling a structure of rules and fiats (including the famous three unities of time, place and action) might well have surprised Aristotle, had he returned to life.

Two French neo-classical dramatists finally succeeded in winning both popular applause and high critical esteem: Corneille, and the even more "regular" Racine. To men like Rymer these playwrights proved that moderns could still write great drama on the classical model, while observing the rules of the critics. How irritating that English writers of tragedy did not know their business!

Rymer, as a matter of course, grounded himself on a favorite neo-classical conception that nature and men are always the same, that man's affections and passions always have the same springs, and result in the same effects, whether he is Greek or Elizabethan. It followed for him that what was sound in Greek drama was sound for all time. But even "were it to be suppos'd that Nature with us is corrupt . . . that we are Barbarians . . . shall our Poet therefore pamper this corrupt nature, and indulge our barbarity? Shall he not rather purge away the corruption, and reform our manners?"[162]

Rymer posited, as given, that the dramatist should not be a historian but a philosopher, should present us with men and women as they ought to be, should not allow of the "unbecoming" even where true, should "confine his fancy to general probability," and should show forth "Poetical Justice." Reason, not fancy, should frame his characters and control his plotting. Laws of cause and effect and, of course, the three unities, should be observed.[163] Rymer's quarrel with Shakespeare and more especially Fletcher was that they offended in these matters, but had no excuse for doing so.

He explores in detail *The Bloody Brother* (or *Rollo, Duke of Normandy*), *A King and No King,* and *The Maid's Tragedy.* Some of his individual dicta are sensible, even at times acute; he spots theatricalities and other weaknesses in these pieces. But his annoyance carries him away; it results in many amusingly picayune absurdities. His submissive royalism is offended, like Flecknoe's, by our playwrights' treatment of kings; and his total perspective is wrenched awry by his neo-classical preposessions.

Of *The Bloody Brother* he says, "Poetry requires the ben trovato, something handsomely invented, and leaves the truth to History; but never were the Muses so profan'd with a more foul, unpleasant, and unwholesome truth, than this which makes the argument of Rollo."[164] He finds the sense of the design to be that "He who sheds the blood of man, by man shall his blood be shed."[165] Of the title character, King Rollo, who wades in blood, he objects that "an obdurate impudent and inpenitent Malefactor can neither move compassion nor terror; nor be of any imaginable use in Tragedy."[166] As for poetical justice, there can be none where there are "so many lives taken away, and but the life of one guilty person to answer for all."[167] In characterization, Rollo is "much stuff lumberd together," who cannot "the least passion stir, that is pleasant or generous"; Aubrey, his successor on the throne, is nothing "shining and extraordinary"; Latorch violates decorum in that no Poet "dare imagine that God Almighty would trust his Anointed with such a Guardian Devil"; and the women characters are weak and unheroic.[168] In addition, much of the dialogue is senseless.[169]

Conceding that the melodramatic *The Bloody Brother*, probably a four-writer job, is a weaker play than the other two, let us see what Rymer makes of *A King and No King*. He selects as the plot only the basic situation, whereby Arbaces in infancy became the supposed king, and the true ruler, Panthea, became his supposed sister—together with the finale of their marriage. "The rest is all episode."[170] He does not like the deft way in which Beaumont and Fletcher concealed the denouement, for he says, "We blunder along without the least streak of light, till in the last act we stumble on the Plot lying all in a lump together."[171] Moreover, "The Characters are all improbable and improper in the highest degree," and, like all the lines, "run so wide from the Plot, that scarce ought could be imagin'd more contrary."[172] Arbaces, braggart and swaggerer, who detestably draws his sword against a woman above him in rank, is insufferable even as supposed king, for "crown'd heads by Political right are Heroes." His treatment of his prisoner, the King of Armenia, is abominable; "Bajazet in his Cage was never so carried about, or felt half the barbarous indignities."[173] Panthea behaves with Arbaces like some "Wastcoateer of the Village"; indeed, "if we consider them Brother and Sister, 'tis horribly wicked." She lacks the spirit to reject Arbaces as husband; she should have "call'd to mind his late brutish insolence, and have call'd him impudent Slave, . . . or commanded him to be nail'd to the floor as false coin, and a counterfeit stamp of Majesty."[174] As for the entertaining humour character, Bessus, so popular with playgoers, decorum is offended to "find the King drolling and quibbling" with him and his buffoons, and it is "worse that they should presume to break their little jests upon him,"[175]—though that is just what little courtiers actually did with King James.

Whatever truth there may be in some of Rymer's charges, it is sadly distorted out of all justice by his intolerant spirit. So it is with *The Maid's Tragedy*. Once again, "nothing in History was ever so unnatural, nothing in Nature was ever so improbable, as we find the whole conduct of this Tragedy." In this case Rymer gathers "that the Poets intent was to show the dismal consequences of fornication."[176] Once more Rymer's royalism raises its head; a king should be allowed his little peccadillo without being slain for it.

But why continue? Rymer was apparently as much disturbed by the "immorality" of our dramatists as Coleridge and other later critics were to be. And he was firmly convinced that these playwrights (and Shakespeare) had taken "a by-road, that runs directly cross to that of Nature Manners and Philosophy which gain'd the Ancients so great veneration."[177] It never seems to have occurred to him that he was bringing together under one critical standard things incompatible in kind: the grave, serious, almost religious Greek tragedies, and bright, gilded theatrical butterflies fashioned to entertain.

Rymer's corrosive criticism, had it been generally accepted, might have put an end to the popularity of our author's tragicomedies and tragedies on the stage. But he overshot his mark. Among the protests was a sharp if brief reproof from Samuel Butler, the author of *Hudibras*. Writing *Upon Criticks Who Judge of Modern Plays Precisely by the Rules of the Antients*, he rapped over the knuckles those who "steal their farfet Criticismes" from Corneille; and he jibed at their "Trover," which was

> Enough to furnish all the Lewd Impeachers
> Of witty Beaumonts Poetry, & Fletchers,
> Who, for a few Misprisions of wit,
> Are chargd by those who tentimes worse commit;
> And for Misjudging some unhappy scenes,
> Are censured for't with more unlucky sense;
> When all their worst miscarriages Delight
> And please more then the Best the Pedants write.[178]

Butler may have had Dryden as well as Rymer in mind. But Dryden, though impressed by Rymer's argument, was himself aroused to partial disagreement. The ablest critic of the century, he was sometimes unduly respectful of authority, but he generally allowed his intelligence a good measure of free and independent play. He was not altogether immune to the pedantries of his age; indeed, his dramatic criticism is more tainted in this fashion than his non-dramatic. But when his judgment was not swung away from its normal balance, it is true, as Ker remarks, that "He is sceptical, tentative, disengaged, where most of his contemporaries, and most of his successors for a hundred years, are pledged to certain dogmas and principles."[179]

According to Theophilus Cibber, Rymer sent a copy of his book to his friend, Dryden, who had already evidenced sympathy with some of the neo-classical dramatic doctrines, and found fault with Shakespeare, Jonson, and Fletcher. But Dryden was not altogether prepared to swallow Rymer's fanaticism. Cibber's anecdote informs us that he judged Rymer's "Model of tragedy" to be "extremely correct, but not the only one"; and he considered the author "better acquainted with the Greek than the English poets."[180]

With *Heads of an Answer to Rymer* Dryden prepared to enter the lists; but unfortunately he never developed his notations into a full-fledged essay, and they remained unpublished until the 1711 edition of Beaumont and Fletcher.[181] In these *Heads,* he objected to Rymer's imposing a dictatorship of the ancients upon modern plays.[182] He protested sensibly that "Shakespeare and Fletcher have written to the genius of the age and nation in which they lived." He admitted that nature and reason are the same in all places; "yet the climate, the age, the disposition of the people, to whom a poet writes, may be so different, that what pleased the Greeks would not satisfy an English audience."[183]

Dryden planned "to make a judgment on what the English have added to [Greek] beauties." He exampled "new passions, as namely, that of love, scarce touched on by the ancients," and insofar as it was treated, "how short they were of Fletcher." He also intended to prove that "love, being an heroic passion, is fit for tragedy."[184] He noted that characters were "neither so many nor varied" in the Greeks as in Shakespeare and Fletcher, and considered that the style is "certainly more noble and more practical in the English than in the Greek."[185] He felt that, in producing the ends of pity and terror commended by Aristotle, "those plays which he arraigns . . . have moved both these passions in a high degree upon the stage."[186]

As for Rymer's censures on the "designs" of our dramatists' plays, Dryden was deeply impressed, but objected that these were "rather wittily aggravated in many places, than reasonably urged." Concerning Arbaces he asserted, "the faults in the character of the 'King and no King' are not as he makes them . . . but only imperfections which accompany human nature, and are for the most part excused by the violence of his love." Rollo, in *The Bloody Brother,* was "too severely arraigned by him"; nor did Dryden agree with Rymer that poetic justice was neglected in this play.[187] Summing up his point of view, Dryden judicially concluded that "if the plays of the ancients are more correctly plotted, ours are more beautifully written. And if we can raise the passions as high on worse foundations, it shows our genius in tragedy is greater; for, in all other parts of it, the English have manifestly excelled them."[188] Dryden's heart was with the English playwrights.

Dryden's answer, even more than Butler's retort, makes it clear why the idolaters of the ancients did not have things all their own way. Returning to the attack fifteen years later with *A Short View of English Tragedy*, Rymer wryly expressed his conviction that Shakespeare, Jonson and Fletcher were "at this day in possession of the stage, and acted with greater applause than ever."[189] Yet his treatise was symptomatic; it does mark the turning of the tide. Dryden himself was influenced by it, as we shall see. The neo-classical point of view, which Rymer expressed with such intolerance, was eventually to act as a blight on our authors.

During nearly forty years of the Restoration period Dryden wrote about the triumvirate on many occasions, whether briefly or at length. On one matter, their comparative stature, he never wavered. Shakespeare was the greatest.[190] He tells us in 1668 that "He was the man who of all modern, and perhaps of all ancient poets, had the largest and most comprehensive soul."[191] A year earlier he had likewise placed first

> Shakespeare, who (taught by none) did first impart
> To Fletcher wit, to labouring Johnson art.
> He, monarch-like, gave those subjects, law;
> And is that subject which they paint and draw. . . .
> If they have since out-writ all other men,
> 'Tis with the drops that fell from Shakespeare's pen.[192]

Jonson came second, with Fletcher third, as instanced in *MacFlecknoe*, wherein Dryden exempted both from the kingdom of dullness:

> Great Fletcher never treads in buskins here,
> Nor greater Jonson dares in socks appear.[193]

Dryden first discussed the three playwrights in some detail in *An Essay of Dramatic Poesy* (1668), his most full-bodied, urbane, impersonal and lively piece of dramatic criticism. The portion of the essay which most concerns us is the argument in which Lisideius (Sir Charles Sedley) upholds the French neo-classical drama as against Neander (Dryden himself), who champions the English.[194]

Lisideius, an admirer of French regularity, dislikes the dual plots of English tragicomedies and other plays.[195] Yet he is impressed with the delayed denouement of "that excellent play, *A King and No King* . . . for the whole unravelling of the plot is done by narration in the fifth act, after the manner of the ancients,"[196]—a point to which Rymer was blind.

Moreover, he thinks that "but one tragedy of ours" has a plot with "uniformity and unity of design in it"—and he names *The Bloody Brother!* He considers this play to be "founded upon the truth of history."[197] Rymer's special attention to these points suggests that he had read this essay.

Lisideius, however, also finds faults. He does not like the farcical element in *The Bloody Brother,* "which is below the dignity of the other parts; and in this all our poets are extremely peccant." Nor does the play observe unity of time.[198] He objects to sudden conversions at the ends of plays, "which is the ordinary way in which our poets use to end theirs," giving as example the conversion of Morecraft the usurer in *The Scornful Lady.*[199] As a good neo-classicist, Lisideius maintains that tragicomedy, "a drama of our own invention," is the most absurd of all the kinds: "here a course of mirth, there another of sadness, a third of honour, and fourth a duel: thus, in two hours and a half, we run through all the fits of bedlam!"[200] Lisideius' scorn for the mixed moods of tragicomedy suggests that our playwrights' frequent use of this dramatic form was one of the reasons for the decline of their reputation during the age of neo-classicism.

Neander, in defending the English dramatists, considers that even Corneille's comedy, *The Liar,* will not stand comparison with many of Fletcher's or Jonson's.[201] Admitting the charge of irregularity, Neander holds that Beaumont and Fletcher offended less than Shakespeare, "yet through carelessness made many faults." But in most of their irregular plays "there is more masculine fancy and greater spirit in the writing than there is in any of the French," and he considers the latter easier to write.[202] He also contends that variety of plot, if properly controlled, as in *The Maid's Tragedy,* is not objectionable; "you will find it infinitely pleasing to be led in a labyrinth of design."[203]

Not only are Beaumont and Fletcher's plays more regular than Shakespeare's, but "they understood and imitated the conversation of gentlemen much better; whose debaucheries, and quickness of wit in repartees, no poet can ever paint as they have done."[204] In fact, Fletcher excelled any French dramatist in repartee.[205] Neander thinks the English language, in Beaumont and Fletcher, had "arrived to its highest perfection," and that they "represented all the passions very lively, but above all, love."[206] Earlier in the essay, Eugenius (Lord Buckhurst) had mentioned "the excellent scenes of passion in Shakespeare, or in Fletcher."[207]

But Dryden was not always to be thus gracious to our playwrights. In 1671 he published, with *An Evening's Love, or The Mock Astrologer,* a preface in which, feeling that the older modes of comedy were worn out, he was trying to explain—not without heat—how his own comedies dif-

fered from Jonson's. He had been stung by the charge that he made debauched persons like the Astrologer of this play his protagonists, and did
not carry out poetic justice by punishing their vices in the end. He answered that neither do Plautus or Jonson, while "As for Beaumont and
Fletcher, I need not allege examples out of them, for that were to quote
almost all their comedies."[208] He also took pot shots at the "folly" of
Fletcher's "superfluity and waste of wit," his little humour, abundance of
adventure in comedy, and ill-chosen characters who interfere with each
other.[209] The preface is not of Dryden's coolest.

One subject which he had prepared to treat, but was obliged to drop
in this preface, is made the point of the "Epilogue" to the second part of
The Conquest of Granada. This is: "the improvement of our language
since Fletcher's and Johnson's days," a reversal of the position which
Neander had taken three years earlier. Now, his own plays under attack,
he declares, in lines spoken from the stage, that

> . . . Jonson did mechanic humour show
> When men were dull, and conversation low. . . .
> And as their comedy, their love was mean;
> Except, by chance, in some one laboured scene,
> Which must atone for an ill-written play,
> They rose, but at their height could seldom stay.
> Fame then was cheap, and the first comer sped;
> And they have kept it since, by being dead. . . .

Only exasperated ambition can account for Dryden's temper here; yet he
insisted that he did not speak from envy or malice, as he continued:

> 'Tis not to brand them that their faults are shown,
> But, by their errors, to excuse his own.

It was criticism of Dryden's plays, then, that had inspired the epilogue—
this, and the characteristic Restoration sense of superiority expressed in
the next lines:

> If love and honour now are higher raised,
> 'Tis not the poet, but the age is praised.
> Wit's now arrived to a more high degree;
> Our native language more refined and free.
> Our ladies and our men now speak more wit
> In conversation, than those poets writ.[210]

The epilogue provoked a storm. In *The Rehearsal,* which was staged
the same year, Mr. Bayes (John Dryden) is made to say, "I despise your
Johnson and Beaumont, that borrow'd all they writ from Nature; I am
for fetching it purely out of my own fancy."[211] And Lord John Vaughan,

writing verses to be prefixed to the published text of *The Conquest of Granada,* says, in blunt reproof:

> Ben Johnson, Beaumont, Fletcher, Shakespeare, are
> As well as you, to have a poet's share.
> You who write after, have, besides, this curse,
> You must write better, or you else write worse.[212]

Dryden therefore penned a *Defense of the Epilogue; or an Essay on the Dramatic Poetry of the Last Age* (1672), in order to explain himself more fully. He seeks to show that on every page of Fletcher's work will be found "either some solecism of speech, or some notorious flaw in sense." Because of the "ignorance" of his times, his plots were lame; he did not understand correct plotting, nor the "decorum of the stage."[213] *Philaster, The Humourous Lieutenant, The Faithful Shepherdess* and many others were "much below the applause which is now given them." You

will see Philaster wounding his mistress, and afterwards his boy, to save himself; not to mention the Clown, who enters immediately, and not only has the advantage of the combat against the hero, but diverts you from your serious concernment, with his ridiculous and absurd raillery. In his *Humorous Lieutenant,* you find his Demetrius and Leontius staying in the midst of a routed Army, to hear the cold mirth of the Lieutenant [One thinks immediately of Falstaff in the Battle of Shrewsbury]; and Demetrius afterwards appearing with a pistol in his hand, in the next age to Alexander the Great. And for his Shepherd, he twice falls into the former indecency of wounding women.[214]

He concludes that "our improprieties are less frequent, and less gross than theirs."[215]

Dryden's patronizing attitude towards both Shakespeare and Fletcher, in attributing their many "absurdities" to their unpolished age, is in itself absurd. "Besides the want of education and learning . . . they wanted the benefit of discourse," he smugly remarks.[216] Hence, "their wit was not that of gentlemen; there was ever somewhat that was ill-bred and clownish in it, and which confessed the conversation of the authors." In an age of lesser gallantry, they did not even keep the best company: "I cannot find that any of them have been conversant in courts, except Ben Johnson."[217] As for their audience, they "knew no better" and "were content with acorns," because they knew not "the use of good bread."[218] How much complacent ignorance of the facts such utterances disclose must, today, be patent.

In fairness, however, it should be added that Dryden averred his veneration for the beauties of our authors, and attempted a judicial summary of Fletcher, thus:

Let us imitate . . . the quickness and easiness of Fletcher, without proposing him as a pattern . . . either in the redundancy of his matter, or the incorrectness of his language. Let us admire his wit and sharpness of conceit; but let us . . . acknowledge, that it is seldom so fixed, and made proper to his characters, that the same things might not be spoken by any person in the play. Let us applaud his scenes of love; but . . . confess, that he understood not either greatness or perfect honour in . . . any of his women.[219]

In fine, he had much fancy, but was wanting in judgment. In spite of the more balanced tone here, is it any wonder that Rymer sent Dryden a copy of his masterpiece of wrong-headed criticism?

The *Defense* did not mend matters with those who differed from Dryden. A characteristic dig of these years comes from John Wilmot:

> But does not Dryden find ev'n Johnson dull?
> Fletcher and Beaumont incorrect, and full
> Of lewd lines, as he calls 'em? Shakespeare's stile
> Stiff and affected; to his own the while
> Allowing all the justness that his Pride
> So arrogantly had to these deny'd?[220]

Dryden's final essay dealing with our playwrights is *The Grounds of Criticism in Tragedy*, prefaced to his *Troilus and Cressida* (1679). He had been studying French critics like Rapin and Bossu, and, most recently, Rymer. He now admits that "How defective Shakespeare and Fletcher have been in all their parts, Mr. Rymer has discovered in his criticisms." Since Dryden finds *A King and No King* moving when read, and "the faults of the plot are so evidently proved, that they can no longer be denied," he suspects that the beauties of this tragedy lie "in the lively touches of the passions."[221] He likewise echoes Rymer's charge that Fletcher's kings are dowered with qualities unsuitable to a monarch. Placed beside the unpublished *Heads,* all this sounds a trifle obsequious.

In this essay Dryden also compares Shakespeare and Fletcher with much perspicacity. Fletcher comes far short of Shakespeare in almost everything, as, for instance, in "manners," or character traits. Those of Shakespeare's persons are "generally apparent, and you see their bent and inclinations." The characters of Fletcher are "but poor and narrow in comparison of Shakespeare's"; they are only "pictures shown you in the twilight," inconsistent, and "either good, bad, or indifferent, as the present scene requires it."[222] Dryden was the first to make this telling contrast.

In plotting, though both were deficient, "Shakespeare generally moves more terror, and Fletcher more compassion: for the first had a more masculine, a bolder and more fiery genius, the second, a more soft and womanish."[223] Apparently as a consequence, "Shakespeare writ better betwixt man and man," and hence about friendship; Fletcher "betwixt man and woman," and so about love. Dryden's acceptance of the conventional view that, in Herrick's words, "none writes lov's passion" like Fletcher, seems related to his association of love with effeminacy.

At the very core of Dryden's contrast was the discrimination that Shakespeare's mind was "universal," Fletcher's "more confined and limited." Shakespeare "comprehended all characters and passions," but Fletcher "either touched not, or not masterly" any passion save love. "To conclude all, he was a limb of Shakespeare."[224]

Now this was getting Shakespeare and Fletcher into at least a reasonable perspective, and it is Dryden's final contrast. But from our survey of the whole range of Dryden's opinions about Fletcher, we can see that his neo-classical pedantries and his harsher remarks, quite as much as such judicious comparisons as this, would tend to reduce Fletcher's stature for his readers. And when we remember how respected Dryden as a critic was in the eighteenth century, and how much read his essays remain to this day, we can appreciate that he played no small part in deflating our playwrights' reputation.

As time went on, even the counterblasts of Dryden's opponents unconsciously betray the effectiveness of his criticism. Brown, satirizing in 1688 Dryden's change of religion, made "Mr. Bays" say:

Then I fulminated Johnsons affected style, his dull way of making Love, his Thefts and Mean Characters; Shakespeares Ignorance, long Periods, and Barbarous Language; Fletchers want of a Gentlemans education; so often, do you observe me Mr. Crites, that scarce one in a hundred had the assurance to offer one good word in their behalf.[225]

Three years later, Langbaine, angry about Dryden's "implacable Thirst after Fame," which led him to "demolish the Statues and Monuments of his Ancestors," was driven to defend Shakespeare, Jonson and Fletcher by the "tu quoque" argument. Dryden, like Fletcher, made a man draw sword on a woman in *The Conquest of Granada,* and he, too, was guilty of "Improprieties in Grammar," of "Solecisms in Speech, and Flaws in Sence."[226] But Gildon, in 1699, responds with a protest against Langbaine's "partiality." He has a lower opinion of Fletcher and Company, for among their plays "there is scarce one regular. Their comedies are much the best; yet of them take away five or six, and they will not bear acting, scarce reading by a nice judge."[227]

Gildon may be harsher than usual on our playwrights, but their glory had dimmed no little since the First Folio of 1647. Shakespeare was clearly about to win the ascendancy among the triumvirate; no longer did any critic assert that Fletcher excelled him, as some had done at mid-century. Even that stout defender of all the earlier playwrights, Langbaine, tells us that though he "extreamly" admired Fletcher (and Jonson), he admired Shakespeare still more.[228] James Drake, answering Jeremy Collier in 1699, explains that "I shall begin with Shakespeare, whom notwithstanding the severity of Mr. Rhimer, and the hard usage of Mr. Collier, I must still think the Proto-Dramatist of England, though he fell short of the Art of Johnson, and the Conversation of Beaumont and Fletcher."[229]

Thus the same century whose middle years saw the fame of Fletcher, Beaumont and Company at its peak, also witnessed, in its closing ones, not only their decreased popularity on the stage but also their waning in critical esteem.

CHAPTER TWO

Obscuration and Re-Emergence

I N the eighteenth century, the reputation of Fletcher, Beaumont and Company went into sharp decline. During the reign of Queen Anne Shakespeare's tragedies permanently established their supremacy, as vehicles for the stage, over the tragicomedies and tragedies of our playwrights. It is true that the lighter plays of Fletcher and his colleagues, for another generation, fared better on the boards than those of Shakespeare; but when, about 1740, the latter's romantic comedies were finally revived in rapid succession, these quickly triumphed. Performances of dramas from our corpus thereafter dwindled in numbers until only two of the comedies—*Rule a Wife* and *The Chances*—remained stock-plays. Even these were snuffed out during the first half of the nineteenth century.[1]

In critical opinion, moreover, Fletcher, Beaumont and Company were definitely taking third place in the triumvirate as early as the age of Queen Anne. By this time Shakespeare and Jonson were usually acknowledged to be the fathers of English drama and the greatest playwrights of their era—the former (in spite of his faults) by virtue of his extraordinary "natural" gifts, and the latter because of his deeply respected "art." Dryden had insistently maintained that Shakespeare was a greater dramatist than Jonson, and by 1700 many had come to agree. Ben continued, however, to have his partisans, though in decreasing numbers until, in the time of Samuel Johnson, Shakespeare's primacy came to be generally accepted.

In the concentration of eighteenth century critical interest on Shakespeare and Jonson, "Beaumont and Fletcher" underwent a relative critical eclipse. Numerous indeed were the comparisons between their fellow triumvirs in which they did not share. In fact, many students of the drama, including some of the ablest critics of the century, wrote little or nothing about them. In the later decades, the occasional critics who did proclaim the excellencies of our playwrights might well have felt that they were voices crying in the wilderness.

With the upsurge of the Romantic Movement, however, there was a change in critical attitude. Lamb, Hazlitt and others, in a burst of ancestor worship, resurrected the old drama of Elizabethan and early Stuart days. Massinger had been coming out of Limbo, to join the earlier triumvirate, for a generation—thanks to collected editions of his plays in 1761 and 1779, and to a successful stage career after 1781 for his usurer, Sir Giles Overreach, in *A New Way to Pay Old Debts*.[2] Now the new quadrumvirate was broadened out into a council, with Shakespeare the adored and almost god-like leader.

Beaumont and Fletcher were thought to have been Shakespeare's co-rivals, and they suffered in the comparison. They were appreciated as lyric poets, but their moral standards and their "witty obscenity" shocked the sensibilities of the romantic critics. Their skilled craftsmanship and their true character as entertainers to the Jacobean gentry were little understood, although their theatrical tendency was spotted. The net result of criticism by the Romantics was to bring them out of their late eighteenth century obscuration, but with a place of decreased honor among the more elect councillors. They were, after all, rather shady and wanton in character.

I

By the age of Queen Anne, the somewhat extravagant esteem in which Fletcher and Company had been held by Caroline and early Restoration gentlemen had vanished. The criticism of Rymer and Dryden, and of other Restoration writers of strong or moderate neo-classical outlook, was proving corrosive. Since neo-classicism was in the ascendancy during the first half of the eighteenth century, such criticism, backed by the authority of Dryden, now prevailed. That Beaumont and Fletcher did not quite join the forgotten men of the elder drama seems to have been due to those plays which still held the boards, and to the availability in print of their complete works.

As Hooker remarks, "Most Augustans knew shockingly little of the great Elizabethans."[3] This widespread apathy towards writers of an "unpolished age" affected even our playwrights. John Dennis, the ablest Augustan critic of the drama, knew Fletcher and, in a letter, mentioned Colley Cibber's piracies from him; but he does not deign to bring him into any of his dramatic criticism.[4] And half a century later Dr. Samuel Johnson fails to mention our playwrights in his introduction to his edition of Shakespeare's works, and draws on them only scantily—and probably at second hand—in his notes. Although he possessed a copy of their works, it is within the bounds of possibility that he never bothered to open it![5]

Critical discussion of Fletcher is surprisingly sparse throughout the century, compared with that of Shakespeare or even of Jonson. For exactly one hundred years, moreover, there were only three editions of the complete works—in 1711, 1750 and 1778—and the introduction to the first of these merely echoes Langbaine, Dryden and others. For much of this century, Fletcher and Company seem to have interested the critics less than they did the playgoer.

This comparative neglect had various roots. In the eighteenth century, as Miss Bradbrook points out, Shakespeare—and he alone—was exempted by "special grace" from the rules.[6] Indeed, as time went on, the power of his "irregular beauties" eventually encouraged a bold minority to question the validity of fixed laws themselves.[7] Ben Jonson, of course, stood in relatively little need of exemption from the prevailing dogmas, and held his own thereby. But at a time when some critics maintained that "Shakespeare, enjoyable as he was, would have been still more enjoyable had he followed the rules,"[8] it is not surprising that the lesser playwrights of our corpus should have been often denied any special dispensation. They had, moreover, sinned in writing a number of plays in that deplorably mixed form, tragicomedy. Eighteenth century critics generally acknowledged Shakespeare's insight in portraying character, and some of them praised him as a philosopher. By comparison, Fletcher and Company clearly did not shine in either respect. Then, too, their "grossness" seemed more of a blemish to many than Shakespeare's, whose greater "natural genius" made it possible to excuse his lapses as due to the "unreformed" character of his theatre, and the "rude conditions" of his audience.Thus, while the groundwork of sound Shakespearean criticism was laid in the eighteenth century, Fletcher seems to have been accepted, in the main, as an agreeable lesser light not worth prolonged discussion, even though educated men still read him with pleasure.[9]

A rebellious note was occasionally struck, however, as early as the age of Queen Anne. George Farquhar, a playwright himself, insisted in 1702 that the writer of comedies must consult, not Plautus or Menander, but

Shakespear, Johnson, Fletcher and others, who by Methods much different from the Ancients, have supported the English Stage, and made themselves famous to Posterity. . . . I wou'd willingly understand the Regularities of *Hamlet, Mackbeth, Henry the fourth,* and of Fletcher's plays; and yet these have long been the Darlings of the English audience, and are like to continue with the same Applause, in Defiance of all the Criticisms that were ever publish'd in Greek, and Latin.[10]

It was in this same year that Farquhar consulted Fletcher to good advantage by deriving his own *The Inconstant* from *The Wild-Goose Chase!*[11]

A more normal note for this age was that of the rigidly neo-classical Charles Gildon, who in 1710 quoted approvingly "another," who thought that

if All that is absurd and irrational should be excluded the theatre, you must banish a great many of the most celebrated Pieces of the Stage; as, *Othello*, which is compos'd of Parts shocking to Reason, and full of Absurdities; the *Maid's Tragedy*, which Mr. Rhimer has justly condemn'd, and several others, which no Man has been able to vindicate from Faults equal to those urg'd against Opera's.[12]

We have already noted Gildon's dismissal of all plays of our corpus except five or six comedies. Now he states that there was not "much of Comedy known before the Learned Ben Johnson, for no Man can allow any of Shakespeare's Comedies, except the *Merry Wives of Windsor*."[13] This farce was regular enough to pass inspection.

Addison did not deal with our playwrights.[14] In one *Spectator* essay he discussed poetic justice in tragedy, but "the best of this kind" were by Restoration writers, except for *Othello* and *Lear*. As for tragicomedy, (wherein our authors faulted), he voiced the widely held opinion that it was "one of the most monstrous inventions that ever entered into a poet's thoughts," an absurd "motley piece of mirth and sorrow."[15] The "monstrous" simply echoes Rymer and Gildon. In a paper dealing with the cultivation of taste, Addison selected, as his three examples of ages when literary men flourished together and profited from association, Socratean Greece, Augustan Rome and Seventeenth Century France![16] The non-classical theatre world of Elizabethan London simply did not exist for him. As his dreary but correct *Cato* further suggests, Addison's "regular" dramatic tastes would prohibit interest in our plays.

But the warmer and more flexible Steele gave them some attention. In *The Tatler* he called *The Chances* "a true picture of real life," and thought that "Don Juan and Constantia are acted to the utmost of perfection," although the piece was not "wholly what a play should be."[17] In a *Spectator* paper he praised the portrayal of a bawd to the life in the third scene of the second act of *The Humorous Lieutenant* as "inimitably excellent" and as having "the true Spirit of Comedy."[18] But his reaction to *The Scornful Lady* was mixed. He thought the heroine was "so just a Picture of the Vanity of the Sex in tormenting their admirers" that it had been drawn by "one who had studied the Sex." But the comic presentation of Sir Roger, the chaplain, moved him "with the utmost Indignation at the trivial, senseless, and unnatural Representation." He found it difficult to believe that "such a Driveler . . . so bereft of all manner of Pride . . . could come into the Head of the same Man who drew the rest of the Play." Not comprehending Beaumont's satiric amusement at the plight of the Elizabethan family chaplain, he considered the characterization a gratuitous insult done Holy Orders "to gratify a loose age."[19] In another *Spectator* essay Steele agreed with Dryden that not even Beaumont and Fletcher could compare with Shakespeare in presenting witches and magic.[20]

Alexander Pope does not mention our playwrights in the introduction to his edition of Shakespeare. But if he is correctly identified as a certain "Dorimant" who wrote four letters to the *St. James' Journal* in the season of 1722-23, he did take an interest in *Philaster*. His second letter, of December 8, praised it as acted by Wilks,[21] and in the third, a week later, he wrote:

I hear several people have thought fit to quarrel with me for my opinion of *Philaster*, which I shall take the opportunity to justify as to the Fable, Sentiments, and Diction, when I have nothing better to entertain you with. . . . At present I shall only declare that a Dramatic Piece finely written, and justly represented, is, in my opinion, a most reasonable entertainment, and is capable of being made a very useful one.[22]

Unfortunately, Pope never found the opportunity; the rest is silence.[23]

In 1718, the editor of Samuel Daniel's poems suggested that a passage in *Hymen's Triumph* did not "fall short of the finest in Shakespeare or Fletcher."[24] In some minds, evidently, the latter two names were still linked. Five years later Jacobs, in his *Poetical Register*, merely repeated the usual bromides about Fletcher's excellent repartee, his wit, Beaumont's judgment, and their fine scenes of conversation. But though he said nothing new, he was appreciative rather than condemnatory. Doubtless many readers agreed with this handbook that "Fletcher express'd his Thoughts with . . . Vivacity, drew the Passions . . . lively," and wrote delightful raillery—whatever neo-classical critics might think.[25]

The major attempt to supply dramatic criticism in London during the decade of the 1730s was Aaron Hill's *The Prompter*, appearing twice a week from November 12, 1734, to July 2, 1736. A certain I. K., in his *Life of Aaron Hill*, informs us that this periodical was "calculated to instruct the actors, and to reform theatrical amusements."[26] Among other efforts at reform was a heavy onslaught in Number 60 on the immoral influence of *The Maid's Tragedy*. Theatre manager, improver of Shakespeare, minor playwright and critic, Hill takes a neo-classical position in his attack, quoting Rymer's criticism as "unanswerable."[27] He may well have contributed to the disappearance of this play from the boards.

Two writers of much greater ability than Hill pay tribute to our playwrights in the next decade. William Collins contributed *An Epistle Addressed to Sir Thomas Hanmer, On His Edition of Shakespeare's Works,* dated from Oxford, December 3, 1743. After asserting that Jonson's plays smack too much of the critic, he continued:

> Of softer mould the gentle Fletcher came,
> The next in order, as the next in name;
> With pleased attention, 'midst his scenes we find
> Each glowing thought that warms the female mind;
> Each melting sigh, and every tender tear;
> The lover's wishes, and the virgin's fear.
> His every strain, the smiles and graces own;
> But stronger Shakespeare felt for man alone:[28]

This is, of course, a versification of Dryden's contrast between Shakespeare's excellence in the manly passions, and Fletcher's in the softer.

The other writer was Edmund Burke. In 1748, when a precocious lad of 18 in Dublin, he was bringing out a periodical, *The Reformer.* In the second issue, he praised Jonson and Shakespeare, condemned the "lewdness" of Restoration dramatists, and stated that Dryden "industriously avoided nature." Then he indicated that, in his hurry, he had forgotten to mention "two authors of great note," Beaumont and Fletcher, who, he added, "are authors of merit."[29] This is tantalizing; one wishes he had been in less of a hurry!

Another assemblage of stereotypes about Beaumont and Fletcher, smacking strongly of Dryden, Winstanley and Langbaine—as in Jacob's *Poetical Register*—was put together for *Biographia Britannica* (1747). The virtues of our authors included plots more regular than Shakespeare's, a better imitation of the repartee of gentlemen, and lively descriptions of the passions; their faults were "luxuriance . . . frequent solecisms of speech, and great incorrectness in general." The account concluded that "envy cannot deny, that their wit is great, and their expressions often noble," and allowed "the absurdities they committed" a Shakespearean dispensation, in that they were "rather the age's fault than theirs." So, "T"; but "K" adds, in a footnote, that the preference between our authors and Shakespeare "lies greatly on his side; whose sublimer beauties of sentiment and poetry Beaumont and Fletcher could never reach."[30] Shakespeare's superiority in beauties was by now generally conceded.

In 1750 the second eighteenth-century edition of our playwrights' complete works was published. The first one (1711) had been merely a reprint of the Second Folio of 1679 and, as has been suggested, its preface had been almost wholly compiled from information and passages in Langbaine and Dryden. In 1742, Lewis Theobald agreed with the Tonsons to undertake a new edition of Beaumont and Fletcher.[31] Two years later the success of Dodsley's *Select Collection of Old English Plays*[32] confirmed their impression that there was a reading public for Elizabethan and Stuart drama.

Theobald, while editing his *Works of Shakespeare* (1734), had already displayed a wide knowledge of the older drama; his references to plays of our authors (and of Jonson) were especially numerous.[33] To him, in fact, Jones credits no small part in reviving interest in old poets, and so in stimulating the nascent romantic movement. Both his critical method and his frequent quotations of earlier authors inspired scholars to resurrect long-buried writers of the past.[34]

Theobald applied his scholarly acumen to that part of the text which he edited: six plays, and most of two others.[35] By careful collation of all available texts and cautious emendation, he produced results commensurate with those of his edition of Shakespeare. But unfortunately he was obliged to associate with him in his work the Rev. Thomas Seward of Lichfield and a man named Sympson, and after his death they completed the edition. Both men, though they tried to follow Theobald's methods as well as they could, were incompetent collators, ignorant of Elizabethan language and life, and rash emendators.[36] Despite the skill of Theobald's portion of the job, the edition as a whole was therefore disappointing. It was, however, noteworthy as "the first serious attempt towards a critical reconstruction of an eclectic text."[37]

For our purposes, the most significant aspect of this edition is the *Preface* by Seward—the first full and independent discussion of our authors to appear in an issue of their works. How far Seward was indebted to Theobald for the ideas he expressed, we do not know. At any rate, he made some very sensible observations and shrewd deductions. He did not confine himself to repeating what others had said, nor was he hag-ridden by a stern neo-classical outlook.

Seward considered as alike unjust the seventeenth century extolling of Beaumont and Fletcher as equal or superior to Shakespeare, and the tendency of his own age to depress their plays "beneath the smooth-polished enervate issue of the modern drama."[38] He noted that Earle ascribed to Beaumont those "three first-rate plays," *The Maid's Tragedy, Philaster,* and *A King and No King.* He thought that "there is scarce a more lively-spirited character in all their plays than Philaster," and surmized that "Beaumont aimed at drawing a Hamlet racked with Othello's love and jealousy." As for Arbaces in *A King and No King,* anathema to

Rymer, he "holds up a mirror to all men of virtuous principles but violent passions," while Bessus and his two swordsmen were "infinitely the
liveliest comic characters of mere bragging cowards that we have in our
language," though not the equals of the more fully rounded Falstaff and
his men.[39]

Comparing our playwrights with Shakespeare and Jonson, Seward held
them to be "in a direct mean," for though "they do not reach the amazing rapidity and immortal flights of the former, . . . they soar with
more ease and to nobler heights than the latter." They had less of "noble
enthusiasm" and "terrible graces" than Shakespeare, but more of these
than Jonson. On the other hand, they were "more regular in their plots
and more correct in their sentiments and diction than Shakespeare, but
less so than Jonson."[40]

When it came to differences between the "twins," Seward considered
that in comedy Beaumont imitated Jonson, while Fletcher followed
Shakespeare—a distinction with some truth in it. In tragedy, they both
painted "from real life." Beaumont was a "hard student," while Fletcher
was "a polite rather than a deep scholar," who studied men as much as
books. Hence sprang "the gay sprightliness and natural ease" of Fletcher's
young gentlemen, which "judges of candour" allow to be "inimitable,"
and superior to Shakespeare's achievement in this kind. After noting
that *The Bloody Brother* and *The False One* were "two of Fletcher's
first-rate plays," despite their borrowings from the "ancient classics," he
concluded that Beaumont, to his credit, was less imitative of the ancients
than Fletcher.[41]

We may be surprised to learn that our playwrights were "not at all remarkable for forming a labyrinth of incidents and entangling their
readers in a pleasing perplexity," since this seems to moderns a definite
skill of theirs. What Seward, however, wished was that readers would
"drop the expectation of the event of each story, to attend with more
care to the beauty and energy of the sentiments, diction, passions, and
characters." Living in a country town, at a time when the plays were performed with decreasing frequency, he was apparently unaware of their
impact in the theatre. Perhaps, too, long familiarity with them as texts
had taken the edge off unexpected turns of plot and situation.[42]

Seward accepted the view that Shakespeare's "first-rate beauties" of
poetry were inimitable, but held that his second-rate ones ranked with
our playwrights' best. To prove his point, he discussed many comparative instances from both bodies of plays.[43] Then he sought to demonstrate that, whereas Shakespeare often excelled not only "in diction and
sentiment" but also "in characters and passions," yet instances occurred
of "the pre-eminence of our authors." He cited Julianna in *The Double*

Marriage, "who, through her whole character, in conjugal fidelity, un-
shaken constancy and amiable tenderness, even more than rivals the
Portia of Shakespeare." He considered her death-scene more pathetic than
that of Cordelia in King Lear's arms. He held that the Cleopatra of *The
False One* compared favorably, in character and passions, with Shakespeare's. On the other hand, he believed the quarrel-scene of Amintor
and Melantius in *The Maid's Tragedy* not quite so dignified and noble
as that of Brutus and Cassius in *Julius Caesar.* Whatever we may think
of Seward's judgment, it is good to find an eighteenth century critic of
our plays getting down to cases.[44]

We need not pause over Seward's discussion of our playwrights' three
styles in comedy—the sublime, the droll poetic and the burlesque sub-
lime—nor over his classification of the plays nor his justification of
Fletcher's inferiority to Shakespeare in ghosts and magic. His defense of
Theobald against other critics is, for our purposes, a tale of far-off things.
What he had to say, however, on the moral issue is worth noting.

Seward felt that he must apologize "for a fault which must shock every
modest reader: it is their frequent use of gross and indecent expressions."
He adds that "they have this fault in common with Shakespeare, who is
sometimes more gross than they are; but I think grossness does not occur
quite so often in him."[45] In thus finding Shakespeare, as well as our playwrights, guilty of coarseness, Seward was more clearsighted than Shakespeare's idolators, for whom that dramatist could do no wrong; and he
justly admitted the lesser frequency of his offending.

Seward had likewise given thought to the fact that some seventeenth
century writers celebrated our playwrights "as the great reformers of the
drama from bawdry and ribaldry." Citing Beaumont's excuse for
Chaucer's indecencies—that he put his "filthiest words" into the mouths
of "low characters"—Seward suggested, with some acumen, that the same
plea might be made for all the older dramatists, whose grossness he ro-
bustly preferred to "the more delicate lewdness of modern plays." This
was more sensible than the "barbarous age" cliché. Yet, though Seward
held that our body of plays, in general, "tend to promote virtue and
chastity," he regretted publishing their "indecencies," and at one time
had even contemplated bowdlerizing the text![46] Our parson seems to
have worried about his own reputation for respectability, but he kept his
balance, nonetheless.

Bishop Hurd, one of the precursors of the romantics in criticism, in
1752 wrote to his friend, William Mason, about the latter's projected alteration of Fletcher's *The Faithful Shepherdess.* As he had expected, the
new version had not interested Garrick, and the bishop consoled his
friend with the prejudiced thought that the play was too good to appeal

to Garrick's "ill-taste," for it left the actor little room for "playing tricks
and showing attitudes."[47] In his *Letters on Chivalry and Romance* (1759)
he again evidenced his esteem for Fletcher in his remark about Jacobean
masques: "we . . . have reason to conceive of them with reverence when
we find the names of Fletcher and Jonson to some of them."[48] Could he
have been thinking of Beaumont's masque?

But despite Seward and Hurd, our playwrights were not faring well.
Hugh Blair, moderately a neo-classicist, in his *Lectures on Rhetoric and
Belles Lettres* (1759), could find nothing of worth in them except "much
fancy and invention" and "several beautiful passages." He objected that
"they abound with romantic and improbable incidents, with overcharged
and unnatural characters, and with coarse and gross allusions." Of the
Elizabethans, he discussed the tragedies of Shakespeare only. As for
Fletcher and Company's comedies, "they have become too obsolete to be
very agreeable."[49] We look in vain for mention of our authors in Edward
Young's *Conjectures on Original Composition* (1759), though we find
Shakespeare's originality contrasted favorably with Jonson's imitative-
ness.[50] Edward Capell, in his introduction to his 1768 edition of Shakespeare, classes Fletcher with Shirley, Middleton, Massinger and Brome as
all alike vastly unequal to Shakespeare.[51]

When we turn to journalistic dramatic criticism such as that of *The
Morning Post* on a revival in 1778 of *A King and No King*, we find the
play reviewer doling out praise and blame as follows:

> The motley drama of A King and No King . . . was revived last night at
> this house, with such alterations as the nature of present manners necessarily
> required.
> The play with all its improbabilities and much heaviness as to the serious parts
> of it contains many noble sentiments, much forcible imagery and powerful
> language in the comic scenes, a considerable share of humour . . .
> The character of Panthea admits no great scope for theatrical excellence,
> but all that could be made of it, was amply effected by Miss Brunton.
> The laughable poltroonery of Bessus was given with admirable humour by
> Ryder, who has never appeared before a London audience to greater advantage.[52]

This hard-headed reviewer was at least won over by Bessus!

The revival of *A King and No King* in this season may have been
prompted by the publication of Colman's edition of *The Dramatic
Works of Beaumont and Fletcher* (1778). Colman, in his preface, returned to his earlier criticism of Garrick, now deceased, for his lack of
interest in the plays of our dramatists,[53] and argued again for presenting
them on the boards. He mentioned by name *A King and No King*, as
well as *The Maid's Tragedy*, *Love's Pilgrimage* and *Monsieur Thomas;*

they "would hardly disgrace that stage which has exhibited The Two
Gentlemen of Verona."[54]

Page considers Colman's edition a capable one, carefully done. In it
were reprinted the prefaces of 1647, 1711 and 1750, with footnotes adding comment on them. There were also many new notes to the plays,
concise and to the point.[55] Perhaps because of the inclusion of the older
prefaces, Colman was more concerned in his own introduction with his
special pleading for the production of Fletcher and Company plays than
with criticism. He did, however, express his opinion that the genius of
Shakespeare should illustrate, rather than obscure, "the kindred talents
of Beaumont and Fletcher." In support of this opinion, he declared:

These plays, we will be bold to say, have the same excellences, as well as the
same defects, each in an inferior degree, with the dramas of their great master.
Like his, they are built on histories or novels, pursuing in the same manner the
story through its various circumstances; like his, but not always with equal
truth and nature, their characters are boldly drawn and warmly colored; like his,
their dialogue, containing every beauty of stile . . . is thick sown with moral
sentiments, interchanged with ludicrous and serious, ribaldry and sublime, and
sometimes enlivened with wit in a richer vein than even the immortal dramas
of Shakespeare.[56]

There is a somewhat defensive tone, here, as in his later statement that
"freely allowing, the general superiority of Shakespeare to Beaumont and
Fletcher (and indeed to all other poets, Homer perhaps only excepted)
yet we cannot so far degrade our authors, as to reduce the most excellent
of their pieces to a level with the meanest effusions of Shakespeare."[57] At
the end of his preface, however, Colman came out strongly for our playwrights:

For our parts we have been incited to this undertaking from a real admiration
of these poets, grounded, as we apprehend, on their genuine excellencies, and a
thorough persuasion that the works of Beaumont and Fletcher may proudly
claim a second place in the English drama, nearer to the first than the third,
to those of Shakespeare; some of their plays being so much in his manner, that
they can scarcely be distinguished to be the work of another hand.[58]

Six years later Thomas Davies, the book-seller, in his *Dramatic Miscellanies,* readily granted Shakespeare's general superiority to Beaumont and Fletcher, but his praise of the latter, though qualified, was not
lacking in gusto. He thought their characters "as various as nature could
produce, and, in most of their pieces, admirably and faithfully delineated"; their sentiments struck him as "tender, pathetic and forcible, as
plot, situation, and character, require"; he declared that "their dialogue

is universally allowed to be free, elegant, pleasant, and witty; in general more adapted to the conversation of gentlemen than Shakespear's."[59]

The last point, a sound one so often made before, is nowadays frequently overlooked. Davies hit upon the reason for this oversight when he said that

though I grant their scenes abound more in liberal and high-seasoned dialect than Shakespeare's, yet, whenever he thinks proper to introduce wits, and treat his audience with gay converse, he is not only equal, but superior, to his imitators. For whom will they match with the sprightly Mercutio or the humourous Benedic? To say nothing of the pleasantness of the amiable Roslind, what dialogue can be put in competition with the lively, witty, varied, mirth—the rapidly-facetious and laugh-winning repartees—of the Prince of Wales and Falstaff?[60]

True; and likewise true that Shakespeare's characters have a vitality that those of our playwrights lack; and yet true also that Fletcher, especially, was adept at the conversation of gentlemen.

In comparing the treatment, by Shakespeare and by our dramatists, of equally improbable plots and situations, Davies suggested a shrewd distinction. Shakespeare's "superstructure is so beautiful, that you forget the foundations," and imperceptibly the sense of improbability lessens, so that "you do not have leisure to think of the enchanted ground on which it stands."[61] Although Stuart playgoers surely held this to be likewise true for Fletcher and Company, by Davies' time only two or three of their plays, at best, created this illusion. Their shallower characterization and treatment had told against them, under difficult production conditions, in theatres ill-adapted to their presentation.

Davies, like some others before him, looked at our playwrights with a stern moral eye; he found their scenes "often blotted with unpardonable licentiousness, and stained with vile obscenity." He thought, indeed, that "they have gone beyond all that I ever read of those times in illiberal freedom." Comparatively, Shakespeare was "modest and chaste," and wrote "like an anchoret." To their "unlimited licentiousness" was due their appeal to the age of Charles II, to the "colour" of which "they approached nearer, in dialogue and character . . . than the plays of any other authors."[62] Whatever its truth, this viewpoint has a neo-Puritan tinge of Victorian prudishness, which descended earlier and has lasted longer in criticism than is sometimes recognized. It is strikingly out of harmony with First Folio attitudes, but anticipates Coleridge.

The Maid's Tragedy really upset Davies. He expected that "a young lady, in the pride of youth and bloom of beauty, such as Evadne, should have warm desires, when ascending the nuptial bed," but he would have the king's mistress modestly reluctant, for this "will heighten her charms, and prove the best incentive to the lover." And then he asked, "But why

not draw the curtains of the marriage-bed? Why will these writers, like
Mrs. Behn, 'Fairly put all the characters to bed, and shew them there?' "[63]
It might be protested that, in contrast with some Broadway plays of the
present day, the young couple of this tragedy are not actually put to bed;
quite the contrary, in fact! Davies did, however, put his finger on a tendency common to our playwrights and many another dramatic entertainer,
past and present: that of skating over the thin ice of piquantly daring
situations between the sexes. Shakespeare himself is not altogether free
from this tendency.

In 1786 Dr. Ferriar wrote an essay in which he placed the newly reviving Massinger second only to Shakespeare. The essayist was, of course,
concerned solely with those plays which he wrote independently of
Fletcher. He considered Massinger "More natural in his characters, and
more poetical in his diction, than Jonson or Cartwright, more elevated
and nervous than Fletcher, the only writers who can be supposed to contest his pre-eminence."[64] Cartwright's name in this select company is indeed a surprise; it is a signpost on the way to the reappraisal of all the
older dramatists.

Dr. Ferriar found one fault with Massinger; he wished that he "had
preserved his scenes from the impure dialogue which disgusts us in most
of our old writers." So Massinger, too, had touched pitch! Ferriar also
objected to the adaptations of Fletcher, as well as of Massinger (and Jonson), because the altered plays were "so mutilated, to fit them for representation, as neither to retain the dignity of the old comedy, nor to acquire the graces of the new."[65]

Philip Neve, in his *Cursory Remarks on Some of the Ancient English
Poets* (1789), made a few of that nature about Beaumont and Fletcher.
He could not draw any conclusion about their merit: "So unequal are
their pieces, that they admit of every degree of estimation, from excellent
to bad." He liked their plots better than "their conduct of them, or their
writing." He singled out for approval *Rule a Wife* (as their best play),
Bonduca, The Knight of the Burning Pestle ("a comedy of peculiar character . . . not without much humour"), and *The Prophetess* (the first
three acts only)—surely an odd selection! He also considered as "beauties"
the scenes with Ordella in Act IV of *Thierry and Theodoret,* and a single
speech in *The Humourous Lieutenant.*[66]

Edmond Malone, as his *Preface* to his edition of Shakespeare (1790)
demonstrates, liked none of the other older dramatists. Attacking the
preference of the 1660s for Fletcher and Jonson, he scornfully remarked
that "To attempt to show to the readers of the present day the absurdity
of such a preference, would be an insult to their understandings." He
cited, as the grounds given for "this presumptuous taste . . . Fletcher's

ease, and Johnson's learning." Presumptuously ignoring Fletcher, he sneered at the uselessness of Jonson's erudition.[67]

Malone's distaste for the Elizabethan-Stuart dramatists other than Shakespeare was extreme, even for Shakespeare devotees. The pendulum was soon to swing in the other direction. More characteristic of the changing temper of the time was Monck Mason's volume of critical notes, *Comments on the Plays of Beaumont and Fletcher,* 1797, which appeared the year before Wordsworth and Coleridge's *Lyrical Ballads.* In his preface Mason protested against a state of obscuration which would not long continue. He informs us that "these elegant writers are now so totally neglected, that many copies of the last edition of their plays still remain unsold, though published nearly twenty years ago." He was as surprised as Colman had been that, in the waxing Shakespeare idolatry, attention was not being paid to our dramatists, "whose language, manner, and spirit, are so congenial to his, and who possess a large portion of his admirable talents." Mason's volume of notes had, as one of its motives, the redemption of our playwrights "from this state of unmerited oblivion."[68]

Thus did Monck Mason's book, in a sense, herald the new age of romantic criticism and appreciation, not only of Beaumont and Fletcher but also, as it was to prove, of all the older dramatists. In the new century, our playwrights would receive less acclaim than the First Folio gave them, and their plays were to vanish all but completely from the stage. They would not, however, be so much slighted critically as they had been, especially by the neo-classicists, in the eighteenth century.

III

The romantic movement brought forth criticism of the Elizabethan and Stuart dramatists as distorted in perspective, in its own way, as the neo-classical had been. To be sure, the newer critical approach had freed itself from the once dominant constricting rules and fixed formulas. But in place of à priori theories of what the technique of a play ought to be— theories which at least assumed that a drama did have a skeleton of structure—it substituted a tendency to treat Shakespeare and his fellow-dramatists as though their plays had been written in a vacuum, not for a specific stage and audience. These plays came to be regarded as poetry in dramatic form—of characterization, beauties, philosophy and ethics all compact. Even Coleridge, the new leader for the cult of Shakespeare in the nineteenth century, was a critic of drama whose soaring wings were crippled because he did not understand the craftsmanship aspect of playwriting.

With Coleridge, the incompletely theatre-minded Hazlitt, and the beauties-culling Lamb regnant over dramatic criticism in the nineteenth century, it is not surprising that the great poets of that century wrote merely closet verse in the ill-fitting garb of drama, to the scandal of the true play-lover. The theatres of the day, with their bad lighting until gas-light improved it, and their elaborate scenery in garish poor taste, were awkward mediums for staging plays, as Lamb emphasized in his *Trage-dies of Shakespeare Considered.* The poets did not care to learn from their "commercial" inadequacies what actual experience in them could have taught.

A play-as-literature attitude, however, when not completed and made healthy by a play-as-stage-entertainment objective, was bound to produce closet-drama. So the theatre, despite its previous brief but brilliant inter-lude of Sheridan in the 1770s, did not begin to develop highly literate playwrights again until towards the close of the nineteenth century. It has remained for modern critics to realize that an Elizabethan drama, or any other, is in itself simply a kind of shorthand in playscript form—however beautiful as poetry and profound in characterization and interpretation of life—until it is transformed into living reality by stage production.

This dichotomy between drama as literature and drama as stage enter-tainment had its roots, so far as English drama is concerned, in the trans-formation of the earlier structural and multiple stage into a semi-picture-frame one.[69] What was needed, as Nicoll has pointed out, was that critics and scholars should accumulate a "sound body of scientific, historical, and appreciative interpretation of past dramatic efforts,"[70]—leading, among other things, to an understanding of the actual theatres, stages, audiences and conditions of production which had shaped Elizabethan dramatic technique. This had, however, to wait until the modern dramatic renais-sance, which was likewise accompanied by improved theatres, lighting, and stage design. Edmond Malone was the sole pioneer of his time in study of the earlier stage. Critics took no interest in discovering, for in-stance, why their own ill-lit picture frame stages, with inartistic scenery, were unsatisfactory for performances of Shakespeare, Jonson, Massinger, or Fletcher, whereas the Elizabethan playhouses had been flexible and appropriate media. Their ignorance led to assertions such as Coleridge's that Shakespeare was "Self-sustained, deriving his genius immediately from heaven, independent of all earthly or national influence."[71] Had Coleridge realized how definitely Shakespeare had written for the Eliza-bethan platform stage and audience, he could never have denied earthly influence.

This serious defect in romantic criticism, with its resultant over-empha-sis on dramatic poetry and characterization, long interfered with the per-

ception that Fletcher, Beaumont and Company were not other Shakespeares, but simply most competent theatrical entertainers to the gentry
of their generation. It has also obscured the fact that, in the main, blank
verse and lyric outbursts of poetry were, to them, but the accepted means
for purveying this entertainment.

The romantic critics were not as original in their treatment of the older
dramatists as has often been supposed. Just as the preference for Shakespeare read, as against Shakespeare acted, did not originate with Lamb,
so the nineteenth century emphasis on analysis of character, on philosophy and ethics, and on poetic beauties is merely the culmination of tendencies which even the lean criticism of our playwrights in the eighteenth
century has already suggested. So also have we discovered, as early as the
Restoration age, the first indications of that growing sense of disapproval
of the "coarseness" and other "moral" laxities of our plays.

It is doubtless the fact that the romantic critics were in reaction against
the neo-classical dramatic dogmas which has tended to obscure the large
inheritance of attitudes they derived from their predecessors. What they
most definitely contributed to criticism of the Elizabethan and Stuart
dramatists—aside from a brilliant crystallization of the idolatry of Shakespeare—was the infectious enthusiasm with which Lamb and Hazlitt, especially, exhumed these old dramatists, some from a long oblivion. In
this enthusiasm our playwrights shared less than some of the new discov-
eries, but it helped them, nevertheless, out of their late eighteenth century doldrums.

How much they stood in need of this help Charles Dibdin illustrates.
In his *Complete History of the Stage* (1800) he made many derogatory
statements, often of a sort to reveal his own incompetence to deal with
dramatic technique. Beaumont and Fletcher were "rather amateurs than
writers, rather gentlemen" than playwrights. Their works had a partial
claim to reputation, but "taking them altogether, there is scarcely a play
but is extravagant, wild, and ill-managed."[72] They "failed as to regularity," were both "weak on the side of judgment," and "perpetually tried
to go beyond the bounds that nature and genius prescribed them." Their
plots were "the crudest and most indigested that can possibly be conceived; . . . there is more good sense in the construction of *Every Man
in His Humour* than in all the works of Beaumont and Fletcher put together."[73]

Comments on the individual plays by this belated neo-classicist were
equally tart. *Rule a Wife* was "no great acquisition to the stage"; it was
"thin," and its plot, "though admirably imagined is poorly treated." *The
Chances*, pervaded with indelicacy throughout, and blotted by the abominable libertinism of Don John, was "a most improper and reprehen-

sible subject for the stage." As for plays no longer acted, *Philaster* was by
many thought the best, but "has never [sic!] been able to keep the stage
. . . because there is not one regular simple grand interest excited, and
because it is ingeniously made up of pieces instead of being one whole."
Dibdin agreed completely with Rymer's blasts against *A King and No
King,* while *The Maid's Tragedy* was replete with our authors' "extravagance and irregularity." *Wit Without Money,* though possessing less of
these defects and "closer to nature" than usual, was so flimsy as to be un-
attractive. *The Bloody Brother* had deservedly been long consigned to
oblivion, and *The Spanish Curate* was "a heterogenous jumble" like
many of the others. Even *The Wild-Goose Chase,* which was, for once,
allowed to have considerable merit, was "ill-conducted."[74]

Dibdin accepted the false notion that our playwrights copied Lope de
Vega.[75] He thought Fletcher copied badly; he "added to the extravagance
of the Spaniard wild and eccentric wit of his own, but perpetually tinc-
tured it with obscenity"; thus, "an unbridled wit grew to licentiousness
and destroyed the legitimate drift" of the plays of our ensemble. Hence
their popularity in the "loose and profligate" days of Charles II's reign,
"when, an indelible disgrace to that monarch and his court, they obtained even to the exclusion of Shakespear."[76] This is as savage a thrust
as will be found in the whole range of Beaumont and Fletcher criticism.

Dibdin went so far as to smear Fletcher and Company with the un-
founded charge of jealousy of Shakespeare, adding that they "arrogated a
false consequence and ridiculously fancied themselves superior to a man,
whom they might have been proud to have followed at a humble distance.."[77] After this mudslinging, he asserted that all had now been set
right; not only was Shakespeare supreme, but "all judges of genius and
taste" place Massinger "very little behind Jonson, and far before Beaumont and Fletcher."[78] It would doubtless have shocked Dibdin to have
discovered how often Massinger had collaborated in the despised plays
with Fletcher.

By Dibdin's standards, William Gifford must have been no judge, for
he did not demote Beaumont and Fletcher to a bad fourth in a foursome.
In the introduction to his *Plays of Philip Massinger* (1805), Gifford traditionally placed Shakespeare, Jonson and Fletcher in the first rank, and
Massinger, along with half a dozen others, in an inferior one, but held
the latter worthy of being on the same bookshelf with Ben and our authors.[79] Massinger lacked wit, and was surpassed in humor by Fletcher,
but his "vigorous metre" escaped the "morbid softness" of Fletcher's
poetry. Beaumont was as "sublime" and Fletcher as "pathetic" as Shakespeare, but the latter possessed other qualities to which Jonson and they
"make no approaches."[80] Thus Gifford, who edited Jonson, Ford and

Shirley as well as Massinger, and planned editions of Shakespeare and of Beaumont and Fletcher he was not able to carry out,[81] showed himself a more judicial-minded critic than Dibdin, as well as a practical contributor to the reviving interest in the older dramatists.

Of far greater influence, however, were the group of friends who set the tone for criticism of Shakespeare and his compeers for a hundred years: Lamb, Coleridge, Hazlitt and Leigh Hunt. To Lamb goes the honor of being prime mover in reviving interest in all the old dramatists. Whereas Coleridge concentrated his attention chiefly on Shakespeare, and did not extend his range beyond the now conventional group of Jonson, Massinger and Fletcher, Lamb read with enthusiasm in all accessible old plays, and sought to bring them to the attention of the reading public.

Lamb culled scenes and speeches from Dodsley's and Hawkins' collections, but also from the extensive body of old plays which David Garrick had left to the British Museum, and from other sources not so easy of access, including private libraries.[82] The first result of his search was his book of 90 selections and some critical and appreciative comments, *Specimens of English Dramatic Poets* (1808). Almost twenty years later, delving further into the Garrick plays, he unearthed 86 new selections and four prefatory poems which delighted him, and these he contributed to Hone's *Table Book* throughout 1827.[83] These cullings, and especially the first book, dispelled all doubt that there were poetic riches to be found in the long-forgotten contemporaries of the foursome; with *Specimens,* the restoration of these playwrights to easy accessibility begins. When Lamb prepared his autobiographical sketch for a friend in 1827, he ended with this statement: "He also was the first to draw the Public attention to the old English Dramatists. . . ."[84] It was no idle boast.

In his preface, Lamb explained that he had chosen entire scenes, or successive scenes, whenever he could, though he had done some "expunging"—notably and "without ceremony all that which the writers had better never have written, that forms the objection so often repeated to the promiscuous reading of Fletcher, Massinger, and some others."[85] He would thus protect his admired selections from the neo-Puritans.

He sought "not so much passages of wit and humour" in his extracts as "scenes of passion, sometimes of the deepest quality, interesting situations, serious descriptions, that which is more nearly allied to poetry than to wit, and to tragic rather than comic poetry." Here is that romantic emphasis on the drama as poetry to which even Lamb inclined, although he was an actual if unsuccessful playwright, and loved the theatre and good acting. As for the ethical emphasis of his century, Lamb avowed that his leading design had been "to illustrate what may be called the moral sense of our ancestors."[86]

But it is probable that Lamb's main intention was really expressed in "another object," namely,

to bring together the most admired scenes in Fletcher and Massinger, in the estimation of the world the only dramatic poets of that age who are entitled to be considered after Shakespeare, and to exhibit them in the same volume with the more impressive scenes of old Marlowe, Heywood, Tourneur, Webster, Ford, and others: to show what we have slighted, while beyond all proportion we have cried up one or two favourite names.[87]

In performing this signal service, Lamb rightly included a dozen selections from our plays, to 78 from others. It is interesting to observe that, in his wide range of choice, he omitted none of the playwrights of any note except Lyly and Greene.

In his comments on some of the twelve selections from Beaumont and Fletcher, Lamb drew several contrasts with Shakespeare. He compared as slighted women, for instance, Aspatia of *The Maid's Tragedy* with Helena of *All's Well That Ends Well*. Aspatia's situation is "artfully contrived," so that "while we pity her, we respect her, and she descends without degradation. So much true poetry and passion can do to confer dignity upon subjects which do not seem capable of it." But Beaumont's characterization does not equal Shakespeare's: Aspatia "does not so absolutely predominate over her situation, but she suffers some diminution, some abatement of the full lustre of the female character; which Helena never does." The latter lacks the weakness which, in Aspatia, "if we do not despise, we are sorry for."

Lamb's explanation was that "After all, Beaumont and Fletcher were an inferior sort of Shakespeares and Sidneys."[88] This shows the normal tendency of critics to recognize a distinction only of quality, but not of kind, between the character-drawing of Shakespeare and that of our playwrights. It did not occur to Lamb that Aspatia, for all Beaumont's lyrical poetry, was theatrically conceived—that is, in terms of stage effectiveness for evoking sentimental response from an audience.

Lamb was, nonetheless, aware of our playwrights' sensationalism. He found Fletcher excellent alike in wit and in serious scenes, but with the qualification that "there is something strained and far fetched in both." Unlike Shakespeare, "He is too mistrustful of Nature; he always goes a little on one side of her."[89] While commenting on "the finest scene in Fletcher" (Act IV, scene 1, of *Thierry and Theodoret*), he calls attention to

the latter's fondness for unnatural and violent situations, . . . He seems to have thought that nothing great could be produced in an ordinary way. The chief incidents in the Wife for a Month, in Cupid's Revenge, in the Double Marriage, and in many more of his Tragedies, shew this. Shakespeare has none of this contortion in his mind, none of that craving after romantic incidents, and flights of strained and improbable virtue, which I think always betrays an imperfect moral sensibility.[90]

Lamb's antithesis has much soundness; but "melodramatic" would characterize the Fletcher situations more accurately than "unnatural," and Shakespeare is by no means lacking in improbable ones. Furthermore, the sort of "imperfect moral sensibility" which Lamb attributed correctly to Fletcher is common among playwrights who are primarily entertainers.

To Lamb's ear, Fletcher's versification was "slow and languid."[91] Lamb detected his trick of laying "line upon line, making up one after the other, adding image to image so deliberately that we see where they join."[92] Hence, the motion of Fletcher's verse "is circular, not progressive. Each line revolves on itself in a sort of separate orbit. They do not join into one another like a running hand."[93] This is a perceptive reader's observation; but if the speeches were rapidly delivered on the stage, the effect of this technique should usually be cumulative, animated and even a bit high-pitched rather than languid.

Only once did Lamb raise a particular moral objection. He considered *The Faithful Shepherdess* spoiled, as a sweet arcadian lyric poem for boys and virgins, by the presence of the shepherdess Chloe. "Coarse words do but wound the ears"; Lamb protested, "but a character of lewdness affronts the mind. Female lewdness at once shocks nature and morality." No doubt Chloe the wanton had been intended as a contrast to Clorin the faithful, but "Fletcher should have known that such weeds by juxtaposition do not set off, but kill, sweet flowers."[94] There comes to mind a whimsical line from an Elizabethan lyric, "Whist, wanton, will ye?"

It was Coleridge, however, and not Lamb, who set the tone for criticism of Beaumont and Fletcher in the nineteenth century and even, in some measure, since then. This has not been altogether fortunate for the reputation of our corpus. Convinced that Shakespeare was "universal" rather than of his own age, Coleridge was predisposed to find Jonson, Massinger and Fletcher, by comparison, inferior in every respect. His genuine gift for the psychological analysis of characters, together with his tendency to treat dramatis personae as real people, had little to operate upon in our plays. Their moral tone could not but displease the solemn, almost neo-Puritan ethical thinker in Coleridge, who found even Shakespeare embarrassing wholly to defend on this score. The plays did not provide him any "philosophy" to discuss, save a monarchist political one. Earlier criticism of the playwrights could be dismissed from consideration (as was

Seward's praise of *A King and No King*) because of "the abject state to which psychology had sunk from the reign of Charles I to the middle of the present reign of George III"[95]—a point of view having a curious resemblance in spirit to the earlier "barbarous age" one. Coleridge's own creative cast of mind was distinctly that of the poet rather than that of the playwright. Moreover, as has been suggested, he lacked that knowledge of Elizabethan-Stuart life and theatrical conditions, and of the whole range of its drama, which alone could have given his penetrating mind a clear perception of our playwrights as, above all, skilled entertainers to the gentry.

In addition, Coleridge had a particular animus against Beaumont and Fletcher. He considered them "always imitators of, and often borrowers from,"[96] Shakespeare, "and in their tragedies most glaringly"; and yet they " (O shame! shame!) miss no opportunity of sneering at the divine man and subdetracting from his merits!!"[97] Now McKeithan, the most thorough investigator of the indebtedness of Beaumont and of Fletcher to Shakespeare, has recently demonstrated that it was never Fletcher's habit, and Beaumont's solely in his first plays, "to refer to Shakespeare satirically." Nothing is clearer from the evidence than that both collaborators recognized Shakespeare's genius "to a far greater extent than has hitherto been realized."[98] Both men, in different ways, did come under Shakespeare's influence; in detecting this, Coleridge was correct, if vague and over-emphatic. But his charge that they sneered at his idol "with a spite far more malignant than" Jonson's[99] is simply not true. Yet Coleridge's indignation—reminding us of Dibdin's—was bound to color his attitude towards our playwrights.

A favorite opinion of Coleridge—also stressed by some later eighteenth century English critics and by the German Schlegel—was that Shakespeare's judgment was equal to his genius.[100] As for Beaumont and Fletcher: "In this (as, indeed, in all other respects; but most in this) it is that Shakespeare is so incomparably superior to Fletcher and his friend—in judgment!"[101]

By this Coleridge meant, in part, that the form of our dramatists' plays was "mechanic" or mechanical—that is, arbitrarily imposed from without—whereas the form of Shakespeare's dramas was "organic," developing from within like a natural biological growth.[102] In other words, "the plays of Beaumont and Fletcher are mere aggregations without unity"— fabricated "just as a man might put together a quarter of an orange, a quarter of an apple, and the like of a lemon and a pomegranate, and make it look like one round diverse-coloured fruit."[103] Their serious plays "are complete hybrids . . . upon any rules, Greek, Roman, or Gothic." Moreover, "the comic scenes are rarely so interfused amidst the tragic as to produce a unity of the tragic on the whole, without which the inter-mixture is a fault."[104] On the other hand, "in the Shaksperian drama there is a vitality which grows and evolves itself from within—a key note which guides and controls the harmonies throughout."[105]

Beaumont and Fletcher thus illustrated, by contrast, a theory about Shakespeare's genuine artistry which Coleridge found effective as a coun-terpoise to the still lingering neo-classical view that Shakespeare "lacked art." Analogies from biology, however, are apt to be dangerous when ap-plied to literature, and this one, though highly suggestive, can be pushed too far. On their own lower level, our playwrights rival Shakespeare as craftsmen, and their better plays are not structurally "mere aggregations," lacking in unity. Their "organic" weaknesses, which create a more "mechanical" effect, largely spring from other sources. The distinction which Coleridge's contrast suggests is actually that between playwrights aiming chiefly at stage effectiveness, and a genuine dramatist.

One of Coleridge's "grave objections" to the tragedies (and tragicome-dies) of our ensemble was that almost all were "founded on some out-of-the-way accident or exception to the general experience of mankind," and hence "proceeded upon something forced and unnatural; the reader can never reconcile the plot with probability, and sometimes not with pos-sibility."[106] In some measure, such charges as these can be brought against great numbers of Elizabethan-Stuart plays—even, be it added, against some of Shakespeare's. William Archer will later bring them—sparing Shakespeare, however. Coleridge also objected that too many of our "comedies, tragedies and tragicomedies . . . are farce-plots."[107] He did admit, however, that our playwrights had one virtue in common with their German counterpart, Kotzebue, who "excels in his mode of telling a story clearly and interestingly, in a series of dramatic dialogues."[108]

Coleridge, as psychologist, evidently found little to analyze in the char-acters our playwrights created. "In Beaumont and Fletcher," he re-marked, with sweeping generalization, "you have description of charac-ters by the poet rather than the characters themselves; we are told, and impressively told, of their being, but never feel that they are."[109] He con-sidered their brave soldiers "self-trumpeters and tongue-bullies," but conceded that doubtless this was "the fashion of the age . . . and deeper than the fashion B. and F. did not fathom." Similarly, all the generals were "pugilists, or cudgel-fighters, that boast of their bottom and of the claret they have shed."[110] He held Rollo, in The Bloody Brother (a four-author play) to be an imitation of Richard III, but a greatly inferior one, "a mere personification of outrageous wickedness, with no fundamental characteristic impulses to make either the tyrant's words or actions philo-sophically intelligible."[111] The tyrants and the loyalist Aëciuses equally disgusted him, "the fantasticalness and gross caricatures" of the personae of the comedies disturbed him, and he felt that "There are few characters that you can really like (even though you should have erased from your mind all the filth which bespatters the most likeable of them, as Piniero in 'The Island Princess' for instance.)."[112]

Coleridge had picked up the mistaken notion that "the opinion once prevailed . . . that Fletcher alone wrote for women." This was merely a fairly recent misconception of Dryden's comment that Fletcher wrote especially well "betwixt man and woman," and so of love. In rebuttal, Coleridge waxes moral: "with very few, and those partial, exceptions, the female characters in the plays of Beaumont and Fletcher are, when of the light kind, not decent; when heroic, complete viragos." By contrast, "in Shakespeare, all the elements of womanhood are holy."[113] One recalls Cleopatra, Cressida and Juliet's Nurse, and marvels.

Coleridge's moral reactions to our plays (perhaps reinforced by Schlegel's) are reminiscent of those of a seventeenth century Puritan criticizing stage-plays. Collier's records of his conversations yield the statement that the situations "are sometimes so disgusting, and the language so indecent and immoral, that it is impossible to read the plays in private society."[114] Since Coleridge wrote, in *General Characteristics of Shakespeare*, that the latter "never clothes vice in the garb of virtue, like Beaumont and Fletcher,"[115] it does not leave one incredulous to find Collier reporting him as saying that these twain "ridicule virtue and encourage vice: they pander to the lowest and basest passions of our nature."[116]

Identifying virtue with chastity, Coleridge remarked (in an extended note on Act I, scene 3, of *Valentinian*) that our dramatists "always write as if virtue or goodness were a sort of talisman, or strange something, that might be lost without the least fault on the part of the owner." Indeed, "their chaste ladies value their chastity as a material thing," and "all their women are represented with the minds of strumpets, except for a few irrational humorists." And so there was a "frightful contrast" between their virtuous women, who were "strumpets in their imaginations and wishes," and Shakespeare's. As for the men, "love is merely lust in one direction—exclusive preference of one object."[117] Wedded love, in Massinger as well as Beaumont and Fletcher, "really is on both sides little better than sheer animal desire."[118] In general, "the grossest passages of Shakespeare were purity to theirs."[119]

Here is expressed, full-fledged, the so-called Victorian attitude. The span of Coleridge's life (1771-1834) marked a deep point of woman's subjection to a man-made milieu—and the return of woman to something like equal status with man was slow throughout the nineteenth century. The double standard of morality had petrified. Only two kinds of women were recognized by society—good and bad—and a single sexual indiscretion usually changed the label. A properly bred maiden, in this neo-Puritan atmosphere, was kept sheltered from "the facts of life," sometimes to her undoing; and she was not supposed to feel the raptures of love until the correct young man had obtained her father's consent to her hand in marriage. She was expected to be innocent of the sexual attraction natural to the young human animal, except as a bait to a proper alliance in matrimony. It was not quite decent frankly to recognize that strong physical attraction is one of the foundations on which marital happiness rests. It is against such a background as this that Coleridge's "strumpets in their imaginations and wishes" needs to be placed.

The inhibited attitudes of Coleridge and other romantic critics towards our playwrights' handling of relationships between men and women could be left without remark were it not that the effect of their criticisms still lingers on. It will be recalled that those who eulogized Beaumont and Fletcher in the First Folio of 1647 gave them, on the contrary, a clean bill of moral health. Neo-classical critics of the Restoration who judged our writers guilty of other breaches of dramatic decorum were the first drama-lovers seriously to call their morality into question. This suggests that a sound judgment in this matter may be bound up with a lucid understanding of their theatrecraft. If the neo-classicist, on principle, disapproved of our playwrights' craftsmanship, and the romantic critic did not clearly perceive its nature, then it is entirely possible that both, as one consequence, went more or less astray in assessing the morality—or immorality—of the plays.

That Coleridge was an unreliable judge of the matter should be apparent from this misleading suggestion: "It would be worthwhile to note how many of these plays are founded on rapes—how many on incestuous passions, and how many on mere lunacies."[120] Swinburne, who recognized the exaggeration in this dictum, will later supply an answer to it.

After Restoration charges that our playwrights were blameworthy for a disrespectful treatment of kings, it is startling to discover Coleridge calling Fletcher and Beaumont "the most servile *jure divino* royalists" and "high-flying, passive obedience, Tories," whose "ultra-royalism" was "carried to excess," was expressed in "hollow extravagance" and "rants," and displayed the "vice" of "servility of sentiment and a spirit of partisanship with the monarchical faction."[121] Massinger had the opposite political vice; he was filled with "rank republicanism," was "a decided Whig," a "sneerer" who took "continual flings at kings, courtiers, and all the favourites of fortune"—perforce because he was discontented at his lot in life, and envious.[122] Shakespeare alone gave "the permanent politics of human nature"; he had "a profound veneration for all the established institutions of society, and for those classes which form the permanent elements of the state." He was "always the philosopher and moralist," who never promulgated "any party tenets," and was "if aught personal, an aristocrat."[123] Thus, he was a measure for the delinquencies of the others.

Obviously, the generous political enthusiasms of Coleridge's youth had hardened into stout Tory prejudices. Yet his charge against Beaumont and Fletcher has carried great weight ever since, despite the quite different seventeenth century views. Here is a dichotomy which must be examined, without party spirit, later.[124]

Coleridge thought Fletcher, Beaumont and Company "the most lyrical of our dramatists," and wished that they "had written poems instead of tragedies"; their blank verse was "constantly slipping into lyricisms."[125] But he considered their style mechanical; it was "a well arranged bed of flowers, each having its separate root, and its position determined aforehand by the will of the gardener—each fresh plant a fresh volition." Shakespeare's style, on the other hand, was "an Indian fig-tree . . . all is growth, evolution."[126] Coleridge was on his own ground here—that of the poet. But, like various criticis since, he does not appear to have realized that our authors' style was intimately bound up with other aspects of their theatrecraft. One also wonders how acutely he listened to conversation, when one reads of Fletcher's comic metre that it is "a far more law less, and yet far less happy, imitation of animated talk in real life than Massinger's."[127]

In the midst of so much disapproval, it is refreshing to discover that Coleridge actually enjoyed some of the Fletcher (and Massinger) comedies; he thought them "the best part of their works."[128] In Collier's records, he even allowed that "at times, and excepting in the generalizing of humour and application," they "rivalled those of Shakespeare."[129] In *Table Talk* he admitted that " 'Monsieur Thomas' and the 'Little French Lawyer' are great favorites of mine amongst Beaumont and Fletcher plays. How these plays overflow with wit!" For him Fletcher's *The Pilgrim* held "the first place in B. and F.'s romantic entertainments," while of a Fletcher-Massinger collaboration he said, "I could read 'The Beggar's Bush' from morning to night. How sylvan and sunshiny it is!"[130] In another informal moment in *Table Talk*, Coleridge acknowledged that some of the serious plays were "very delightful notwithstanding" their being hybrids, and graciously accepted the point that "no doubt, they imitate the ease of gentlemanly conversation better than Shakespeare"[131]—a genuine concession. Would that Coleridge had climbed off his critical stilts more often, and been under less compulsion to use our playwrights as stalking-horses for his "divine man!"

William Hazlitt, like Lamb, was concerned to rescue from "hopeless obscurity" the Elizabethan-Stuart playwrights, and he performed yeoman service for them in his influential *Lectures on the Age of Elizabeth,* delivered at the Surrey Institution, and published, in 1820.[132] With his customary relish he discussed the plays of more than a dozen contemporaries of Shakespeare (as well as some earlier ones), dealing with individual dramas and often quoting from them—sometimes at length.

The first half of Lecture IV dealt with our playwrights, and the remainder with Jonson's tragedies, Ford, and Massinger. Equipped with reading knowledge of many Elizabethan-Stuart playwrights, he was the first to remark that Beaumont and Fletcher were innovators, who "in some measure departed from the genuine tragic style of the age of Shakespeare."[133] He came closer than Coleridge to discovering that they were primarily entertainers. He was, however, withheld from this discovery by his belief that they were "lyrical and descriptive poets of the first order,"[134] and by his lack of knowledge of the Jacobean theatrical milieu. Making due allowance, also, for the fact that Hazlitt's rush of impressionistic gusto tended to sweep him along to over-statement, many of his comments on our playwrights show penetration.

Fletcher, Beaumont and Company had, for Hazlitt, "prodigious merits," but they wanted "something of the sincerity and modesty of the older writers." They had gained facility from their study of preceding playwrights, "and this facility of production, and the necessity for appealing to popular applause, tended to vitiate their own taste, and to make them willing to pamper that of the public for novelty and extraordinary effect."[135] This is a plausible explanation (though not a complete one), for Hazlitt had some share of the "feel of the theatre." In support of his position, he wrote that

. . . they availed themselves too often of commonplace extravagance and trick. . . . They would have a catastrophe in every scene; so that you have none at last; they would raise admiration to its height in every line; so that the impression of the whole is comparatively loose and desultory. They pitch the characters at first in too high a key, and exhaust themselves by the eagerness and impatience of their efforts. We find all the prodigality of youth, the confidence inspired by success, and enthusiasm bordering on extravagance, richness running riot, beauty dissolving in its own sweetness. . . . Their productions shoot up in haste, but bear the marks of precocity and premature decay.[136]

Our playwrights, it should be remarked, were not as heedless craftsmen as Hazlitt seems to imply. His final sentence points towards the charge of decadence sometimes brought against our playwrights by modern critics.

Hazlitt considered them "dramatic poets" of the second order,

in point of knowledge, variety, vivacity, and effect; there is hardly a passion, character, or situation, which they have not touched in their devious range, and whatever they touched they adorned with some new grace or striking figure; they are masters of style and versification in almost every variety of melting modulation or sounding pomp, of which they are capable. . . . [In their serious plays] their fault is a too ostentatious and indiscriminate display of power. Everything seems in a state of fermentation and effervescence, . . . the characters in general do not take a substantial form, or excite a growing interest, or leave a permanent impression. The passion does not accumulate . . . but wastes itself in the first ebullitions of surprise and novelty.[137]

With regard to our playwrights' morality, Hazlitt found in their works

a . . . weakness . . . of moral constitution struggling with wilful and violent situations, . . . In the heyday of their youthful ardor, and the intoxication of their animal spirits, they take a delight in tearing up some rooted sentiment, to make a mawkish lamentation over it; and fondly and gratuitously cast the seeds of crimes into forbidden grounds, to see how they will shoot up and vegetate into luxuriance, to catch the eye of fancy. They are not safe teachers of morality: they tamper with it, . . . Shakespeare never disturbs the ground of moral principle: . . . Beaumont and Fletcher constantly bring in equivocal sentiments and characters, as if to set them up to be debated by sophistical casuistry, or varnished over with the colours of poetical ingenuity.[138]

It will be noted that Hazlitt offered the explanation of "youthful ardor" and "animal spirits" for what he considered their moral perversity; and he went on to add that their "laxity of principle" was a mental phenomenon not displayed in their actual behavior. Though partly in sympathy with Coleridge's charge of deliberate immorality, Hazlitt thus gave it a different emphasis and, like Lamb, refrained from severe condemnation.

In discussing the tragicomedies and tragedies, Hazlitt characterized *The Maid's Tragedy* as "one of the poorest." He found the basic situation "disagreeable and repulsive," shrewdly exposed some of its improbabilities, condemned Amintor as weak and effeminate, but praised the characterizations of Aspatia, Calianax and especially Evadne.[139] *A King and No King* was very superior, though "on a strangely chosen subject as strangely treated," and having gross love-scenes. His analysis of Arbaces is admiring.[140] *The False One* especially delighted him: "It is something worth living for, to write or even to read such poetry as this is," and he thought the play came nearest to Shakespeare's manner of all written by our ensemble.[141] *The Faithful Sheperdess* also aroused his enthusiasm, except for Thenot, for in this pastoral Fletcher had "given a loose to his fancy, and his fancy was his most delightful and genial quality." In reading it, "we find ourselves breathing the moonlight air under the cope of heaven, and wander by the forest side, among fresh dews and flowers."[142] *Philaster*, likewise, was admirable, with "innumerable passages of extreme romantic beauty."[143] Other serious plays among their best were

The Bloody Brother, Bonduca, Thierry and Theodoret and *A Wife for a Month*.[144] In a newspaper criticism of 1817 for *The Examiner* on a revival of *The Humourous Lieutenant,* he made this judgment: "a bad alteration from one of the most indifferent of the Beaumont and Fletcher plays."[145]

In another criticism for *The Examiner,* in 1815, on a performance of *Rule a Wife,* Hazlitt had commented that "the morality of this excellent comedy is very indifferent."[146] But in 1820 he wrote of our playwrights that "In comic wit and spirit, they are scarcely surpassed by any writers of any age."[147] *Rule a Wife, The Chances* and *The Wild-Goose Chase* were "superior in style and execution to anything of Ben Jonson's. They are, indeed, some of the best comedies of the stage. . . . They show the utmost alacrity of vision in contriving ludicrous distresses."[148] The comedies next in excellence were *The Night Walker, The Little French Lawyer,* and *Monsieur Thomas*.[149] Resembling Coleridge, therefore, in his enjoyment of Fletcher's comedies, Hazlitt was the romantic critic most appreciative of our dramatists' plays, as well as the one who most nearly considered them from the point of view of the theatre.

We are likely to think of Sir Walter Scott in the same breath as Lamb, Coleridge and Hazlitt, because of his romantic poems and novels. Yet his viewpoint on Beaumont and Fletcher is curiously neo-classical, though of a modified, late eighteenth century sort. In *An Essay on the Drama,* written for the *Supplement to the Encyclopedia Britannica* (1819), Scott emphasized the point that our dramatists having taken "the boundless license of the Spanish stage" for their model, they badly neglected their plots. These "can scarce be said to hang together at all." Despite this serious structural defect, however—as well as violations of character and the discarding of probability—he credits them with "a high poetical value . . . the most beautiful description, the most tender and passionate dialogue; a display of brilliant wit and gaiety, or a feast of comic humour." Interestingly, it was Jonson whom he blamed for "filthiness of dialogue," —the worst offender, among eminent English writers, save Swift.[150]

In one sense, Leigh Hunt sums up the romantic writers on Fletcher and Beaumont. To read him after Lamb, Coleridge and Hazlitt is to see in his attitudes a blend of theirs, with some coloring and spice of his own. He echoed Lamb's distaste for the wanton Chloe in *The Faithful Shepherdess,* Hazlitt's for Thenot (but not his enjoyment of this pastoral drama), and contributed his own objection to Clorin, "who is made such a paragon of chastity, . . . that the virtue itself is compromised, and you can see that the author had very little faith in it."[151] Hunt sounds rather like Hazlitt on our playwrights' catering to their audience and on their extravagance, Coleridge on their improbable plots and their royalist servility, and both (abetted by the German Schlegel) on their debased morality—adding a rather strident and squeamish Victorian note all his own.

To Leigh Hunt also goes the dubious honor of bowdlerizing 47 plays of our authors who, in his opinion, were "destined to survive only in fragments." The full title of his book is worth quoting: *Beaumont and Fletcher; or, the Finest Scenes, Lyrics, and other Beauties of these two Poets, Now first Selected from the Whole of their Works, To the Exclusion of whatever is Morally Objectionable.*[152] The announced object of this purge was that "The most cautious member of a family may take up the volume at random, and read aloud from it, without misgiving, in circles the most refined."[153]

In a surviving fragment of a letter, written from Chelsea in 1835, we catch a glimpse of Hunt in the process of reading through the plays of our group. In part, the fragment reads,

Am more astonished (ever) at the amazing coarseness they mingle with their delicacies, and the true love they mingle with their false; am delighted with their wit, poetry, and high gentlemanly style, &c.&c. But Lord! what a gentleman, after all, was Shakespeare, even to *their* gentlemen! . . . The woolstapler's son . . . was a born prince compared with the bishop's and judge's sons.[154]

Again, that fatal comparison with Shakespeare!

Leigh Hunt made much of the paradox of "poetry of the highest order and of the loveliest character" continuously "mixed up with inconsistent, and too often, alas, revolting matter." To him our playwrights seemed "different men when writing in their own persons, and following the taste of the town" for "ditch water . . . (as if two different souls were writing one passage)." His explanation was that, partly to recruit their purse, they sold their birthright "for the mess of loathesome pottage of the praise and profligacy of the court of James I."[155] The "lively and flattered young men" fell in with the tone, servile royalism, and licenses of "a court which was the vulgarest in its language, and the most profligate in its morals, of any that has ever disgraced the country"—worse, even, than that of Charles II. Hence came "the very spite and riot of the tongue of a disordered incontinence," which was like "a torrent of feculence beside a chosen garden."[156] Their moral disease, however, had not corrupted them to the core.

This paradox explained the juxtaposition "of a noble tender imagination, of great fancy and wit,"[157] and of gentlemanly refinement, with "improbable plots, gratuitous and disjointed scenes, extravagant effects, and all those other substitutions of the surprising for the satisfactory, that lower the dramatist into the melodramatist, . . ." Hence, too, their "mis-

takes of sentimentalism for sentiment, violence for sincerity, and heap-
ings of superlative phrases for paintings of character." Other phrases of
condemnation follow thick: "ribaldry . . . want of truth . . . positive
trash . . . exits and entrances that have no ground but the convenience
of the writers . . . childish adventures . . . inconsistent speeches . . .
sudden conversions of bad people to good . . . heaps of talking for talking's sake," and, always recurring, "those foul places . . . which nauseate
a modern reader to the soul."[158] Unless one remembers the other term of
the paradox, he might wonder why Leigh Hunt bothered to produce a volume of their carefully pruned beauties.

Thus, the efforts of the romantic critics to arouse interest in the long-
forgotten Elizabethan playwrights extended to Fletcher and Company,
and caused them to re-emerge from the obscuration which had threatened
them. But they now faced a wider and stiffer competition, and they were
stigmatized as more or less disreputable. It was acknowledged that they
had great lyric gifts as poets, with something of the gentleman about
them—and that in farce, especially, they could be delightful. Yet, as entertainers to the Jacobean gentry, they were seen almost solely as panders
to the depraved tastes of a vile court. Hazlitt alone had a somewhat imperfect sense that they were able theatre craftsmen, although both Coleridge and Leigh Hunt negatively reprobate some aspects of this craftsmanship.

Our corpus of plays may have lost most of their stage appeal during
the eighteenth century, and may not have attracted the attention of many
—nor the ablest—critics of those years. But such criticism as was written,
sometimes was fairer and nearer the mark. The romantic critics, despite
their fragmentary perceptiveness, had one eye too much on Shakespeare,
and the other too much on our playwrights' dreadful licentiousness, for
clear-seeing. They were also, of course, limited by their lack of knowledge of the Jacobean milieu. One positive effect their attentions to
Fletcher, Beaumont and Company did, however, have: our playwrights
were not again to be relatively neglected by the critics as they had been
in the eighteenth century.

CHAPTER THREE

Towards an Historical Approach

T HE attitudes expressed by the romantic critics towards the plays
of Fletcher and his collaborators did not immediately or completely supplant the older ones. Neither did statements and opinions of earlier critics and editors entirely disappear from view. But because of the power, insight and gusto which Coleridge and his friends
displayed in dealing with Shakespeare and his fellow-dramatists, the romantic appraisals soon became pervasive in moulding critical reactions
to all the older playwrights. Despite wide fluctuations of individual opinions, there was scarcely a Victorian interested in Beaumont and Fletcher
who was not influenced in some degree by the romantics' criticism of
them. Indeed, their verdicts, and Coleridge's notably, are still sometimes
reflected in pronouncements of twentieth century scholars and critics.

One factor, however, which originally sprang from the very enthusiasm for the Elizabethan-Stuart drama kindled by Lamb and Hazlitt, has
tended towards a new evaluation of it. This is the historical approach.
As the whole range of this drama was explored, a gradually increasing
curiosity developed about the circumstances which had produced it. The
resultant research of many scholars, especially in the last sixty or seventy
years, has flowered in a large, various, detailed and still expanding body
of factual information about the milieu which conditioned this drama,
and determined its nature. One important result is that our playwrights
—as well as Shakespeare and all their compeers—can now be understood
in terms of their environment and, if we choose, more justly appreciated
than formerly.

The authorship dilemmas presented by our corpus teased many minds
in the nineteenth century. Some thought the problems insoluble, but
others made occasional shrewd guesses, perhaps because of a good ear for
style, perhaps because of careful weighing of the external evidence. The
presence of Fletcher's second collaborator, Massinger, was strongly suspected in several pieces—not always the right ones—but the full extent of

his involvement was not realized. Only in a few instances was the hand of others than Massinger or Beaumont recognized to be present in a play. Finally, in the last three decades of the nineteenth century, scientifically objective verse and style tests were devised which proved practicable, though by no means infallible, in giving clues to authorship of plays and scenes. Fleay, then Boyle, then Oliphant were the pioneers in these new methods. These investigators, and specially Boyle, were the first to recognize how large was Massinger's share in the corpus.

Throughout the Romantic and Victorian ages, the same tendency which led its poets to write unactable dramatic poems in blank verse, in imitation of the Elizabethan-Stuart playwrights, continued to show itself in criticism. If the gradual growth of the historical approach partly revealed the fact that our playwrights were, in good measure, stage entertainers, this ordinarily counted against them. More often, however, they continued to be treated in the way which Lamb had established—as dramatic poets with lyric gifts but deplorable morals.

I

The upsurge of interest in the Elizabethan-Stuart dramatists resulted in four new editions of the works of Fletcher, Beaumont and Company between 1811 and 1846. Two of these appeared in 1811 and 1812, less than five years after Lamb's *Specimens*. The remaining two were published in the ensuing generation: 1839 and 1843-46. Thereafter nineteenth century readers of drama had to depend on reissues of these last editions.

The edition of 1811 contributed nothing new; it was merely a reprint of the earlier Colman one.[1] But that of Henry Weber in the following year (1812)[2] was another matter, for it contained a long introduction by the editor, an eclectic text, and notes making full use of Monck Mason's.[3] In the next generation, Weber's labors were to be rendered obsolete by those of the Rev. Alexander Dyce; but his edition was, in itself, an improvement on eighteenth century ones, despite its textual shortcomings.

Weber's introduction shows him to have been a sympathetic yet judicial critic of a slightly pre-romantic cast. He dealt with the lingering neo-classical viewpoint by insisting that "In considering the general merit . . . of the works of Beaumont and Fletcher, the state of dramatic composition at the time must always be kept in view." While conceding that "the new dramatic school" of Shakespeare, Massinger, Jonson and our playwrights was, "in regularity and unity of design," less perfect than that of the ancients and the French, he nonetheless thought their technique "founded more immediately on nature, better calculated for the display of striking events, and indulging to the imagination more extended limits." On the basis of these distinctions—for apparently he was unaware of Coleridge's seminal theory of the organic unity of Shakespeare's plays—Weber asserted that "the general conception of our poet's plots is most happily imagined."[4]

He did, however, concede that, especially after Beaumont's retirement, our playwrights too frequently betrayed "haste and carelessness in the progress towards the catastrophe." This haste he blamed on the players. As evidence, he quoted a footless sentence about Fletcher from *The Mysteries of Love and Eloquence* (1685): ". . . his importunate comedians would not only crowd upon him such impertinencies, which to him seemed needless and lame excuses, his works being so good, his indignation rendered them [the impertinencies] as the only bad lines his modest Thalia was ever humbled with." This jumbled utterance also supplied Weber with the plausible explanation that to Fletcher's "good-natured but ill-timed complaisance to the actors" was due many of the worst blemishes of his pieces.[5]

Weber also thought our play-fabricators "too fond of introducing incidents strained to the highest pitch of probability, and sometimes surpassing the bonds of nature." Moreover, "the events are often too much crowded together, and not always connected with sufficient art." In fact, "In the general mechanism of their plots . . . they were . . . surpassed by Massinger." But he did perceive that Fletcher and Company deserved "the praise of generally supporting the interest throughout, and of fixing our attention in a lively manner," and holding it,[6]—the prime requisite, be it noted, of a successful playwright.

Informing us that "in the scale of the dramatic poets of that age, the second place has generally been awarded" to Beaumont and Fletcher,[7] Weber found the latter deplorably coarse and careless, but "in every other species of poetical talent he equalled, and in most respects, excelled" Beaumont, especially in "richness of fancy, and the delineations of peculiar descriptions of character."[8] Fletcher yielded to his younger colleague in the portrayal of men of strong character, but excelled him "in pathos, and in his female characters, which, making allowance for his disposition to overstrain their virtues and vices, may be pronounced superior to those of almost any dramatist."[9] Beaumont did, however, join "great eloquence of language, power of description, and sublimity of diction, to a strong and manly humour, and a powerful and indignant personification of the vices and follies of the time."[10]

True to his late eighteenth century inheritance, Weber devoted much attention to characters. He considered them, in general, "well discriminated and well sustained," though confined in scope compared to Shake-speare's. Fletcher's sprightly conversation and gay repartee empowered "his uncommon facility in pourtraying gentlemen of high rank and honour, and of easy, genteel deportment," who "exceed those of all other poets."[11] Weber praised their great variety: Don John, Mirabel and Cleremont as "young men of spirit and fashion;" "the steady honour" of Don Jamie and DeGarde; the "sprightly" Piniero and Leander; the "madcap" Monsieur Thomas and Wildbrain, and the profligate Valentine and younger Loveless. He thought Fletcher also "peculiarly happy in de-lineating the passions of a lover," citing Demetrius, Armusia, and the Francisco of *Monsieur Thomas*—and Beaumont's Amintor as well.[12]

As for heroic characters, "our authors yield to few dramatists,"—wit-ness Caractacus, Melantius, Arcas, Aëcius and Maximus. Hengo was "su-perior not only to Shakespeare's Arthur, but to any generous heroic boy who has ever been exhibited."[13] Other types in which our playwrights ex-celled were "the blunt sturdy Englishman, an enemy to foppery and affectation of all kinds," (Tibalt, DeVitry, Norandine, Leon, Jacomo), and "old men, agitated by violent anger" (Cassibelane, Alberto, Baptisto, Champernel).[14]

Weber considered our playwrights' villains decidedly less successful; they were merely invested "with every mark of downright depravity." Septimus of *The False One* was their most finished delineation. Their evil women were "still less happy." Hippolyta, Lelia, Brunhalt were "too vicious for the stage;" the priestess of *The Mad Lover*, Megra, Panura were defilements, "disgusting beyond endurance."[15] But "the brighter side of the female character" was another matter; here was "a profusion of ad-mirable portraits:"

> The meekness and patience of Aspatia, the saintlike purity and devotion of Ordella, the ardour of affection of Euphrasia, the burning love and resignation of Juliana, the firmness and heroism of Edith, and the tenderness of Evanthe furnish specimens of every virtue estimable in the female character, which these authors, particularly Fletcher, must have studied in every shade and variation.[16]

"No less happy" were "the sprightly girls and jolly widows," such as the widow in *Wit Without Money,* the scornful lady, Alinda and Frank. The roguish Estafania of *Rule a Wife* was "delineated . . . with the truest colouring."[17]

Weber also liked the Jonsonian "humour" characters of our corpus; they "yield the palm to none" except Ben's; many, such as LaWrit, La-zarillo, Bessus and the humourous lieutenant, approach his excellence "very nearly."[18] He thought highly, likewise, of the strictly "Fletcherian" comic characters, as droll as Jonson's, but more natural: the peevish Calianax, for instance, and the pedantic Sir Roger the chaplain, the fortune-hunting Michael Perez, and the group of Bartolus, Lopez and Diego in *The Spanish Curate*. He held Fletcher to be more versatile in comic creation than any of his fellow-dramatists except Shakespeare.[19]

Our editor anticipated Fleay in detecting the main differences between the versification of Beaumont and that of Fletcher, though he did not apply his findings rigorously to the problem of authorship. The distinctions he made were these:

[In Beaumont] the general cast of the versification has some degree of affinity with Shakspeare. The sense of one line is continually run into that of the next, the breaks in the middle are very frequent, and the recurrence of female, or double terminations of the lines, is even less frequent than in Shakspeare. . . . [In Fletcher] the greater number of verses end with some division of a sentence, the breaks in the middle occur more sparingly and are less striking, and the number of double and treble terminations considerably exceeds that of the single or male[20]

A footnote adds: "Another peculiarity of Fletcher's metre . . . is the introduction of dactyls, principally at the pause in the middle of a verse." Weber was on the scent which finally led Fleay and his successors to much success in dealing with the problems of collaboration.

Weber judged Beaumont and Fletcher "reprehensible in an equal, perhaps a superior, degree with the other dramatic writers of the age, for the frequency of gross and indelicate allusions" in their pieces. He noted their Caroline reputation for chasteness, however, and took into consideration "the great change of manners" since their time. He also recognized that the Restoration, "while it partly banished these gross phrases and direct allusions, introduced a more covert, and therefore more dangerous, kind of indelicacy." With more than a grain of truth, he pointed out that "a corrupt imagination in the higher ranks" may "shrink with disgust" from the Beaumont and Fletcher plays, while complacently dwelling on "the genteel and seductive licentiousness of Dryden, Etherege, Otway, and Vanbrugh, where the preponderance of mischief indubitably rests." But he agreed with Dryden in thinking *The Custom of the Country* the grossest play of the corpus.[21]

Weber also thought our playwrights nearly as pathetic, at their best, as Shakespeare.[22] He conjectured rightly that Massinger had a hand in *The False One*, but wrongly supposed him a collaborator in *Love's Pilgrimage*.[23] This partial success was characteristic of his attributions. His comments on the individual plays, as much factual as critical, resemble in tone his more general discussion.[24]

The first of the two early Victorian editions of *The Works of Beaumont and Fletcher*, published in 1839, contained Weber's text, with an introduction by George Darley.[25] It is regretable that Robert Southey decided against editing the 1839 edition, for Darley, a minor romantic poet, was a reluctant substitute with an obvious disrelish for Fletcher. He confessed that his criticisms were "the thoughts which struck me on a hurried review of Beaumont and Fletcher, read desultorily long before. . . ." This hasty hack-work, his postscript informs us, had no critical pretensions "except great desire for truth, and determination to speak it."[26]

This desire for truth appears to have been simply an emotional drive to "debunk" our playwrights. Darley was irked by the conviction that they were usually thought to rank "next below Shakespeare," and also by the fact that in Stuart years they ranked above him. He blamed this latter situation, "scarce credible now," on "new-fangledness" and "the decadence of English manners since Elizabeth's sterner times."[27] He thought the bulkiness of fifty-odd plays the cause of their continued pre-eminence.[28]

Darley had given thought to Henry Hallam's treatment, two years earlier, of Fletcher as a master of stage technique. He gladly conceded that our playwrights were "much better theatrical writers than Ben Jonson, Webster, Ford, etc.," but insisted that they were "less imbued with the genuine dramatic spirit." They lacked the artistic power, purpose, and care in attaining properly their end, which distinguish the true dramatist from the mere theatrical playwright; "while Shakespeare catered for the popular taste, Fletcher pandered to it," regardless of its viciousness.[29] Since the plays of our corpus were too immoral even to compete, on their own low level, with "tasteless contemporary entertainments" in the minor Victorian theatres, he came to the Alice-in-Wonderland conclusion that they should "be considered rather as dramatic poems than plays."[30] So considering them was, in effect, unconsciously acknowledging that they were more witty, sprightly and literate than the average commercial theatre product.

The comedies of Fletcher and his colleagues were, with two exceptions, cheap theatrical pieces. Nowhere had they developed "a plot or group of characters so skillfully, so consistently, so harmoniously" as had Jonson in his best plays. In fact, not one comic character had the "force, through understanding . . . and uniform self-sustainment, of any principal portrait" of Ben's; their imitations of him were markedly "servile."[31] A fastidious reader perpetually regretted that, even in their most popular comedies, "so much *vis comica* has been frittered away" by lack of compactness and mere theatricality. *The Wild-Goose Chase,* however,—"wild-witted and mercurial"—did move with an agreeable swiftness; and Beaumont's *The Knight of the Burning Pestle* had "an art almost equal to Ben Jonson's; with nativer and mellower humour, though less caustic."[32]

Disagreeing with Hallam, Darley thought our playwrights better in tragedy and tragicomedy. He considered *Philaster* and *The Maid's*

Tragedy, "if not equi-valuable with all the other plays together," at least
the ones on which their chief renown rested.[33] And yet these did not equal
Webster and Ford in "the essence itself of drama—impassioned action."
Our playwrights could not "direct the storm of passion" they raised; their
tragic poetry was "apt to become an ambitious fustian, their action un-
fanciful extravagance." Their forte was merely "a certain gentle and almost feminine pathos." They could turn out solely "such plays as will
fill theatres."[34] Darley's contempt for filling theatres was characteristically nineteenth century in spirit.

Beaumont and Fletcher, unlike Shakespeare, had no pretensions that
could be justified to "skilful and nice conduct" of plotting or to "harmonious combination of effective circumstance."[35] They filled "their
scene with motion instead of action," and did not even allow a plot to
grow spontaneously, let alone shape one up; "they cut it short, and graft
upon the stump any exotics that lie near, till their plays become . . .
one intertangled knot of heterogeneous ramification,"—a loose "nosegay"
with only a title to tie it together.[36]

Darley held it a mark of impotency and debauched taste that our playwrights founded "almost every" play on love, which "too often degenerated . . . into mere sensuality." One result of this "eternal love-lolly-
ing" was that woman was "too much treated as a fair animal, . . . degraded into an object of voluptuous pursuit." Only a few tragedies displaying Beaumont's hand represented love "as a noble passion," but
never with "as much native purity and wholesome intensity" as in Shakespeare.[37]

In characterization, Fletcher and Company usually "unnaturalize,"
"often making beautiful chimeras of their virtuous characters . . . and
hideous or grotesque monsters of their bad."[38] Only a handful—and these
mostly in tragedies—"have a sufficient groundwork of truth." The playwrights "keep upon the surface of their subjects rather than penetrating
them," and represent only "the caprices, oddities, fashions, manners of
artificial life rather than genuine human nature."[39] They do not allow
characters to develop, and they "mistake particular nature for general
(which alone is true nature)."[40] Their idealized women, such as Ordella
and Juliana, are "improbable as characters," though possible in life. But
the playwrights reflect one "truth of nature . . . their women are either
far more angelical or diabolical than their men."[41]

Laxity of morals, inspired by their libertine age, "pervades their
dramas." Fletcher "prostituted his Muse with less reserve than Beaumont, while Massinger, "though a stern . . . moralizer, is bytimes yet
more immodest" than either. "We have here the key to the Puritan
horror of the drama." All except Puritanism's "most extreme procedures

and prejudices" were justified "whilst playhouses were so like the devil's preserves as playwrights made them."[42] Though Darley asserts that he was not of a Puritan temper, the reader is privileged to doubt him.

Our playwrights' "indelicacies and indecorums" were, however, more repellant than alluring. Their "beau-ideal of gentlemen" was "a very vulgar one, . . . they mistook fashionables" for them, and excelled in portraying "court rakes and roués, but could no more have delineated such inborn gentlemen as Hamlet and Romeo than conceived such poetic characters." Fletcher was "adept at Tyburn gibberish . . . ribald wit and farcical nastiness;" his ladies "scatter the rankest flowers of rhetoric." Darley considered this "heap of rubbish" totally absent in Shakespeare, who "never used a vulgar expression," though many gross ones.[43]

Darley distinguished certain characteristics of Fletcher's style but appears to have attributed them to both playwrights. He believed this style "the freest and feeblest" of all the great dramatists, and that it marked "the first sweetening and softening, united with the weakening of our poetic language. . . ."[44] Its dramatic merits almost escaped him. It was "Seldom vigorous except when inflated, nor often melodious without being mawkish," even though it had "a certain openness, and abandon, and ever-varying elasticity."[45] It "mingled together . . . different laws of metre," and therefore was "broken-backed, full of ridges, an incessant joggle from one rut to another."[46]

The poetic "beauties" which the playwrights achieved were "wheat grains lost in a bushel of chaff."[47] Even the charming song in *The Nice Valour*, "Hence, all you vain delights," (on which Milton drew for *Il Penseroso*), epitomized for Darley "the valetudinarian interestingness, the delicateness implying want of perfect wholesomeness, which hangs all about Beaumont and Fletcher's more serious productions,"[48]—even, apparently, their best ones.

Hallam's account of Beaumont and Fletcher[49] had confirmed the opinion of this minor poet, contemptuous of stagecraft, that in the main our playwrights were merely rather shoddy little men of the theatre, despite such mild poetic gifts as they had. In thinking that Beaumont was less blameworthy than Fletcher, since he had the dominant share in most of the few good plays they wrote, Darley anticipated a frequently expressed modern viewpoint. With his introduction—derogatory in spirit in spite of scattered seasonings of praise—and with Weber's text, the 1839 edition was scarcely an improvement on that of 1812.

The Works of Beaumont and Fletcher, 1843-46, edited by the Rev. Alexander Dyce, was a happy contrast. This second and last Victorian edition offered the first carefully collated text yet to appear. In addition it had scholarly and often sensible notes, and a biographical-critical introduction which was the result of careful research. To Dyce goes the distinction, for instance, of discovering the date and place of Fletcher's birth.[50] If the edition is now partially obsolete, it is still useful.

Dyce's *Some Account of the Lives and Writings of Beaumont and Fletcher*[51] interwove the biographical narrative of the two playwrights with individual discussions of each play (and poem), in a pattern as nearly chronological as the data then available allowed. This method made for little general comment. The only extended discussion was à propos *The Custom of the Country,* which Dyce considered a superior play "for interest and happy management of the plot, for contrast of character, and for beauty of style,"—unusual admissions—but "unfortunately the very grossest of them all." Thus echoing the charge of Dryden and Weber, he felt that our playwrights could "only be extenuated on the plea, that they had sacrificed their own taste and feelings to the fashion of the times," when " 'to be like the Court was a playe's praise.' "[52] In deforming "their dramas with ribaldry . . . they sinned more grievously than any of their contemporary playwrights."[53] Dyce had, however, the fairness to add that "most of the others have enough to answer for; nor was Shakespeare himself completely proof against the contaminating influence of his age." He agreed, moreover, with Weber that "If Dryden and the other dramatists of Charles the Second's time did not equal their predecessors in open licentiousness . . . they far exceeded them in wanton innuendoes and allusions."[54]

In his critical remarks on the individual plays, Dyce showed the nineteenth century tendency to put much stress on characterization and poetry, while giving some attention also to plotting, situations, scenes and—less often—dialogue. Back of his treatment lay solid acquaintance with the comments of Lamb, Hazlitt and Coleridge, as well as of Hallam, Darley and Weber, of eighteenth century editors, and of Dryden and other seventeenth century writers. Dyce's viewpoint was, on the whole, romantic; his spirit seldom harsh and often warmly appreciative.

Two, only, of the tragedies of our corpus altogether escaped censure. Beaumont and Fletcher's *The Maid's Tragedy* was, to Dyce, the greatest achievement in this form by our playwrights—"unrivalled for the growing interest it excites and for the ultimate impression which it produces." Evadne was "a daring character . . . finely conceived and happily preserved;" Aspatia, "the very personification of blighted maiden love, meekly submitting to unmerited suffering." The brave, blunt, honest soldier, Melantius, was well contrasted with the weak, irresolute Amintor. The Fletcher-Massinger *The False One* had regular plotting, consistently good characterization and "general elevation of style." Cleopatra, though not the equal of Shakespeare's, had a "fresh morning beauty;" she was "in all respects a fit object to captivate the master of the world." Caesar was "equal, if not superior, to any" portrait of him by other dramatists, while Septimius was a skilfully drawn cold-blooded murderer.[55]

Of the other tragedies, Fletcher's *Valentinian* was well managed and effective in character delineation until its true ending, the death of Valentinian; thereafter it went awry. Lucina, despite Coleridge, was "remarkable for truth and delicacy of painting;" Aëcius and Maximus good portraits for the first three acts. Fletcher's *Bonduca,* praiseworthy for its serious scenes, was equally blameworthy for its comic ones. Caratach was the most successful brave, rough, honest soldier of our corpus. Hengo had a "delicious freshness," (though he was not invariably child-like), and his death had true pathos. In both *Thierry and Theodoret* and *The Double Marriage* the depiction of major characters was overstrained; but the former was "one of the most energetic of the tragedies" and the latter well plotted and not too improbable in incident. Dyce found little, however, to praise and much to condemn in *The Bloody Brother,* while *Cupid's Revenge* was "a wretched drama."[56]

Among the tragicomedies, Dyce ranked *A King and No King* as one of the masterpieces of our corpus, though its subject was unpleasing, its plot "liable to great objections," and its "passages of poetic merit" few. Arbaces was "a character . . . strangely compounded." His instantaneous changes of temper were dramatically effective, if a trifle mechanical, and his inconsistencies when in love with his supposed sister were "displayed with a truth and vigor worthy of all praise." Dyce agreed with Hallam that the plot of *Philaster* was absurdly managed, but thought Philaster and Arethusa "delineated with great skill and spirit," and Bellario "one of our authors' most perfect creations—unequalled in the romantic tenderness and deep devotedness of her affection." The play was studded with "Passages remarkable alike for poetic beauty and felicity of language."[57]

Fletcher's pastoral tragicomedy, *The Faithful Shepherdess,* when compared to the perfection of Milton's *Comus,* was "a gem with several flaws and clouds." These included an unskilful and uninteresting plot, the wanton Chloe, and the ridiculous passion of Thenot for Clorin.[58] The gem-like quality of this drama came from the lyric portions, "steeped in the most delicate and brilliant hues of fancy," and written in "exquisitely modulated . . . verse."[59]

Among the various other tragicomedies, Dyce considered one, *The Honest Man's Fortune,* "a drama of superior merit," sustaining our interest in Montague's plight to the very end. *Women Pleased* was "very entertaining," with a plot shaped by "the nicest art" from three tales of

Boccaccio and one of Chaucer, and with an effective "original" comic role: Penurio, the hungry knave. *The Knight of Malta,* despite a rambling plot and few "vigorously" drawn characters, had some "highly dramatic . . . scenes and a profusion of beautiful writing." *A Wife for a Month* was disagreeable in plot, marred by "coarse and commonplace" villains, and sullied by grossness in certain dialogues between Valerio and Evanthe. Yet it managed to hold the reader's attention up to the very denouement. But the remaining tragicomedies were second-rate, like *The Loyal Subject* and the badly told but sometimes animated *The Humourous Lieutenant*—or else, like *The Island Princess,* definitely inferior. As for *The Mad Lover,* it was "little else than a tissue of extravagance."[60]

Above all other comedies by Fletcher, with or without the aid of Massinger, four stood out for Dyce: *The Chances, The Elder Brother, Rule a Wife,* and *The Spanish Curate.* The first of these gave pleasure through "a throng of incidents brought out with high dramatic effect," and through "sprightliness and ease of dialogue." It also afforded three fine character delineations: the gay, impetuous and gallant Don John, the less mercurial Frederick, and the richly grotesque landlady, Gillian. *The Elder Brother* provided a well-balanced dramatis personae, including a hero drawn with "skill and delicacy"—as well as "many poetical passages." In the Fletcher-Massinger *The Spanish Curate,* the interest never languished despite the loose-jointedness of the two plots. Incidents were "heightened with great dramatic skill," and a group of well contrasted characters yielded first place to the curate Lopez and the sexton Diego who, though essentially caricatures, possessed a "firmness of outline and richness of coloring, which Fletcher has never surpassed and seldom equalled." And that playwright's *Rule a Wife* had

always been esteemed, and justly, as one of the author's masterpieces in comedy. The main plot and the underplot are very skilfully connected, and both so judiciously conducted that the interest never flags, and the unpleasing nature of the fable is entirely overlooked. The dramatis personae are forcibly delineated, with no unwarrantable heightening of their peculiarities. . . . The dialogue . . . is everywhere full of animation, often richly humorous, and, in some of the serious portions assigned to Leon, remarkable for the neat and forcible expression of the sentiment.

Beaumont's *The Knight of the Burning Pestle* was the fifth comic masterpiece of our team—the first in merit, as in time, of English mock-heroic plays. The whole piece was "highly artistic and in perfect keeping; the humor of great breadth and raciness."[61]

Others of the comedies had excellences which placed them among our playwrights' better work. *Wit Without Money* was prominent among these, because of a well handled plot, "a constant flow of humorous dialogue," and masterly depictions of the spendthrift Valentine and the free-spoken Lady Heartwell. *The Little French Lawyer* had to its credit, besides many beautiful serious passages, "the pleasant whimsicalness" of La-Writ, whose first three scenes displayed "infinite ease, smartness, and rapidity of dialogue." The strength of *Monsieur Thomas* lay chiefly in "the exuberant animal spirits, the whim, and the madbrained freaks" of its name character, consistently maintained. *The Beggars' Bush,* with romantic story, well-conducted plot, and its spirited "ragged regiment," was highly amusing. *The Pilgrim,* despite desultory plot and featureless characters, "charms us by the rapid succession of events, the well-contrived situations, the vivacity of the comic scenes, and the unstrained grace . . . of the serious portions." And *The Night-Walker,* while not deserving as high rank as Hazlitt gave it, was nonetheless "a merry play."[62]

Clearly, more comedies impressed Dyce favorably than either tragedies or tragicomedies. He disagreed, however, with previous high estimates of both Fletcher's *The Wild-Goose Chase* and the Beaumont-Fletcher *The Scornful Lady.* The former was "by no means agreeable," since the characters "excite our mirth, but none of our esteem;" the latter, despite certain merits, had "unusual coarseness of feeling throughout the entire play." As for other comedies in which Beaumont had a hand, his *The Woman-Hater* deserved its failure, while the Beaumont-Fletcher *The Coxcomb,* though amusing, was "extravagant in plot, character, and incident."[63] Thus, except for *The Knight of the Burning Pestle,* the genuine comedy successes were Fletcher's.

Darley and Dyce represent respectively the negative and the positive poles of their day in criticism of Beaumont and Fletcher. Their editions, supplanting Weber's, were also the two most often read until the early twentieth century, and hence their appraisals had an impact on Victorian readers. Neither critic fully understood our playwrights' skill in terms of theatre. Darley saw the theatricality of Fletcher and Company solely as pandering to depraved tastes. Dyce, without ignoring technique, gave fuller attention to character delineation and poetic beauty. The latter also enjoyed the plays sufficiently, despite "grossness" and other defects, to avoid the former's acidulous distaste for Fletcher, and to strike a more judicious balance of praise and censure. It should be added that their editions were the last two to carry critical introductions, for those of the twentieth century lack them.[64]

II

The advance in knowledge of many long-buried Elizabethan and Stuart dramatists which followed the advent of Lamb's *Specimens* is reflected in various handbooks of the time. Early comparative evaluations of the playwrights, however, show interesting divergences from modern ones, as Nathan Drake's *Shakespeare and His Times* (1817)[65] and S. A. Dunham's *Lives of the Most Eminent Literary and Scientific Men of Great Britain* (1837)[66] will suffice to demonstrate.

To Drake, Shakespeare was easily first, Fletcher and Massinger were of nearly equal merit, and Jonson completed the major foursome. Ford followed, with Webster sixth, and Middleton, Dekker, Heywood and perhaps Chapman sharing the seventh position. Surveying this whole field, Drake marvelled, of many of these, that "even the talents of Shakespeare should, for so long a period, have eclipsed their fame."[67]

Dunham reflects the advance in knowledge made during the intervening twenty years. His allotments of space, in his biographical and critical accounts of the various playwrights, proves a fairly accurate gauge of his opinions about their respective merits. Major attention in volume two was given to the now traditional quadrumvirate. Though Beaumont and Fletcher appeared as an appendage to the chapter on the greater Jonson, they received full treatment, as did Massinger. Of the others, it was Ford and Webster who achieved the dignity of moderately extended discussion. Dunham's range of at least bowing acquaintanceship is indicated by the ten "minor dramatists" accorded brief handling: Chapman, Middleton, Marston, Dekker, Heywood, Rowley, Field, May, Davenport and Cartwright. In volume three there was a long chapter on Shirley and a shorter one on Davenant—both newcomers to posts of honor.[68]

Neither Drake nor Dunham was a critic of any exceptional penetration. Drake believed that Fletcher wrote most of the plays of our corpus, assigning Beaumont a share in only ten, and Massinger, Field and Rowley hands in still fewer.[69] He also held a not uncommon illusion that Fletcher sought to emulate Shakespeare, with resultant painful "labour and contortion." Granting him mastery in delineating "softer passions, especially of love," Drake nonetheless often found the final impression of his plays to be that of "feebleness and effeminacy, a sickliness of sentiment, and a want of dignity." While the comedies, his best work, had "grace and legerity," and coruscated with wit, repartee, and "intellectual smartness of dialogue," they had "little humour, and consequently not much strength of character."[70]

Dunham, on the contrary, thought neither playwright "had much genius for comedy." The "most tedious" *Rule a Wife*, with its "grotesque situations," was judged to lack wit, even though its dialogue had "something like animation." *The Woman-Hater*, incorrectly attributed to Fletcher, was paraded at tedious length as generally bad work, as well as "disgustingly obscene." In tragedy, however, Dunham considered our playwrights "worthy of very high praise," standing next to Shakespeare in both the sublime and the pathetic: witness *The Maid's Tragedy*. But *Philaster* won the faint acclaim of "a very respectable performance," while *The Faithful Shepherdess* was dismissed as "frigid, unimpassioned, unnatural," and void of all merit.[71] On the remaining plays Dunham was silent. The inference is plain that he did not really like our playwrights. One wonders if Darley may have read him, before he wrote his introduction.

A critic of greater shrewdness than these was Henry Hallam, whom it is certain both Darley and Dyce read. His *Introduction to the Literature of Europe*[72] was published in the same year (1837) as Dunham's book. Perhaps aided by suggestions from Hazlitt's lectures, Hallam grasped more clearly than either Darley or Dyce the fact that Fletcher and Company were primarily dramatic entertainers. Indeed, this seems to have been the core idea of his critique.

Thinking Fletcher "much superior to Shakespeare in his knowledge of the stage," Hallam called attention to "the great fertility of his mind in new combinations of circumstance."[73] It was his contention that, with the stage picture ever in their vision, our playwrights directed their main efforts to the "plot . . . the rapid succession of events, the surprises and embarrassments which keep the spectator's attention alive." Hence "the numerous and striking incidents" in their pieces.[74] In some plays, however, he found "a want of unity in the conception," "as if the authors had gone forward with no clear determination of their catastrophe."[75] And in their more serious dramas the denouement was often baffling to "reasonable conjecture," "unnatural," and "generally mismanaged,"[76]— in other words, calculated to surprise theatrically rather than to fulfill expectation.

In characterization, Hallam considered Fletcher far inferior to Shakespeare, both in variety and in depth. His comments, while true enough, do less than justice to our playwrights' best work. The characters delineated by them were, he pointed out, "sometimes lightly sketched," and "usually . . . but vehicles to the story; they are distinguished for the most part, by little more than slight peculiarities of manner, which are easily caught" by theatregoers. New combinations of circumstance gave "as much appearance of novelty to the personages themselves as an unreflecting audience requires." The characterization seldom approached "the elaborate delineations of Jonson, or the marked idiosyncrasies of Shakspeare," yet provided a sufficient "degree of individual distinctness" for stage success.[77]

Lacking "that large sweep of reflection and experience" which resulted in Shakespeare's strong conceptions of male characters, Fletcher was best at portraying females. "None of his women delight us like Imogen and Desdemona, but he has many Imogens and Desdemonas of a fainter type"—pleasing pictures of "faithful, tender, self-denying female love, superior to everything but virtue." He was successful, too, "in the contrast of minds stained by guilty passions," though sometimes exaggerating almost to caricature.[78] Some characters, apparently "intended to surprise by incongruity," sadly lacked consistency; striking examples included Ruy Dias of *The Island Princess* and Edith of *The Bloody Brother.*[79]

Hallam agreed with Coleridge that *The Maid's Tragedy* and many other dramas poured out "the unlimited loyalty fashionable at the court of King James."[80] It did not, however, escape his attention that the plays were "full of implied satire" of the court, discernable to spectators. "The warm eulogies on military glory, the scorn of slothful peace, the pictures of dissolute courtiers seem to spring from a dislike, very usual among the English gentry, . . . for that ignominious government."[81] This shrewd suggestion has been often ignored by later critics.

There is a right Victorian ring to Hallam's notion that *The Maid's Tragedy* (and other plays) ought not to be read "by any respectable woman," because of "that studiously protracted indecency which distinguished Fletcher beyond all our early dramatists."[82] But he genuinely regretted that it was impossible to produce the comedies "without such changes as destroy their original raciness, and dilute the geniality of their wit,"[83] thereby acknowledging that their raciness was often genial and witty. He held, moreover, in common with some seventeenth century eulogists, that the comedies "never descend to the coarse buffoonery not infrequent in their age."[84]

Unlike Shakespeare's winged utterance, Fletcher's "pleasing, though not profound or vigorous language," was, Hallam believed, "understandable to all spectators alike." Yet "we are seldom arrested by striking beauties; good lines occur in every page, fine ones but rarely."[85] In this, as in all other aspects of our playwrights' craftsmanship, what Hallam found chiefly lacking was—and he quoted from Schlegel—"seriousness and depth."[86] His criticisms of a number of the individual plays are in harmony with his more general viewpoint.

Bodham Donne is another early Victorian writer whose viewpoint on Fletcher, Beaumont and Company has, like Hallam's, a strong individual flavor. A critic who was to become official "Examiner of Plays" for the London stage, his distinction is to reflect the nascent historical approach in a partial tendency to consider the qualities and defects of Beaumont and Fletcher in terms of Jacobean court life and theatre. His review for *Fraser's Magazine* (March, 1850) praising Dyce's edition of our playwrights, condemned the carelessness of earlier ones; only Weber's had "any pretensions to merit on the score of editorial competence." But Dyce's provided "a well restored or corrected text, and . . . a full but not burdensome commentary." The qualifications of the editor for his task included "skill in old books and archaic lore, . . . sound judgment . . . good taste . . . erudition and acumen," as well as caution in amendation, sagacity in detecting obscure or doubtful meanings, and a fine ear for metre.[87]

"The respective shares of Beaumont and Fletcher in the dramas which bear their joint names" was to Donne "an insoluble problem," interesting only because its solution might show how much each owed to Shakespeare and to Jonson. He did, however, doubt the "superior judiciousness" traditionally assigned Beaumont, because he found plays written after Beaumont's death "neither more nor less judicious" than those ascribed to the partnership.[88] Here was an original conclusion, and one of much soundness, since both men were expert craftsmen.

Donne considered Fletcher (and, by inference, Beaumont) "an artist of the second order." Fletcher moved more "gracefully and spontaneously" on the lower levels of art, but was "constrained to unnatural and spasmodical movements" on the higher, as in *A King and No King, Philaster,* and *The Faithful Shepherdess.*[89] Donne thought him probably indifferent to those imperfections which were due to rapid writing. "He knew well what suited the players and pleased the public and had no deeper artistic yearnings," except in the instance of *The Faithful Shepherdess.* He also lacked such earnest sympathy with his characters as Shakespeare evinced. He was "more studious of effect than of consistency or even probability." Donne therefore urged that "it is not fair . . . to try such pieces as the 'Island Princess,' the 'Sea Voyage,' or the 'Coxcomb,' by a strict standard of dramatic propriety,"[90]—a plea which deserves more consideration than it has received.

He also believed, however, that "There is a moral decadence, an imaginative decay" in the plays of our corpus which was not present in "the manlier drama of Elizabeth. . . . The hues of autumn have begun to streak the poetic foliage; . . ." Whereas "the irony of Sophocles and Shakespeare regards man struggling impotently with circumstance, . . . the irony of Beaumont and Fletcher is the utterance of the satirist on men and manners," who is "conversant only with the superficial emotions and conventional forms of life." Hence their temper, which "contemplates and derides the phenomena of society without attempting to solve them by any higher law of reconcilement," is that of "Lucian, Montaigne and Voltaire," and we do not rise from reading them "much the happier or the wiser."[91]

The point of irritation to our Victorian critic seems to have been that our playwrights' "flashes of wit and fancy, their crowded incidents and startling contrasts, even the voluptuous music of their verse, are things of the sense and the scene, not echoes from the fontal deeps of humanity." Unlike Shakespeare, they were wanting in "the imaginative expression of the strife between Fate and Free-Will." They were not "genuinely humorous or earnest,"—and so Donne, like Hallam, quoted Schlegel on their lack of seriousness of mind.[92] Yet if these playwrights are to be judged on their own basis as entertainers, as Donne had also suggested, why the sober concern about this lack?

Our critic was not, however, harsh about the so-called moral decadence of Fletcher and Company. True, he spoke of "The bias of Fletcher's mind to prurient sentiments and images, his fondness for the debatable ground between virtue and vice, his microscopic trials of a foible or an emotion," and held them to be blemishes alike to man and artist. But he called for "some allowance in the verdict." He recognized that Beaumont and Fletcher catered to "worshipful society," and he roundly told his contemporaries that "our ancestors tolerated grossness; we endure and applaud sentimental and melodramatic fiction." In explanation of this tolerance of coarseness, Donne instanced the delight of the courtiers in public hangings, as well as the corruption and vice of James I's court, shared even by that monarch's upstart favorites, Carr and Buckingham.[93] If the language of the court was by no means always finical or refined, the language of the plays was only its echo. "The stage may have added to the impurities of the stream; it did not originally corrupt the fountain."[94]

On the basis of the recorded language and manners of the Court, compared with the banter and love-making of our playwrights' gentlemen, Donne suggested that Fletcher and Company "copied more faithfully than Shakespeare the language of the Court and the Mall,"—thus agreeing with Dryden and many others. But if Fletcher "caught the trick and passing fashion of the spruce gamesters and curled darlings of his age," Shakespeare better depicted the "true English gentleman."[95]

Donne also gave an historical explanation for the coarse language of heroines in Elizabethan plays: that boys played these roles. Even Shakespeare was not immune to the temptations afforded by this situation. But Fletcher took far more liberties; and in his plays the convention of girl-masquerading-as-boy "is repeated *ad nauseam*." Since the audience knew that these masqueraders were boys indeed, they were easily reconciled to female license, as of Lelia, Bacha and Hippolyta.[96] But Dryden, "who surpasses Fletcher in indecency, had not even his excuse for it," for women by that time acted feminine roles.[97]

Like Hallam, Donne perceived that Fletcher, Beaumont, Massinger and their assistants were not altogether in sympathy with the court life which they portrayed. He singled out the "arrogant and unveiled despotism" of their scenic kings, dukes and counts as resembling in some measure the attitude of James. If "the virtuous suffer unreasonably" at their courts, "and female purity and manly honour are exposed to extravagant trials," this but shadowed forth the corrupt atmosphere of the actual Jacobean court. Donne brought out the point, moreover, that in various plays the favorites of rulers came in for satire, "veiled, but . . . pungent and significant"; witness Boroskie, Latorch, Sorano and Heimskirk.[98] It was therefore Donne's conclusion, in evident disagreement with Coleridge's, that our playwrights were, "for their age, free-spoken, and implied more than they thought it politic to set down."[99]

Interestingly enough, Donne considered *The Maid's Tragedy*, despite "striking stage effects and passages of brilliant declamation," an overvalued play. Aspatia he held, with some justice, to be "a poetic rather than a dramatic creation"; the other characters were "uninteresting and even heartless." Pierre of Otway's *Venice Preserved* was a better stagesoldier than Melantius; Amintor offended by his "fickleness in love," and disgusted by his "fantastic loyalty"; Evadne (her sin "rank" and her repentence "worse") was "unendurable."[100] Herein, as elsewhere, our critic betrayed some little tincture of stuffy Victorianism, blended with the gold of his fairminded allowances for the Jacobean milieu of our playwrights.

But Donne's essay was solid gold compared with the febrile and telltale outcries which, foreshadowed by Leigh Hunt and Darley, flowed forth from many pens in this age. As amusingly absurd as any—and perhaps, too, a little pathetic, since it suggests festering inhibition—was this *ex cathedra* fiat, pronounced by George Gilfillan in 1855 to "the uninitiated" into Beaumont, Fletcher, and Massinger:

that more beastly, elaborate, and incessant filth and obscenity are not to be found in all literature, than in the plays of these dramatists; and that we, at least, could only read one or two of them through. They repelled us by the strong shock of disgust, and we have never since been able to understand of what materials the men were made who have read and reread them, paused and lingered over them, dwelt fondly on their beauties, and even ventured to compare them to the plays of Shakespeare; . . .[101]

And the American Edwin P. Whipple insisted in flushed tones that Beaumont and Fletcher were generally conceded to be

more effeminate and dissolute than the band of dramatic writers to which they must still be considered to belong. . . . Their tragic Muse carouses in crime, and reels out upon us with bloodshot eyes and dishevelled tresses. . . . The atmosphere of their tragedy is too often hot, thick, and filled with pestilential vapors. . . . Their strength is flushed, bloated, spasmodic, and furious. They pitch everything in a high key, approaching to a scream.[102]

There was such a bounteous lifting of the hands in horror among the lesser Victorian critics[103] that the robust if not profound voice of Thomas Babington Macaulay, reinforcing Weber and Dyce, is a relief. In *The Comedy of the Restoration* (1841), he admitted that

> There is undoubtedly a great deal of indelicate writing in Fletcher and Massinger, and more than might be wished even in Ben Jonson and Shakespeare, who are comparatively pure. But it is impossible to trace in their plays any systematic attempt to associate vice with those things which men value most and desire most, and virtue with everything ridiculous and degrading. And such a systematic attempt we do find in the whole dramatic literature which followed the return of Charles the Second.[104]

Though itself not untinged with Victorianism, this passage, so far as it concerns our playwrights, makes sense.

III

During the first seven decades of the nineteenth century there was little progress in solving the authorship puzzles of the "Beaumont and Fletcher" corpus. The group of romantic critics made no effort to sift through such evidence, external or internal, as was available; indeed, Coleridge frankly admitted that he had "never been able to distinguish the presence of Fletcher during the lifetime of Beaumont, nor the absence of Beaumont during the survival of Fletcher."[105] Hallam let the matter alone, and Craik agreed with Donne that puzzles of joint authorship were insoluble, since neither "the contradictory accounts that have been handed down," nor the plays themselves, furnished any decisive evidence.[106]

The three nineteenth century editors, however, all made attempts to assign the plays, though Darley was interested only in the problem of Beaumont. The results were not particularly happy. Weber, amidst his unreliable if interesting conjectures, made one useful clarification. From Sir Henry Herbert's manuscript he drew the evidence that several plays must have been written by Fletcher alone, and that Beaumont could not possibly have co-authored several other disputed ones. Moreover, his enlargement of the troup of collaborators to include not only Fletcher, Beaumont and Massinger but Daborne, Field, Jonson, Middleton, Rowley, Shakespeare and Shirley as well, was sound, even though his opinions about particular partnerships have sometimes not been sustained by modern scholars. Darley helpfully analyzed the metrical qualities of the plays, and suggested that, with some differences, Massinger resembled Beaumont and Fletcher in versification. He also had some flair for detecting

Beaumont's presence in a play. Yet he did not attempt the further step of distinguishing the three playwrights' styles as a means to determining their shares in joint work. Dyce, taking stock of his predecessors' labors and sometimes relying too much on shaky external evidence, arrived by literary instinct at only a modest proportion of correct assignments in doubtful cases.[107] None of the editors pretended to omniscience in their hazarded opinions.[108]

It is, therefore, not surprising that Minto should acknowledge the existence of "ample materials for forming an estimate of Fletcher," because of his unassisted pieces, but not for arriving at one of Beaumont. Minto had to confess that "there is no passage in any of the joint plays that I could affirm with any confidence not to be Fletcher's." So he inclined to accept the opinion "current during the reign of Charles I . . . that Beaumont's chief share in the plays lay in correcting the exuberance of Fletcher," though "it is quite possible that he contributed whole scenes, if not whole acts."[109]

In the year 1874, the authorship log-jam which Minto's remarks so clearly indicate was broken. The Rev. F. G. Fleay devised the new method of attack. He had already applied a system of metrical tests to the doubtful dramas of Shakespeare with rewarding results. He now devised similar ones for the plays of our corpus. To determine Fletcher's metrical characteristics he chose 12 pieces by that playwright, in only one of which, *The Custom of the Country,* has a second hand—that of Massinger—been discovered. For Beaumont's characteristics he selected the first two one-acters of *Four Plays or Moral Representations in One,* still sometimes claimed for that author.[110] Working from this basis, Fleay uncovered six metrical peculiarities of Fletcher and four of Beaumont. The most important of these he rightly held to be a prevalence of double (and triple) endings and of end-stopped lines in Fletcher, as against a preference for single or masculine endings and run-on lines in Beaumont. He also examined Massinger's verse-characteristics.

Fleay then applied these tests to the individual plays of joint or doubtful authorship, assigning to each playwright his share in terms of acts, scenes, and even parts of scenes. He isolated, to his own satisfaction, the shares not only of Fletcher, Beaumont and Massinger but also of all the other dramatists suggested by Weber, with the further addition of Dekker. Then he presented his results in a paper read before "The New Shakspere Society" in 1874, with discussion by its members following.[111] This discussion brought out limitations and dangers in Fleay's method, and challenged some of his results. In 1886, after further consideration, Fleay modified his conclusions, and tried to establish a more accurate chronology.[112]

His initial investigation provoked one immediate counter-reaction: from Algernon Charles Swinburne, poet of hypnotic melody, and impressionistic, sometimes flamboyant critic. Swinburne's approach to criticism was aesthetic, appreciative, nonscholarly; his outlook was romantic rather than historical. As Chew points out, he was averse to source-studies, verse-tests and other scholarly methods. He cared nothing for understanding Elizabethan-Stuart drama in terms of its own milieu or as theatre; its literary qualities were what concerned him.[113]

Encountering Fleay's paper, Swinburne made a study of it and then, according to Gayley, wrote his own essay, *Beaumont and Fletcher,* (1875).[114] Fleay's methods appeared to him ridiculous. Relying solely on his own poetic "instinct" or intuition, he proceeded to distinguish the plays in which Beaumont had had a share. His results, interestingly enough, now appear to be somewhat more accurate than those which Fleay arrived at by his pioneering verse-tests. Swinburne did not, however, condescend to indicate shares by act and scene.

The outcome of his study of Beaumont and of Fletcher was to convince him that "the loss of their names from the roll of English poetry"—note that it is "poetry," rather than "drama"—"would be only less than the loss of the few greatest names inscribed on it."[115] At the same time, "we must admit that Beaumont was the twin of heavenlier birth."[116] Indeed, "in that tragic field where the freshest bays were gathered Beaumont was the worthiest and closest follower of Shakespeare,"—except, perhaps, for Webster.[117] Here was a cue that later Beaumontians picked up.

What gave the younger twin primacy was "those tragic poems of which the dominant note is the note of Beaumont's genius,"—*Philaster* and *A King and No King* no less than *The Maid's Tragedy.* In them "a subtler chord of thought is sounded, a deeper key of emotion is touched than ever was struck by Fletcher. The lighter genius is palpably subordinate to the stronger, and loyally submits itself to the impression of a loftier spirit." One observes here, as so often in modern criticism, unawareness of the contribution Fletcher's skill in stagecraft made to these plays, which Swinburne considered "the most precious part" of our corpus. "Outside it we shall find no figures so firmly drawn, no such clearness of outline, no such cunning of hand, as we recognize in the three great studies of Bellario, Evadne and Aspatia." Not even Fletcher's Ordella in *Thierry and Theodoret* had "such cunning touch of tenderness or delicate perfume of pathos" as Bellario and Aspatia. "These have in them a bitter sweetness, a subtle pungency of mortal sorrow and tears of divine delight, beyond the reach of Fletcher." Unfortunately, however, Philaster and Arbaces showed "something of that exaggeration or inconsistency" more usually characteristic of Fletcher.[118]

True to his nineteenth century heritage, Swinburne conceived of our playwrights as busy, in their serious plays, at "studies" of human nature. Fletcher's "highest studies of female character have dignity, energy, devotion of the heroic type"; the trouble was that "they never touch us to the quick." His meeker ones were "too servile" and, in devotion, "too dog-like," for more than "modest pathos. . . . To excite compassion was enough for Fletcher, as in the masculine parts of his work it was enough for him to excite wonder, to sustain curiosity, to goad and stimulate by any vivid and violent means the interest of readers or spectators." The death scene of the child Hengo in *Bonduca*, however, aroused our poet to enthusiasm; it was "a scene which of itself would have sufficed to enroll his name forever on the list of our great tragic poets."[119]

Swinburne did perceive that Fletcher's forte was comedy. He granted him "a special province . . . of his own discovering, where no later colonist has ever had power to settle or share his reign:"

> His crown of praise is to have created a wholly new and delightful form of mixed comedy or dramatic romance, dealing merely with the humours and sentiments of men, their passions and their chances; to have woven a web of emotion and event with such gay dexterity, to have blended his colours and combined his effects with such exquisite facility and swift light sureness of touch, that we may return once and again from those heights and depths of poetry to which access was forbidden him, ready as ever to enjoy as of old the fresh incomparable charm, the force and ease and grace of life, which fill and animate the radiant world of his romantic imagination. . . . The quality of his genius, never sombre or subtle or profound, bears him always toward fresh air and sunshine. His natural work is in a midday world of boyish laughter and hardly bitter tears. . . . What with him is the noon of night would seem as sunshine on the stage of Ford or Webster.[120]

Purple prose though this may be, Swinburne saw to the heart of Fletcher's true gift with a poet's intuition. Fletcher was indeed a born merry and romantic farceur. Swinburne also saw that, because this was so, Fletcher's more serious plays and plots veer inevitably towards a kind of melodrama difficult to take with full seriousness: "Even his Brunhalts and Martias can hardly persuade us to forget for the moment that 'they do but jest, poison in jest.' "[121]

Swinburne did not consider Beaumont and Fletcher "in any exact sense the founders of a school either in comedy or in tragedy." Massinger was "in some points akin to them as a workman," but "the deepest and most distinctive qualities of his genius" set it apart. Shirley, however, he classed as "a pupil who copied their style in water-colour," and in Middleton's finest work "we recognize an almost exact reproduction of Fletcher's metrical effects—a reverberation of that flowing music, a reiteration of those feminine final notes." Too, his best later tragicomedies showed the beneficent effect of Fletcher's impact on him. Scattering other influence there was, also; but the Caroline debasement of tragic poetry was the work of a "mass of playwrights" little indebted to Fletcher and Beaumont.[122]

Swinburne did not fail to find some Victorian fault with our playwrights' moral laxity. But he was not inclined to be too harsh with this, even though he thought that Fletcher's heroines "are apt to utter sentiments worthy of Diana in language unworthy of Doll Tearsheet," and Fletcher himself too prone to "stain the ermine of virtue and palliate the nakedness of vice."[123] For

There is the glory and grace of youth in all they have left us; if there be also somewhat too much of its graceless as well as its gracious qualities, yet there hangs about their memory as it were a music of the morning, a breath and savour of bright early manhood, a joyous and vigorous air of free life and fruitful labour, which might charm asleep forever all thought or blame of all mortal infirmity or folly.[124]

Again, the poet's intuition—of youth, be it noted, not of decadence. And it is true that Beaumont died young, and Fletcher never lost the youthful heart, as one of his latest plays, *Rule a Wife,* should demonstrate.

Although Swinburne accepted the notion of our playwrights' "extravagant and boyish insanity of prostrate royalism,"[125] he dealt summarily with other aberrations of Coleridge, whom he considered "now and then, by fits and starts—a very great critic." Coleridge's inability to distinguish between Fletcher and Beaumont proved his criticism to be "throughout vitiated by prejudice or paralyzed by incapacity to appreciate aright" their merits—"so patent, so glaring, so palpable" was the superiority of the first "as a comic dramatist," of the second "as a tragic poet."[126] As for Coleridge's "so foul and injurious a suggestion" that many of their plays were founded on rapes, incestuous passions, and lunacies:

Among fifty-two plays there are exactly two which are founded upon rapes, *Valentinian* and *The Queen of Corinth*; there is not one which is founded on an incestuous passion, for the whole action of *A King and No King* hinges on the fact that Arbaces and Panthea are not brother and sister, but absolute strangers in blood; and if we except *The Mad Lover* and *The Nice Valour*, which may fairly be held liable to such a charge, I cannot discover an example of the 'plays founded on mere lunacies.' "[127]

Swinburne did not publish his valuable essay immediately. Even if he had done so, it would doubtless not have deterred others from entering the promising new field of scholarly investigation which Fleay had pioneered. Robert Boyle published his findings in the 1880's,[128] and Oliphant vented his early investigations in 1890-92.[129]

Boyle was especially interested in Massinger, as was Oliphant in Beaumont, and each showed a tendency to claim much for his favorite. Boyle laid great stress on the literary qualities of Fletcher, Beaumont and Massinger as corroborating metrical characteristics, and he revised Fleay's tests, which he considered inadequate. Oliphant, though not rejecting the aid of metrical tests, considered literary qualities the safer basis for conclusions.

Various other scholars have since entered the lists, with the result that, though many tangles still remain, and some will doubtless always stay knotted, there is now general agreement on the authorship of the majority of the plays. Moreover, the extent and nature of the collaborated shares of Beaumont and of Massinger have become relatively clear.

The investigations of Fleay and his various successors, Swinburne to the contrary notwithstanding, have been useful to critics. The first who attempted to distinguish one of our playwrights on the new basis was G. C. Macaulay, who constructed his portrait of *Francis Beaumont* (1883) on the foundation of Fleay's tests. Like the later Oliphant and Gayley, he was drawn to the younger "twin," and like them, too, he tended to exalt his favorite at the expense of Fletcher.

Macaulay found it necessary to establish Beaumont's metrical mannerisms by contrast to Fletcher's, since the latter could be much more readily ascertained. Making use of Fleay's method, with such revisions as he thought desirable, he discovered "the most marked characteristic" of Fletcher's verse to be an exceptional "freedom in the use of redundant syllables in all parts of the line, but especially at the end;" in fact, "out of every three lines generally two at least have double or triple endings." The playwright's redundant syllable, moreover, often had weight, and was sometimes an emphatic monosyllable. Frequently he threw in an additional word like *sir, too, lady,* at the end of the line to maintain his cadence.[130] Scarcely less in importance was his tendency to make a definite pause at the line's end. This mannerism perhaps arose from the "unconscious influence" of the old rhyming couplet. As a consequence, the line rarely finished on a "light or insignificant word," such as *and, but, with, that.*[131]

Sound as this analysis was, so far as it went, Macaulay's explanation of why Fletcher adopted these verse mannerisms was even more pertinent. They were obviously different in their effects from the conventional blank verse characteristics of *The Faithful Shepherdess*. Macaulay concluded that Fletcher employed them deliberately to "avoid solemnity and weight, to make the line less 'mighty' and more flexible." His free use of redundant syllables resulted in "a breaking away from the rigidity of the older style," with its mouth-filling lines, into a livelier one. This could "supply the place of prose in the lightest interchange of fashionable repartee," while still serving adequately for serious scenes.[132] The end-stopped lines, lacking the flow of the periodic style, produced "a rather marked discontinuity," whose effect was

less appearance of premeditation and more of spontaneous development of thoughts from the circumstances of the moment. Impulses seem to work before the eyes of the spectators, the speakers correct themselves, explain by parentheses hastily thrown in, or add afterthoughts as they occur to the mind. In short, the expression of thought becomes less narrative and more dramatic.[133]

Macaulay believed, however, that Fletcher "gained ease rather than strength" by these devices of style, since his verse was weak in "metaphorical conciseness" and in "rapidity of movement." He also quoted Lamb approvingly on the playwright's slow, "circular" expression of thought, and found a "tiresome monotony" in the frequency of end-stopped lines.[134] It is worth recalling that the royalist writers of First Folio commendatory verses, contrariwise, agreed on the "fluency" or "flow" of Fletcher's lines. Many of them had heard his lines often delivered on the Stuart stage, whereas Lamb and Macaulay judged the movement of Fletcher's verse solely from reading. Macaulay did, however, recognize that the playwright's "absence of confusion" and "presentation of ideas in due succession and fully expressed" probably contributed to the stage popularity of his plays in Stuart times.[135]

Assigning *Philaster* to Beaumont alone,[136] and using its versification as his touchstone, Macaulay found its metrical characteristics "a complete contrast to Fletcher's." The blank verse had "a serious and stately character," was comparatively free from redundancy, and showed "unrestricted freedom" in running on from line to line. Its tendencies were to "the periodic structure of sentence" and "a rounded melody of cadence in the more rhetorical passages." Unlike Fletcher, whose verse was more flexible, Beaumont used prose "For that which requires not dignified expression, that which is neither heroic nor mock-heroic."[137]

Summing up his more general findings, Macaulay concluded that Beaumont was, on the whole, a follower of the older school, though he used run-on lines as freely as Shakespeare in his later plays did. Beaumont resembled Fletcher in the one respect of avoiding a weak syllable at the end of the line, but in hardly any other. His style was "vigorous, and ornamented rather by metaphor than by simile." The balanced sentences were "suitable to the lofty tone which he adopts in tragedy, and to the picturesque descriptions in which he always delights." Macaulay considered Beaumont's blank verse, though "somewhat monotonous," a more poetic and stately vehicle than Fletcher's.[138] It was one suitable to a playwright whose "serious work is deeply tinged with the 'irony' which

is characteristic of the graver and more thoughtful of the world's dramatists."[139]

On the whole, Macaulay's analysis of metrical characteristics is basic,
sound and definitely useful; it provided a somewhat firmer foundation
than had previously existed for distinguishing the individual work of the
two playwrights. But there is a trap for the unwary in the fact that, of
the more than fifty surviving plays, only two and a half, on the most liberal count, can be solely Beaumont's: the immature *Woman-Hater* (with
Fletcher?), *The Knight of the Burning Pestle* (with Fletcher?), and the
frame and first half of *Four Plays in One* (probably by Field). Moreover,
as we have noted, Macaulay assigned *Philaster* to Beaumont alone—a
dangerous first premise.[140] Like other Beaumontians, too, he overlooked
the strong probability that these particular co-authors shared more
closely than was common in every stage of the planning and development
of their joint plays—the actual writing of which in verse or prose is (as
every dramatist knows) merely the final step. And so Macaulay, out of
enthusiasm for Beaumont, set the modern fashion of making an over-
sharp distinction between Fletcher and his younger colleague.

This may be clearly seen in Macaulay's comments on plotting and construction. He appears to have found only weaknesses in Fletcher's playcraft. The latter's plots were "often very loosely put together;" he frequently pursued two stories whose only link was "some accident of
locality or relationship;" he threw in scenes unconnected with the story.
Unlike Shakespeare, he lacked that "unity of idea . . . which fuses together the most varied forms of life into a harmonious whole," and that
"artistic earnestness which aims at a single end." He was "content to
produce a series of effective situations." He strove after "immediate and
startling effect," and consequently liked "violent situations" and "the representation of extreme physical agony."[141]

In contrast, Beaumont showed "considerable skill" at construction,
"especially as regards the introduction of his characters and the preparation for situations." He liked novelty of incident, but was otherwise an
apt pupil of Shakespeare and other older dramatists, from whom Fletcher
learned little. He observed "the essential rule of unity of action," and
generally invented his own plots.[142] So, Macaulay. But Fletcher's technique was not so unlike his companion's as all this suggests. He, likewise, learned from Shakespeare and Jonson; and with his more fertile
and inventive mind he was not likely to have left all the labor of evolving and building plots to his colleague. Macaulay overplayed Beaumont's
"judgment," and ignored the common interest of the collaborators in
stage effectiveness.

He also rejected for Beaumont, though not for Fletcher, the charge of "penetrating no deeper than the fashion." As instances of the younger playwright's seeing below "the superficial manners of men and women," he cited Viola and Violante: "charming creatures, with all the woman's self-sacrificing affection, and the maiden's purity of thought and feeling, though one of them is indeed no maid."[143] There was, moreover, that "type of female character which belongs especially to Beaumont:" the love-lorn damsel, "unhappy victim of unrequited love." Euphrasia (Bellario) of *Philaster* and Aspatia of *The Maid's Tragedy* "find pretty and fantastic ways of expressing their griefs and desires; their minds are not unhinged by their situations, but in a sense they may be said to 'walk distracted.' Quaint and picturesque imaginings occur to them, and poetical language flows naturally from their lips."[144] Sweetly pure and sentimental Ophelias, fabricated with lyric grace to make the playgoer misty-eyed—these, to Victorian taste, Beaumont had wrought well. But Fletcher's spirited and resourceful young Rosalinds, with their merry but deplorably racy tongues, lived in an atmosphere of dubious health, and there was "something overstrained and unnatural even in their virtues."[145]

Accordingly, Macaulay's view of these playwrights' morality was bifurcated. Fletcher, as others had claimed, was wanting in moral earnestness. This was especially evident in his portrayal of gentlemen and men of honor as profligates.[146] But Beaumont, whose morality was much more satisfactory, had suffered from his involvement with his older compeer, and also from "fearlessly" presenting "human nature as it is."[147] In reality, only Fletcher had justly incurred Coleridge's charges, such as that "Lucina and the rest . . . 'value their chastity as a material thing—not as an act and state of being.' Female chastity is by Beaumont represented under more attractive forms."[148]

Macaulay accounted for this difference between the two collaborators in terms of the fashionable if dubious concept of decadence. Stating the already growing opinion "that our authors especially represent the decline of the great dramatic age," he found in *A King and No King* "some unmistakable signs of decadence," despite its power. Nonetheless, Beaumont himself was representative not of the decline, as Fletcher was, but rather of the transition to it. He was at once "the religious admirer of Shakspere and Jonson, yet the associate of Fletcher," and thus "bound by strong ties" to both old and new.[149]

The critical or turning point Macaulay placed in the years 1611-13, as others have since done. Fortunately for this theory, Shakespeare retired at just this time, and no other dramatist of anything like his stature emerged thereafter. Macaulay reasoned that Chapman, Webster and Dekker wrote "little of importance" after 1613, that Beaumont abandoned the theatre then, and that Jonson henceforth "occupied himself mainly with masques. In fact, the impulse which had moved the older generation was by that time almost exhausted." Under the disillusioning impact of James I's rule, the theatre was less and less expressing the sturdy older patriotism, and a drama that had been national was becoming the idle amusement of gilded gentlemen and of anti-Puritan members of the lower classes. The chief new, and decadent, dramatic writers catering to an audience of blunted moral and aesthetic tastes were Fletcher, Massinger and Ford.[150] Beaumont's years in the theatre happily antedated this decline.

Perhaps because Beaumont was concerned in the matter, Macaulay also made a useful protest against Coleridge's "servile *jure divino* royalists" charge. Sensibly he remarked:

Surely if these authors were such devoted royalists, and aimed so constantly at exhibiting their loyalty on the stage, it is strange and even unaccountable that so few sovereigns are represented in their plays as a sovereign would desire to be represented, and that so many are set up as objects of contempt and hatred. . . . The arrogant pride of these tyrants is usually the pride that goes before a fall, and the loyal sentiments of an Amintor or an Aecius serve as foils to the opposite feelings of a Melantius or a Maximus.[151]

Macaulay's book was the first to present a relatively clear picture of Beaumont. In this book, moreover, points of view since popular with modern critics were given full and lucid presentation. But, like later Beaumont admirers, Macaulay did not appear to recognize that his subject was vitally interested in stage effectiveness. Like them, too, his distinctions between "the twins" were sometimes less than just to Fletcher.[152]

Another critic who took full advantage of the results of Fleay's new attack on the authorship problems of our corpus was Adolphus William Ward. The first edition of his *A History of English Dramatic Literature to the Death of Queen Anne* (1875) had followed on the heels of Fleay's first paper; but twenty-four years intervened before the publication of the revised second edition of 1899.[153] Ward's rewritten chapter on Beaumont and Fletcher[154] now made careful use not only of the metrical testing but also of the source-hunting and other research of recent years. It therefore not merely expressed Ward's own critical views of our playwrights but reflected as well the state of historical scholarship on them at almost the turn of the twentieth century.

Ward's method of treatment was, first, to deal with the lives and personalities of Fletcher and of Beaumont (Massinger is missing[155]); then to give individual critiques of all the plays of the corpus, with actual or probable assignments as to authorship; and finally to sum up the general aspects of the two playwrights' achievement. In commenting on metrical tests, he acknowledged their value towards alloting the shares of the collaborators in the joint plays. At the same time, he sensibly recognized that at any point in these pieces either dramatist might have added touches to the other's writing. Unlike the later Gayley, he thought it improbable that any mental or moral test would be useful in distinguishing between the two playwrights.[156]

According to Ward, Beaumont and Fletcher were still generally ranked second only to Shakespeare.[157] But there was a decided gap, for our playwrights lacked that true greatness which would have placed them above their age and made them teachers of it. Instead, they reflected all its littleness and corruption, without aspiring to anything better. Hence, although their plays would continue to "dazzle and delight" because they had exceptional stage effectiveness, perhaps none of them could satisfy the mind or give full emotional satisfaction.[158]

Adjusting the level of their plays to the manners and behavior of James' shameless court, our playwrights displayed no glimmer of understanding of "female purity." Here Fletcher was a greater sinner than Beaumont, because he confused good and evil in the relations of the sexes, looking upon love merely as a game of chance or skill, and paying only formal homage to women's virtue. Such ethical grossness was a far worse "self-prostration" than coarse diction, for which excuses could be made.[159]

All this sounds much like Darley and other Victorians. But Ward also thought Beaumont and Fletcher unaware of their moral coarseness of fibre; they were neither cynical nor affectedly frank about it.[160] Now and then, indeed, he directed attention to the "moral earnestness" he discovered in such plays as *The Little French Lawyer* and *The Lovers' Progress*.[161] He praised the powerful representation of the conflict of moral forces in *Valentinian*, and held that *The Knight of Malta* showed its authors to be in sympathy with the high chivalric code of the knightly order.[162]

As might be surmised, Ward accepted the Coleridgean tradition of the servile royalism of Fletcher and Beaumont. He cited in evidence the time-honored but dubiously conclusive Act I, scene 3 of *Valentinian*. Yet he also noted, as an exception to their general attitude, *The Maid's Tragedy*, the climax of which implied a distaste for tyranny.[163]

Ward adjudged the productive power of Fletcher and his collaborators to be amazing. Like some First Folio eulogists, he also commended the absence (except for *The Woman-Hater*) of any sign of strain in either construction or writing. That Beaumont and Fletcher were well educated and socially trained gentlemen could only partially explain their ease. Of far greater importance was the fact that they began writing after Shakespeare and Jonson had developed individual techniques to the

point of excellence. The fertility and readiness of the younger playwrights owed much to these elders, whom they had the wit to study.[164]
The result was deftness, and occasionally skill of the highest order in
construction, all the more surprising because the materials drawn upon
might be heterogeneous indeed. Fletcher, however, often handled his
double plots with undesirable looseness, thus diffusing the interest. At
the same time, certain of his plays, such as *The Chances* and *The Woman's
Prize*, were as cleverly constructed as any of the joint pieces.[165]

Aside from frequently licentious or coarse treatment of the relations
of men and women, our playwrights often were felicitous in character
studies, if within a limited range: witness their "Violas" and pages, their
blunt soldiers and tyrants. In comic characterization Fletcher had a relatively wide range. His high comedy figures were sometimes unpalatable
to modern taste, but a few low comedy ones were unquestionably original, like the title character of *The Spanish Curate*.[166]

Ward found the special distinction of our playwrights to lie not in
technique nor in characterization but in diction. Tragic elevation was
beyond them; but their pathos, seldom cloying, was usually phrased with
grace, and revealed as well some understanding of woman's "softness"
and of "that well of true sentiment," her heart. However extravagant
their ideas and passions, the diction of both authors was never inflated
nor bombastic, but normally stayed within the bounds of appropriateness.
In addition, it was often beautiful.[167] And it was this beauty of their
plays which made Fletcher and Beaumont more attractive than any of
their fellow-dramatists save Shakespeare.[168]

That Ward's chapter on our playwrights should now seem partially
obsolescent testifies, no doubt, to the advance of twentieth century scholarship in the field of Jacobean drama. It is also partly due, one suspects,
to Ward's characteristically late Victorian outlook. He was fairminded
if highly moral, he was even at times enthusiastic, in his criticisms of the
various plays. But he continued the tradition of judging them as dramatic poems, however he may have acknowledged their theatrical effectiveness. Be that as it may, his estimable dramatic history summed up, in
many ways, the nineteenth century achievement, both scholarly and
critical, in the field of Elizabethan-Stuart drama. It well deserved its
now declining day in the sunshine of authority.

CHAPTER FOUR

In Recent Years

I
N the twentieth century, that body of accumulating historical data
about the Elizabethan-Stuart dramatists which we saw at times reflecting itself in Victorian criticism has multiplied abundantly. It
has brought much new understanding of the London world of the theatre
in which the playwrights worked, the stage for which they built their
plays, and the audience upon whose response their success depended.
Criticism has often, though by no means always, gained fresh insights
from the laborious research and scholarly interpretations of the many
workers in this field.

Holding in mind this fruitful advance in understanding the milieu of
a drama written for a very different actor, audience and stage than our
own, let us examine two clusters of critical writings which, during the
first quarter of this century, added to the interpretation of our body of
plays. And with that, our long pilgrimage ends, for at some ever-advanc-
ing point the history of the reputation of Fletcher, Beaumont, Massinger
and Company must undergo an imperceptible sea-change into present-
day criticism. To locate this point in the 1920s will, for our purpose, be
a convenience, even if arbitrary. By then the present complex of opinion
about our playwrights had taken form with reasonable completeness.
Foundations which, in some cases, go back to Coleridge and other romantics, or even farther, were well laid.

Familiar many of the books we are about to examine may be, for their
impact has not faded away, nor are they usually inaccessible. Hazardous the
selection certainly is, for perspective is shortening, and time's sifting-out
process is barely in operation as yet in this area. These relatively few instances may, however, suffice to suggest how the dwindling reputation of
our playwrights, and especially of Fletcher, was then shaping towards our
contemporary groupings of scholarly and critical attitudes—attitudes
which will more properly concern us in suceeding chapters.

I

Two volumes published in the first decade of the century dealt, from different points of view, with only the more serious plays of Fletcher, Beaumont and Company. The first of these, Thorndike's *The Influence of Beaumont and Fletcher on Shakspere* (1901),[1] concentrated mainly on a half-dozen tragedies and tragicomedies of these two playwrights, together with three dramas of their greater fellow-worker. The second, Ristine's *English Tragicomedy* (1910), included in its survey all plays of our corpus classifiable as of that type.

Thorndike's purpose was to demonstrate that the Beaumont-Fletcher "romances," notably *Philaster,* influenced Shakespeare to write his three final dramas, especially *Cymbeline,* in the same new manner. By a review of all plays produced between 1601 and 1611, so far as dates could be determined, Thorndike demonstrated beyond question that the "romances" of these three playwrights were a new departure in the drama of that decade.[2] Disagreeing at some points with Fleay's chronology, he concluded that the circumstantial evidence about dating justified the deduction that *Philaster* might well have preceded *Cymbeline* on the stage.[3] He also examined Shakespeare's probable collaboration with Fletcher on *Henry VIII* and *The Two Noble Kinsmen.* As a result, he concluded that Shakespeare would have seen no indignity in experimenting with the innovations in form and treatment which the younger men had introduced into his own King's Men's Company with the successful staging of their *Philaster.*[4]

Turning to direct consideration of the plays involved,[5] Thorndike analyzed in detail the plotting, characterization, style and stage-effects first of the Beaumont-Fletcher plays and then of the Shakespearean.[6] He followed this with a more specific cross-comparison of *Philaster* and *Cymbeline.*[7] Discussion of *The Winter's Tale* and *The Tempest,* a concluding summary, and an appendix placing *Pericles* in a different category than the "romances" completed Thorndike's case.[8]

In addition to showing that Shakespeare, Fletcher and Beaumont were the leaders in the return to romantic drama, this study should convince a fairminded reader that there was certainly some degree and direction of cross-influence, even if Thorndike's conclusions be not accepted. Whether Shakespeare's *Pericles* might have been the real trail-blazer, however, and what relationship *Philaster* had to *Cymbeline,* remained moot questions. As Sampson was quick to point out (1902),[9] the dating of the two latter depends on circumstantial evidence alone. Miss Hatcher (1905) concurred, adding that even Thorndike's evidence could not indisputably establish priority for *Philaster.*[10]

In 1914 Gayley made a slashing onslaught on Thorndike. He protested against calling any play whatsoever a "romance."[11] He objected to associating Beaumont's name with *Thierry and Theodoret* (Fletcher's "clumsy failure"), with *Four Plays in One* or even, except in a minor way, with the worthless *Cupid's Revenge*. He refused to admit that *The Maid's Tragedy* made sacrifices to emotional thrills—a point characteristic of Gayley's tendency to underestimate Beaumont's concern for theatrical effect. Somewhat arbitrarily he held that any "novelty" which could have influenced Shakespeare must therefore be discovered in either *Philaster* or *A King and No King*, the latter of which certainly postdated *Cymbeline*.[12]

Gayley could find no such novelty which Shakespeare had not already anticipated in *The Two Gentlemen of Verona* and *As You Like It*, *Much Ado About Nothing* and *Twelfth Night*, *All's Well That Ends Well* and *Measure for Measure*, and the recent *Pericles*.[13] He considered *Cymbeline* closer in resemblance to these than to *Philaster*. He found the main motive force of the three chief Beaumont-Fletcher collaborations to be "the contrast between sentimental love and unbridled lust," whereas Shakespeare's plays, from *Pericles* to *The Tempest*, all centered around the idea of disappearance and discovery.[14] Moreover, Shakespeare's treatment was "romantic," while our playwrights' was "melodramatic." The only novelty of *Philaster* and *A King and No King* lay in emphasis upon "sensational properties and methods." In this emphasis, these plays were most akin to the earlier *The Gentleman Usher* of Chapman and to *Measure for Measure* and *All's Well* of Shakespeare.[15] In fine, "Beaumont did not influence Shakespeare."[16]

Gayley's attack exposed some weaknesses in Thorndike's chain of demonstration, but was itself open to some criticism. His observation of resemblances, including the melodramatic denouement,[17] between the romantic plays of all three playwrights and Shakespeare's earlier dramas did not prove that there was no influence at all from *Philaster* to *Cymbeline*. No more decisive was his prejudice that the long-experienced and abler dramatist could not possibly have been influenced by his less established juniors.

Much more recently (1936), Middleton Murray joined Gayley in finding no substance in Thorndike's theory; he asserted positively that he could discover no debt in *Cymbeline* to *Philaster*, whether of thought, attitude, or verse. As for plot, he believed *Twelfth Night* a much more credible source of influence.[18] But in 1938 Tillyard considered the question rather "warehoused" than settled. He brought forth new evidence of influence, especially of *The Faithful Shepherdess* on *The Winter's Tale*. Like Gayley, he also called attention to the large common stock of romantic incident, which had its most striking prose rehandling in Sidney's *Arcadia*.[19] And there the whole matter rests.

Regardless of Gayley's attack, Thorndike's analysis of *Philaster, The Maid's Tragedy, A King and No King, Cupid's Revenge* and *Thierry and Theodoret*[20] was a capable one. He discovered that in plotting and construction our playwrights made theatrical effectiveness their aim. Inventing their plots, or adding many incidents to their adapted sources, they provided an abundance of action throughout. Rarely was a scene written for purely narrative or expository purposes; even byplots, and "operatic" passages of lyrical description, normally carried the action forward. Great care was also taken in the development of each situation, however improbable or violent, so that variety and intensity of action might be gained from it. At the same time, the collaborators gave their plots more unity and coherence than was usually found in Jacobean plays.

Contrast, likewise, was more fully employed in these plays than before. In construction, this meant a concern with various, and often opposed, emotional impacts—idyllic, tragic, comic—rather than a concentration on a single emotion or character. The plots tended to resemble each other in counterpointing a story of "pure, sentimental love" with another of "unbridled sensual passion." Yet all lines of emotion and action, however varied, were so directed as to point towards a tragic outcome, and to culminate in a strong, complex denouement. This, in itself, was composed of a skilfully contrived sequence of actions giving a "sharp succession of surprises." The denouement was thus, in truth, the unpredictable, melodramatic yet powerful climax of the whole play.[21]

Since "collections of situations" giving "vivid momentary pictures of passions" was our playwrights' aim, characterization was of necessity secondary. Consistency and shading were sacrificed in their handling of the characters; these had to speak and behave as each successive situation required. Type delineations resulted. Emphasis, as in plotting, was placed on strong contrast—in this case, of clearly marked good and evil types, whose predominant qualities were exaggerated and intensified.

Naturally enough, a tendency to characterize by description rather than by more strictly dramatic means prevailed. Characters were often introduced through dialogue, sometimes in passages by Beaumont of great lyrical beauty, as with Bellario and Aspatia. Thereafter the dramatis personae kept up a running play of comments on one another, whether in praise or in blame. By these means, the sympathy of the audience was steadily directed to the correct persons to receive it.

Thorndike considered that five types of denizens of the court, repeated with slight variations, comprised most of the principal characters in the romances: the sentimental, love-lorn maiden; the "lily-livered" hero; the depraved woman; the base poltroon; the faithful friend. The devoted maiden, all purity, meekness and self-sacrifice, was given much romantic stage charm by the lyric poetry lavished on her. The heroes were likeable, noble, generous but otherwise situation-figures. The shameless, brazenly evil women, especially Evadne, were the least unlifelike. The poltroons were not only cowardly but scoundrelly and bestial.[22] These two types supplied the strong character contrasts to the first two. The faithful friends were blunt, brave, devoted, given to rough humour, impatient of deceit and eager to act.[23]

In his discussion of style, Thorndike called special attention to both playwrights' frequent use of parenthesis to give an effect of spontaneous rather than rhetorical speech, and also to Fletcher's fondness for colloquial abbreviations. In fact, he proposed that Fletcher's preference for *'ems* over *thems* provided an additional metrical test for confirming or rejecting scenes as his. He found the styles of both playwrights dramatic in structure and excellently suited to be spoken and acted on the stage. Beaumont's, in addition, was free from his partner's over-stereotyped mannerisms, while Fletcher's conversational tone and metrical freedom were "revolutionary."[24]

As for stage effects, the romances drew freely on the spectacular devices of the increasingly popular Jacobean court masques. Sometimes, as on Evadne's wedding night, a small masque itself was presented, together with a comic delineation of the crowds who wished to attend it.[25] Or an antimasque dance which the King's Men had already performed at court might be fitted, costumes and all, into the play. The first large use of such effects, Thorndike believed, was in these "romances" of Beaumont and Fletcher and those of Shakespeare.[26]

Thorndike's analysis clarified the characteristics of the Beaumont and Fletcher "romances," and so gave a solider picture of the collaborators' technique than had previously appeared. Ristine, whose *English Tragicomedy* was written under Thorndike's direction, acknowledged his indebtedness to this analysis for his own account of the tragicomedies of our corpus.

Ristine found the true essence of this "intermediate" type soundly diagnosed by the Italian pastoralist, Guarini, who evolved his theory as a defense of his own *Il Pastor Fido:*

The gist of his argument is that tragicomedy, far from being a discordant mixture of tragedy and comedy, is a thoro blend of such parts of each as can stand together with verisimilitude, with the result that the deaths of tragedy are reduced to the danger of deaths, and the whole in every respect a graduated mean between the austerity and dignity of the one and the pleasantness and ease of the other.[27]

Hence the simple inclusion of a comic plot and a tragic one in the same play would not, of itself, constitute the piece a tragicomedy.

English tragicomedies of the seventeenth century, however, while conforming to this essence, developed their own peculiarities. Selecting six which spanned most of the century, from *Philaster* to Dryden's *The Spanish Friar*,[28] Ristine enumerated the special characteristics that these, as representative of the whole group, displayed. Aside from the general impression of "startling unreality," the usual stigmata included: setting in a distant, romantic world of its own; imaginary history and strange happenings; men of "superhuman" traits; love of some sort as motivation for the action; a main focussing on the "chequered fortunes" of royalty and aristocracy; a subordinate concern with "war, usurpation, rebellion," whether threatened or actual; comic relief, ranging from slight to considerable; intrigue and villainy in stark contrast with exalted behavior. "In the course of an action teeming with incident and excitement, and in which the characters are enmeshed in a web of disastrous complications, reverse and surprise succeed each other with a lightning rapidity, and the outcome trembles in the balance." But then comes the surprising and ingenious denouement, which deftly averts the threatened tragic outcome; ". . . wrongs are righted, wounds healed, reconciliation sets in, penitent villainy is forgiven, and the happy ending is made complete."[29]

This seventeenth century variety of tragicomedy, initiated by Beaumont and Fletcher, "presents no transcript from life; it neglects portrayal of character and psychological analysis for plot and theatricality; it substitutes dramatic falsity for dramatic truth; it emphasizes novelty, sensation, surprise, startling effect." As a result, "all is unreal, artificial, inadequate"; so that inevitably the form became, by the age of Queen Anne, "an absurdity of the past."[30]

Ristine considered Fletcher's pastoral tragicomedy, *The Faithful Shepherdess*, to have been "the source of the inspiration" for those of Beaumont and Fletcher.[31] Though this lyric drama failed on its first performance because of deficiency in plot and lack of an effective denouement, it showed Fletcher's knowledge of stagecraft in its quick introduction, rapid movement, constant suspense, and "serious situations multiplied."[32] Moreover, the pastoral atmosphere of this play became transmuted into the forest scenes of *Philaster;* its shepherds and shepherdesses renewed themselves as the woodlanders and aristocratic men and women of the latter's equally romantic "no-man's land." In both plays, evil slander confused the course of true love. Amintor, in wounding Bellario and Arethusa, was simply acting according to a common pastoral pattern of the jealous shepherd swain.[33]

It was not, however, *The Faithful Shepherdess* but the idyllic *Philaster* and the martial *A King and No King* which Ristine adjudged "the forerunners of the new type of English tragicomedy." These displayed, full blown, its normal characteristics, including exotic background, melodramatic action, warring passions, ingenious and complicated plot, surprises, fluctuations and reversals, and fates hanging in the balance until the finale. The "tragic romances," for which *The Maid's Tragedy* set the pattern, likewise possessed these attributes; what distinguished these from the tragicomedies was chiefly the fatal instead of happy denouement. Both of these twin forms, as practiced by our playwrights, sacrificed character delineation, probability and ethical meaning for immediate stage success.[34] Of such material was the new mold cast.

Ristine conceded that the Beaumont-Fletcher innovations in *Philaster* might have influenced Shakespeare's *Cymbeline*. But in spite of the many parallels in character, plot and treatment, the latter play, and even more *The Winter's Tale,* followed in structure the old school of rambling romance and epic drama. *The Tempest,* compactly built, and telling a story of sentimental love contrasted with villainous intrigue, never reached a really threatening crisis, though the play was pitched above ordinary romantic comedy. Thus, none of Shakespeare's last plays was altogether a tragicomedy of the new type. Yet all were closely related to this form.[35]

Alone or in collaboration with Massinger (and others), Fletcher continued, for a dozen years after Beaumont's retirement, to write a whole series of influential tragicomedies. These shaded, in various gradations, from those close to tragedy, such as the Fletcher-Massinger-Field *The Queen of Corinth,*[36] to those so close to the borderline of comedy, like Fletcher's *Women Pleased,* as to be "composite in tone."[37] This range in treatment, backed by success on the stage, was of decisive effect on other dramatists.[38]

In the main, Fletcher simply amplified the types of character and the technique already developed in *Philaster* and *A King and No King.* But his gay, effervescent humor, often involving non-aristocratic characters, was sometimes given freer play. Likewise, sentimental youths and maidens tended to be replaced by "stauncher types."[39] In those tragicomedies which he wrote alone, death never overtook even the basest villain; instead, such scoundrels were often seized with sudden repentence and, most unethically, were forgiven.[40]

Ristine considered Fletcher exceedingly fertile in conceiving extravagant motives and situations, the aim of which was to startle and electrify his audience. He completely disregarded probability, logic and ethical value. Moreover, all his tragicomedies made pervasive use of tragic elements: "lust, jealousy, revenge, intrigue, murderous designs, torture, rape, duels, poisons, and the like." Villainy often beset lovers or perchance threatened ruin to the court of king or duke. The tone and style, likewise, maintained a dignity, in the serious scenes, nearly akin to that of tragedy.[41] Thus did Fletcher, alone or in partnership with Massinger and others, stereotype the ingredients which Beaumont and he had blended into *Philaster* and *A King and No King*.

It was, above all, the denouement of our playwrights' tragicomedies which, as Ristine saw it, set these pieces off from those of Elizabethan days. This climactic point was carefully devised, with situations leading up to it so ingeniously that it would often unravel of itself. At the same time, it was deliberately "concealed," instead of forecast, so that suspense might be maintained to the last. The audience would thus be unaware whether the outcome was to be catastrophic or happy until the surprises, reversals and disclosures of the final scene had unfolded themselves. This technique of completely concealing a sensational denouement largely explained, in Ristine's opinion, the theatrical success of the plays. Succeeding writers of tragicomedy were quick to learn this lesson in deft stagecraft, and seldom neglected to apply it in their own pieces.[42]

One further book published during the early years of the century, Miss Hatcher's *John Fletcher* (1905),[43] contributed a helpful study of the characteristics displayed by a selected group of our plays—in this instance, those pieces which were Fletcher's own handiwork. Miss Hatcher concentrated on a detailed and analytical examination of the dramatic methods which Fletcher employed in fifteen of these.[44]

She appears to have been somewhat perturbed that Fletcher should have accepted the applause of theatregoers as the final standard of his work, thus blithely sacrificing "fundamental principles of high literary art."[45] Nor did she like his moral tone any better than his "flippant and ignoble conceptions" of his task. Yet, aware that Fletcher was not aiming at permanent literary fame, she acknowledged that it would be only fair —at least for a time—to consider his plays at their own level. She recognized that a reader had simply to visualize them as though he were himself a playgoer to discover in them countless elements of popular appeal —often the very ones to "vex and weary" him, should he read them solely as literature.[46] And so she founded her treatment on the acting quality of Fletcher's plays.

Miss Hatcher's exploration of his dramatic method convinced her that modern critics had not given him his due. They had truthfully, she felt, brought out his various weaknesses, but had overemphasized his obvious "moral taint" and consequently had often neglected his genuine gifts.

These were, in particular, two: dramatic artistry of the first rank, and a liberal poetic endowment.[47]

Much of Miss Hatcher's study, as we shall see, was devoted to demonstrating that Fletcher had a large share of the artist's discriminating intelligence. Miss Hatcher was impressed by his "well nigh incomparable" sense of the theatre and command of stagecraft. He had, in especial, a shrewd ability to select, arrange and add to his material so as to make full use of all the resources of the Jacobean stage, and even to overcome its limitations. Whatever he may have sacrificed in his constant and eclectic striving for stage success, he was a dramatic artist; he would have been one above reproach had he also had "deep spirituality" and "profound intelligence" instead of a gay, pleasure-loving nature subject to "moral inertia."[48]

Miss Hatcher also insisted, briefly but succinctly, on Fletcher's poetic gift. His verse was that of a "musician"; it had a limpid, rhythmic fluency too often discounted by critics. It adapted itself with admirable flexibility to all moods from grave to gay—ranging easily from quiet conversation or brisk repartee to passages bristling with movement or rising to a dignity consonant with serious situations. Fletcher had not received the full recognition due his mastery in adapting his verse to the shifting dramatic requirements of his plays without impairing its poetic quality.[49]

Miss Hatcher made a careful study of Fletcher's use of his various sources: classical, historical, Italian, Spanish.[50] She discovered that, in combing through any story material, Fletcher had a sure instinct for spotting its picturesque and effective dramatic situations, whether developed or only latent. These, and not some central personage or passion, were what he was seeking. With unerring skill, he separated the promising situations from their useless trappings, then rearranged and very freely added to them so as to produce a crowded series of adventures. These he built up to a succession of slight but arresting and sometimes startling crises, which in due course all converged on the denouement. In order to provide a sufficient variety of activities and points of tension, he frequently combined several very different stories. All of these, however, he sought to harmonize with the general tone of the play. He was not satisfied until he had a full but elastic framework into which an abundance of stage activity could be inserted.[51]

After analyzing Fletcher's "general dramatic practice" in choice and presentation of theme, setting, plot and characters, Miss Hatcher concluded that each of these aspects was controlled by the same end: immediate stage effectiveness.[52] In terms of this aim, for instance, Fletcher's perennial theme, romantic love, was not only felicitous but necessary.

Accordingly, only *Valentinian* and *Rule a Wife* entirely dispensed with it. Whatever the web of difficulties in which the lovers became involved —grave, comic or both—the outcome always met the audience's desire by being happy.[53]

Fletcher's varied settings would satisfy many tastes. Locales were often remote enough to be exotic, but the actual atmospheres of foreign lands were barely suggested. Much more fully elaborated were splendid stage effects. Audiences at courts of kings and dukes, masques, processions, cathedrals, temples, flowers—these and such homelier displays as country festivals, morrice dances and the antics of madmen feasted the spectators' eyes and ears.[54] Moreover, many fine lyrics, rollicking songs and instrumental effects were appropriately and artistically introduced into the plays.[55]

In both plotting and characterization Fletcher's dependence on stage conventions was marked. Since he lacked depth, subtlety and strong creative faculty, he could not highly individualize the type, whether in character or situation. But his choice of conventions was discriminating, and he wove them into the structure of his plays with rare agility.[56]

Among his conventions of plot, disguise (especially of girls as boys) was the one most overworked; yet the gay mix-ups and mischief of his comic plots owed much to it.[57] The most unconvincing one, except in some farcical instances, was his unmotivated use of "conversion," in order to give rise to new situations or speed the denouement.[58] Retribution, or the deed returning upon the doer, was happily used for comic purposes, as were the abundant asides, unnatural, unsubtle, yet helpful in keeping spectators abreast of the briskly moving turns of action. But these "commonplaces of the theatre" were often inappropriate and vexing when used in tragicomedy or tragedy.[59]

Conventional types of character were the natural outgrowth of such plotting, since behavior patterns were determined by the action. The figures, frequently resembling one another from play to play, echoed the exaggerations and absurdities of the situations in which they were placed. Diverse stories did, however, give some differentiation to individuals of the same type.[60] They were, in general, conscienceless creatures.[61]

The main characters were, for practical reasons, of the upper classes; they thus lent themselves readily to spectacle, and had leisure for adventure and merry intrigue. But a sympathetic interest in the lower classes was reflected in a host of minor figures.[62] Fletcher's major types were the clever maid-in-love,[63] the merry scapegrace, the sentimental hero or "mooning youth," and the brave soldier; minor ones included the chaste maid or matron, the clever servant, the wrathful gentleman, the merry old man, the evil king or duke, and the scheming favorite. If these figures, seldom much individualized and never original, had small human interest compared with Shakespeare's, Fletcher nonetheless selected perennial favorites almost unerringly.[64]

From her study of our playwright's stagecraft, Miss Hatcher concluded that he had a nearly infallible "stage manager's instinct."[65] He expended much energy upon stirring his audience to a sense of bustling activity. His characters came and went constantly; the stage group kept shifting in "kaleidoscopic fashion." Anyone bound for anywhere crossed the stage, but paused to tell his errand. Changes in scene, normally not involving much distance, were numerous. Characters frequently had just returned from their travels or were about to set out on them, and there was much talk of journeys; trips were sometimes prepared for with much bustling about, and then countermanded.[66] Moreover, Fletcher could visualize to the full the possibilities of the inner and upper stages, of the doors, windows, balconies and other structural features of his playhouse. Hence he could, with rare flexibility, bring two or more groups to interact on each other, whether in eaves-dropping scenes, serenades, battlefields, masques or the play-within-a-play.[67] All this made for an "air of commotion" well suited to comedy, if unrestful in more serious plays.

In his "technique," Fletcher observed the unities of time and place adequately; the first by creating the impression of an almost continuous time-sequence, and the second by making careful transitions between his frequent, but short-distance, changes of place. He flagrantly violated unity of action, however—a grievous fault in his serious plays. Since he sought to combine in one drama as many groups as he could, he did not focus on "some powerful personal center." So, as Coleridge had suggested, he gave his plays no "inner coherence" or "strongly vitalized relations."[68] Two or more plots might be joined so loosely as to be virtually independent; linking devices were usually the flimsy ones of kinship or service. Such plotting, however, always provided abundant activity, and sometimes furnished a contrasting tone, or intensified the mood.[69] But only in the comedies was the absence of "general centralization" relatively harmless or even, at times, almost advantageous.[70]

As for other matters of technique, Fletcher quickly sketched-in the essential "exposition" in the opening conversation of a play, and thereafter allowed his loquacious characters to talk everything into crystal clearness.[71] Preferring the fillip of surprise to adequate motivation, he left many major turns of the action unprepared, a "fault" which "ran riot" in the tragicomedies and comedies.[72] His denouements were always spectacular if dubiously dramatic, with every possible closing-scene convention packed into them, and every effect heightened indiscriminately.[73] To create conflict, except of the more tangible kinds, was beyond his powers;

his "whole moral endowment was against the portrayal of the tragic life," with its deeper, spiritual issues. Hence tragic heroes—even the Caratach of *Bonduca*—lacked any inner struggle, and villains were base and bestial without adequate motivation. Only in comedy could Fletcher handle conflict skilfully; here, the interplay of alternating give and take between two characters or groups of characters was often brilliantly executed.[74]

From this summary of Miss Hatcher's findings it should be clear that, while she appreciated and ably demonstrated Fletcher's mastery of his craft as a practical playwright, he yet vexed her in various ways. To her, his tragicomedies were his least convincing work. He undertook to create "a world at least half serious" and then made no effort to "solve its problems reasonably," thus arousing resentment in his reader.[75] Of much better quality in this kind were the plays done jointly with Beaumont.[76] Throughout her analysis, Miss Hatcher had sought to show that Fletcher's essentially comedy methods were ill-suited to serious drama.

It was in a deft combination of romantic comedy and comedy of manners that he shone.[77] Sweeping us along on a rapidly moving and exhilarating current of highly improbable but amusingly audacious happenings, with no concessions "to a sober common sense," Fletcher was in his own element.[78] Unmoral and fun-loving, he lacked perception of the deeper ironies;[79] but his lively, bustling stagecraft and even his extravagances were here in place. Combined with touches of mild satire,[80] and with the sprightly sense of humor and the light sentiment which gave charm to his many good companions,[81] they contributed to the gay result. In this domain, at least, Beaumont could not equal Fletcher.[82]

Here, at last, in Miss Hatcher's study, was a detailed presentation of most of the elements which went to make up Fletcher's unusual command of craftsmanship. With even more penetration than Thorndike or Ristine, she laid part of the technical groundwork for a modern understanding of Fletcher, Beaumont and Company as entertainers to the Stuart gentry.

II

A few facets of the criticism which appeared in print between 1914 and 1923 remain for briefer consideration: the tendency towards downward revision in estimates of our playwrights; the move to rescue Beaumont from this fate while throwing Fletcher to the wolves; and one effort to reduce the stature not only of our corpus of plays but of the whole Elizabethan-Stuart drama except for Shakespeare.

Ten years after Swinburne's death in 1909, his *Contemporaries of*

Shakespeare[83] was published. Included in this volume was a section on Beaumont and Fletcher written much later than his article of 1875. While he had remained enthusiastic about some aspects of their plays, and there are many resemblances between the two appraisals, there was likewise a perceptible lessening of his previous high estimate of them.

Philaster, he asserted, had no characters deserving comparison for either power or truth with Marlowe's Faustus or Edward, Webster's Vittoria or Bracciano. The superior *The Maid's Tragedy* demonstrated the utter inability of our playwrights to create a protagonist of heroic mould like Faustus or Webster's Virginius. In fact, they had a "boyish or feminine incapacity" to create a serious hero who should be lifelike and conceivable, though they could do the "gallant and roistering humorist" better than Dumas. Amintor was "abject," Melantius "absurd," Philaster "the wraith of a living man," and Arbaces an excessively "blatant braggart and swaggering swashbuckler." While Swinburne still thought well of Bellario and Evadne, he now held that Aspatia could not compare, for vitality and truth, with Webster's women, and that Fletcher's Ordella, abnormally good, was not quite human.[84]

As a tragic poet, Fletcher had "magnificent but far from supreme power." His tragedies could not stand a moment's comparison with those of Shakespeare, Marlowe or Webster.[85] *Thierry and Theodoret*, his best, was not equal even to the collaborated *Philaster*, but did manage to sustain the reader's interest breathlessly. Its style, in its own "impulsive fashion," was as creditable for its purpose as were those of Shakespeare, Webster or Marlowe, which were nobler and more serious, as befitted their "higher and sincerer inspiration."[86] If Fletcher's fame had been eclipsed by the greater dramatists, it had not been completely effaced.[87]

Swinburne also put heavier emphasis than formerly on our playwrights' "besetting sense of the theatre." Readers of Fletcher's tragedies could not escape it; indeed, *Bonduca* was, in this respect, a triumph of skill.[88] The collaborated *A King and No King* was a brilliant achievement in "theatrical magnificence of incident and effect." But it sacrificed "all serious study of character, all rational or moral evolution of conduct . . . wantonly if not shamelessly" in order to create "vehement if not sometimes galvanic sensation or surprise."[89] *The Maid's Tragedy*, though exquisite as a poem, likewise subordinated everything else to stage effect.[90] Evidently Swinburne—lover of character studies and sublime truth in dramatic poetry—had grown wearied that the tragedies and tragicomedies of our corpus, which had the form of dramatic poetry, should be, in purpose, theatrical entertainment.

Just as he had tilted against Coleridge in his earlier essay, so Swinburne now challenged the opinions of other critics. Despite Dryden of the "dirty and greasy" comedies, and Hallam and Dyce as well, *The Custom of the Country* was neither coarse nor obscene, but an "audacious" and "magnificent" tragicomedy. Apparently of an opinion similar to Richard Lovelace's, he found no dirty words in it, and no "whiff" of "Swiftian or Carlylesque impurity."[91] It was the Beaumont-Fletcher *The Scornful Lady* which, while not "so impure an abortion of morality" as one of Richardson's novels, deserved the epithet of "coarsest."[92] He also considered as inept the efforts of Lamb and others to apply an ethical standard to the characters and their conduct in "the fairyland" of *The Faithful Shepherdess*. These conventional woodland figures, with their pastoral patterns of behavior, were scarcely conceived as possible men and women.[93]

Swinburne also singled out for attack "that typical Oxonicule" and " 'seraphical preacher,' " William Cartwright, whose damning offense consisted of proclaiming, in his First Folio commendatory verses,[94] that Shakespeare was dull, inartistic and scurrilous as compared with Fletcher. This "so ridiculous a promotion" had wrought much harm, for justice had not been done our playwrights ever since "their work was set up against Shakespeare's."[95] Whether or not Swinburne was fair to Cartwright, the course of our playwrights' reputation should have made it clear that his diagnosis was shrewd—and it certainly needed saying. The outmoded irritation at such comparisons as Cartwright's, which were rooted in a special milieu, should long since have ceased to bedevil criticism of Fletcher, Beaumont and Company.

Swinburne's moderated appreciation of these playwrights reflects their changing status in the last fifty years. Much more drastic, however, was the youthful attack on them by the Georgian poet, Rupert Brooke. In the brief pages devoted to them in his *John Webster and the Elizabethan Drama* (1916),[96] their reputation—and notably that of Fletcher—reached its twentieth century nadir.

To Brooke, Beaumont and Fletcher were the most significant cause of the degeneration of Jacobean drama. As long as the collaborators wrote together, however, they did fairly good work, though of a "fatally new kind." Its vices were not yet fully developed, and the degradation did not go far, because of Beaumont's satire, his sense of humour, the "strength" in his sentimentality, and his traditional metre. Fletcher, however, when free from his colleague's control, accelerated the "downhill course" of Stuart drama. He had nothing in him but "a kind of wit, a kind of prettiness, and an inelastic blank verse line."[97]

Like Macaulay before him, Brooke placed the turning-point in Elizabethan-Stuart drama about 1611. He blamed Fletcher for the decline; if the causes lay deeper, then he stood "a figure-head for our abuse."[98] His tragedy, *Bonduca*, with its lack of serious purpose, its sole aim of pleasing, its "mild" jokes and its unreality, was itself an example of the "dreary and fifth-rate" stuff which, through Fletcher's influence, overwhelmed the London stage. Five years before 1611, great tragedy was still "thunderous" through England; five years after 1611, "Fletcher and the silly sweetness of tragicomedy" carried all before them. Webster, in fact, appeared grander than he was as "the last of Earth, looking out over a sea of saccharine."[99]

Concerning Brooke's influence, Tillyard has recently reported that, since the "sea of saccharine" jibe, people have tended to avoid Fletcher's tragic work for fear they might "like it too well."[100] Yet it should have been clear that the ebullient young poet was too bent on iconoclasm to recognize any merits Fletcher's work might have. The "saccharine," which may describe with some aptness Beaumont's love-lorn maidens or Fletcher's mooning youths, is flippant rather than sound when flung out indiscriminately.

Two years before Brooke's passage was published, Gayley had also dealt with the issue of "decadence," in his *Beaumont the Dramatist,* from a much broader standpoint. Desiring to exculpate his hero, he suggested that signs of degeneration were palpable in many plays before these dramatists formed their partnership. Specifically indicted for trial were Heywood's *The Royal King and the Loyal Subject;* Chapman's *Bussy D'Ambois* (for its "glaring colours"); his *The Gentleman Usher* (for its "artificial atmosphere of court romance" as well as its surprises and reversals of a melodramatic order and its huddled-up poetic justice); Marston's *The Malcontent* (for its sensational effects, its "passionate unrealities and sepulchral action"); his *The Dutch Courtesan* (for its "sophistical theme and callous pornography"); and his *The Insatiable Countess* (for its "inhuman imaginings"). Also requiring consideration were Middleton's "heartless irresponsibility and indecency," and the way in which his early romantic plays warped tragic actions to comic endings.[101]

Here, indeed, was a formidable set of faults, such as had often been charged against our playwrights, in dramas that had preceded their *Philaster.* Pondering these blemishes of earlier works, Gayley repudiated the indictment of "decadence" for Beaumont, although not exempting Fletcher, who "hastened" it. Neither playwright initiated the decline. Not alone their joint-plays but some of these others—and some, like *All's Well* and *Measure for Measure,* by Shakespeare—were forerunners of the "melodramatic development of tragicomedy and sentimental tragedy," which soon grew to abuse and had its *reductio ad absurdum* at the hands of Restoration dramatists.[102] In these findings, whether fully accepted or not, are clear indications that Brooke's singling out of Fletcher as "figurehead for our abuse" over-simplified and distorted the facts.[103]

Gayley's book, as the foregoing suggests, sought to rescue Beaumont from the stigma which he felt had fallen on that dramatist because of his collaboration with Fletcher. He considered Beaumont second only to Shakespeare among the Jacobean playwrights as a dramatic poet. Webster, it was true, occasionally surpassed him; but *The Maid's Tragedy* was "breathless and heart-breaking," whereas the atmosphere of *The Duchess of Malfi* was essentially lurid and unhealthy.[104]

Since Gayley was intent upon demonstrating that there was "a wide and clearly visible distance" between the twin stars, even in their joint work,[105] and since he was himself not untouched by American Victorianism, he developed a bias against Fletcher. He was concerned to disassociate Beaumont from the hedonistic morality (or immorality) of Fletcher and from his "extravagant artistry,"[106] for he did not clearly recognize to what degree Beaumont, also, was intent upon immediate stage effect.

He therefore hailed with delight Paul Elmer More's statement that Fletcher's plays appeared to be the work of a man utterly lacking in conscience, but resented and tried to disprove More's further assertion that by nature Fletcher was of sounder fibre than Beaumont.[107] Examining that playwright's "heroic-romantic comedy," *The Humourous Lieutenant*, which More had praised as resembling Shakespeare's "strain" except for its lack of insight into human motives,[108] Gayley agreed that it was Fletcher's best piece in this kind. He accepted the Rabelaisian wit of the piece as tolerable, and added that it was Fletcher's only comedy in which objectionable qualities such as grossness and bawdy intrigue were not "ineradicable." But he thought it showed little insight, compared to plays of Beaumont, into ethical conflicts.[109]

Proceeding to dissect *A Wife for a Month*, whose Evanthe had impressed More favorably, Gayley found her, not a finely drawn woman but one who spoke billingsgate and behaved like a trollop, in spite of her chastity. Zola's *L'Assomoir*, compared to this play, smelled sweet, and a nightmare was equally probable. Fletcher could write poetically and express noble sentiments when he chose, as at points in this play; but his fancy was perverse and beastly, and he prostituted his art sordidly to sensationalism. He did not demonstrate the manly fibre of Beaumont, even when collaborating with him, much less when writing alone, regardless of his "surpassing excellence" in the field of comedy.[110] Indeed, Gayley's central irritation with Fletcher appears to have been that the collaborators had been jointly blamed for weaknesses that properly were Fletcher's alone, even in such plays as *The Maid's Tragedy*.[111]

Gayley believed that the latter play and *A King and No King* were not antiquated. Neither was there anything neurotic nor insidious in them, even though the latter was a "spoiled tragedy" by virtue of its ending.[112]

Beaumont's sense of moral conflict was dominant in them, and the characterization and handling of situation consistent, except in Fletcher's few scenes.[113] Gayley objected strenuously to More's charge that *The Maid's Tragedy* tangled up a group of passions incomprehensibly; he insisted that it had unity of interest and of emotional effect.[114] Properly cut, this play and *A King and No King* should both still delight on the stage. And if *The Knight of the Burning Pestle* had been written by Shakespeare, he would zestfully have been compared to Cervantes, and the play often performed by professionals to enthusiastic audiences.[115]

Like his contemporary, Oliphant, Gayley thus reveals himself to have been a belligerent champion of Beaumont who was correspondingly harsh towards Fletcher.[116] When due allowances are made for this bias, however, *Beaumont the Dramatist* remains a scholarly and valuable book. Its longer biographical half is particularly useful, for Gayley made full use of a vast fund of information about Beaumont's ruling class ancestry, relatives and associates, and also about the friendships he made, or may have made, in each circle his life intersected, whether university, inns of court, theatrical, literary or aristocratic. Fletcher, though given much slighter treatment, emerges as a popular, modest and independent gentleman, for Gayley conceived of him as of higher personal quality than his plays would suggest.[117] Massinger, later to be Fletcher's friend and colleague, was absent, since he never collaborated with Beaumont. The portrait of the latter, imaginatively treated, and occasionally a little tenuous in its foundation of facts, was a full-bodied one. Part I thus gives the best account that has yet appeared of the lives of Beaumont and Fletcher.

William Archer, in his heterodox book, *The Old Drama and The New*,[118] did not concern himself with any objective so limited as re-estimating our playwrights, whether upward or downward. True, *Philaster* and *The Maid's Tragedy* came under his scalpel, but simply as two among five specimens infected with Elizabethan deficiencies into which he was probing. His larger attack was on Elizabethan-Stuart drama and its descendants of the Restoration and the eighteenth century. These he considered a semi-barbarous and illegitimate hybrid. They had the purity neither of the lyric and operatic dance-drama of Greece, nor of the carefully motivated and genuinely life-imitating drama of the modern theatre. Inconsistently and awkwardly, they compounded elements of both, being dominated by lyricism but struggling sometimes towards a genuine realism.[119]

The point of irritation that inspired Archer's book was the superior prestige which he conceived the old drama still enjoyed over the new. This prejudice was based, he thought, upon a confusion between drama and lyric poetry.[120] His contention was that this mass of English plays from Elizabethan times to the nineteenth century had nothing to say to present day audiences. The reasons for this failure in communication were that these dramas belonged to "primitive and transitional types of art," that they were highly exaggerative in a delineation of manners which were "gross and unpleasing," and that they required "forms of virtuosity" in production which no longer were existent. Shakespeare alone had the supreme genius to transcend the inherent imperfections of his theatre.[121]

Narrowing down to our own field, Archer contended that the Elizabethan playwright's medium, blank verse, tended to cheapen rather than ennoble his work. Such verse was not hard to write, though the result might often be wooden rhetoric; it allowed the dramatist to pad his lines almost at will; and its artificiality made natural and simple expression unnecessary. In fact, the writer need have no ear at all for the patterns of ordinary, every day speech.[122] Moreover, the semi-barbarous platform stage contributed to the resulting "softness" by the licenses which it permitted. Some of these "facilities" were the fuzziness about time and place due to lack of scenery and the consequent rapid changes of locale; the unnatural soliloquy and aside, whereby much could be baldly told that would otherwise have to be dramatized; the ever-ready convention of disguise, encouraging other incredible devices; and the ease with which horrors thrilling to the spectators could be created.[123]

One result of these laxities was that, if characters behaved with enough violence, weak motivation of their passions and actions did not trouble the theatregoer, who wanted to have his flesh made to creep with horror, or his sides split with laughter. Since Elizabethan life itself was "harsh, coarse and cruel," dramatists wrote "savage satires" such as *Eastward Ho!* and Massinger's *The City Madam,* or "cynical tales of debauchery" like *The Chaste Maid in Cheapside* and the Beaumont-Fletcher *The Scornful Lady.* When there was some humanitarian feeling in a play, as in *A Woman Killed With Kindness,* this was outweighed by puerilities and barbarities.[124]

The standards by which Archer judged the shortcomings of Elizabethan-Stuart drama were the ones to which the plays of his own generation conformed: consistency and probability in plotting; careful psychological motivation of lifelike characters; and a colloquial speech imitating the natural and individual idiom which each of the dramatis personae would use if a real person. The touchstone was "the sober and accurate imitation of life."[125] As part of his demonstration that the older drama was sadly deficient, when looked at in this light, he selected for dissection five "Elizabethan masterpieces," including the Beaumont-Fletcher *The*

Maid's Tragedy and *Philaster*.[126] His choice of these two plays was buttressed by the opinion of St. Loe Strachey that they excelled all others except Shakespeare's.[127]

Archer found *The Maid's Tragedy* "brutally gross" and "full of psychological improbabilities and enigmas." It was incredible that Evadne should select as husband a man already in love with another woman, or that a king should agree to such a dangerously "cruel fooling" of the man, when a willing scapegoat could easily have been found. Yet this was the foundation on which the whole play rested. Moreover, Evadne's motivation was obscure. Why should she be ambitious merely to be the king's mistress in secret, when she had no apparent influence over him? The relationship of the pair lacked any interest it might have developed from such influence, and in consequence the king, the keystone of the play's arch, was nothing but a "rhetorical puppet." Nor was the bullying of Melantius anything but the slightest of motives for Evadne's sudden "conversion."[128]

Philaster, with much beautiful writing, was more attractive and less gross than *The Maid's Tragedy*; indeed, it was one of the most pleasing of the Jacobean "romances," with its charmingly drawn Arethusa and Bellario. Yet that the disguise of the latter should have deceived everybody—her father Dion, her princess Arethusa, her beloved Philaster—at a court where she had been well known, was most improbable. Moreover, her failure to reveal herself as soon as she heard Megra's slanderous charge of her misconduct with Arethusa was sheer whimsy and actually wicked. Bellario, in truth, kept silent solely that the plot might not fall to pieces there and then. Dion's acceptance of Megra's charge was out of character, nor should Philaster so easily have accepted Dion's false testimony. Moreover, the "transparent candour" of Arethusa and Bellario should have allayed any suspicions that Dion had aroused. The whole play was built up around "elements of unreason"; yet this was one of the "more civilized" dramas written by another playwright than Shakespeare![129]

There can be little question but that, from the standpoint of his modern criteria—consistency in plotting and well motivated characterization, resulting in realistic imitation of life—Archer diagnosed with acuteness some of the weaknesses of these two Stuart plays. So it was with the others. His knowledge of the technique of modern playwriting, and of the problems involved in staging dramas in picture-frame theatres, was considerable; it sharpened his perception of differences, and since he was defending modern standards, resulted in his unfavorable view of older ones. In so far as his defense counteracted an over-enthusiasm for the elder drama, it was healthily astringent. It was doubtless also useful in counteracting the nineteenth century tendency to over-emphasize Elizabethan-Stuart drama as poetry.

Archer's criticism, however, like Rymer's, raises a larger issue: whether any one standard is applicable to the plays of all times. Just as Rymer would have had all serious plays weighed in the scales of Greek drama and the theorizing about it, so Archer believed that the plays of the past should be submitted to the test of the realistic standards accepted by the playwrights of his own day. Subjected to the criteria of either, the Elizabethan-Stuart drama appeared the product of an ill-conditioned theatre and of a barbarous age.[130] From a less exclusive standpoint, however, the central deficiency of both critics would seem to be an insufficient historical insight—in Rymer's case alone, be it added, combined with a malignant spirit.

The Achilles' heel of Archer's argument was his exemption of Shakespeare from diagnosis. As Miss Bradbrook has indicated,[131] the modern standards which Archer applied might, with much the same cogency, be extended to the greatest exemplar of the old drama with strikingly like results. Dr. Samuel Johnson, that great realist of the eighteenth century, would never have left this heel exposed. He would have perceived at once the mistake in "leaving out Hamlet," for he wrote, of Shakespeare's plotting:

The plots are often so loosely formed, that a very slight consideration may improve them, and so carelessly pursued, that he seems not always fully to comprehend his own design. He omits opportunities of instructing or delighting, which the train of his story seems to force upon him, and apparently rejects those exhibitions which would be more affecting, for the sake of those which are more easy.

It may be observed, that in many of his plays the latter part is evidently neglected. When he found himself near the end of his work, and in view of his reward, he shortened the labour to snatch the profit. He therefore remits his efforts where he should most vigorously exert them, and his catastrophe is improbably produced or imperfectly represented.[132]

This criticism has a familiar ring, as though Fletcher were the playwright under discussion instead of Shakespeare. It suggests that the latter cannot be exempted simply on the score of his transcendent genius. His craftsmanship, like his actors, audience and stage, was that of his fellow dramatists, however greater his stature than theirs. And just that suggests the unbalance of Archer's position. His shrewd but limited outlook recalls Henry Weber's admonition, given in 1812, to be historically rather than provincially minded; for, in judging the work of playwrights, "the state of dramatic composition at the time must always be kept in view."[133]

III

As the supposed seamless weave of our ensemble has been unravelled, the component colors of Fletcher, Beaumont, Massinger and minor collaborators have been distinguished, in spite of the many knots and tangles that remain. Beaumont has risen and Fletcher fallen in critical approval; the wheel of fortune has brought the latter, for a time at its top, lower than his once less visible twin. And yet not only Shakespeare and Jonson but also Marlowe and Webster, so long unknown, today take precedence even of Beaumont in many comparative judgments. Massinger has continued to gain more attention in his own right than as Fletcher's second colleague. Both of these are conceded to outrank such dramatic hacks as Field, Rowley and Brome—but which outranks the other might be matter of argument. Both rub shoulders uncomfortably with playwrights as diverse as Middleton, Dekker, Marston, Heywood and Ford. Beaumont and Fletcher, but more especially the latter, even stand accused of heavy responsibility in the decay of Stuart drama. All this is a far cry from the glory of the First Folio.

O tempora! O mores!

PART 2

Re-Interpretation

CHAPTER FIVE

The Time, the Place and the Men

As we emerge from considering the long yet selective history of the reputation of Fletcher, Beaumont and Company, the multiform variety of opinions about their plays is, no doubt, one dominant impression. The body of work under discussion has remained almost constant down the ages, despite such an accession as was brought to light by the first printing, in 1883, of *Barnavelt*.[1] Yet the attitudes of the playgoers of Caroline days towards this corpus had little in common with those of Coleridge and Lamb, nor did Dryden see eye to eye with Darley, nor Colman with either Gayley or Brooke. If the perspective has thus continually altered, as new times and new men looked at these plays, will it ever cease to do so until our corpus has been swallowed up in the limbo of forgotten things?

Probably not. That there is a relativity in criticism, as in other mundane matters, needs no further illustration; the point in time-space of the observer, no less than his own temperament, inevitably colors his observations. But just for this reason there arises periodically a need for reinterpretation of our playwrights, as when the romantics enlarged the quadrumvirate of the late eighteenth century, or when reasonably practicable methods were devised, two generations later, for disentangling the clotted skeins of authorship. These were times when some of the accumulated encrustations of previous generations were scraped away; times also when new accretions began to blend with the old that remained.

So it is again today. The materials are now at hand for a revaluation of our playwrights in terms of the theatrical milieu in which they lived and moved and had their being. Thanks to the devoted labors in research of countless men and women, capped by such brilliant reconstructions as Adams' *The Globe Playhouse*[2] and Harbage's *Shakespeare's Audience*,[3] most of the necessary spadework has been done, even though much that we should like to know will never be recovered. As we have already seen, the accumulating data have often, and increasingly, made themselves felt in the more recent criticism of our playwrights.

Nonetheless, accretions from the past still blur the newer perspective. Sometimes they throw an eerie and distorting light on what our entertainers were trying to do under the conditions that surrounded them, what the nature of their resulting product was, and why it was thus and no other. Emphasis upon a view of Elizabethan-Stuart plays as dramatic poetry still persists with enough strength, in some quarters, to dim the perception that the drama is a mixed form of art whose ultimate test is performance on the stage, not reading in the study—rewarding as the latter pursuit may be, and not to be left out of account in critical judgments.

Sufficient regard is still too seldom given to the fact that Fletcher, Beaumont and Massinger, like other Elizabethan-Stuart dramatists, were bent on writing—often under pressure of time—successful plays shaped for the stage of their day and to the tastes of an audience which they were obliged to please if they were to earn even a modest living thereby.[4] Beaumont alone, as a younger son of a prominent county family, appears to have shared Shakespeare's freedom from urgent financial necessity. But even for these latter dramatists a *succès d'estime* would be inadequate compensation for failure in the playhouse. We easily forget that all of these playwrights were attempting to supply the current demand of their actors and their audiences rather than courting the fair regard of posterity. From the care which Shakespeare gave to publishing them, it would appear as though it were by *Venus and Adonis, The Rape of Lucrece* (and possibly the *Sonnets*) that he hoped chiefly to be remembered. Fletcher showed a similar concern solely for *The Faithful Shepherdess*. Both were modest men and, in general, plays written for the London stage still were less esteemed than poetry.

If, then, a just evaluation is to be given the achievement of Fletcher, Beaumont, Massinger and Company in the light of present knowledge, we need to see them not only against the floodlighted background of the sometimes revealing, sometimes obscuring criticism of the past, but in their human relationship to their youthful environment and to the workaday world of the London playhouses in Jacobean years, so far as these can be reconstructed. For what our playwrights wrote sprang not only from their own prepossessions and talents but also from the demands which their particular time and place made on them. And it was not, precisely, Shakespeare's time and place, in spite of overlapping careers.

I

When William Shakespeare was born to prospering middle-class parents in the small town of Stratford-on-Avon in Warwickshire towards the end of April, 1564,[5] Queen Elizabeth had been ruler of England less than five and a half years. When John Fletcher was born into a rising clerical household in Rye, Sussex, a few days before December 20, 1679,[6] Shakespeare—now almost sixteen—had probably completed his formal education at the excellent Stratford Grammar School.[7] When Philip Massinger, son of a gentleman in the service of Henry Herbert, Earl of Pembroke, was born at Salisbury in November, 1583[8] Shakespeare was a married man of nineteen and father of a six months' old daughter.[9] And when Francis Beaumont was born, sometime between February, 1584, and February, 1585—probably at the family estate of Grace Dieu in Charnwood Forest, Leicestershire[10]—Shakespeare was nearing the end of his apprenticeship and, with five mouths to feed after February, 1585, was soon to leave Stratford and turn country schoolmaster.[11]

Shakespeare appears to have abandoned school-teaching to try his fortune on the London stage within a year or two of the time when the English fleet and a subsequent storm made havoc of the Spanish Armada.[12] To the twenty-four year old man of Stratford, as to all his generation, this overwhelming English victory was a vital and shaping experience. His chronicle-history plays of the 1590's were one expression of the deep patriotic enthusiasm which the event had evoked. To the other three, however, the crisis of 1588 was only a childhood memory; Fletcher was a schoolboy of eight at the time, Massinger five, and Beaumont only three or four.

When, in 1591, Shakespeare began to emerge into some notice as an actor and a playwright, John Fletcher's father, now Bishop of Bristol, Almoner to the Queen, and possessed of a house in Chelsea, sent his promising twelve year old son up to Cambridge University as a pensioner of Bene't (Corpus Christi) College, of which he himself had once been President. No doubt John was at this time expected to follow in his father's footsteps, for two years later he was a Bible-reader, performing this office at the services in the college chapel.[13] Whether lack of vocation or the sudden death of his father, now Bishop of London, in 1596, caused the abandonment of the family calling is uncertain, like the rest of the youth's career until he emerged as a playwright. Since he was apparently left unprovided for by his father, it may have been his uncle, Dr. Giles Fletcher, who now took him in charge.[14] Indeed, it would have been strange if the bishop's brother—diplomat, scholar, and author of the sonnet-sequence, Licia—should have taken no interest in this lad of literary bent, left an orphan at sixteen.

By February 4, 1597, when Justice Beaumont sent the twelve year old Francis, with his two elder brothers, to the fashionable Oxford college of Broadgates Hall (now Pembroke),[15] Shakespeare was already in the main of light as London's most popular dramatist, with such recent successes as

Richard III, Richard II, A Midsummer Night's Dream and *Romeo and Juliet* to his credit. His erotic mythological poem, *Venus and Adonis*, had taken the universities by storm after it was published in 1593;[16] we can reasonably surmise that Fletcher, who drew upon it for his *The Faithful Shepherdess* years later, first read it as a youthful undergraduate. Perhaps he saw *A Midsummer Night's Dream*, also of influence on his pastoral play, during one of his vacation trips up to London. Near the time that Beaumont entered Broadgates Hall, *Romeo and Juliet* likewise became a favorite of the students at both universities.[17] It is, therefore, hardly surprising that echoes of his play are found in the writings of both playwrights.

On November 3, 1600, Francis Beaumont, now a lad of fifteen or sixteen, and probably just down from Oxford, was admitted to membership, with his brothers, in the Inner Temple, and, according to Gayley, took up residence and legal studies at one of the nearby lesser Inns of Chancery attached to it.[18] John Fletcher became of age a few days before December 20 of this year. At this time Shakespeare, now thirty-six, having written such recent "hits" as *Julius Caesar, As You Like It* and *Much Ado About Nothing*, was about to embark upon his great tragedies for the new Globe Theatre. At this time, too, the aging Elizabeth, who had reigned some forty-two years, was destined to live scarcely two and a half more, and the problem of the succession to this childless queen was deeply troubling many minds.

In the spring of 1603, when James VI of Scotland safely ascended the English throne as James I, Shakespeare was nearing forty, and his life-work in the London theatres was more than half over. His formative years were behind him; he was truly of the age of Elizabeth. But Beaumont was still a law student of eighteen or nineteen, Massinger an undergraduate of twenty at his father's college, St. Alban's Hall, Oxford,[19] and Fletcher a young gentleman of twenty-three—whereabouts unknown but probably London. As yet the playhouses, private and public, knew them only as spectators. These three youths, with their careers still ahead of them, were, thus, of the new Jacobean generation of young manhood, and less firmly rooted than Shakespeare in the Elizabethan past.

Had they been coevals of their great predecessor, their careers would inescapably have been different. Fletcher and Massinger, forced to earn their livings, and choosing the theatre as the most pleasant means, would have been subject to the same dramatic influences as the young man from Stratford: Lyly, Marlowe, Kyd, perhaps Peele and Greene. The developed techniques of Shakespeare, Jonson, Chapman, Marston and others would not have been ready-made to their use. In the 1590's they would have been obliged by financial necessity to write for the public playhouses, possibly in Henslowe's slave-market, and certainly for a more various and catholic audience than later. Catering to this widely representative play-going public, and molded by it, Fletcher might well have escaped becoming a figure-head for the abuse of Rupert Brooke and others.

As for Beaumont, he would most probably be remembered today as a minor poet; his family and his connections were too prominent to have permitted his debasing himself, under the eagle eyes of Elizabeth and her councillors, as a writer for the commercial London theatres. He might have contrived entertainments for the private delectation of Queen and court, much as he concocted his *Masque of the Gentlemen of Grays-Inne and the Inner Temple* for performance before James I.

It was their particular point in time which allowed Beaumont, and Fletcher, to write for the Jacobean private theatres, and then for the best London public company which, when they established connection with it, had recently acquired the private Blackfriars playhouse for use as winter home. It was this time-point, too, as much as their gentlemanly breeding, education and social outlook, which made both Fletcher and Beaumont entertainers to the gentry in special. The dramatist must write to his audience, even if, as with Shakespeare, there be somewhat in his plays beyond the capacity of some fraction of the playgoers. The oft-repeated charge of decadence brought against Beaumont and Fletcher is, thus, a two-edged sword.

In point of time, Shakespeare was more fortunate than these younger men and Massinger, for his broadly based, predominantly middle-class audience was just the one, as Harbage has shown,[20] to draw out the best he had to offer. Not so the more exclusive clientele, with money to spend, that developed, especially at Blackfriars, towards the end of Shakespeare's career, and for which he soon ceased to write. By 1613 he had fulfilled his creative urge and had made his fortune. He could retire to Stratford confident that, even if Beaumont were also withdrawing, Fletcher, the neophyte Massinger, and Nathan Field, the leading actor of twenty-six who had recently succeeded as playwright, could carry on with the kind of entertainment that audiences of his King's Men's Company now were desiring.[21]

II

In the winter of 1600-1601, when Fletcher came of age and Beaumont was settling into his legal studies, the circumstances of Queen Elizabeth's death and its peaceful consequences were as much concealed from our two youths' knowledge as were their own later intimate friendship and collaboration. Perhaps one or the other, however, occasionally discussed

with his friends the much mooted and dreaded possibility that the demise of the aged queen might entail civil war. There was much concern
over the facts that she was childless, had not named her successor, and
more than a dozen persons had some claim to the throne. The rebellion
and execution of the Earl of Essex must have brought some realization
of the dangers even to these youths. Assuredly, like Shakespeare, they
shared the general relief when the peaceful accession of James belied all
bleak forebodings. They were still young enough in 1605 to have been
deeply impressed by the Gunpowder Plot of certain Catholic fanatics to
blow up King, royal family and members of Parliament. Certainly this
train of events left its mark on Beaumont, some of whose Catholic relatives were involved;[22] the stinging treatment of informers in *The
Woman-Hater* (1606) is sufficient evidence of that. One suspects that, as
with many another gentleman, these two crises resulted for our playwrights in a conviction that even an unsatisfactory king was better than
the chaos which twice had threatened. That would not, however, necessarily make them sympathetic to James' theories of absolutism.

Fletcher, Massinger and Beaumont, by birth and upbringing, were all
quite naturally of the aristocratic party. John Fletcher had seen his father
rise to be a Lord Spiritual through "the gratious aspect and favour" of
Queen Elizabeth, and had known the life of an episcopal palace.[23] The
bishop's sudden death, which appears to have had some relationship to
the withdrawal of the Queen's favor because of his second marriage to
the widow of Sir John Baker,[24] could have taught the lad, still in his
teens, how insecure was dependence on the whims of monarchs. Philip
Massinger had, no doubt, because of his father's important position in
them, been brought up in the households of Henry and then William
Herbert, Earls of Pembroke, and perhaps had received from the latter
some assistance towards his university education.[25] Francis Beaumont was
the third son of a country squire with a Cambridge and Inns of Court
education, who had aristocratic connections both of his own and through
his wife, and who was member of one Parliament and later a Queen's
Justice of the Court of Common Pleas.[26] Francis himself was educated to
follow the same county family career when he should have made a suitable marriage—as he was to do when he was twenty-eight or nine.

All three may have shared the instinctive belief of the aristocracy and
gentlemen-commoners that their stability was bound up with that of the
monarchy. Even Shakespeare, who established his gentility by a grant of
coat of arms, stressed the need of "degree" in his Roman history plays, as
Phillips has convincingly shown.[27] Not yet the day of John Milton's *Ten-
ure of Kings and Magistrates*.

There was little in their background, however, to make any of the three younger playwrights susceptible to the "divine right" propaganda of James I. The gentleman-commoners of the House of Commons were notoriously at loggerheads with the King throughout his reign, in asserting the rights of Parliament. Fletcher had to make his way, not by favor of a Queen, but by the plaudits of playhouse audiences which were largely out of sympathy with James' pedantic claims, in spite of a sprinkling of sycophants among the theatregoers. Massinger, an admirer of William Herbert, whose bounty appears on occasion to have relieved the son of his faithful and able steward, was immune to divine right doctrine through sharing the independent political views of this Earl of Pembroke, who was largely in opposition to James, and wholly to Buckingham.[28] Beaumont belonged to just that station in life which was later to furnish many leaders of the Parliamentary party in the Civil War, and others who espoused the Cavalier cause with regret that the conflict could not be avoided. They were men long trained to exercise authority in their respective counties, and restive at dogmas of divine right and at autocratic practices, even when they finally threw in their lot with the King.

Nor was there anything in their university education to make our three youths "servile divine rightists." Quite the contrary, in fact. No doubt their university years cultivated a social class consciousness, but it was that of a ruling class which looked forward to leadership in the affairs of the land rather than to servile compliance with dictatorship or tyranny. Moreover, the study of the Greek and Latin languages and literatures, history and philosophy, confirmed aristocratic rather than absolutist leanings. For the classical authors whom the undergraduates studied belonged to mature and esteemed civilizations whose form of society was, in the main, aristocratic. Those who had received most favor in the books they were studying were such active men in public affairs as writers, orators, lawyers and statesmen. The students of that "queen of sciences," theology, would add clergymen to such leaders; and these, in contemporary England, were often likewise writers and orators—and sometimes politicians.

The university undergraduate would thus normally be strengthened in a conviction which many had brought from their homes that neither democracy nor absolute monarchy was desirable. The fact that most governments of the day, including their own, were monarchies, would be offset by the flattering belief that their own class was the really effective support of the state, and that some of their own number would, in due time, represent the interests of their class in parliament. It would also seem probable that our three youths, who found in their lectures and readings that kings of the ancient world were frequently denounced as tyrants and "ravening wolves," were being provided as undergraduates with an antidote against the mental poison of absolutism.[29]

The number of vile despots and contemptible favorites in the plays of our corpus is not, therefore, a remarkable coincidence. Their prevalence would appear to be an indirect reflection of the dramatists' distaste for the theory and practice of absolutism. Nor is it strange that Massinger and Fletcher should have joined in writing a dangerously political play about the contemporary Dutch statesman who was the titular hero of *The Tragedy of Sir John Van Olden Barnavelt*—how daring a play, its non-appearance in print until recent times should indicate. Fletcher, leading playwright of the King's Men as he was in 1619, need not have joined Massinger in writing a tragic drama about this independent Dutchman, had he preferred not to do so.

Considering the vital interest of the upper classes in James I's theories of absolute monarchy, it was natural enough that the issue of divine right should be debated in certain dramas of our corpus. But for each weak-kneed Amintor, paralyzed by "the divinity that doth hedge a king," there was, as Macaulay pointed out,[30] an opposing Melantius. Aëcius had Maximus as a foil, and the rulers of both *The Maid's Tragedy* and *Valentinian* died for their misdeeds. Without question, it was politic to give Barnavelt a sentimental closing speech directed to his old enemy, the Prince of Orange, which seemed to hint the virtue of servility to monarchs, thus:

> Commend my least breath to his Excellence,
> tell him the Sun he shot at, is now setting,
> setting this night, that he may rise to morrow,
> for ever setting: now let him reign alone,
> and with his rays, give life, and light to all men,
> May he protect with honor, fight with fortune,
> and dye with general love, an old, and good Prince;[31]

But Fletcher's sop to Cerberus must have been determined upon by both playwrights to make possible the tragedy's production; a Barnavelt defiant to the end would not, under the conditions of censorship, do. Many members of the audience were intelligent enough, if some sycophants were not, to understand the drift of the play and to discount the ending. Indeed, the sop did not prevent the play's suppression, though it apparently helped to get it past the licenser and onto the stage.

That our authors were not divine rightists was, we have seen, clearly perceived by the eulogizers of the First Folio who pointed out that the political drift of their plays was not favorable to tyrants or tyranny. The complaints of Restoration critics that kings and dukes were not treated in our corpus with the proper dignity or respect point to the same conclusion. So does Langbaine's report that the libertine King Charles II forbade the playing of *The Maid's Tragedy,* with its murder of a licentious monarch—whatever the degree of truth or falsity in the rumor.[32] Symptomatic, too, were Edmund Waller's three efforts to rewrite the last act of this play so as to clear its king of all guilt and leave him triumphant in the end.[33] Had Fletcher, Beaumont and Company been lickspittle monarchists, Restoration critics would not have been thus aggrieved at their treatment of rulers.

Seventeenth century perceptiveness contrasts favorably with Coleridge's misleading Tory prejudices. This is not a matter for bias but for truth, and one's own political convictions are irrelevant. In spite of Coleridge's persuasive dogmatism, we have found other nineteenth century critics besides Macaulay who were aware that something was wrong with the charge of servility to James' absolutism. Hallam, for example, noted much implied satire of the court in our plays, as well as much warm praise of military valor and scorn for ignominious peace, such as expressed the sentiments of upper class theatre-goers—and middle-class ones, too—dissatisfied with James' conduct of court and foreign affairs.[34] And Donne recognized that, in a reign during which the government kept a firm hand on acting companies and plays, our dramatists were as free-spoken as it was practicable to be and still continue playwrights. He indicated that their dramas shadowed forth the actual corrupt atmosphere of James' court—in the midst of their land-of-romance trappings—and called attention to their satirical treatment of the favorites of stage-tyrants, during a reign notorious for its ignoble ruler's sudden advancement of, and dependence upon, unworthy men like Carr and Buckingham.[35] Today he might have gone farther, thanks to Oscar James Campbell's studies of dramatic satire,[36] and indicated that such blunt-spoken advisers as Mardonius in *A King and No King* fulfilled somewhat the role of satirical commentators on their princes' weaknesses.

Donne showed good judgment in thinking our playwrights, for their age, free-spoken; they would be obliged, by the danger of censorship and penalties, to imply more than they said. Had not one of their own companies, The Children of the Revels, been forced to stop playing in the spring of 1608 because of royal disapproval of Chapman's *Charles, Duke of Byron?* It was, in fact, as a consequence of this contretemps—not the first for that company—that the Blackfriars Theatre became the winter playhouse of the King's Men.[37]

It is against such a background as this that the third scene of Act I of *Valentinian,* sometimes urged as a striking example of servile royalism, must be considered. No doubt the present-day reader finds fantastic and even disagreeable such lines as these, spoken by Aëcius concerning the tyrannous and libertine emperor, Valentinian:

> yet remember,
> We are but Subjects, Maximus; obedience
> To what is done, and grief for what is ill done,
> Is all we can call ours: The hearts of Princes
> Are like the Temples of the Gods; pure incense,
> Until unhallowed hands defile these offerings,
> Burns ever there; we must not put 'em out,
> Because the Priests that touch those sweets, are wicked;
> We dare not, dearest Friend, nay more, we cannot,
> While we consider who we are, and how,
> To what laws bound, much more to what Law-giver;
> Whilst Majesty is made to be obeyed,
> And not to be inquired into, . . .[38]

That may sound like arrant divine right nonsense, with a vengeance. But who speaks these lines? Aëcius, a sturdy believer, like Amintor, in their truth. Fletcher accordingly puts these words into his mouth, but that does not make them his own sentiments. Wise students of Shakespeare have learned the danger of considering, as being that dramatist's private thoughts, any striking or beautiful expression of attitude with which he invests his characters—even Prospero's magical lines incorporating the thought that "we are such stuff as dreams are made on." The same perception that Fletcher is a playwright creating characters and telling a story, and not a lyric poet unpacking his heart with words, should temper the reading of Aëcius' speeches. Indeed, that character himself, before the scene is over, will point out to Valentinian with what vices the common report accredits him.[39] He was, at least, not one of our playwrights' fawning courtiers, and hence not subjected to ridicule.

And yet so recent and, in many ways, valuable a book as Ross' *Milton's Royalism,* published in 1943, continues the old attitudes. It cites three dramas of our corpus as significant instances of "a crop of plays glorifying monarchy," written in "self-conscious defiance of the city"— a city, incidentally, that attended these plays in large numbers. Ross found our authors' royalism "a tawdry, blatant thing."[40]

The Maid's Tragedy is considered to portray a dissolute king as above criticism because he is the monarch; Amintor's attitude is, thus, given more weight than the impact of the play as a whole. Arbaces in *A King and No King* (actually not of royal blood) is seen as ardently seeking to commit incest. But this simplifies too much; it ignores Arbaces' inner struggle, Panthea's being none of his kin, and Mardonius' pungent criticism of Arbaces, to his face, for his defects of character—as well as the cowardly Bessus' servile willingness to act as pander, which shocks Arbaces himself. Archas of *The Loyal Subject* is stigmatized as "a servile creature" who, after submitting to various indignities, is finally rewarded by gaining the Duke of Moscovia's favor.[41] This statement suggests that Ross did not discern the main satirical drive of the play, which is directed somewhat against the Duke of Moscovia himself, more fully against the corrupt atmosphere of his court, and, above all, against Boroskie, his unworthy favorite.

That so many critics, including Ross, should have missed the point of *The Loyal Subject,* as the majority of Jacobean playgoers assuredly did not, is in part Fletcher's own fault.[42] He did not bring out as clearly as he should the fact that the Duke's father, realizing his son's weaknesses of character, had arranged for Archas to act as a sort of unofficial guardian over him. It is, however, there in the play, as in the old Duke's leaving a portion of his wealth under the custody of Archas, not to be yielded up until a time of crisis, such as he feared his son's bad judgment might precipitate. Under these circumstances, Archas' loyalty becomes more understandable. Fletcher also failed dramatically at a key point; depending on the convention of "conversion," he did not take the pains to motivate the young Duke's change of heart out of the events of the play—in particular, out of his respectful interest in Honora. Hence, his change in attitude towards Boroskie and towards Archas comes as a largely unprepared surprise.

Fletcher's characteristic concentration, moreover, on a sequence of sensational and melodramatic situations towards the end of the play, involving the testing of Archas, tends to make the casual reader forget the satire which colors many earlier scenes. Furthermore, the easy forgiveness of the base but repentant Machiavellian favorite, Boroskie, at the end of the play obscures the satirical drive—as it was doubtless intended to do. Fletcher was not only concerned to give the play a generally happy ending; he also desired to moderate the boldness of the play's attack on unworthy favorites, in view of King James' own addiction to such parasites. The title, the setting in Moscow, and the loyalty of Archas also helped to cloak the attack.

Fletcher's satire is apt to have a merrier, less incisive quality than that of Jonson or even of Beaumont. But, when seen on the stage by the sharp-eyed Jacobean, its direction in this play could not have been missed. The cowardly and self-seeking favorite, Boroskie, was the hard-hit central target. But there is some very plain speaking to the Duke himself, even occasionally by Archas—and various commentators on our corpus have drawn quotations from this play dealing with the corruption of the court. This is dramatized not only in the speeches of the country-bred Honora and Violet, when faced with the necessity of going to court, and in the arguments of Alinda (Young Archas) and of Theodore and the soldiers, but also in such satirical scenes as the one (Act III, scene IV) in which Theodore, while presenting his newly arrived sisters to the gentlemen of the court, drives them out of his presence, silent and abashed, by his withering scorn of their lecherous tendencies.[43]

Fletcher's treatment may not be to modern tastes; the plain-spoken if wittily satiric bawdry may not please. But a careful reading of the play, with alertness to its central intent, should convince the reader that this play was hardly written in praise of tyrannous monarchs and their favorites, or of a corrupt court, however persistent Archas' loyalty. Keen visualization of the play as it would act before a Jacobean audience should also persuade him that, under a sufficient protective coloring, Fletcher's play was expressing distaste for favorites, and for an immoral court atmosphere—a distaste shared by the majority of his spectators.

It is probable that the introspective and philosophically-minded Massinger thought through his political convictions more searchingly than did either Fletcher or the youthful Beaumont. But as the willingness of the first two to collaborate on *Barnavelt* would suggest, there was a substantial amount of resemblance in the basic attitudes of these three playwrights. It is therefore pertinent to note certain conclusions which Benjamin Townley Spencer reached in his brilliant study of Massinger's ideas.[44]

After a comprehensive and well documented discussion of that dramatist's conception of the prince, as seen in the plays of his sole authorship, Spencer presents the following summary of opinion:

A constitutional monarchy is the best form of government. In such a state the king owes a duty to his people and they, in turn, owe a duty to him. He is to enforce rather than to make the laws of the country, and to abide by the fundamental statutes of the land as well as by the Divine laws. His will is not the law. The prince must respect the will and opinions of his citizens; . . .[45]

Coleridge's "rank republican" thus proves, under sound analysis, to be a constitutional monarchist.

Like Fletcher's Aëcius, Massinger also believed that citizens "are to hold their monarch sacred, for, if he is not directly appointed by God, he is in His special care."[46] Such a conviction does not necessarily imply a belief in divine rightism. Massinger's constitutionalist views that a king is subject to the laws of the country, and that he is not directly appointed by God, were contrary to those of King James and other divine rightists. Accepting God's special care of rulers, however, like Aëcius and most pious Jacobean Englishmen, the playwright further maintained: "Therefore, it is not the duty nor is it the right of any individual to assassinate" the ruler, "however unworthy he may seem."[47] A similar conviction would be shared by most citizens of modern democracies concerning their elected executives.

That God might sometimes bring vengeance on evil rulers was acknowledged by our playwrights—as the murders of the monarchs in *The Maid's Tragedy*, *Valentinian* and other plays demonstrate. But this did not exculpate the human instruments. In *The Maid's Tragedy* Lysippus, the new king, explicitly underscored these attitudes in the final lines of the play:

> May this a fair example be to me,
> To rule with temper: for on lustful Kings
> Unlookt for sudden deaths from heaven are sent!
> But curst is he that is their instrument.[48]

From this point of view, therefore, certain plays of our corpus could be looked upon as warnings to princes. And precisely this appears to have been clear to certain First Folio eulogizers who, by 1647, had experienced the civil strife provoked by the absolutism of James' son.[49]

The persistence of the Coleridgean misconceptions of our playwrights' politics alone justifies the treatment of this matter at so much length. That the dramas of our corpus do reflect the court of James, and likewise his theories of government and of foreign relations, is true enough; but not in the spirit so often assumed. Indeed, it is time that the baseless fabric of the charge of "servile divine rightists" against our playwrights should melt into unsubstantial air. That they were monarchists was inevitable from their aristocratic background, and normal to Englishmen of all classes in the Jacobean age. Natural enough also was the appearance of absolutist doctrine as matter of debate in their plays, since this material would deeply interest Jacobean audiences of whatever opinions. But that none of them saw eye to eye with James I's view of the kingly function should be evident from the nature of their upbringing, education, and experience in the early 1600's. It should also be clear from any careful appraisal of the total impression of their individual work.

If, as Baldwin Maxwell plausibly contends, the playwrights of the King's Men were obliged to take up the cudgels against duelling after 1615 or 1616, as part of James' campaign to stamp out that practice,[50] this indicates the strength of the King's control over his own company of players, but not that their dramatists were servile royalists. They had no other choice if they were to eke out their livelihood by writing plays for the Globe and Blackfriars theatres. If the same playwrights could indicate their real opinions of the King's absolutist views and of his court by indirect means only, that, too, does not make them divine rightists. They ran the risk of being misunderstood by a posterity for whom they were not writing, but they do not appear to have been misunderstood by the seventeenth century playgoer whom they were seeking to entertain.

III

It would be useful to know more than we do about what Fletcher, Beaumont and Massinger were reading, aside from their assigned Latin authors, during the impressionable years when they were in residence at the universities. Something, however, can be reconstructed from the fashions of the time and from the plays they later wrote. Anthony á Wood made the statement, in Restoration days, that Massinger "applied his mind more to poetry and romances . . . than to logic and philosophy."[51] This seems probable not only for him but for Fletcher and for Beaumont as well, both of whom went up to their university at twelve—even then an early age for matriculation.[52] Boys so young as they usually found their studies anything but easy and attractive, unless they had been exceptionally well prepared. It is likely that all three youths thus found extra-curricular reading more to their taste than that which their tutors assigned. Possibly, also, they took the time while in residence to begin their acquisitions of such foreign languages as they mastered, in order that they might read Renaissance writers in the original.

As well-born youths of literary bent, our three playwrights must have been familiar with those English writings of the past then fashionable among the undergraduates. No doubt they read "the father of English poetry," Chaucer; Fletcher, in fact, was indebted to *The Canterbury Tales* both for the plot of *The Two Noble Kinsmen* and for the serious main story of *Women Pleased*. They were also surely acquainted with some of the Elizabethan anthologies of lyric poetry; among them, the earliest of these, *Tottel's Miscellany*, with its lyrics by Wyatt, Surrey and other poets of Henry VIII's court.

Doubtless, too, the sonnet-sequences which Sidney's *Astrophel and Stella* introduced in 1591 interested our youths. Indeed, Fletcher's uncle, Dr. Giles Fletcher, brought out his *Licia* in 1593. The fashionable attitudes towards love and one's lady-on-a-pedestal which the majority of these sequences embodied must have delighted them, as they did young Romeo, who first saw the light of the stage in 1595. Years later, when the sonneteering fashion had passed, John Fletcher was to burlesque one of their attitudinizings, the exchange of hearts, in *The Mad Lover,* whose title character was to take the giving of his heart to his lady with literal seriousness.[53]

Probably Fletcher and Beaumont, at least, devoured not only *Venus and Adonis* but various other erotic narrative poems such as Chapman's *Ovids Banquet of Sence,* and Marlowe's and Chapman's *Hero and Leander.* Certainly, if *Salmacis and Hermaphroditus* was penned by the youthful Beaumont, as Gayley thinks,[54] the lad knew these poems well. Treatments so frankly sensual of the relationship of young man and woman, read at adolescence, might well have had some lasting effect on Fletcher's own later conceptions. Indeed, even Spenser's *Epithalamion,* written to honor his wife in lieu of wedding gifts that had failed to arrive on time, is downright enough about the bridegroom's impatience for the wedding night to come, and about the bedding of the bride.[55] There was little "modesty" in Elizabethan days, even in the most idealistic of poets.

Fletcher, and doubtless Beaumont as well, read Edmund Spenser, who himself had been an undergraduate at Cambridge not many years before. Both the epoch-making *Shepherd's Calendar* and that pictorial storybook, *The Faerie Queene,* have left traces in *The Faithful Shepherdess,* not only in the names of various characters but also in the style and in poetic echoes. It may be, too, that the third (and fourth) books of *The Faerie Queene,* with their series of stories illustrating various aspects of love and lust as bodied forth in typical knights and ladies, is responsible for Fletcher's adoption of a similar framework for his pastoral tragicomedy. When Fletcher went up to Cambridge, the first three books of Spenser's major poem, just published, were the literary sensation of the moment. The remaining books of this poetic effort to "fashion a gentleman or noble person in vertuous and gentle discipline,"[56]—including the pastoral cantos of Book VI—appeared in the year that Fletcher's father died. With Spenser and Sidney both reinforcing the authority of the ancient and Renaissance pastoral, it is not surprising that the play in which Fletcher strove most definitely to satisfy high artistic standards should have been written in that aristocratic mode.

The vogue of the lyrics about shepherds and their Bonibels had also not ended; and Drayton began to publish his pastoral poems in 1593, with his *Idea, the Shepherd's Garland.* Beaumont, whose family home was not many miles distant from Polesworth Hall in Warwickshire, where Drayton had spent his youth, became his loved friend, and through him, well acquainted with other bucolic poets like William Browne. Fletcher, perhaps through his friendship with Beaumont, knew them, too.[57] An interest in Spenser and the pastoralists, moreover, appears to have been common to this generation of Fletchers. John's younger cousins, Phineas and Giles, were poets of the Spenserian tradition. Phineas wrote both a set of *Piscatorial Eclogues* and a play of arcadian fishermen, *Sicelides*. It is quite possible that, had John not been church-outed by his father's embroilment with Elizabeth and sequent death in debt, we should know of him today only as a clergyman who, like his cousins, wrote poetry mainly in the pastoral vein.

Probably more important as a formative influence on Beaumont's tastes than any of these, and equally important with the pastoral influence even on Fletcher, was Sir Philip Sidney's romantic prose "epic," *Arcadia*, published in 1591, the year when Fletcher matriculated at Cambridge. It was the prose volume most in fashion during their university days; nor was it less admired at the time Massinger was at Oxford.

Sidney had been, for many, the deeply admired incarnation of the Elizabethan gentleman or courtier. His extensive romance, pastoral in atmosphere, chivalric in much of its content and spirit, and influenced in form both by the classical epic and by such late Greek romances as Heliodorus' *Theagenes and Chariclea*, was highly respected even by scholars. As Tillyard points out,[58] Sidney's treatment of his material with academic correctness lifted the whole status of romance for late Elizabethans and Jacobeans. His romance was written with gentlemanly urbanity, and it embedded some serious political thought.

With its lyrical and "conceited" style, its complicated web of heroic adventures and chivalrous combats, its entangled and romantic love intrigues, and its loquacious if rather shadowy and unreal characters, the *Arcadia* must have delighted our lads. It was just the book to become a major formative influence on the tastes of these youthful gentlemen, whether or not they fully grasped Sidney's noble spirit. When Beaumont ridiculed the plebian romances of the lower classes in *The Knight of the Burning Pestle*, it was not as an opponent of romance in general, but because he found these writings absurd in comparison with Sidney's aristocratic masterpiece and, possibly, Ariosto's wittily disenchanted treatment of his *Orlando Furioso*.

The *Arcadia's* employment of disguisings, its somewhat melodramatic heroics, its aristocratic atmosphere, its courtly manners, its centering of interest on a web of stories and a variety of characters rather than on one commanding figure, its emphasis on the friendship of Musidorus and Pyrocles, its artificial but eloquent passions and sentiments, its chivalric and ardently amorous young knights—these and other ingredients are not altogether unrelated to the manner of tragicomedy and tragedy later developed by Beaumont and Fletcher. They were, in fact, to draw upon the romance directly for plot materials, notably in *Cupid's Revenge*. Moreover, Massinger's chivalrous quality in such plays as *The Great Duke of*

Florence may quite probably owe something to the spirit of Sidney's "epic." Indeed, it would be difficult to over-estimate the effect which the *Arcadia* had on the imaginations of upper class youths of our playwrights' generation.

With the *kudos* which the *Arcadia* conferred upon romances in general, it would be surprising if our youths did not feel justified—should they feel any justification to be needed—in exploring the range of the fiction of their day. Fletcher's command of Italian not only enabled him to investigate Italian pastoral drama but gave him the key to reading the racy or melodramatic stories of Boccaccio's *Decameron* in the original. This collection of tales was later to be one of his hunting-grounds for plots. Other Italian *novelle* were also available to our playwrights; particularly accessible were such omnibuses of translated stories as Painter's *Palace of Pleasure*. These collections, levied on by Shakespeare and his fellow-dramatists, were also pleasantly adapted to whiling away our undergraduates' idle hours.

These Italian tales, and their English counterparts, put their emphasis on story—on dark passions and sensational deeds, or on comic situations, often of the fabliau sort. Improbabilities abounded, and strange, fantastic events. Atmosphere might be built up, but characterization was usually rudimentary; indeed, the characters were rarely more than puppets of the story. English romances, such as those written by Lodge and Greene, likewise placed emphasis on plentiful story rather than on characterization. Sometimes they also exploited a euphuistic style, and gave their characters long soliloquies of love-casuistry. Euphuism was, however, a dead fashion by the time our playwrights began to write; and the long soliloquies and dialogues about love were too static for dramatic purposes. These elements were, therefore, useless to them, though Beaumont's fondness for metaphors may bear some faint resemblance to Sidney's use of conceits.

The fiction which the Elizabethans read, then, whether of foreign or native growth, gave little attention to motivation of actions or to realistic truth to life. Even as in the *Arcadia*, abundance and variety of event and striking, even daring situations were emphasized. Of the dramatists, Shakespeare most successfully brought to life such wooden figures as were endemic in the fiction purveyed for Elizabethans and Jacobeans: witness his signal success in transforming Lodge's *Rosalynde* into *As You Like It*, or Arthur Brooke's flaccid poem, *Romeus and Juliet*, into its brilliant stage successor, pulsing with ardent, young first-love.

In view of our playwrights' much lesser success in this respect, it is worth glancing at the fact that the strong modern demand for consistency in characterization appears to be a concomitant of the development of modern science. A pervasive awareness of cause and effect relationships in scientific matters leads to a concern for proper motivation of passions and actions. Such an awareness was not strong before the Restoration era; it is no accident that modern realistic fiction was born in the eighteenth century. Even Shakespeare, with his extraordinary intuitive grasp of the workings of human nature, was content to retain from his sources glaring improbabilities of plotting and motivation which a modern dramatist would hardly dare to employ, except in fantasy.

Fletcher was, on the whole, satisfied to make theatrically effective use of the kind of story materials he had found, in his younger days, in the *Arcadia* and a wealth of other fiction, or which he later discovered in D'Urfé's *Astrée* or in Spanish narratives. So, though perhaps to a lesser degree, were the other two playwrights. Allowance must be made for the influence of the "humour" technique, introduced by Chapman and developed by Jonson. But none of our playwrights had a highly evolved sense of character in our own understanding of the term; careful, realistic motivation or rounded individualization usually concerned them relatively little or, in Fletcher's case, hardly at all. They might, on occasion, improve on the character drawing they found in their plot sources; but to them, as to the writers of narrative, situation mattered more.

Our three playwrights were thus, in considerable if unequal measure, transmitters rather than transmuters of the sort of materials they had first discovered in the *Arcadia* and other fiction of their youth. All, and especially Massinger, may have caught something—more or less—of the underlying political seriousness and the sophisticated urbanity of Sidney's romance. Massinger, at any rate, had developed an interest in political history in his undergraduate days. But their major aims as playwrights were: to select piquant situations and arresting, contrasted passions from the abundant stock of these in tales and other plot-sources (even when they were not drawing directly on any particular narrative); to handle these technically with all the up-to-date theatrical devices they could muster; and to shape their treasure-trove to the taste of upper-class spectators, to many of whom Sidney's masterpiece was familiar. And what was this, in one sense, but a return to the tradition of the *Arcadia?*

IV

Sometime in the summer of 1599, the handsomest public theatre which had yet been built in Greater London, the octagonal Globe near Maiden Lane on the Bankside, Southwark, was opened by the Lord Chamberlain's Men. Its acting star was Richard Burbage, whose father, James, had erected the first public playhouse, The Theatre, adjoining Finsbury Field, in 1576. Among the five other "householders" who, in addition to the Burbage brothers, jointly owned the new building was William Shakespeare, a leading actor as well as the outstanding dramatist of the company. As for the playhouse itself, it had been partially constructed out of the timbers of The Theatre, dismantled for this purpose.[59]

In the following year, the Fortune, north of London wall not far from Cripplegate, arose to furnish a new home for the Lord Admiral's Men, driven to abandon the old Rose on the Bankside as outmoded because of the resplendent new Globe nearby. The Fortune was built by Philip Henslowe and by Edward Alleyn, Burbage's rival in acting prestige, to the specifications of the Globe except for a shape square instead of octagonal. By the end of November or early in December, 1600, it was ready for the occupancy of the Lord Admiral's players.[60]

Meanwhile the private theatres, with their companies of child actors and their smaller, more select clienteles, were stirring once more, after ten dormant years, into renewed activity. Sometime during the season of 1599-1600 the Children of St. Paul's resumed acting,[61] probably at their old hall in a building near the Cathedral.[62] In the autumn of 1600, the Children of the Chapel Royal at Windsor began their eight years' reign at the finest of private indoor theatres, the Blackfriars, owned by the Burbages and located within the city walls but outside the city's jurisdiction.[63] Thus, the turn of the century saw three of the leading companies of the next decade splendidly housed.

Among the young gentlemen of literary tastes and playgoing inclinations who must have responded to the stimulation of these vigorous new theatrical ventures were the youthful law student, Beaumont, and Fletcher, just come of age. Possibly they were already beginning to entertain aspirations to write for the private playhouses, for whose child actors their first plays were, a few years later, to be created. Certainly they must, on various occasions, have been rowed across the Thames to see Burbage as Hamlet and in various other roles of Shakespeare's plays, new and old, at the Globe. Probably, too, they made visits beyond Cripplegate to watch the acting of Edward Alleyn at the Fortune. But we can be especially confident that our two young men attended many of the Paul's and Blackfriars productions. For the new children's companies, and notably the one at Blackfriars, were rapidly becoming the fad of the moment among the denizens of the Inns of Court and among other young aristocrats and gentleman-commoners.

If the old and small play-hall of Paul's Boys was not altogether up-to-the-minute in equipment, the recent and much admired Blackfriars assuredly was. Indeed, it provided the model for later private theatres such as the Salisbury Court and the Phoenix or Cockpit.[64] It is probable, as we shall see, that this new second Blackfriars had a thoroughly satisfactory multiple-stage structure very similar to that which had been developed at the old Theatre and that which was built into the new Globe, likewise Burbage theatres.

The new Blackfriars, in fact, had been constructed to house the Lord Chamberlain's company. James Burbage had spent considerable sums of money in 1596 to purchase the old Frater building of the former Black-friars monastery, and to equip it as a theatre.[65] Had Burbage not been frustrated in his plans by the dwellers in the precincts, who successfully opposed the theatre's use by professional players,[66] Fletcher and Beaumont would doubtless have found Shakespeare's company domiciled at Blackfriars. As things stood, however, James Burbage's sons must have been pleased to rent the idle playhouse in 1600 for the use of the Children of the Chapel.[67]

Before being checkmated in his plans, James Burbage had thrown together the Parlor and the adjoining hall of the Frater Building to create his theatre. We know that the resulting auditorium measured 66 feet in length and 46 in width. Moreover, the Parlor, which seems to have been originally the dining room of the monastery must, together with the Hall, have had unusual height.[68] Burbage, after twenty years of experience with The Theatre and other public playhouses, was not likely to have invested heavily in a building in which the rooms used for the auditorium would not permit a stage structure equivalent in flexibility to that of the public theatres.

The "tiring-house" facade, and the abutting rear edge of the stage, measured forty one feet across at the Globe, according to Adams' calculations.[69] Since Blackfriars was forty six feet across, there would have been no difficulty in creating a facade for it of the same width. It may, however, have been somewhat narrower.[70] As for height, the plays written especially for the children's company which occupied this theatre from 1600 to 1608 call for all the features which Adams has so fully described in his *The Globe Playhouse*. Careful observation of stage directions will at once reveal that full use was made not only of the platform stage, the inner stage and the side doors of the first level, but also, on the second level, of the upper inner stage or chamber, the bay window balconies at each side of the facade above the doors, and even of the tarras which ran between the bay windows at the front of the chamber.

It should be evident from these facts that the Blackfriars stage had at least two levels—and this suggests that it would have the corresponding two galleries. For Burbage, as a practical builder, would be certain to get as much seating space as he could into his relatively small hall. And indeed, without galleries it is hard to estimate how anything like a thousand persons—the round figure normally alluded to in contemporary references to the hall's seating capacity[71]—could have been crowded into this auditorium.

There may even have been a third stage level, and a corresponding third gallery. Plays written after 1608 or 1609 had to be technically suitable for playing in both the Blackfriars and the Globe, regardless of which theatre was the scene of their premiere, if they were to be acceptable to the King's Men's Company. Yet Adams has shown, in his *Globe Playhouse*, that certain plays belonging to this category, including *The Tempest* and the Fletcher-Massinger *The Double Marriage*, appear to have made use of the Musician's Room on the third level directly above the inner stage—in the latter instance as a mast-top from which an approaching ship was distinguished.[72] The Frater Parlor and Hall need not have had the full 35 foot height of the Globe to permit the construction of three levels.

Whether the tiring-house structure provided three levels, however, or two, it is significant that James Burbage, in equipping the theatre in 1596 with an eye to its use by his own men's company, appears to have given it the same sort of multiple stage with which he had been familiar in the public playhouses. As a result, the boy actors, and later the King's Men, doubtless had an acting structure almost if not exactly as flexible as the Globe or the Fortune. Budding playwrights could study the technique of writing for a multiple stage quite as well here as they could at the public theatres. Fletcher's skill in utilizing all features which his acting areas provided—a skill on which Miss Hatcher remarked—could thus have been at least partially acquired at Blackfriars.

This theatre, and in some respects Paul's as well, possessed certain advantages over the outdoor playhouses. Since the private theatre was roofed in, its patrons were free from the danger of drenchings by sudden showers, and in cold weather the auditorium could be heated. The stage likewise had the advantage of artificial lighting, even if only by clusters of candles. Although such lighting could not be controlled to produce effects in the manner of the modern theatre, it could set off costumes and stage pictures to greater advantage than the plain daylight of outdoor playhouses.[73] It is therefore not surprising to find, as J. Isaacs has brought out,[74] that spectacular effects—no doubt often of great aesthetic charm—flourished increasingly down to 1642 in the plays written for Blackfriars.

Since the auditorium was small as well as completely enclosed, it was peculiarly suited to songs and music. From the first, the new Blackfriars was notable for its concerts, apparently of about an hour's length, that preceded the performances.[75] Moreover, most of the plays written specially for its boys made opportunities for the introduction of music, songs, dancing or even small masques. The youths of the company were often accomplished dancers, musicians and singers as well as actors. Ostensibly they had been taken up to be trained as choir boys of the Chapel Royal at Windsor.[76]

It was because of these practices of the Blackfriars children during the eight years following 1600 quite as much as because of the increasing popularity of Jacobean masques[77] that Beaumont, Fletcher and Shakespeare included such elements in the dramas which Thorndike discussed. About the time that *Philaster* and *Cymbeline* were written, all three playwrights became aware that their dramas would be performed at the new winter home of the King's Men as well as at the Globe. Indeed, one reason why Beaumont and Fletcher may have begun writing for the King's Men at this time may have been that they understood so well how to supply the ingredients desired by Blackfriars audiences. Accustomed, even during Elizabeth's reign, to delight in spectacular court entertainments, these theatregoers did not cease to relish such garnishings of plays when the Children of the Revels Company gave way to the King's Men.

Thus the tendency, which grew upon Jacobean drama, to include elements of spectacle actually goes back, in the private theatres, to 1600—and beyond, into lavish entertainments devised for Elizabeth and her courtiers. The aristocratic taste for spectacle was thus created long before Fletcher or Beaumont appeared on the dramatic horizon. But in 1600 and succeeding years both were young enough to have delighted in the effects of music, song, masquing and pageantry that graced the plays of the "little apes," especially at Blackfriars. Here, then, appears to have been one of the significant roots of our playwrights' gentlemanly tendency towards the spectacular.

V

Boy actors such as Fletcher and Beaumont often watched at Blackfriars and Paul's were no new phenomenon on the English stage. Such youngsters had dominated the theatrical world from 1515 to 1580, and had been active in it until 1590—but almost exclusively as purveyors of entertainment to the royal courts, or in the halls of aristocrats.[78] Except for John Lyly, however, the boys' companies ceased, in the 1580's, to attract the ablest playwrights; it was for the new commercial playhouses, now in the ascendency, that such men as Kyd, Peele, Greene and Marlowe found it profitable to write their best plays, if not all of them. The children had held their own for as long as men and boys alike performed the same kinds of immature drama—moralities, farces, classical romances—before undemanding audiences avid for plays.[79] But the more masculine new drama such as the "university wits" introduced was beyond the youths' acting capacities. As Hillebrand remarks, "If the lads had sprightliness, vivacity, pertness and charm, they lacked power to portray serious and deep emotions."[80] So the last sixteenth century company of child-actors—Paul's Boys, whom Lyly's plays had kept afloat—were forced by a government inhibition to give up the unequal struggle by 1590,[81] when Shakespeare was about to begin his career as playwright.

Thus, when the boy companies of Paul's, and of the Chapel Children at Blackfriars, were revived about 1600, they faced formidable competition from the men, whose dramatic fare had advanced rapidly in the intervening decade. The new private theatres were, moreover, now operated on a commercial basis, like the public ones.[82] The problem of their managers was, therefore, how to create productions which would successfully rival those of the men's companies, and in such a way as to compensate for the limitations of the boys as actors.

One solution, as we have seen, was to exploit the talents of the lads for singing, dancing and instrumental music, because of the known appeal of these to such theatregoers as could afford the high scale of prices.[83] This was an important element in the Blackfriars' success, especially from 1600 to 1603. Another was to lure away experienced playwrights from Henslowe and other managers to provide suitable new vehicles for the boys. Then, too, the patrons might find a special charm in bawdry issuing from the pert mouths and actions of young lads; Fletcher and Beaumont were far from the first playwrights to introduce piquant situations and witty indecency as spicery to entertain the gentry and the upper middle-class theatregoers.

Partly because bawdry could be more safely dispensed under cover of apparent moral purpose it was, moreover, a happy thought to exploit the new trend for "humour" characters, comical satire and personal lampoon. The impudent grace of the boys might well allow them to carry off remarks which might lead to trouble in the mouths of men. Moreover, the Inns-of-Court students, courtiers, university graduates and other such patrons of these theatres would, no doubt, especially enjoy the witty, and even derisive, comic or satirical exposure of figures dominated by absurd humours and social affectations—especially when these seemed to glance at persons of their own acquaintance.[84] Though the Blackfriars managers were to find, by more than one unpleasant clash with the authorities, that satire even in the mouths of lads might be dangerous, they were not to succeed in digesting this lesson.[85] After all, daring passages in the plays filled the auditorium.

Here was a variety of ingredients, then, well calculated to amuse a more limited and aristocratic clientele than that of the public playhouses. A few romantic or Senecan melodramas—perhaps flavored with satire also —would vary the dramatic fare, but obviously the staple would have to be comedy of some sort. That Blackfriars, and in lesser degree Paul's, succeeded by these means in draining off some part of the better paying customers from the public theatres is well attested by the famous passage in Hamlet about the "little eyases."[86] Fletcher and Beaumont must have found no difficulty in grasping the reasons for this popularity.

It is significant that we discover Jonson and Chapman writing for Blackfriars, and Marston for Paul's Boys, soon after these companies began playing. In 1597 George Chapman had initiated the comedy of humours with *A Humourous Day's Mirth* while both he and his good friend, Ben Jonson, were laboring for Henslowe and the Admiral's Men. The next year Jonson followed this example with the much superior *Every Man in His Humour*, produced by the King's Men. Then, on June 1, 1599, the Archbishop of Canterbury and the Bishop of London issued their restraining order against the verse and prose satirists, Marston among them, decreeing also that "noe *Satyres* or *Epigrams* be printed hereafter."[87] This led Jonson immediately to attempt to distil the dramatic equivalent of classical satire into *Every Man Out of His Humour*, his first derisive "comicall satyre." Blackfriars then secured his second and third ones, *Cynthia's Revels* and *The Poetaster*, in 1600-01. It is perhaps illustrative of Jonson's careful workmanship that both the latter were excellently adapted to the abilities of the boy-actors.

The young Oxford graduate and Inns-of-Court law student, John Marston, had established his reputation as a satirist in 1598 with *The Metamorphosis of Pygmalion's Image and Certain Satires* and *The Scourge of Villainy*. Shortly after his two volumes were banned by the restraining order of the next year, Paul's Boys secured his services as a playwright. He appears to have paralleled Jonson in the effort to circumvent the censorship by losing no time in preparing for this company his own first venture into comical satire, *Antonio and Mellida*.[88] Thereafter he supplied the private theatres, in a gentlemanly way, with seven or eight other vehicles, most of them satiric in purpose. About 1608, however, he retired from playwriting and took holy orders.[89]

Apparently in 1602, Chapman appeared as Jonson's successor at Blackfriars, supplying the lads for some years with humour comedies, and tragedies based on French history. Probably in 1604, Thomas Middleton furnished Paul's Boys with a comical satire, *The Phoenix*, and then proceeded to turn out a series of satirical comedies of London life for the two children's companies.[90] Thus, at least until 1608, Middleton, Chapman and Marston were all giving their playwriting services exclusively to the private theatres. It is worth noting, in this connection, that they and Jonson were four of the five dramatists—the other being Shakespeare— whose work attracted the closest scrutiny from Fletcher and Beaumont during the years of preparation for their own careers as playwrights.

A few of the ablest satirical plays of the decade were performed by the King's Men. Notable among these were Shakespeare's *Troilus and Cressida, Measure for Measure* and *Coriolanus,* Jonson's *Volpone,* and Marston's *The Malcontent.* The reservations should be made, however, that *Troilus and Cressida* is now thought to have been written for a special Inns-of-Court performance,[91] and that *The Malcontent,* a Blackfriars play, was requisitioned by the King's Men as compensation for the boys' illicit production of their own *The Spanish Tragedy.*[92] Indeed, a decided majority of the plays with satirical elements appear to have been performed either at Blackfriars or else at Paul's. Even Chapman's best tragedy, *Bussy D'Ambois,* had long passages of satire which provided this form of amusement for the gentleman patrons of the latter theatre.

It is therefore readily understandable why Beaumont's first play, *The Woman-Hater,* acted by Paul's Boys, should have devoted itself to presenting satirically a group of humour figures, and why the drama he may well have written next, *The Knight of the Burning Pestle,* given at Blackfriars, should have been a burlesque. Likewise, that humour characters such as Bessus of *A King and No King,* and satirical elements such as we have noted in *The Loyal Subject,* should have been incorporated into romantic plays of our corpus is the natural afterglow of our playwrights' theatregoing in these years.

VI

On some occasion in the years immediately following Beaumont's arrival in London, and while satiric comedy was the dominant mode of the private playhouses as Shakespearean tragedy was at the Globe, our two young gentlemen met. Aside from mutual personal attraction and a joint delight in wit, there must also have been, from the start, sufficient congruence of tastes so that they would be drawn towards the dramatic collaboration which was so evidently the fruit of warm friendship.

A shared interest in upper-class forms of literature and drama was assuredly a strong sympathetic link between them. We have already seen that one of their conditionings towards an exotic, aristocratic world in their more serious plays was the type of fiction which they read in youth and of which Sidney's *Arcadia* was the honored exemplar in prose, Spenser's enchanted realm of faerie in verse. We have also noted that Fletcher was steeped in the whole pastoral tradition, and have only to consider certain descriptive speeches in *Philaster*[93] to realize that Beaumont was not untouched by it, even if we discount his friendship for Drayton and other bucolic poets. Equally a bond would be the young men's delight in the prevailing comedies with satiric intent of Jonson, Chapman, Marston, Middleton and, perhaps, Shakespeare.

As young men of marked, if somewhat different, natural endowments, it was with considerable eclecticism that Fletcher and Beaumont diligently studied or unconsciously absorbed their craftsmanship from these playwrights. Nor can such absorption always be pinned down specifically. The two young men were open to all the dramatic trade-winds of their milieu—even to learning what not to do from some of the characteristically middle-class plays of Heywood and others. This recreation at such inferior theatres as the Rose and the Curtain was, in fact, to pay dividends of laughter in *The Knight of the Burning Pestle*.

Yet it has become conventional to assume that Jonson was the master of Beaumont and had a lesser but still considerable influence on Fletcher. The rest of the field, if we except Shakespeare, has been relatively little emphasized. Thus Miss Kerr, in her *Influence of Ben Jonson on English Comedy, 1598-1642*, asserted that "As playwrights Beaumont and Fletcher learned most from Jonson in ideals of constructive excellence."[94] From him, also, was derived their technique in humour characters and in satire, while Beaumont was his disciple in blank verse.[95]

Let us admit at once that Jonson could, and indeed did, teach our playwrights something—and Beaumont probably more than Fletcher. In their first years of theatre-going they may have managed to see performed —and they could certainly have read and studied as well—Ben's four achievements in humour comedy and comical satire for the King's Men and Blackfriars. Moreover, they could have imbibed some quantity of dramatic wisdom direct from him. For by 1606 or 1607 and doubtless somewhat earlier they were his friends—and Chapman's and Shakespeare's as well, since all were of the Mermaid Tavern fellowship. Of the convivial meetings, Beaumont has left us a picture; there he had

> heard words that have been
> So nimble and so full of subtle flame
> As if that everyone from whom they came
> Had meant to put his whole wit in a jest,
> And had resolved to live a fool the rest
> Of his dull life; . . .[96]

Jonson loved jesting and good fellowship. He was also never averse to discussing his theories of play construction, nor the ancient dramatic practices which gave them foundation. Nor was he chary of trenchant criticisms on the dramas of others.

That our playwrights, and especially Beaumont, admired Jonson's dramatic principles and his plays, their prefatory poems to the first editions of *Volpone* and later dramas make clear.[97] So does Beaumont's famous verse-letter to Ben, already quoted from, and probably written at Grace Dieu, whence the young playwright hoped that "strong destiny, which all controls," would soon return him to London:

> 'twill once again
> Bring me to thee, who wilt make smooth and plain
> The way of knowledge for me, and then I
> Who have no good in me but simplicity,
> Know that it will my greatest comfort be
> To acknowledge all the rest to come from thee.[98]

But despite the flattering and graceful compliment conveyed in these lines, and Jonson's statement to Drummond in 1619 "that Chapman and Fletcher were loved of him,"[99] it is possible to read too much into this friendly relationship. Indeed, Miss Kerr herself acknowledged that Jonson, in his thirties, was a less awesome figure among his fellow-dramatists than he was later to be with a new generation of literary youths. It is therefore pertinent to consider Miss Kerr's unilateral claims for Ben in the light of what Beaumont and Fletcher may have absorbed, by means of theatre-going and occasional reading, from the plays of other dramatists.

Miss Kerr considered the two young men to have been "quick and intelligent pupils" of Jonson in several respects. One of these was "In the management of detail with constant reference to the entire plot and regard for complete unity of impression."[100] If so, they learned their lesson but indifferently. Both playwrights, and notably Fletcher, were as much concerned with the management of details so as to make the individual scene or the immediate sequence of scenes effective as they were with detail in relation to the whole. Although they aimed to draw all threads together into an elaborate, and often concealed, denouement, this particular method for insuring some degree of unity of effect was probably developed, as we shall see later, from various sources. There may be some cross-influence between the denouement of *The Silent Woman*, wherein the name character is discovered to be a boy, and that of *Philaster*, in which Bellario reveals herself as a maiden. But both Julia in *The Two Gentlemen of Verona* and Viola in *Twelfth Night* similarly unmask at the end, although the audience is not surprised thereby; and such masqueradings are a stock ingredient of prose romance as well as of drama. Moreover, the evidence is insufficient to determine which play was produced first.[101]

And yet it is certain that Beaumont and Fletcher did acquire from Ben a regard for some aspects of construction which make for unity of impression. The young playwrights themselves testify to this. Beaumont, in his commendatory verses on Jonson's *Volpone,* lauded

> the art which thou alone
> Hast taught our tongue, the rules of time, of place,
> And other rites, delivered with the grace
> Of comic style, which only is far more
> Than any English stage hath known before.[102]

The prefatory lines by Fletcher on the same play are to somewhat similar, if more generalized, effect; Ben's friends, he asserted, could not "praise Enough the wit, art, language of the plays."[103]

We have noted that the neo-classical Dryden considered Beaumont and Fletcher "more regular" than Shakespeare, and that Miss Hatcher adjudged Fletcher, in his own plays, satisfactory as to the unities of time and place.[104] So with Beaumont. None of the plays in which either had a main share sprawls, in these respects, as does Shakespeare's *Anthony and Cleopatra* or *Pericles.* Here Jonson's theory and practice evidently made an impression on our playwrights. In addition, Beaumont especially appears to have had something of Jonson's interest in shaping up a plot to create unity of impression, as the best plays in which he had the sole or an important hand reveal. Indeed, Beaumont's own temperament, which won him the epithet of judicious, bore some resemblance to Jonson's, though he had little of the latter's determination to enforce moral lessons through his dramas.

But whatever the younger men may have learned from Jonson about construction, neither was quite so rigorous as Ben in the pursuit of the unities. Both had no hesitation in blending diverse elements of farce, romance and tragedy into a single drama—a practice to which Jonson, with his concern for correct literary forms, was not prone. And as Miss Hatcher demonstrated, Fletcher, in his concern to supply his plays with abundance and variety of action, sometimes ran two or more plots side by side with the lightest of connections,[105] in quite the old-fashioned Elizabethan and, indeed, Middletonian way. Yet he, too, could blend his plot materials skilfully into a unified effect when he chose, as in *Rule a Wife,* or secure a deftly juxtaposed emotional variety from his two or more plot-strands, as in *The Custom of the Country.*

In order to increase the liveliness of a play, Fletcher sometimes violated unity with amusing but irrelevant scenes. This was not dissimilar to the practice of satiric dramatists in introducing into their comedies, purely to arouse laughter or derision in the spectators, minor ridiculous characters unconnected with the plot. It would prove illuminating to cut from the comedies of Marston, Chapman and Middleton characters who, so far as the stories go, would never be missed. Indeed, one could thus eliminate the whole of Beaumont's disconnected minor strand in *The Woman-Hater* wherein the mercer, enamoured of scholarship, is gulled by the pander, posing as a student, into marrying a whore.[106] Fletcher may well have acquired the trick of the irrelevant but entertaining character or scene from observing satirical comedies. He could not notably have done so, however, from those of Jonson.

Another respect in which Miss Kerr found our playwrights to be pupils of Ben was in the sound preparation for the entrances of important characters.[107] But Shakespeare had demonstrated skill in this aspect of craftsmanship before Jonson made his first success as a playwright. Moreover, one of the devices of comical satire was to present a description of a character's follies or traits before he began to expose himself in action.

Furthermore, it may be well to point out, in this connection, that the satirical plays in general are loaded with passages in which the figures describe one another's characters. This device of characterizing, from the outside, by means of a running commentary from the dramatis personae was also, as Thorndike perceived,[108] relied upon to a great degree by Beaumont and Fletcher. Shakespeare likewise used this method markedly in *Cymbeline* and his two following dramatic romances. It is, for instance, worth noting how much of the characterization of Imogen in *Cymbeline* proceeds from the mouths of other characters. Our playwrights and Shakespeare all acquired this technical device from the general practice of comical satire by Jonson and others—and, in Shakespeare's case, from his own experience with this kind of play as well.[109]

Miss Kerr also visioned Fletcher and Beaumont as under the tutelage of Ben in "the clever invention of tricks and skilful conduct of intrigue."[110] No doubt there is some truth in this, especially as regards Beaumont. Nor is Miss Kerr's statement contestable that the younger men included, in some of their plots, "tricks equal in wit and ingenuity to those invented by Jonson."[111] But her mention of *The Tamer Tamed* (or *The Woman's Prize*) calls to mind at once the play to which it is indebted and of which it is the inverse sequel, *The Taming of the Shrew*. And that suggests Shakespeare's witty skill in presenting, in *Much Ado About Nothing*, the gulling of Beatrice and Benedict into acknowledgement of love for each other—a series of situations precisely of a sort to delight the man who wrote *The Wild-Goose Chase*. The unmasking of Parolles in *All's Well That Ends Well* is quite as likely to have been on the fringes of Beaumont's consciousness, when he was creating Bessus, as the posturing of Bobadil and his exposure by Downright in *Every Man in His Humour*.[112]

Nor are the dramatists of the private theatres to be overlooked. All of them could manage clever intrigue. Marston's impact on our playwrights may have been greater in other directions than in this. But the intrigue is ably handled in *What You Will*. Therein Francisco is disguised as Albano, the missing husband of Celia, with a resulting series of farcical confusions when Albano turns up, confronts his identical image, and both are taken for imposters.[113] These situations (slightly reminiscent of *The Comedy of Errors*), like the tricks which Cockledemoy plays on Mulligrub in *The Dutch Courtesan* and those whereby Dulcimel wins her man in *The Fawn*, are ingenious and witty in a way sure to have appealed to the farceur in Fletcher, and doubtless to Beaumont as well.

Chapman, too, may have added to their fund of instruction in the art of intrigue. His comic force, as Parrott has observed, lay "in incident and situation rather than in character or dialogue."[114] The strategems are cleverly executed by which, in his well-plotted *All Fools*, the various characters cross-gull each other, under the prompting of the roguish young scholar, Rinaldo, until all have been fooled, as the title promises—even Rinaldo. *May Day*, though unmoral and rather bawdy in tone, is also amusing in its intrigues. Like *All Fools* and some of Fletcher's plays, it undoubtedly needs staging to come fully alive. Its intriguer, Lodovico—goodhumored, abundantly full of animal spirits, witty, harebrained—strikingly foreshadows some of Fletcher's most ebullient young gentlemen. *The Widow's Tears* has as fantastic a set of intrigues, in Tharsalio's wooing of the widow Eudora and in the courting of Cynthia in the supposed tomb of her husband, Lysander, as can be met with in any play of our corpus. It would, moreover, be difficult to match, in any of our dramas, the completely cynical tone which Chapman gave this play.[115]

Unlike Jonson and Marston, however, he does not ordinarily treat his characters derisively. He normally puts them through their antics without showing his hand, and such plays as *All Fools*, *May Day* and *Monsieur D'Olive* have a merry, if unmoral, note. Chapman had, in comedy, less depth and intensity than Jonson, but greater lightness of touch, and in these respects he anticipates our playwrights. Except for his treatment of the informers in *The Woman-Hater*,[116] Beaumont handles his intrigue in somewhat the merry spirit most often encountered in his friend's comedies.

Except when Chapman could lean on some other playwright, such as Terence in *All Fools* or Piccolomini in *May Day*, Middleton was a defter craftsman in handling intrigue. It is from the latter that Fletcher may well have learned most, from the standpoint of stagecraft, in this matter. Dunkel, in his study of Middleton's technique as practiced in his London comedies, has shown that the playwright's chief purpose was to present humorous intrigues and escapades one after another, and with such rapidity of motion that they aroused increasing interest in his audience.[117] The exposition is simple but clear, the complications are developed briskly, and the strategems frequently have the extravagance of farce, as in the clever sequence of scenes in *A Mad World, My Masters*, during which Follywit and his companions rob Sir Bounteous Progress.[118] As Miss Hatcher has pointed out, Fletcher's plays show the same tendencies.

Middleton was not so much concerned with binding his intrigues into a rigid unity. He linked his plots more skilfully than usual in *A Mad World, My Masters*, because the courtesan, Frank Gullman, was central to both of them; and *Your Five Gallants*, with part of the structure of a comical satire, is controlled by the intriguer and exposer, Fitsgrave. More commonly, however, such jointure consisted of the bonds of kinship or friendship between certain characters, or their mere presence in two or more plot strands. Miss Hatcher has shown that Fletcher used similar devices of linking, including the master-servant relationship.[119]

Middleton, moreover, with his interest in action and in stage effectiveness, was more concerned with the motivation of situations than of characters. This, too, was characteristic of Fletcher and, to a lesser degree, of Beaumont. All three dramatists had a tendency to place the preparation for a new turn of the action in the scene preceding its occurrence. Beaumont and Fletcher, however, often preferred surprise to such motivation. Middleton, with his sense of the irony of situation, normally took his audience into his confidence and thus aroused anticipation. But in his desire to keep his intrigues moving forward and in new directions, he sometimes failed to prepare for a change in a character's attitude, as when Thomasine, the wife of Quomodo in *Michaelmas Term*, surprisingly decided to aid her husband's victim, Easy.[120]

Middleton may also have made some contribution to the technique of the Beaumont and Fletcher denouements. He builds up to them skilfully, places them in the last scene, makes them theatrically effective, and then ends his play quickly. His rascals, if clever, often escape retribution, just as Jonson's do. His denouements, however, are simpler than those of our playwrights and, in part at least, anticipated by the audience.

If Jonson was, thus, not the only playwright who had something to teach our young men about "the clever invention of tricks and the skilful conduct of intrigue," neither was he their sole guide to the creation of the "humour" figure.[121] That they studied such characters in Jonson's first popular success, *Every Man in His Humour*, his sequent comical satires, and his later masterpiece, *Volpone,* is, however, indisputable. Jonson, by both his practice and his theorizing, had made himself an authority on the matter.

The type character of Elizabethan comedy had previously developed its own conventions, partly from the native tradition and partly from Roman and Italian comedy. The new kind of figure was a simplification of it. A humour character's talk and actions, from start to finish of a play, were dominated by a single ruling passion, affectation or even mannerism, although he might also have congruous subsidiary ones. As a result, he was less human than the more complex type figure, but better suited to satirical purposes because of his very simplicity.

The popular "characters" of Theophrastus, which likewise inspired the widespread character-writing of the seventeenth century, contributed to the conception of the humour figure. So did the derisive portraits in the verse satires of the 1590s, modelled on those of the Roman satirists. The humour character also had a considerable resemblance to the allegorical figure: to the personified vice, virtue or other abstract quality of the morality play, and to their descendants in Spenser's *The Faerie Queene.*

Other playwrights besides Jonson employed the humour character, and from these, also, Fletcher and Beaumont assuredly learned. Chapman, for instance, handled such figures as Monsieur D'Olive, and Quintilliano in *May Day,* with an amused detachment similar to his friend Beaumont's treatment of Lazarillo in *The Woman-Hater.* Marston's and Middleton's plays were also replete with characters whose humours were displayed, (and, in Marston's case, usually derided), while, as everyone knows, Shakespeare did not leave this field untouched.

Gondarino of *The Woman-Hater* may strike one as Jonsonian, but the informers of the same play possibly owe something to Dogberry and Verges of *Much Ado About Nothing.* The delightful Merrythought of *The Knight of the Burning Pestle* brings to mind rather the Clown, Feste's, singing in *Twelfth Night* than any figure in Jonson. The usurer, Morecraft, in *The Scornful Lady,* reforms from his greediness in a manner characteristic of Fletcher, but not of Jonson. Indeed, Fletcher, like Middleton, was always inclined to handle his humour characters farcically, as with Monsieur Thomas, the humourous lieutenant, or Lopez and Diego of *The Spanish Curate.*

Miss Kerr did note a difference between the treatment of types in Jonson and in Beaumont and Fletcher. While the former "seeks to emphasize the individuality of his representation of the type, they dwell almost always upon the class qualities."[122] In so far as this dictinction holds true of the simplified humour figures, it suggests an influence from Chapman and Middleton. The former succeeded in individualizing only a few such characters: Bassiolo in *The Gentleman Usher*, Monsieur D'Olive, and Quintilliano in *May Day*. Since intrigue took precedence over characterization with Middleton, it is not surprising to find that most of his humour figures lack individuality, and simply represent an affectation or folly characteristic of a certain social group, or else a particular sort of knavishness to be found in a special occupation. The Fletcher and Beaumont humour characters do not always lack individuality—for instance, Lopez or Lazarillo—but our playwrights had warrant for class figures in many plays they had witnessed.

There was, however, a way in which the technique developed by Jonson, and also used by Marston, for displaying the humours of many of their dramatis personae did influence Fletcher—and because of him, Beaumont and Massinger as collaborators. With this Miss Kerr does not deal, but Waith analyzes it with much penetration,[123] on the basis of Campbell's study of "comicall satyre."[124] This technique evolved by Jonson and Marston was their answer to the problem of employing the humour figure successfully in plays which transferred the derisive intent of verse satire to the stage.

In these plays, the one passion or mannerism which obsessed such figures was conceived of as a deformity to be displayed, censured, and eventually punished. Yet descriptions of these characters, and comments on their actions, although required by such a conception, involved a dangerously large amount of sheer exposition. Hence Jonson and Marston leaned heavily on the dramatic principle of antithesis.

The clear-headed censor and the buffoonish railer, as commentators, provided one such antithesis. Moreover, motion was imparted to scenes which could easily have degenerated into static character-sketches by bringing together figures of contrasting satirical types, such as the prodigal would-be gallant, Asotus, and the foppish returned traveller, Amorphus, of Jonson's *Cynthia's Revels*. In the interplay of such figures, the audience's interest was held, while the follies displayed by one character drew forth those of the other. Moreover, the entire structure of the play might be built upon an antithesis, as in *Every Man Out of His Humour*, or upon several nicely adjusted contrasts, as in *Cynthia's Revels*.[125]

As Waith expresses it, the basis of the comical satires of Jonson and Marston was "the conflict between extreme types of character—vice against vice, or vice against virtue. . . ."[126] He contends that Fletcher learned, from these plays, methods of throwing situations and character types into sharp antithesis, while eliminating the satirical purpose which underlay the methods. Hence, too, may have come Fletcher's tendency to simplify a character to a few traits, and then to exaggerate these traits for the sake of emotional conflict.[127]

It might be well to point out here that Spenser also made effective use of contrast in the whole structural plan of certain books of *The Faerie Queene,* as well as in his treatment of allegorical characters and situations. Romances of the type of *Arcadia,* moreover, may well have taught Fletcher something about the emotional possibilities of antithesis. Nonetheless, Waith has isolated an important dramatic influence on Fletcher —one which resulted from that playwright's keen observation of the methods of presenting humour characters in satirical comedy.

Miss Kerr, in discussing Jonson's influence on Fletcher's and Beaumont's humour figures, also found "a censor and satirical commentator on personage and action"[128]—apparently in the person of the Count—in *The Woman-Hater.* The Count, however, does not display the derisive scorn nor the buffoonish railing of the satirical commentators of Marston and Jonson, except in his biting deflation of the informers. He is a level-headed, non-impulsive gentleman, quite capable of pointed remarks. But he is much amused by the eccentricities of Lazarillo, whom he treats in a friendly way, and he is not too much disturbed by the behavior of his sister, Oriana, to keep his common sense. As for the robust Grocer and his literal-minded wife in *The Knight of the Burning Pestle,* also cited by Miss Kerr,[129] these personalities are genuinely original commentators, with ancestry but mistily traceable beyond their own creator's observation and wit. They do not censure other dramatis personae in the manner conventional to comical satire.

Finally, Miss Kerr asserted that "In his blank verse Beaumont certainly followed Jonson as master and teacher." His strict adherence to the regular line of ten syllables, his largely masculine caesura or internal pause, his "free dignified phrasing with many run on lines" she attributed to Jonson's influence.[130] There may be much truth in this position, though Beaumont used feminine endings, or eleven syllable verses, with more freedom than "strict adherence" suggests. But other critics have thought that his verse bears some resemblance to that which Shakespeare wrote from, say, *Romeo and Juliet* to *Twelfth Night.* Chapman may also have had some influence on Beaumont's blank verse technique.

Fletcher's verse Miss Kerr found essentially different from Ben's,[131] and so it is. In fact, it is highly individual, and was devised by Fletcher to give him a flexible medium which could range from the witty badinage of young gentlemen to the serious rhetoric of tragic scenes. Nonetheless, he may have acquired from Jonson a distaste for the flashier sorts of bombast and rant, and for obscurity in expression. Moreover, Middleton had already succeeded in writing dialogue which almost photographically reproduced the speech of actual men and women. Chapman had written *May Day,* as Parrott phrased it, "in the raciest and most idiomatic prose,"[132] and the blank verse of *All Fools* and *The Gentleman Usher* has just such a ready flow as we associate with Fletcher. Indeed, Parrott comments that "if a model for Fletcher's easy mastery of colloquial blank verse in comedy scenes is to be sought, it is to Chapman . . . that we must look."[133] Here, as elsewhere, then, our playwrights were doubtless eclectic in learning what the drama of their time had to teach.

VII

The popularity of comical satires, and of comedies of humor and intrigue, for the nine or ten years following the production of *Every Man in His Humour*, was a fact of major significance in the milieu of Fletcher and Beaumont. The native bent of both was towards light romance and comedy; neither had a profoundly tragic view of life, though Beaumont doubtless had a deeper sense of human destiny than Fletcher. The former appears to have had by nature an amused, satirical eye for the behavior of his fellowmen, combined with sober judgment. The gayer-hearted, more mercurial Fletcher had the sprightly wit and liveliness of the born farceur, joined to a liking for honesty and independence. Both had a taste for the aristocratic prose romance and for the fashionable pastoral. But if the chief non-dramatic source of their technique was the kind of romance first encountered in their youthful reading, the main dramatic one was the comedies which they watched with laughter but with appraising eyes during the years when they were haunting the theatres—one hopes together—in order to ferret out the mysteries of stage effectiveness.

In these comedies, Fletcher and Beaumont discovered certain ways of treating comic material which had continuing appeal to audiences, and especially to the more select clienteles of the private theatres. When, therefore, our playwrights turned to romantic and passionate substance in *Philaster*, they simply carried over into tragicomedy much of what they had learned at Paul's and Blackfriars—and from Jonson and Shakespeare. Their lively use, in this drama, of theatrecraft which had been time-tested in comedy was one of the main reasons for its success. Henceforth such stagecraft became one of the distinctive features of all their more serious plays.

It is for this reason that the basic ingredients of the theatrecraft in all the plays of our corpus tend to be surprisingly similar, and in tragicomedy and tragedy almost indistinguishable. From this springs the perception of critics that *The Maid's Tragedy* might have been so handled, in its later scenes, as to become a tragicomedy, and that *A King and No King* could easily have been given the tragic ending which some believe this drama needed. Largely from the same cause arise both the difficulty of classifying some of the plays as to type, and the recognition that the tragedies of our corpus, even at best, tend towards the operatic and sensational.

Several of the particular aspects of technique which we have already considered were employed in the more serious dramas of Beaumont and Fletcher. Dryden's comment on the superior regularity of our corpus to Shakespeare's dramas was made without distinction as to kind of play. Appropriating the originally satirical devices of characterizing by means of set descriptive speeches and of frequent comments by the dramatis personae on each other, our playwrights leaned heavily on them for character delineation, even in tragicomedy and tragedy. They were temperamentally drawn to the lively and sometimes extravagant sorts of situation and intrigue which they had witnessed in comedy, and so they adapted its technique of one scrape and embroilment after another to the emotional demands of serious drama. To make emotional conflicts more theatrically effective, they adopted the methods of providing arresting contrasts they had observed in comical satires.

Fletcher and Beaumont gave more attention to the motivation of situations than of characters, even in tragedy, and, indeed, added a much higher voltage of surprises and reversals than they had found in their mentors' plays. Their dramatis personae in tragicomedy and tragedy, however well portrayed, were shaped to the demands of plot as surely as many of the humour figures of Chapman and the greater part of Middleton's. Our playwrights also sought to create a dynamic and easily grasped manner of speech as like that of comedy as they deemed compatible with the dignity of serious drama. Writing with colloquial wit when they could, they avoided the close-packed imagery of Shakespeare, the sometimes turbid and static declamations of Chapman, and the mouth-filling bombast of the lesser dramatists of the minor theatres.

These particular aspects of craftsmanship are not the only outgrowths of their dramatic milieu to which Beaumont and Fletcher gave expression in their innovating tragicomedies and tragedies. They apparently picked up other useful hints towards evolving their hybrid product from a number of specific plays by Shakespeare, Marston and Chapman. The constellation of things observed and digested which coalesced into *Philaster,* their first popular success, was, in fact, a complex fusion of ingredients from divergent sources.

Gayley, however, would have us believe that this play and *A King and No King* contained "nothing . . . that had not been anticipated by Shakespeare." He further contended that Shakespeare's *Cymbeline* embodied no novelty not already to be found in seven of his preceding plays.

Four of these are romantic comedies written during the first half of his career: *The Two Gentlemen of Verona, As You Like It, Much Ado About Nothing* and *Twelfth Night*. The others are the comical satire, *Measure for Measure*, the so-called "dark" comedy, *All's Well That Ends Well*, and that dramatic romance, *Pericles*.[134] Gayley considered that the Beaumont and Fletcher tragicomedies were influenced not only by aristocratic romances but by these seven Shakespeare plays—and by *A Midsummer Night's Dream* and *Love's Labour's Lost* as well.[135]

It is difficult to find much grist in Gayley's claim for the four romantic comedies which he listed together as ancestors of *Cymbeline*, and still more so for *Love's Labour's Lost*. McKeithan, who has gathered with painstaking thoroughness every evidence, from strong to tenuous, of the indebtedness of our corpus to the plays of Shakespeare, found not even the faintest verbal echo of these four comedies, or of *Love's Labour's Lost*, in *Philaster, The Maid's Tragedy, A King and No King* and *Cupid's Revenge*.[136] In truth, *A Midsummer Night's Dream* has the only claim, among Shakespeare's romantic comedies, to any marked influence—and this because it appears to have been, in some measure, a shaping force on Fletcher's pastoral tragicomedy, *The Faithful Shepherdess*.[137]

Indeed, there is no reason why these four Shakespearean romantic comedies should have been of much effect on the Beaumont and Fletcher innovation, aside from their being admired examples of their own genus. Equally romantic in spirit are *Pericles*, the *Arcadia*, and Montemayor's *Diana*, which have a better claim to impact.[138] Following a widely used convention, Julia, Rosalind and Viola all mask as boys; but in no instance is the disguise, as is true with Bellario, concealed from the audience. The world of the forest of Arden in *As You Like It* is a variety of no-man's land, a realm of artificial unreality with pastoral overtones. But it is not the kind created by Beaumont and Fletcher; they do not provide their "spectators with satiric glasses which distort all the characters and all that they do."[139]

Nor do any of the four plays, despite hindrances to the course of true love, veer far in the direction of the tragic. *Much Ado About Nothing* has a main plot which might have done so had Shakespeare willed it. In fact, this plot is, in itself, tragicomic in its general structure. But while Shakespeare gave free rein to his delightfully individualized Beatrice and Benedick, he deliberately made Claudio and Hero colorless plot characters, and combined the serious charge against the latter, and her feigning death, with the low comedy of Dogberry and Verges in such a fashion that the audience could never doubt a satisfactory outcome. A situation serious enough in itself was not allowed to develop genuinely tragic complications, nor a surprise ending. Indeed, the danger of death, though frequently present in Shakespeare's romantic comedies, never becomes as threatening as it normally does in the tragicomedies of our corpus.

Measure for Measure, as Campbell has convincingly shown, was "Shakespeare's second attempt"—_Troilus and Cressida_ was his first—"to adapt to his genius some of the conventions of comical satire,"[140] despite material of tragicomic possibilities. Ristine says of the play: "The tone is serious thruout and tragic situations are plenty; but the plot is stripped of the real theatrical effectiveness of tragicomedy by the interposed soliloquies of the Duke, which act as a kind of chorus and forecast for the audience the happy solution of the difficulties."[141] The denouement of this comical satire is, thus, not concealed, though its carefully built and theatrical elaborateness may have repaid our playwrights' study. Isabella's dilemma, in which she can save her brother's life only by sacrificing her chastity—and to the supposedly incorruptible man who had sentenced her brother to death for a similar offense—is of a kind that was often employed later in the plays of our corpus. But Vincentio, the Duke of Vienna, as satirical commentator and intriguer, is a figure not paralleled in the serious plays of Fletcher and Beaumont. The buffoonish Lucio considers sexual promiscuity a merry joke, like some of the aristocratic young men of our corpus. He is, however, not a witty and companionable gentleman but a base fellow who is derisively exposed and deflated by the Duke. _Measure for Measure_ may, thus, have made some contribution to the constellation of things that resulted in _Philaster_, but its treatment and much of its technique is of a different order of drama.

All's Well That Ends Well is closer in spirit to that of Shakespeare's earlier romantic comedies. As Hazelton Spencer has pointed out, its "bed-trick" has—like that of _Measure for Measure_—brought forth from the critics such adjectives as "shocking," "revolting" and "corrupt." Yet this was simply a conventional plot ingredient of Renaissance fiction. Spencer makes the commonsense rebuttal that the Elizabethans saw nothing immodest in such situations. In fact, Helena's husband, Bertram, imposed on her the conditions which justified her trick.[142] Spencer's recognition that piquant situations such as these were not considered subversive to morality by Shakespeare's audience is worth pondering when considering the employment of similar "shocking" situations by Beaumont and Fletcher. Aside from this example and possibly the Parolles situations, the carefully built up and elaborated denouement of _All's Well_—fulfilling in part, however, the audience's expectation—is most likely to have made its iota of contribution to our playwrights' innovation.

Thus, apart from *A Midsummer Night's Dream* and *Pericles*, which will be considered later, the plays selected by Gayley do not explain a great deal of the novelty of *Philaster* and its successors. *Hamlet*, which Gayley did not mention, made a larger individual contribution to both *Philaster* and *The Maid's Tragedy*.[143] Indeed, the heroes of the two latter plays are simplified modifications of Hamlet himself.

In *Philaster*, the title character's relationship to the usurping king is a reworking of Hamlet's to Claudius. Philaster talks much about the wrongs the hated king has done him, and about his father's dangerous spirit within him. But although he is, like Hamlet, much admired, and although he actually has the full support of the nobility, he makes no effort to secure his rights. Instead, he discourages his supporters with the opinion that the time is not yet ripe. The King of Calabria and Claudius are both aware of their victims' popularity, and so hate them; both likewise realize that their misdeeds make them unable truly to pray. Philaster, moreover, rails against Arethusa and all women in a manner reminiscent of Hamlet upbraiding Ophelia.[144] In his jealousy of Arethusa, however, he bears more resemblance to Othello.[145]

The parallels are more numerous between *The Maid's Tragedy* and *Hamlet*. Apparently Amintor, like his prototype, was intended to typify the well-rounded Elizabethan gentleman. He swings from elation to melancholy, just as Hamlet does, and it is feared that he will go mad. His inaction, however, springs from different causes: his horror at his wife's shamelessness, and the "divinity" about the King which strikes dead his rising passions.[146] The King's relationship to Evadne was doubtless suggested by Claudius' to Gertrude; and Melantius chides his sister in terms quite similar to Hamlet's chiding of his Mother.[147] The over-ripe, cowardly and meddlesome councillor, Calianax, in some measure resembles Polonius, similarly in his dotage, just as Melantius' contemptuous treatment of the former does Hamlet's of the latter. Furthermore, each has a daughter who has been spurned. The cast-off Aspatia becomes pathetically dejected, instead of going insane, like Ophelia; but her "sad song" recalls Ophelia's mad lyric outbursts.[148] Melantius suggests both Horatio in his loyalty to Amintor, and Laertes in having a sister to revenge and in going actively about it.[149] But the famous quarrel scene between Amintor and Melantius is imitative of that between Brutus and Cassius in *Julius Caesar*.[150]

There are likewise certain more general resemblances between Shakespeare's tragedy and the Beaumont-Fletcher *Philaster* and *The Maid's Tragedy*. Like the two latter plays, *Hamlet* has an exotic setting, its characters are almost all royal or aristocratic, most of the action is located within or about the palace, there are alarums of war (Fortinbras) and of rebellion (Laertes), sexual passions are involved (Claudius, Gertrude, Ophelia), and there is a variety of emotional appeal and some comedy (Polonius, the gravediggers).

Most of these last points could also be made regarding that popular comical satire, *The Malcontent*, itself indebted to *Hamlet*.[151] This is the play by Marston which, in some ways, most definitely foreshadows *Philaster*. It combines a "comical satire" treatment with a tragicomic plot and construction. We can ignore the former, and the role of Malevole, the malcontent, as satirical commentator. But the tragicomic aspects of this play—which Fletcher and Beaumont must have witnessed—is another matter. Here, again, are the court setting, aristocratic characters, sexual passions and a comic element. Here, also, are a lustful and vicious Megra (in the person of Pietro's duchess), a lustful Pharamond (though in this instance, the completely Machiavellian villain, Mendoza), and a wronged prince (the true duke, in disguise as Malevole), his faithful friend (Celso), and the usurper (Pietro). A gallant is theatrically stabbed but recovers from the wound; in the fourth act there is a hunting expedition with scenes in a forest; some slight use is made of a citadel, and of a pretended poison. The intrigue of the final acts mounts up to a theatrically effective masquing scene which supplies the happy—but largely anticipated—denouement, in which the villain is banished (a frequent Elizabethan punishment) rather than condemned to death.

Satiric treatment and Machiavellian villainy are missing from the Beaumont and Fletcher tragicomedies; and romantic young love, absent from *The Malcontent*, is one of their central ingredients. These and other differences make it inadvisable to push the effect of Marston's comical satire too far; yet it should be evident that this play, like *Hamlet*, definitely lies in the background of *Philaster* and its successors.

None other of the Marston comical satires does so, except most tenuously.[152] That playwright's absurd initial compound of satire and romance, *Antonio and Mellida*, may have lingered vaguely in Fletcher's consciousness. The sensational stratagem whereby Andrugio, in the denouement, marches into the court of Piero, clad in a suit of armor with the beaver down, to claim the reward of twenty thousand pistolets set upon his own head, and then lifts the beaver to reveal himself, might, perhaps, have found a place in one of the more fantastic romances of our corpus. Antonio's entrance in a coffin, and his arising out of it alive at the right theatrical moment, are duplicated by Polydor in Fletcher's *The Mad Lover*, but coffin effects were a popular convention.

Parrott and Ball find in Chapman's *The Gentleman Usher* "a distinct anticipation" of the tragicomic mode of our playwrights.[153] In this comedy, the hero, Vincentio, and Strozza both come near death; Vincentio is treacherously attacked by Medice's guard and reported slain, while Strozza is seriously wounded by a forked arrow during a hunt. Moreover, Margaret, when she believes Vincentio dead, destroys her beauty by rubbing a blistering poison on her face. Strozza and Margaret likewise "escape by something like a miracle."[154] The former recovers because—as he has been predicting with the foreknowledge his wound has amazingly given him—the arrowhead falls out after seven days. Could Ralph's forked arrow through his head in *The Knight of the Burning Pestle* have been a burlesque of Strozza's predicament? Margaret is granted an unexpectedly happy outcome because a doctor is able to restore her blasted beauty with a wondrous ointment.[155] This reversal might well have come out of our corpus; and it dowers the denouement with at least one element of surprise.

Though some of the later scenes and situations are thus handled in a tragicomic manner, Chapman's play is actually a curious medley. Activities involving an entertainment and a small masque—providing opportunities for the Blackfriars lads to display their range of talents—occupy much of the first two acts, just as a masque opens *The Maid's Tragedy*. The satiric bedevilment of the dullwitted and pompous Bassiolo by Vincentio and Margaret is given a major prominence in the play; and it is barely possible that Bassiolo as well as Polonius may have been in our playwrights' minds when Calianax of *The Maid's Tragedy* was conceived. But Chapman's almost tragic occurrences do not resemble any situation in the collaborated tragicomedies of Beaumont and Fletcher otherwise than in bringing certain characters near death and in providing unexpected recoveries. As for Medice's being "let off with banishment,"[156] this follows a convention which, when enacted in the actual life of the time, meant a fate often more dreaded than death. But although Chapman's comedy actually foreshadows *Philaster* and its immediate successors less directly than *The Malcontent*, it must be reckoned a part of their background.

It was a later play than any of these, however, which appears to have set Beaumont and Fletcher to thinking about the possibilities of romantic drama, and so to devising a tragicomic mode which would appeal to theatregoers. This was the well received *Pericles, Prince of Tyre*. It was apparently the first Globe Theatre play, in years, replete with romantic adventures by land and sea and with theatrically effective tugs at the heartstrings. Its success,[157] after the long dominance of tragedy at the Globe and of satires and other varieties of comedy at the private theatres, would have afforded evidence that audiences were ready once more for the romantic treatment of materials. It might well have convinced our playwrights that a return to the spirit of the *Arcadia* and the *Diana,* or perhaps of the pastoral, would now gain the applause of upper class spectators, if the ingredients were rightly compounded.

In *Pericles*, Shakespeare is believed to have rewritten almost completely the last three acts of a manuscript in possession of his company, and perhaps to have added touches to the first two acts. Since the Venetian Ambassador, Zorsi Guistinian, saw the play not later than November 23, 1608,[158] and since the plague apparently had closed the theatres by the end of July in that year,[159] it was most probably first produced during the season of 1607-08, though an earlier date is possible.

It would be logical to suppose, although it cannot be conclusively proved, that Fletcher's pastoral tragicomedy, *The Faithful Shepherdess*, was the first attempt made by either of our young playwrights to meet the new demand for romantic drama. It may very well have undergone its failure at Blackfriars in the winter of 1608, before that company was inhibited from playing in March. Having diagnosed the causes of its failure to their satisfaction, Beaumont and Fletcher may then have experimented, in *Philaster*, with another adaptation of tragicomic materials and technique.

Ristine, it will be recalled, thought that some of the ingredients of *The Faithful Shepherdess* were transmuted into *Philaster*. It seems improbable that Fletcher, so adept at denouements, would have failed at this structural point in his pastoral drama after experience with Beaumont in building to an effectively climactic series of events in *Philaster*. A lack of Fletcher's usual theatrical deftness in other respects as well suggests that this lyric drama was an earlier experiment. And so Harbage's dating of 1608 seems the probable one,[160] although a premiere between December, 1609, and March, 1610, is possible, in spite of the difficulties the Revels Children were having about a home for their company at that time.

In any case, *Pericles* lies in the immediate background of *Philaster*, and of *Cymbeline* as well. The story traces back to Greek romance, though it was transmitted to later ages through Latin versions. It has the sensational elements of wanderings by land and sea about the eastern Mediterranean world, of shipwrecks and piracies, and of the long trials and hardships of its central figures, that comprise, in part, the narrative ingredients of the *Arcadia*. Indeed, as is often remarked, the traditional name of Apollonius may have been dropped by Shakespeare for Pericles because of resemblances between his sea misadventures and those of Pyrocles in Sidney's prose epic. Thus, Beaumont and Fletcher, while perhaps deploring the loose structure of *Pericles*, may well have been influenced by it to turn the pages of romances and of pastoral dramas in search of materials which might be shaped up into plays.

Thorndike, since his main interest was to demonstrate the probable influence of *Philaster* on *Cymbeline,* minimized the impact of *Pericles* on either. He found the last "a return to the old chronological, narrative dramatization of stories of wonderful adventures"—a loose, rambling play, in large measure undramatic, and lacking a highly developed denouement.[161] These criticisms are true enough, with the important qualification that some of Shakespeare's more sensational scenes are handled with theatrical skill and sentimental impact. Aside from the play's employment of many tragic situations, which bring some major characters near death, as well as minor ones actually to it, the main technical suggestions for our playwrights doubtless lay in Shakespeare's stagecraft in individual scenes. It is also possible that the discovery of Thaisa, in the final situation of the play, suggested Bellario's revealment of her true identity at the denouement of *Philaster.* As Thorndike noted, however, our playwrights avoided the lax structure of *Pericles* in *Philaster,* whereas Shakespeare did not do so in *Cymbeline.*[162]

Nonetheless there appear in *Pericles* some of the hall-marks of Beaumont and Fletcher's tragicomic innovation. The play lacks a dominant central figure, as does *Philaster;* its interest is split between Pericles, Marina and, less importantly, Thaisa. The dominant theme of the play is that of loss and recovery (of Marina and Thaisa by Pericles); but there is also a minor contrast of lust versus romantic love (Antingonus and his daughter versus Lysimachus and Marina). In *Philaster* the relative importance of these two themes is reversed; the contrast of romantic love and lust becomes the major one, whereas disappearance and recovery is significant only in providing the concealed element of the denouement. The appearance of both themes in contrasted patterning in the two plays is arresting, however, in view of the fact that Fletcher likewise reversed, though in another manner, the two plots of *The Taming of the Shrew* in *The Woman's Prize.*

There is as much violence to probability and to normal human existence in the events of *Pericles* as in those of *Philaster.* These events produce a variety of emotional impacts on spectators, as in our playwrights' tragicomedies, and there is notable use of the technical devices of surprise, unexpected twists to situations, and reversal. Moreover, the exotic locales of Shakespeare's play are in the favorite Mediterranean world of our playwrights.

Finally, there is Marina, "a piece of virtue," Shakespeare's first portrait of the faithful and true little maiden of romance. She moves spotless through compromising circumstance, and shines so virtuously in a brothel that she reforms Lysimachus. While Bellario is put through no such trial of her chastity, she, too, is a spotless little maiden who, in the end, emerges triumphantly from a series of compromising situations, and clears herself of the charge of unchastity. The delightful Marina may thus have been one of the sources of inspiration for the creation of Bellario. She is also the more successful immediate predecessor of the somehow wooden though "perfect" woman, Imogen of *Cymbeline,* whose personality lacks integration because of the strain induced by the variety of extravagant situations to which her creator subjects her.

The importance of *Pericles* as a determining drama in the immediate background of *Philaster,* as well as of *Cymbeline,* has been very largely overlooked. And yet, considered in connection with what else our playwrights had been observing on the stage over a period of seven or eight years, it should be clear that this play has a strong claim to being the catalyzing agent which finally precipitated the new brand of tragicomedy in *Philaster.* Had *Cymbeline* never been written, Beaumont and Fletcher, out of their complex background of literary and dramatic experience, rounded out by *Pericles*—and *The Faithful Shepherdess*—could have created their first joint tragicomedy just as we have it today.

And this has a bearing on the "warehoused" question of the influence of *Philaster* on *Cymbeline.* In the light of *Pericles* as—in some respects— the predecessor of both, the answer to this question may be of less importance than has sometimes been thought. But it is worth noting that while *Philaster* is a fresh, spontaneous, lively production of our playwrights in their best serious vein, *Cymbeline* is surprisingly inept for a dramatist of Shakespeare's genius and experience—as wooden a play as he ever wrote, despite its over-rated if charming Imogen. To an experienced playwright this would immediately suggest that if any one were the imitator, it would be Shakespeare, making his trial effort to adapt to his own genius aspects of technique alien to his former practices.

Why the master should, quite possibly, have sought to adopt some elements of the technique of his juniors is a perplexing and incomprehensible enigma to Shakespeare idolaters. But it is understandable enough in terms of the common, everyday, bustling world of the theatre. England's greatest dramatist was a humble man; he did not recognize his own towering pre-eminence. He was an artist devoted loyally to the interests of the King's Men, with whom for many years he had been a businessman shareholder taking his profits, and a leading actor, as well as chief playwright. He had a weather-eye to whatever pleased audiences at any particular time, and *Pericles* had made a hit. What, then, should he provide the Globe spectators next in the way of romantic drama, to capitalize on its apparent return to fashion?

At this point, the King's Men began negotiations to make Blackfriars their winter home. This added a new element to the situation. From now on, Globe plays must be so devised as to please the more aristocratic tastes of a more upper class audience as well. At just this time, too, Shakespeare's young gentlemen friends, Beaumont and Fletcher, were desirous of writing for the King's Men. The Children of the Revels were now inactive, and no one knew when they would be allowed to resume playing. Since our playwrights had already had experience in concocting plays for Blackfriars (and Paul's), it might be well to give them an opportunity at the Globe. So it may be that they talked over with Shakespeare the ideas they had, or possibly their friend suggested that they write something for the King's Men. In any case, all three playwrights now found themselves confronted by the same new playhouse situation.

It is unnecessary to assume, as is usually done, that *Philaster* must have been performed before *Cymbeline* was written in order to explain an influence on Shakespeare. In fact, it is by no means impossible that there was a cross-influence during the writing of the two plays. When Beaumont and Fletcher had thoroughly worked out their scene by scene "plat," or scenario, of *Philaster*, they would doubtless have taken the normal step of reading it to the King's Men.[163] Shakespeare, whether acting in a play or not, would usually have been at such a reading; he was, in addition to being a shareholder, undoubtedly valued as a judge of new pieces. In the ensuing talk he would come to understand clearly what his younger friends were about. He would probably later read the completed manuscript, and might well be present at rehearsals. Long before *Philaster* was actually performed before an audience, he could have come to the conclusion that our playwrights had hit upon effective techniques, characters and situations, and have decided to experiment with some aspects of their new vein in his own new play.

Confronted with the necessity of writing romantic drama which would appeal to Blackfriars as well as Globe audiences, it is only natural to suppose that the three friends were not tongue-tied, but to some extent talked over their common problems. Playwrights for Jacobean companies did not live in their writing-rooms alone; they were much about the theatre, and haunted the same taverns and inns. The theatrical world of London was, after all, a small one, and the King's Men had many attributes of one large family.

What the actual situation was we shall never know, unless the dates of first production for both *Philaster* and *Cymbeline,* and other data, are discovered. The controversy on the subject, however, has somewhat obscured the fact that these two plays show differences as well as resemblances. Some of the major characters of each show more unlikeness than Thorndike would have us believe. To the rambling structure of *Cymbeline,* and the main emphasis on disappearance and recovery, might be added Shakespeare's use of old-fashioned chronicle-history material from Holinshed, and his stress on the theme of forgiveness. None of these are present in *Philaster*.

It is, after all, a matter of importance that the background of dramatic experience and practice which the three playwrights brought to bear in getting plays ready for the opening of the theatres in December, 1609, was in many respects different. The resultant products, springing from highly individual creative temperaments, were thus bound to be diverse—whatever the three men may have learned from one another in trying to solve their common problem. It is therefore sounder to think of the two plays as attempts to meet precisely the same demand, rather than as vehicles one of which was fully and directly imitative of the other.

VIII

Whether or not we accept the hypothesis that Shakespeare's *Cymbeline* was influenced by the Beaumont-Fletcher *Philaster*, or that there was mutual exchange of ideas, it is more significant that Shakespeare worked at his own particular form of dramatic romance until he had wrought out, in *The Tempest*, one of his finest artistic successes. This done, he was ready to retire. Meanwhile, our playwrights, in *Philaster* and *A King and No King*, created with high gusto and theatrical effectiveness the new Jacobean tragicomedy—and extended its technique to *The Maid's Tragedy*. If this was a lesser achievement, it was, in its own way, original—though compounded of various ingredients brought together, as we have seen, from many sources.

Gentlemen by birth, by education and by literary and dramatic tastes, Fletcher and Beaumont had used their eyes and ears well at the private theatres and the Globe, had written their own first ventures for Paul's and Blackfriars, had acquired by trial and error a keen sense of what elements of stagecraft appealed to Jacobean playgoers, and finally, for the King's Men, had hit upon the formulae which brought into being a new brand of entertainment for the gentry. As Lyly, Kyd and Marlowe had been the first, so they were the last important innovators in Elizabethan-Stuart drama.

If they placed their emphasis on technique, so had others before them. Elizabethan theatrecraft had matured since Shakespeare had arrived in London. Moreover, the varieties of source materials that the drama could draw upon had already been pretty well exploited, and intensification of theatrical effect appeared to offer the chief remaining means of novelty. Tragicomedy was the answer of Beaumont and Fletcher. In developing it, they in no way lowered the standards, moral or dramatic, which had been set by the comedies written for the upper class audiences of Paul's and Blackfriars.

If there is any decline in Jacobean drama, its roots must be traced back through the boys' companies of the private theatres. In all probability their final rootlets will be found in the fashion of verse satires on classical models during the 1590's. Therein something of the tone of the private theatre plays was set. Jonson's sane moral attitude in dealing with human follies and vices, in his comical satires, was not everywhere maintained. Compare the essential nastiness of some areas in Marston's comical satire of professed moral purpose, *The Dutch Courtesan,* with the merrier and wittier treatment of sex relations in the Fletcher-Massinger *The Custom of the Country,* and Lovelace's lines will take on fresh meaning:

> Heare ye foule Speakers, that pronounce the Aire
> Of Stewes and Shores, I will informe you where
> And how to cloathe aright your wanton wit,
> Without her nasty Bawd attending it.
> View here a loose thought said with such a grace,
> Minerva might have spoke in Venus face;
> So well disguis'd, that 'twas conceived by none
> But Cupid had Diana's linnen on;
> And all his naked parts so Vail'd, th 'expresse
> The Shape with clowding the uncomlinesse.[164]

Fletcher, Beaumont, Massinger—all are free from Marston's neurotic and unhealthy obsession with sex. Many of their expressions are not comely by modern standards, but neither are Shakespeare's or Jonson's, Middleton's or Chapman's, always so. If due allowance is made, however, for downright speech later banished from polite society and from plays, Fletcher can be seen to have handled sex themes with a cold, swift, surface brittleness that compares not unfavorably with similar treatments in modern sophisticated comedies. He was not more unmoral in his plays than Chapman and Middleton had been in the comedies they wrote for Blackfriars and Paul's. It is worth recalling that the healthy-minded Sir Walter Scott considered the moralistic Jonson as the coarsest offender in dialogue among the Elizabethan-Stuart playwrights.[165]

Moreover, as Thomas Babington Macaulay pointed out, our playwrights did not stand accepted moral conventions on their heads,[166] as Ford was to do. For that matter, the theatrically effective scene in Middleton's *A Mad World, My Masters,* in which Frank Gullman, the harlot, holds Harebrain in hypocritically deceiving conversation while his wife and Penitent Brothel are consummating their passion in the next room,[167] can hardly be matched again in any play until the days of Restoration comedy. It staggers the imagination to picture Leigh Hunt as reading *Measure for Measure* or *All's Well That Ends Well* with perfect aplomb to a proper Victorian family circle. Nor is the completely cynical tone of Chapman's *The Widow's Tears* duplicated in our corpus.

Our playwrights appear to have taken their dramatic milieu pretty much as they found it. They wrote abler plays than the majority that had held the stage at Paul's or Blackfriars because they put their ingredients together with greater technical skill and power. They thus fulfilled a development in drama for gentlemen which had been under way since 1599. In addition, they had an original idea, which crystallized as tragicomedy. Thereby they not only achieved popular success at Shakespeare's Globe Playhouse; they also solved for the King's Men the problem of how to entertain their new audiences of gentlefolk at Blackfriars.

The decision of London's outstanding professional company to occupy Blackfriars regularly during a winter season of at least six months was fateful not only for the King's Men but for Beaumont and Fletcher as well. Indeed, this decision was the true turning-point in Jacobean drama; it made irrevocable the cleavage between upper and lower class audiences which had been growing since 1599. It should not be forgotten, however, that Shakespeare's company still played at the Globe also.

Partly as one consequence of the new arrangement, Fletcher, Beaumont and Company began their emergence, immediately afterwards, as popular entertainers to the gentry. The twin stars, Castor and Pollux, were at last in the ascendancy. Because the tragicomedies and other plays they wrote were so well adjusted to the time-spirit of their theatrical milieu, they henceforth became leaders in Stuart drama, and Fletcher, after Shakespeare's death in 1616, master playwright with the King's Men.

CHAPTER SIX

Prologue to Success

BEFORE Beaumont and Fletcher tasted the heady wine of enthusiastic acclaim at the première of *Philaster*, their first play acted by the King's Men, they had both known failure. We have seen that it was almost inevitable they should have fixed their attention, from the start, upon gaining the applause of genteel audiences. But at first, neither of our young playwrights hit upon the precise substance and technical methods destined to earn them their dominant position as entertainers to the gentry. In *The Knight of the Burning Pestle* and *The Faithful Shepherdess* each wrote a play which grew out of his own aristocratic tastes and diverged, with some originality, from the accepted dramatic fashions. Only after the chastening experience of seeing these "first heirs of their invention" fail were they to devise togther a kind of aristocratic entertainment combining the right mixture of ingredients to achieve instantaneous success.

Significant though they are, the social backgrounds of Fletcher and Beaumont, their university education, their friendships with other dramatists, and their acquisitions from literature and from stage plays, do not completely account for the nature of their work. The two novices in playwriting had tried to please the audiences of Paul's and Blackfriars with lighter pieces, written for child actors, before they joined forces on their first collaborated tragicomedy. They had learned lessons—some of them bitter—from the reactions of theatregoers to their first ventures. Beaumont had shown a definite talent for satirical comedy, and Fletcher had assuredly given indications of his gift for farce. In *The Faithful Shepherdess*, moreover, the latter had experimented with the "middle mood" of tragicomedy, and had worked out some of the craftsmanship which came to successful fruition in *Philaster*.

Thus, the earlier experiences of Beaumont and of Fletcher in writing for the private playhouses determined, in some measure, the characteristics of their first drama for the King's Men. And it was the enthusiasm which greeted this tragicomedy which marked the end of our playwrights' groping for the means to evoke a favorable response from playgoers. Accordingly, with *Philaster* their technique began to crystalize.

Some consideration of the first stage in the dramatic careers of Beaumont and Fletcher is, therefore, desirable, if we are fully to understand how their theatrecraft for the gentry came into being. So is a re-examination of their method of collaboration on the major tragicomedies and on *The Maid's Tragedy*. And since the later plays of Fletcher, written with as well as without assistance, resemble in craftsmanship those in which Beaumont and he established their reputation, it might be germane also to inquire whether Fletcher worked with his later co-authors in the same way as he did with Beaumont.

I

The exact time at which Fletcher and Beaumont each began writing for the private theatres, and the precise number of their dramas produced before *Philaster,* are facts which have not been conclusively determined. Oliphant considered it a "reasonable surmise" that Fletcher "was at work as early as 1602 or 1603."[1] This opinion appears to be based on the assumption that Fletcher must have begun contributing to the theatres well before he was 27 or 28, and on D'Avenant's round figure that Fletcher had been "full twenty years" a dramatist.[2] The assumption is unsupported by evidence, and the round figure may just as well have represented an actual 18 or 19 years of playwriting as 22 or 23. Harbage is probably not far from the truth in assigning only *The Woman-Hater* (1606), *The Knight of the Burning Pestle* (1607), and *The Faithful Shepherdess* and *Cupid's Revenge* (1608) to dates earlier than *Philaster*.[3]

It is reasonable to suppose that *The Woman-Hater* may have been Beaumont's first play. The lad was barely in his later teens when he came up to London in 1600. As a younger son, his immediate business was to secure the legal training at the Inns of Court which would prepare him for a suitable marriage into a county family. There is no reason to think he shirked his task; he was noteworthy for common sense, and at 28 or 29 he made the sort of marriage which was expected of him. Social obligations are implied in his many aristocratic connections and friendships; some attendance at the Royal Court was natural to—and even expected of —a gentleman of the Inns of Court; and his later masque suggests that he entered into the normal activities of his legal milieu as enthusiastically as he cultivated literary and dramatic friendships. Surely 21 or 22 seems early enough for a youth of such varied activities to turn playwright.

Oliphant, who admired Beaumont and disliked Fletcher, was convinced that he had detected the former playwright's hand in many plays of our corpus. Indeed, Oliphant had a marked tendency to identify Beaumont, if he could manage to do so, with any writing in these pieces which he considered of high quality. But it is doubtful whether that dramatist was actually active in any large number of the plays. He remained in London for only seven years following the production of *The Woman-Hater*. He was not driven into writing for the stage by financial pressure, as Fletcher may well have been. Though he appears to have delighted, for a few years, in sharing the bohemian world of the theatre with his comrade, he must often have felt obliged to give precedence over play-writing to his other interests and duties. The responsibilities which he undertook with his marriage, in 1613, to an heiress of Kent could have left him little time for writing, and three years later he was dead. He may have been concerned in more than the eight plays with which we can most confidently associate him,[4] but it is a plausible conjecture that the number was not much greater.

With Fletcher the available data are few. His father died in 1596, his commendatory verses to *Volpone* were published in 1607, and *The Faithful Shepherdess* was probably produced during the winter season of 1607-08, perhaps in January or February of the latter year. The rest is speculation. It is almost certain that the lad of sixteen was taken under the protection of his paternal relatives following his father's death.[5] At some later juncture he may well have travelled on the continent in the entourage of his uncle, Dr. Giles Fletcher, the diplomat. It is also possible that this gentleman found the young man useful to him as a secretary, or else used his influence to place him in a similar position elsewhere.[6]

As a gentleman-commoner of breeding but of no income other than that his relatives could furnish him, Fletcher assuredly must have sought means of support suitable to his rank in life. He may even have had a harassing experience in trying to make a place for himself, as his comments on poverty in his poem, *Upon an Honest Man's Fortune*,[7] seem to hint. Moreover, in his verses to Sir Robert Townesend, prefixed to the first quarto of his unsuccessful *The Faithful Shepherdess*, he penned the significant line, "As sour fortune loves to use me."[8] However much attracted he may have been to literary and dramatic pursuits, it is questionable whether he would have incurred the risk of declassing himself by turning professional playwright, until he had tried all gentlemanly expedients for earning a living.

And so only incontrovertible evidence could prove that Fletcher wrote for the theatres as early as 1602 or 1603, when he was yet in his early twenties, and Elizabeth was still Queen of England. Even the large number of plays in which he had at least a finger affords no genuine evidence of an early start. His whole output could be accounted for as belonging to the years between 1608 and 1625, without straining the hypothesis that his average—alone or with collaborators—approximated three plays a year. It may be questionable whether *The Faithful Shepherdess* was Fletcher's first dramatic effort, but no clear evidence exists to show what dramas, if any, preceded it. Possibly the best claimant for priority would be the merry farce, *The Woman's Prize*.[9]

To prove that a Fletcher play was performed earlier than 1608, inferior or careless workmanship, or later revision by some other dramatist, are not sufficient evidence. Such plays must bear indications of having been written for boy actors to present before private theatre audiences. They would almost certainly be comedies, romantic elements would be slight, satire would normally be present, and humour figures might well be found among the cast of characters. The plays would not be tragicomic in effect, nor would they conspicuously resemble in dramaturgy *Philaster*, *The Maid's Tragedy* and *A King and No King*, or later Fletcher comedies. Evidence of collaboration with Beaumont would be acceptable, with Middleton barely plausible, but with other playwrights almost inadmissible. Unless a given play can pass all these tests, the likelihood is that it dates from about 1610 or thereafter.[10]

It would be a satisfaction to know beyond doubt what plays by Beaumont and Fletcher were performed by boys' companies before March, 1608. As matters now stand, however, *The Woman-Hater*, *The Knight of the Burning Pestle* and *The Faithful Shepherdess*, as dated by Harbage, have the strongest claims to belong to this category. *Cupid's Revenge* stands in more doubtful case. Since it is inferior to *Philaster*, and since both its plots are indebted to Sidney's *Arcadia*, it might have preceded our playwrights' crucial tragicomedy. It has, however, somewhat more the appearance of being a hurried job turned out after *Philaster* and *The Maid's Tragedy* had been acclaimed, in order to supply the immediate need of the Second Queen's Revels Company of boy actors. Significantly, *The Coxcomb* falls into this class, and both plays were presented at Court by this company in 1612—*Cupid's Revenge* on January 5, and *The Coxcomb* between October 16 and 24.[11] This suggests, as the most likely date for the former, 1610 or 1611, when the boys were acting at Whitefriars.

Fortunately, hypothetical early plays need not concern us further. If *Cupid's Revenge* antedated *Philaster*, this would merely demonstrate that our playwrights had worked out most of their dramaturgy, less effectively, before they succeeded with it in *Philaster*. In that case, they had not yet mastered the art of the concealed and surprising denouement, since it is obvious, as early as the first act of this tragedy, that Cupid will secure his revenge. Perhaps this is the main reason why the less likely date of 1608 is sometimes selected for this tragedy. In any event, it is noteworthy that our playwrights were making use of the *Arcadia* at a point in time so close to *Philaster*. As for other possibly early pieces, it is doubtful if they would contribute largely to an understanding of how our playwrights attained to the theatrecraft of their first collaborated tragicomedy.

II

One of the determining factors in the dramatic careers of Beaumont and Fletcher was the failure of plays upon which they had hopefully expended their best efforts. Since they were young playwrights of genuine talent and originality, it was natural that each should early have attempted to please private theatre spectators with a drama which grew out of his own tastes and interests. Doubtless each had encouraged himself in the hope that upper class audiences would understand such a drama and applaud it. When, instead, the play into which he had put the best work of which he felt himself capable met only hostility and lack of comprehension, the shock must have been considerable.

Beaumont sensibly began his career with a conventional play, written under the influence of Jonson and Chapman—no doubt already his friends. This was the satirical comedy of humours, *The Woman-Hater*, which, probably with slight assistance from Fletcher,[12] he supplied to the boys of Paul's. A creditable apprentice-piece, high-spirited but stiff and overwritten, in vivid prose but of somewhat loose construction, it deserved the moderate success which its publication in 1607 indicates it had.

It was then that Beaumont conceived his original idea: that of a comedy burlesquing the literary and dramatic tastes of the lower classes. Walter Burre, the publisher of the first quarto (1613), speaks of *The Knight of the Burning Pestle* as "this unfortunate child, who in eight daies (as lately I have learned) was begot and borne. . . ."[13] But though the play could very well have been written, in a spate of creative energy, within a period of eight days, it must have been longer in gestation. Beaumont and Fletcher doubtless enjoyed discussing it during the time it was taking shape. Indeed, while the hand of Fletcher cannot clearly be traced at any specific point in the writing, one suspects that he may have contributed here and there to the evolution of its ground-plan.[14] The friends must have gleefully anticipated the playgoers' enjoyment of this or that bit of parody, satire or irony. Both must have come to think well of its chance of success with an upperclass audience.

But this effervescent and original burlesque, which has appealed to various later critics as Beaumont's freshest and most characteristic work, was scorned at Blackfriars. Burre informs us that the playgoers rejected it "for want of iudgement, or not understanding the priuy marke of Ironie about it."[15] In other words, the comedy was too novel; the audience did not catch its burlesque spirit. They were accustomed to comical satire of individual human beings and their follies, and they recognized at once the satirical commentator, whether seriously lashing follies or making buffoonish remarks. But an ironic lampooning of vulgar literary and dramatic fashions was beyond many of them, no doubt because they themselves were not free from a taste for such crudities. And though they could understand a Mistress Quickly or a Simon Eyre, they did not relish the Grocer and his Wife, installed as literal-minded commentators. These characters were too uncomfortably like some of the worthy burgesses seated in the audience.[16]

These were not the only causes for the play's failure. Gentlemen might also have felt themselves touched by some of the satire, especially if they did not grasp the spirit of the play. Should the burlesque tone of the sentimental little love-plot be missed, this sequence of situations would, no doubt, have appeared silly, as well as offensive to some in its treatment of the London merchant class. Moreover, Ralph, the title character, may have grown tedious to many spectators. It is the weakness of this delightful play that the frequent intrusions of the grocer's apprentice do not result in any well-connected story. Though the scenes in which he appears may delight in the reading, on the stage they would be weak in dramatic cohesion. Since the type of play being lampooned was itself most loosely constructed, this weakness may have been intentional. But if so, Beaumont miscalculated his effect, for theatregoers wanted, above all, story.

Fletcher, soon after Beaumont's rebuff, had his own taste of an audience's displeasure. He, also, is likely to have launched his career with one or more comedies of a conventional mode, though what these were, and whether he had Beaumont's assistance in them, remain, as we have seen, unknown. And then to him, likewise, occurred a novel idea: the creating of a pastoral drama for a private theatre audience. So *The Faithful Shepherdess* was born.

Fletcher must have felt he was on reasonably safe ground. Daniel's *The Queen's Arcadia*, a relatively stodgy play both in poetry and in dramatic treatment, had been produced for Queen Anne and her entourage at Christ's Church, Oxford, by members of the college on August 30, 1605. This pastoral had been well received; one comment had been that it made amends for the other plays, "being indeed very excellent."[17] If Fletcher had read its printed text (1606), he must have concluded that he could do as well, and that if the courtiers had liked such a play, the spectators at Blackfriars, too, might well enjoy a pastoral.

He, like Beaumont, was to be disappointed. The Blackfriars audience proved to be immune to the spell of the true pastoral, even though Fletcher had provided them with the finest play in this kind, both as lyrical poetry and as theatre, that was to be written in England.[18] It did not fail because it dealt with various love-relationships without highlighting any one of them, or because it lacked a striking denouement. The spectators, indeed, appear not to have sat through the play to the end.[19] Nor was there anything in the moral tone that would have disgusted them, as nineteenth century critics sometimes thought. Fletcher diagnosed the cause of the drama's ill-success correctly when he wrote, in *To the Reader,* prefixed to the first quarto (1609-10), that the audience had concluded a pastoral tragicomedy "to be a play of country hired shepherds in gray cloaks, with curtailed dogs in strings, sometimes laughing together, and sometimes killing one another; and, missing Whitsunales, cream, wassail, and morris-dances, began to be angry."[20]

Both playwrights had miscalculated their audience. Their dramas might both have been well received had they been presented before spectators of literary sophistication.[21] But the private theatre audience, although much less widely representative than that of the public playhouse, was nonetheless of mixed, if more genteel, composition. Aristocrats of taste, literary men, lawyers and Inns-of-Court students could never have kept the private theatres in operation.[22] What made Blackfriars commercially profitable was the large infusion of purely amusement-seeking courtiers, of more prosperous middle-class playgoers, and of less respectable elements of the London citizenry who could manage at least the sixpence admission cost.[23] Though they may have liked to think of themselves as members of a select clientele, a goodly share of this audience could have had little or no cultivated taste in literature and drama such as both *The Knight of the Burning Pestle* and *The Faithful Shepherdess* presupposed.

Here was an unpleasant lesson, but one needful to be learned if our playwrights were to analyze clearly what material and treatment such an audience would welcome. That their failures nettled both Fletcher and Beaumont should be clear from the prefatory matter which they wrote for the first quarto of *The Faithful Shepherdess.* Fletcher's careful explanation, in *To the Reader,* of certain elementary points about the pastoral and about tragicomedy, and his cavalier conclusion that "to teach you more for nothing, I do not know that I am in conscience bound,"[24] show a measure of pique unusual in a man so evidently unassuming and companionable. Beaumont's commendatory verses likewise have a tartness that reveals his own scars. He questions whether such a play should be exposed on the stage at all, since audiences so lack judgment. He even utters the suspicion that more than half of Fletcher's spectators lacked the ability to read.[25]

A contempt for the general run of private theatre playgoers, springing from wounded self-esteem, would seem to have been the fruit of these humiliating failures. Our playwrights had cast their pearls before theatregoers, and the latter had trampled on them. Both Fletcher and Beaumont were young and relatively new dramatists, and such an experience must have gone deeper than later failures would have done. No doubt they gleaned what comfort they could from the discerning few—Jonson, Chapman, Field and others.

But they refused to accept defeat; Fletcher's living, and the self-respect. of both, depended on going forward to success. What would their "hydra-headed" audiences relish? Beaumont's *The Knight of the Burning Pestle* had shown that he knew what had been well liked in the lesser public theatres. *Pericles* had made a hit at the Globe. Fletcher had introduced tragicomedy in *The Faithful Shepherdess*. There was the *Arcadia*, and D'Urfé's recent *Astrée*. With stubborn determination Beaumont and Fletcher went to work to put together a variety of content and theatre-craft carefully adjusted to the capacities for response of a playgoing public unappreciative of their best. The result was the epoch-making *Philaster*. So this was the sort of play their public wanted. Our playwrights never forgot this lesson.

III

John Fletcher's *The Faithful Shepherdess* was the first drama written by either of our playwrights which definitely foreshadows things to come in *Philaster* and its successors. The slight love interest of *The Woman-Hater*, which merely provides a conventional plot element, is almost submerged by the satiric display of humours which is this comedy's main purpose. *The Knight of the Burning Pestle*, though it deals with the romantic excesses of the popular play and tale of lower class consumption, does so in the spirit of shrewd-eyed burlesque and lampoon. Even the sentimental love story of Jasper and Luce is too much immersed in the pervading atmosphere of mockery to be taken seriously as romance; witness, for instance, the absurdly simple-minded diction of the foolish Master Humphrey.

Now Miss Ellis-Fermor, who approaches our playwrights as accomplished theatre craftsmen, finds that "the element of romance, the withdrawal from the pursuit of reality," is the quality most distinctive of their tragicomedies and tragedies, and not entirely absent even from their comedies. She compares the detached world which, for her, they evoke to "the moonlit stage of an exquisite opera-set, become suddenly real and co-extensive with life itself." And so "we accept enchantment." In the "clear, remote radiance" of this world of escape, withdrawn from the problems and dilemmas of every day living, she finds the dramatic novelty of Beaumont and Fletcher.[26]

It might, to be sure, be questioned whether a Stuart audience was so conscious of this distinctive "fairy tale" atmosphere as a modern reader is. By most Jacobean playgoers, a drama was frankly accepted as make-believe. They did not demand, as so many present day spectators do, that it should give them an illusion of reality. Indeed, their structural stage, with its several acting areas and its three levels, was not so well adapted to naturalism as our own less flexible picture-frame one. Whatever may be true for the modern reader, certainly Stuart theatregoers did not find the emotions of our playwrights' characters so "endowed with remoteness" that they failed to respond vigorously to them. These drama-lovers lived in a milieu sufficiently resembling the world of the plays so that, according to Shirley, they found Blackfriars under the reign of Beaumont and Fletcher an "Academy" where gentlemen could have their wits sharpened and gain a valuable social polish.[27] Other contributors to the First Folio testify that spectators could learn political and moral lessons from our dramatists' plays as well. After these reservations have been made, however, it remains true that Fletcher and Company did give to the emotions and events of most of their dramas, including even comedies, some degree of detachment from mundane actuality.

It is arresting to observe how perfectly the phrase, "clear, remote radiance," describes the atmosphere of *The Faerie Queene,* or even, though perhaps in lesser force, of the *Arcadia.* Both of these writings, moreover, had their pastoral elements. It would appear to have been such writings as these—quite as much as the Italian pastoral dramas of Guarini and others, *The Queen's Arcadia* of Daniel, or the *Pericles* of Shakespeare—which inspired the quality of romantic detachment in the plays of our corpus. For it was Fletcher who, in his *The Faithful Shepherdess,* first created a world withdrawn from ordinary life—a world of bucolic shepherds and shepherdesses, of river god and friendly satyr. In doing so, he also created the first "moonlit" atmosphere of "an exquisite opera-set" to be found in our plays. Even though denizens of the court largely replaced, in the collaborated *Philaster,* the pastoral figures of *The Faithful Shepherdess,* and the idyllic notes of the two dramas were correspondingly different, it thus appears to have been Fletcher who pioneered in the particular romantic treatment which distinguishes our playwrights' tragicomedies and tragedies.

As has been suggested, Fletcher was probably stimulated to write his first play in the romantic vein by the popular success of Shakespeare's *Pericles*. No doubt he witnessed the latter, and observed with alertness its remote and exotic settings, its abundant and varied action, the incidents that threatened death yet led to an ultimately happy outcome, theatrical situations that tugged at the playgoers' heart-strings, and a spread of interest between several characters. At any rate, his own immediately following romantic drama for the boys of Blackfriars, although it was based on the pastoral rather than on the more adventurous Greek romance tradition, bore some resemblance to *Pericles* in at least these respects. Moreover, these same special characteristics reappeared in *Philaster,* this time blended with others garnered from *The Faithful Shepherdess* and from such plays of fellow-craftsmen as *Hamlet* and *The Malcontent.*

But though *Pericles* thus appears to have been the immediate stimulus to the creation of *The Faithful Shepherdess,* the influences which came to bear on Fletcher in devising and writing his play were diverse. Many of them were pastoral in nature. Some have already been sufficiently indicated.[28] The debt to Guarini has usually been underestimated because there are few obvious resemblances between *Il Pastor Fido* and *The Faithful Shepherdess*—although Fletcher's borrowing from the Italian for his theory of tragicomedy has often been recognized. One reason for this inadequate recognition of influence is our playwright's fertile inventiveness, which often results in his transposing what he has borrowed. For instance, in *Il Pastor Fido* the title shepherd, Mirtillo, is faithful to his beloved Amarillis even unto his threatened execution. His death is averted only towards the end by just such a delayed and elaborate denouement as marked our own dramatists' later practice. Transferring the common enough pastoral name, Amarillis, to a character who, as intriguer, resembles Guarini's Corisca,[29] Fletcher reversed the Mirtillo situation by making his faithful one, the shepherdess Clorin, a woman, and by having her constant to a lover who was dead. He then proclaimed his transverse parallel in the title of his drama.[30]

Mirtillo probably suggested Perigot, whose name, however, like others, came from *The Shepherd's Calendar.* But Fletcher took distrust, a minor note in Mirtillo's character, and made it the major one in Perigot's, who once wounds Amoret for her supposed lasciviousness, and a second time stabs her thinking that she is Amarillis in disguise.[31] Perigot is thus a first study for the jealous hero of *Philaster* who, in the woods, wounds both Arethusa and Bellario. It might be added, by the bye, that the word, Philaster, at once suggests Astrophel and Sir Philip Sidney, and that Arethusa is the name of the Sicilian river loved of pastoralists. Moreover, Arethusa's father is the ruler of Calabria and Sicily. No wonder the woodland scenes of *Philaster* struck Ristine as transmutations of the pastoral mode of *The Faithful Shepherdess!* The idyllic note, despite transformation of shepherds into courtiers and woodsmen, was carried over from Fletcher's tragicomedy to the sequent collaborated one.

The Faithful Shepherdess, like *Il Pastor Fido,* conforms to the classical unities in the Italian pastoral manner. In especial, the time-interval of the latter play extends from early morning to the sunset hour. Fletcher here makes another reversal, his drama beginning in late afternoon about the time of vespers, and ending soon after sun-up the next morning. The idea of making his play a nocturne may also have been suggested by *A Midsummer Night's Dream*. Shakespeare, however, did not observe unity of time so rigidly in his sylvan drama as did either Fletcher or Guarini.

If Fletcher found Shakespeare's play—the newest candidate for priority of influence—useful to him for many suggestions, these were controlled by one significant divergence. *The Faithful Shepherdess* is true pastoral drama throughout, whereas *A Midsummer Night's Dream* has no pastoral features at all in spite of its woodland settings for three acts. The latter play, with its young courtier-lovers in the forest and Theseus' morning hunt, may well have linked with the fourth act of Marston's *The Malcontent* to reveal to our playwrights how the idyllic notes of *The Faithful Shepherdess* might be transformed in *Philaster*. But because of the differences in mode between the gay sylvan comedy and the pastoral tragicomedy, their resemblances can be over-emphasized. It is, for example, clear enough that Fletcher carried the poetry of *A Midsummer Night's Dream* well in mind for, as McKeithan demonstrates,[32] he wrote many lines and even passages reminiscent of ones in Shakespeare's play. But others as clearly echo Spenser's *The Shepherd's Calendar,* the traditional bucolic elegy, or the details of the arcadian shepherd's life as described in lyric and eclogue from Theocritus and Vergil to his own day.

Structural resemblances may also be misleading. It has been demonstrated that Clorin and Theseus have a somewhat similar function of framing-in their respective plays, and controlling the destinies of certain characters.[33] But Theseus' sole effect on his two young couples is, through his unwise decree, to drive them into the woods. On the other hand, Clorin, who symbolizes a neo-Platonic conception of spiritualized love free of all sensuality,[34] is a most active agent in healing the physical wounds and emotional ills of other shepherds and shepherdesses. Her moral significance for the theme of Fletcher's drama—chastity—demands her central structural position in the play. Such similarity in function as she has to Theseus may, therefore, be purely fortuitous. In any case, whatever suggestion Fletcher got from Shakespeare's comedy he developed independently.

The fact is that Fletcher, steeped in the ancient and Renaissance pastoral literature, was eclectic in his borrowings. His materials were carefully chosen and blended so as to present a picture of shepherd life true to pastoral tradition and, in the episode of the water god, the related piscatorial one. The result of such eclecticism, resembling Edmund Spenser's on a lower creative level, was a genuinely original play which yet, as the scholarly George Chapman acknowledged,

> Renews the golden world, and holds through all
> The holy laws of homely pastoral, . . .[35]

The idea of organizing *The Faithful Shepherdess* on the theme of the power of chastity probably came to Fletcher from the third book of *The Faerie Queene* rather than from the comical satires of Jonson and Marston. Spenser gives his ethical conceptions of chastity narrative form by embodying various aspects of love and lust in allegorical characters, and then illustrating these aspects in action through the adventures of his figures. Although Fletcher avoids an openly allegorical treatment of his theme, nine of his characters, as Wells has shown,[36] have a "central import"; through speech and action they rigidly symbolize divers attitudes, chaste and unchaste. The scale of values runs from Clorin's neo-Platonic devotion at the top to the "unredeemable lust" of the Sullen Shepherd at the bottom.[37] The interrelations of the dramatis personae, and the course of the play's lines of action, are controlled by this symbolism.

Greg, whose Victorian moralism blocked his comprehension of *The Faithful Shepherdess,* except for its lyrical beauty, expressed the opinion that "the various complications arise and are solved, leaving the situation at the end precisely as it was in the beginning."[38] This is far from true. From the standpoint of the theme, much progress has been made at the conclusion of the play. Thenot has been cured of his strange but not unhuman obsession for Clorin; Perigot has learned to trust the ever-loyal Amoret, and their love has been deepened through adversity; the passionate Alexis and the longing virgin Cloe—whom Greg unkindly called a "yahoo"[39]—have learned what it means to love chastely; Amarillis has been terrified into firm temperateness; and the Sullen Shepherd, who remains unrepentantly animal, has been banished. Thus, with the help of Clorin, several characters have been "dishumoured," as Wells puts it. They have learned that chastity consists in loving faithfully, not wantonly or, like Thenot, fantastically.[40] Nathan Field understood, far better than most nineteenth century critics, the explicitly moral intent of Fletcher in this drama when he spoke of his hope

> To live to perfect such a work as this,
> Clad in such elegant propriety
> Of words, including a morality
> So sweet and profitable. . . .[41]

Miss Ellis-Fermor considers that, in this drama, "chastity, like the player-queen, doth protest too much."[42] She finds the characters so weakly motivated, and so wantonly subordinated to plot and situation, as to give the play "a pervading atmosphere of falseness and unreality." This typically modern attitude would probably have baffled a Stuart reader. He expected pastoral literature to have an air of unreality; he took it for granted that symbolic characters would behave strictly in terms of the quality they represented rather than as normal human beings; and he was aware of the enthusiasm for chastity, as an ideal, which even worldly people were capable of feeling. The church had fostered this enthusiasm; so had the apostles of neo-platonic love. Edmund Spenser had chosen chastity as one of the twelve private virtues which went to fashion the complete gentleman. There was doubtless a dichotomy in Fletcher's mind, characteristic of his age, which enabled him honestly and fervently to urge the power of chastity in *The Faithful Shepherdess,* and yet to handle love, in other dramas, with a gaily cynical sophistication reminiscent of Ovid's. Shakespeare, it should not be forgotten, wrote both *Romeo and Juliet* and *Venus and Adonis.*

To base the structure of a play on the symbolic treatment of an idea may be, and often is, a hindrance to its theatrical effectiveness. In *The Faithful Shepherdess* it resulted in the creation of a number of different strands of story interest, nicely adjusted and interrelated from the standpoint of theme. Fletcher's perennial concern with variety of emotional (or comic) appeal to an audience was thus well taken into account. But dramatically the result was a dispersal of the spectator's attention not offset by definite emphasis on one or two plot strands. Moreover, while the action reached a conclusion which satisfied the demands of the theme, it did not build up to a denouement of any theatrical power.

In *Philaster* our playwrights dispensed with a strongly emphasized and controlling theme, contrived fewer threads of plot, and developed a striking denouement. It therefore appears likely that Fletcher, perhaps aided by criticism from Beaumont, put his diagnostic finger on a schematic choice of characters and arrangement of situations, so as to "point a moral," as one of the causes for the failure of *The Faithful Shepherdess* on the boards. Certainly, from the standpoint of central idea, that

drama had been carefully organized; yet thereafter neither of our playwrights used this method of integrating their plays. It is possible that
the failure of *The Knight of the Burning Pestle,* with its marked burlesque purpose, also contributed to their preference for the incidental de-
bating of controversial topics, for aphorism and partial satire, rather
than for serious and complete treatment of themes.

The form of structural integration which was to prove successful in
Philaster, that of emotional patterning, began to emerge in Fletcher's
drama. The various contrasting aspects of love and lust symbolized by
his characters made possible, at times, the juxtaposition in relatively
swift succession of diverse emotional attitudes and reactions. But the demands of his theme and symbolism put restraints on continuous use of
this arrangement; and emotional patterning was further submerged by
the countless lyrical and descriptive passages or touches which, with a
happy effect of spontaneity, give richness of poetic texture to his "golden
world" of the arcadian shepherd. Vesper and matin rituals in the worship of Pan, Clorin's telling over of her medicinal herbs and flowers, the
water god's account to Amoret of his liquid realm: such graceful lyric
passages as these, endowing the drama with an exotic pastoral atmosphere, prevented a constant play of emotion as effectively as the necessity of developing the theme.

So far as his self-imposed limitations allowed, however, Fletcher sought
to create a variety of emotional impact. Indeed, what most drew him to
the tragicomic mode, aside from Guarini's theories about it and practice of it, was doubtless just the diversity of emotional effect—tragic, sentimental, idyllic, comic—which it permitted. This was adumbrated in the
brief explanation of tragicomedy which Fletcher was willing to give the
reader "for nothing." It was not that a tragic plot was combined with a
comic subplot, a common enough Elizabethan-Stuart practice:

A tragi-comedy is not so called in respect of mirth and killing, but in respect it
wants deaths, which is enough to make it no tragedy, yet brings some near it,
which is enough to make it no comedy, which must be a representation of
familiar people, with such kind of trouble as no life be questioned; so that a
god is as lawful in this as in a tragedy, and mean people as in a comedy.[43]

This statement obviously takes the form of an answer to specific objections which had been made to his play (Had his River-god been questioned?), and goes no deeper into the matter than that. But if a variety of
people ranging from the gods and aristocrats of tragedy to the "mean
people" of comedy were admissible, the implication is that as wide a
range of emotional effects was likewise allowable. And however a modern
critic might haggle about it, a practical Jacobean playwright would con-

sider any situation or remark appealing to an audience's risibilities as inducing an emotional response. Tragicomedy, while wanting the "deaths" of tragedy, and at the same time creating crises too serious for comedy— or "bringing some near" death—blended elements of both in an intermediate form.[44] Of such nature, as we have seen,[45] was Guarini's theory of tragicomedy, with which Fletcher was familiar, and which underlies the latter's curt definition.

Fletcher's method of construction in *The Faithful Shepherdess* can be clearly perceived in the first act. In scene one, Clorin, the faithful shepherdess, recounts her constant love for her dead shepherd, in the manner of the pastoral elegy, and describes the healing powers of her herbs and flowers. The uncouth but kindly Satyr, amazed at Clorin's chaste beauty, addresses her as a goddess, and offers her a gift of nuts, grapes, and berries. After he leaves, Clorin expresses her wonder at the "private hidden power" which can "draw submission From this rude man and beast,"[46] and establishes the theme of the play in a eulogy of "strong chastity."[47]

In scene two Fletcher begins to employ those methods for producing sharp contrast which Waith contends he learned from the comical satires of Jonson and Marston.[48] The scene opens with the last rite in a festival in honor of Pan, wherein the Priest, sprinkling a group of shepherds and shepherdesses with holy water, purges away any "wanton quick desires"[49] which the day may have brought. After a concluding song in praise of Pan, Amoret and Perigot linger to evince their chaste love, and to plan a meeting in the woods that night to plight their troth.

Amoret leaves, and Amarillis, whose unbridled passion for Perigot strongly contrasts with Amoret's chaste love, enters at once. Without hesitation, she declares her passion for Perigot, who rejects her advances, telling her of his plan to meet Amoret that evening. Amarillis, left alone, expresses her determination to win Perigot to her will and to enlist the aid of the Sullen Shepherd, who delights in breaking up true love matches. The latter, entering, completes the vivid contrast with Perigot and Amoret by wooing Amarillis lustfully. She readily agrees to yield to him after he has helped her gain Perigot as lover. Thus this scene exploits striking antitheses both of character and of juxtaposed situations.[50]

Scene three is taken up with the attempts of the "green-sick" virgin, Cloe—scorner of chastity—to allure the three other symbolic shepherds, each a different type of lover. After Cloe's opening soliloquy, which reveals her state of feeling, Thenot enters, and she at once attempts to entice him. But Thenot repulses her with his account of his infatuation with Clorin's constancy and departs. Here is a striking parallel to the earlier Perigot-Amarillis situation. Daphnis, in contrast to Thenot, is willing to meet Cloe in the woods in the evening, but bashfully assures her she need not fear any unchaste word or deed from him. After he leaves, Cloe expresses her discontent with so cold a lover. But Alexis, who now enters, is as forward as Daphnis was bashful; he meets her warmth with equal ardor, and they, also, plan a meeting in the woods. The structure of this scene is, therefore, built on antithesis, re-inforced by parallelism.

In this first act Fletcher has thus established—with a minimum of retrospect and exposition—the main threads of his plot. He has announced his theme, and presented contrasting situations which dramatize the diverging attitudes towards love of his ten embodiments of chastity or unchastity. In scene one he has foreshadowed the healing powers which Clorin, with the help of the Satyr, will later display. In scenes two and three he has set in motion his several strands of action, and aroused the audience's interest in them. At the same time, by means of an abundance of incidental descriptive detail appropriate to the various situations, he has established the exotic atmosphere of the pastoral world.

Furthermore, Fletcher has handled his situations with relative swiftness. A sympathetic playgoer will have been moved to a rapid succession of differing reactions, one of which would doubtless be amusement at the bashfulness of Daphnis and at the "green-sickness" of the longing virgin, Cloe.[51] It is, of course, evident that, in this opening act, the full tragicomic range of emotion and mood has not yet been employed. Moreover, the farcical situation, except in the cases of Daphnis and Cloe, will be avoided throughout the play as out of harmony with its theme and mixture of tones.

Because of his somewhat complicated story and his thematic treatment, Fletcher has not fully exploited each individual situation, with many fluctuations of emotional reaction within it. Instead, a number of situations have illustrated many attitudes, chaste and unchaste, towards love. This tendency to the relatively short scene is, in some measure, characteristic of Fletcher, who likes to keep action moving at a fast pace. In *Philaster*, with simpler story and dominant emotional patterning, there will be half as many lovers as in the pastoral drama. Lust will be concentrated in the figures of Pharamond and Megra, in marked contrast to the romantic loves of Philaster, Arethusa and Bellario. Emotional oscillation, and reversal of feeling, especially within longer-held situations, will tend to be greater.

And yet, in both these plays, there is a comparable use of simplified characters, whose traits are exaggerated, whose emotions are intense, and who can be brought into vivid contrast with one another. No doubt, as Waith contends, the methods developed by Jonson and Marston for presenting satirical figures have been appropriated. Indeed, Waith argues pertinently for a special indebtedness which *The Faithful Shepherdess,* as the first of Fletcher's more serious plays, may have owed to certain situations in comical satires of Jonson and Marston.

In these situations, a strong emotional effect of a kind unusual to such plays is achieved by combining satire with romance. The figures involved are themselves otherwise targets of satire. Ovid and Julia in *The Poetaster* "represent the loose morality of the [Roman] nobility," and the title character in *Volpone* is an incarnation of greed. Yet the intensity of the erotic emotion which Ovid displays when he parts from Julia to go into exile (Act IV, scene 9), and the glittering splendor of the verse in which Volpone pours out his passion for Celia (Act III, scene 7), arouse "a romantic—even a sensational—interest" in spectators.[52]

Waith argues that these situations, and somewhat similar ones in Marston's *The Malcontent* and *The Dutch Courtesan,* were of a sort especially to impress Fletcher. They stimulated his interest in further exploring "the emotion of unbalanced personalities like Ovid or Volpone," while eliminating Jonson's satiric purpose. The resultant tone, which Fletcher first achieved in *The Faithful Shepherdess,* was different from Jonson's; in fact, it was "an intermediate tone, not entirely that of romance, and not that which previously was found in tragedy, comedy, or tragicomedy."[53] By comparison, Guarini, in his *Il Pastor Fido,* gave a merely conventional treatment to his pastoral characters. "Fletcher's emphasis on the emotions of morally opposed, extreme types" was entirely lacking.[54]

Fletcher's own technique of characterization undoubtedly was aided by that devised by Jonson and Marston for presenting butts of satire in their own comedies. It is worth noting, however, that the enmeshing of characters in a web of situations to which they respond with displays of intense emotion is more characteristic of the *Arcadia* than of most of the satirical comedies. Sidney's romance, and also *The Faerie Queene,* were earlier well-springs of Fletcher's desire to explore the emotional possibilities of exaggerated figures than were the comedies of Jonson and Marston.

The Faithful Shepherdess, as Waith remarks, "is built around scenes in which the lustful characters oppose the chaste by means of infamous stratagems, only to be themselves vanquished in the end."[55] Of *Philaster* much the same remark could be made. The collaborators on this tragicomedy, however, exploited more fully the emotional relationships between three main characters—Philaster, Arethusa, Bellario—than was done in any instance in *The Faithful Shepherdess.* Yet, despite lesser leeway for developing any single plot-thread, Fletcher presents, beginning with Act III of the latter, "every conceivable complication" which can result from Perigot's illusion that the disguised Amarillis is Amoret.[56]

Indeed, a kaleidoscopic activity is even more evident in the third act of the pastoral play than it was in the first. We have the typical Fletcherian rapidity of movement, with the surprises, reversals and mistakes in identity that we expect in plays of our corpus—combined with an unusual degree of picturesque lyrical beauty. Characters rush on and off the stage; we see Amarillis turned into a replica of Amoret through the agency of a magic well, and later released from the spell in dire need; various amorous passions are aroused; and the wounding of Alexis by the Sullen Shepherd and of Amoret by Perigot bring two of the characters near death in the fashion of tragicomedy.

Perhaps the most suprising reversal comes when the God of the River arises with Amoret in his arms and heals her wound after the Sullen Shepherd has flung her into the magic well to drown. If a spectator were caught in the spell of the play, the swiftly moving action, the sharply contrasting situations and contretemps, and the diverse emotions displayed by the characters, would not permit his tension, throughout this act, to relax for a moment. For all its alternation of blank verse with shorter lyrical measures and its charming touches and passages of description, the third act has a theatrical liveliness which resembles that of the collaborated plays to come.

The pastoral atmosphere of *The Faithful Shepherdess* is not the only cause of this play's "clear, remote radiance." The emotions of the characters are painfully intense. Yet these figures' symbolic, simplified construction, and their exaggerated traits (as of figures in comical satire) remove them, in Waith's words, "to a theoretical world remote from one's own experience."[57] We watch, as it were, the conflict of distilled and concentrated emotions, in characters who have been delicately balanced against each other to produce this effect. We respond to the often painful feelings which the characters express, but with our interest rather more strongly in the series of emotions they are expressing than in their ultimate fate. We may experience the thrill of tragic horror when the wounded Amoret is thrown into the well by the Sullen Shepherd; but the water-god immediately allays our horror by rising with Amoret in his arms and restoring her to life. Never do we feel that the outcome of the play will be tragic, though some of its situations are threatening, and some of its characters become entangled in a web of distressing circumstance. Thus, Fletcher's "middle mood" is neither tragic nor comic, but subtly blends elements of both into a "refined form of sensationalism"[58] alike new to the pastoral, and to the Jacobean, drama.

It should now be clear that *The Faithful Shepherdess* anticipates, in good measure, and in various ways, the idyllic tragicomedy, *Philaster*. Of these, perhaps the most important are: Fletcher's tragicomic treatment of his materials, with a wide range of effects—passionate, threatening, iydllic, comic—blended into a harmony; his evocation of an exotic atmosphere and a sense of a world remote from actuality; his concern with attitudes of love and lust; his concentration upon almost violent contrasts between characters and between successive situations; and his anticipation, in some degree, of the lifting of emotional patterning to dominance in *Philaster.* If, as appears probable, *The Faithful Shepherdess* preceded the latter play, then Fletcher was the originator of some of the elements most characteristic of the collaborated dramas which brought the "twins" to fame.

IV

Embedded in Robert Herrick's eulogy, *Upon Master Fletchers Incomparable Playes,* are these lines:

Here's a *mad lover,* there that high designe
Of *King and no King* (and the rare Plot thine)[59]

This statement that Fletcher was the deviser of the plot for *A King and No King* is unequivocal. Moreover, Herrick was in a position to have known the truth of the matter. When the play was first performed, he was a London apprentice to his uncle, a goldsmith—and doubtless a theatregoer. Furthermore, after proceeding M.A. at Cambridge in 1620, he assuredly became acquainted with Fletcher if, indeed, he had not done so earlier. For he was "sealed of the tribe of Ben," and a participant at "lyric feasts" at the Sun, Dog and Three Tuns taverns;[60] while Fletcher, loved of Ben, would also have been sometimes present. Herrick's statement, therefore, may well have been based on conversation with the playwright himself. In any case, he must have felt certain of its truth, since he gave it emphatic position in the couplet, and then called further attention to it by enclosing it in parentheses.

Herrick's testimony is of importance because Fletcher's share in the design, construction and theatrecraft of *Philaster, The Maid's Tragedy* and *A King and No King* has often been either underrated or ignored, in spite of the ways in which we have found the craftsmanship of these plays skilfully foreshadowed in *The Faithful Shepherdess.* Through verse and style tests Beaumont has been hailed as the main author of the major collaborated pieces and, in consequence, the chief planner of them as well. But Herrick's assertion casts a reasonable doubt over at least the latter claim as it concerns *A King and No King,* and adds support to a conjecture that Fletcher also had much to do with the construction of *Philaster* and *The Maid's Tragedy.* It would seem, then, that the respective achievements of our two playwrights cannot be so easily separated as the application of verse-tests and other such mechanical determinants alone would appear to warrant.

It might, in fact, be questioned whether Fletcher had so small a role in the actual writing of these dramas as the final state of the manuscript has led critics to believe. It has been generally agreed that the collaboration of these two comrades was closer and more leisurely, at least in these three instances, than was normal in Jacobean days, when so many plays were hastily thrown together to meet the pressing demands of the actors. Fletcherian touches have often been suspected in Beaumont scenes, or the reverse, and some scenes have been thought to have been written jointly. This situation is further complicated by the facts that Beaumont had a gift for parody, and that *The Faithful Shepherdess* demonstrates Fletcher's ability to write a more conventional verse than was usual with him. Either author may have been able to imitate the other's style and manner, at least for short stretches of dialogue.

Most important of all are the indications that the critically minded Beaumont, as the stronger personality in this Damon and Pythias partnership, was the chief polisher and reviser. The seventeenth century tradition that Ben Jonson sought the advice of his judicious young friend about his own plots is significant, even if not literally true. Humphrey Moseley, in *The Stationer to the Reader,* prefixed to the 1647 Folio, informs us that "Mr. Beaumont was ever acknowledged a man of a most strong and searching braine . . ."[61] William Cartwright, in his commendatory verses, tells us that, after Fletcher had written, Beaumont

> Added his sober spunge, and did contract
> Thy plenty to lesse wit to make't exact:[62]

There would be nothing surprising in Beaumont's pruning of Fletcher's effervescent fluency. Amidst all the seventeenth century testimony to Beaumont's judgment, we need not consider statements to this effect by Cartwright and others valueless merely because these gentlemen did not recognize how large a creative as well as critical share Beaumont had in the three plays under discussion.

It is, thus, credible that the more flexible and easy-going Fletcher granted his analytical partner the major responsibility for the final revision of these plays, which, indeed, bear no earmarks of hurried work.[63] Hence it is a reasonable assumption that some of the scenes which now appear to be, in poetic expression and treatment, Beaumont's may have been originally drafted by Fletcher. For it is an odd phenomenon that the fertile older playwright appears, on the surface, to have contributed

so few scenes to these plays, especially since he pioneered in the tragicomic mode, and in other ways, with his pastoral drama.

It is, in fact, not utterly beyond possibility that Fletcher (perhaps
aided by Field or another) wrote an unsatisfactory first version of *Philaster* under the title of *Love Lies a-Bleeding*, and that Beaumont then re-
worked the whole play, with advice and help from his comrade, for the
King's Men. The curious opening and closing passages of this drama, as
first printed in quarto one, and as then consciously corrected by the publisher in quarto two,[64] admit of the interpretation that in their first
form they were fragments of an earlier version. So does the disputed
epigram 206 by John Davies of Hereford, addressed about 1610 to
Fletcher, which begins

> *Loue lies ableeding,* if it should not proue
> Her uttmost art to shew why it doth loue.[65]

For Davies might have known of, or seen, the hypothetical earlier version. And then there is the piquant double listing of *Philaster*, once under that title and again as *Love Lies a-Bleeding*, among the fourteen
performances given by the King's Men at Court during the season of
1612-13.[66] Did this company repeat the play in a somewhat revised version, and under the original—or a new—title? Or was the scribe simply
avoiding duplication in his list by using an alternate one for the second
performance—and, if so, where did he get his title? The solution of these
mysteries may yet prove to be that there was an earlier Fletcher version
of the play.[67] If so, the elder dramatist originated the plot of *Philaster*
as well as that of *A King and No King*.

In any event, it cannot be taken for granted that the construction and
the theatrecraft of the three major collaborated plays were mainly the
work of Beaumont. Herrick's explicit statement about the plot of *A King
and No King* gains further support from Beaumont's own temperament.
It is worth pondering that, after his first two satirical comedies, Beaumont wrote no further plays alone which have survived.[68] He was endowed with a temperament rather more strongly critical than creative.
His two independent dramas, in their keen-edged satire, reflect this vigorous bent of mind. Thereafter he evidently preferred to cooperate with
Fletcher, whose facility in devising situations, shaping plots, and ex-
ploiting theatrecraft with emotional or comic virtuosity, is abundantly
clear from his handiwork in some fifty plays.[69]

Beaumont thus appears to have been that kind of playwright who,
originating relatively few dramatic ideas of his own, makes an exceptional collaborator, because of his sound judgment, with a more fluent

but perhaps less deeply gifted talent. In all probability his well developed critical sense of theatre ordinarily needed a catalyzing agent to set it in motion. Fletcher had precisely the lively if more superficial mind that could fertilize Beaumont's. They thus complemented each other. Fletcher spawned plots, situations, theatrecraft, the mode of patterning their joint plays; Beaumont seized upon and improved these, was stimulated to make contributions of his own, and controlled Fletcher's natural exuberance. The result was true collaboration—the most skilful of the whole Elizabethan-Stuart drama—with Beaumont's final imprint on the majority of scenes in their three main serious plays. To such an actual *modus operandi* the Royalist tributes to Fletcher's fluency and Beaumont's judgment all point.

V

Fletcher never found another collaborator who complemented his own gift for playwriting so well as Beaumont. Fortunately for him, the two comrades developed a solid command of their own particular theatrecraft in their major collaborated plays. Their experimental period behind them, they achieved their first fully characteristic blend of dramatic methods in *Philaster*, extended them from tragicomedy into tragedy with *The Maid's Tragedy*, and solidified them in *A King and No King*.

Though Beaumont soon departed from London, Fletcher, in his own more volatile manner, continued to employ throughout the rest of his career the basic elements of their now well-tested technique. He made only such modifications in it as his stage-manager's instinct and the varying types of the plays suggested. Frequently, under the pressure of time, he secured the aid of other playwrights. Shakespeare did not disdain to work with him temporarily, just before he dropped completely out of the King's Men's affairs. Fletcher's star pupil, the less spirited Massinger, was easily his most frequent assistant, and Field shared with them both in several plays. The pieces in which Fletcher had the sole or a main hand made a lively impact on other playwrights. As Ristine pointed out,[70] Fletcher's various tragicomedies, whether written alone or in collaboration with others, established the popularity of this type of play in later Jacobean and Caroline drama.

Massinger proved an adequate assistant in collaboration because, when he joined forces with Fletcher, the latter had already attained acknowledged mastery of his craft through his experience with *The Faithful Shepherdess* and through his observant collaboration with Beaumont. The inexperienced Massinger brought to his junior partnership a more reflective mind and a stronger bent towards unifying a play by means of a tight hold on the plot. Nonetheless, he willingly submitted himself to the tuition of stage-wise Fletcher as regards emotional patterning and other fundamentals of theatrecraft. The mark of this schooling remains in the craftsmanship of Massinger's later unassisted plays, for all the fact that they reveal a personality different from Fletcher's. Field, like Massinger, was dominated in joint work by Fletcher, and occasional other assistants made such adjustments as might be needed when working in the "studio" of the master.

As a result, the plays of our corpus usually display, in differing emphases, the theatrical qualities which first, as a whole, fused in the major collaborated dramas of Beaumont and Fletcher. Even the many pieces which were carelessly and hastily turned out to supply an immediate demand[71] do so. *The Faithful Shepherdess,* as we have seen, anticipated many of these things to come—but not all of them. With *Philaster* the full complex of basic elements in the new theatrecraft for the gentry begins to come clear. Against the perspective of our playwrights' milieu, of their preceding experience in writing, and their method of close collaboration, *Philaster* and its successors can now be made to reveal the nature of that theatrecraft, so often misapprehended in the criticism of the past.

CHAPTER SEVEN

Theatrecraft for the Gentry

T HAT the time was ripe for a return to dramas of a romantic appeal when the King's Men acquired Blackfriars was fortunate for Beaumont and Fletcher. Awake to the promise of so sophisticated an exotic as *Philaster,* Shakespeare's company proceeded to realize this promise on the stage. They thus launched Stuart tragicomedy on its long career of popularity. Moreover, the production of *The Maid's Tragedy* by the King's Men first brought to theatregoers that "twin-form" of tragicomedy, a variety of tragedy incorporating all the features of the "middle mood" except its happy outcome. Shakespeare and his confréres were thus, in a very practical way, contributors to the success of these Jacobean innovations.

If the distinctive quality of the Beaumont and Fletcher plays was largely the result of a skilful blending of ingredients from many sources, there was also something fresh and spontaneous in the mixture. For although both men lacked the penetrating insight into aspects of human life and destiny which characterizes the dramatic genius, neither was content wholly to write in the conventional veins of the past. Having gained a clear sense of the tastes of their audience through the failure of plays expressing their own temperaments with some originality, they joined forces to fabricate dramas designed to hold theatregoers enthralled, and not quite like any that had gone before.

Because Beaumont and Fletcher, in their more serious plays, so subtly fused elements of both comedy and tragedy, as well as the emotions appropriate to each, Miss Ellis-Fermor declares that these dramas were "something not only in a new mood but in a new kind."[1] And she explains that "something . . . in this mood . . . has disabled us from distinguishing, in the world we are now moving in, the characters, emotions and events that will lead to tragedy from those that will lead through romantic stress to escape."[2] Miss Bradbrook, however, censures this novelty. To her, "the blurring of the tragic and the comic" is a symptom of "the coarsening of the fibre" which they introduced into Jacobean poetic tragedy.[3] Miss Ellis-Fermor considers Beaumont, Fletcher and Massinger "consummate dramatic journalists," and calls their dramas "as nearly perfect theatrework as is possible to imagine."[4] But Miss Bradbrook treats these playwrights scornfully as decadents. She weighs them in the balance against the earlier dramatists, and finds them wanting.[5]

Here, in a nutshell, is the present point of conflict in the criticism of our corpus. Against the perspective of our playwrights' gentleman-commoner background, their university education, their aristocratic literary taste, their particular dramatic milieu and their first experiences in playwriting, the newer approach of Miss Ellis-Fermor would, on the whole, appear to be both the sounder and the more illuminating. Those who espouse it seek to understand Beaumont, Fletcher and Massinger as men of the theatre who were a natural product of their point in time and place. They accept the gulf between Shakespeare, a dramatist for the ages, and Fletcher and Beaumont, playwrights to the sophisticates of their own era. They acknowledge that, by 1600, a change had begun to take place in theatregoing which more and more sorted out those spectators who attended the private theatres—and even, in time, the Globe[6]— from those who haunted the lesser playhouses. Holding that, under the circumstances, the emergence of entertainers to the gentry was inevitable, such critics are concerned to understand the exact nature of our playwrights' craftsmanship. They are likely to find it superlatively good on its own theatrical level.

Recognizing, also, that the older modes of romantic comedy, tragedy and satirical comedy had been rather fully exploited by 1608 or 1609, these critics are not surprised that our young and talented playwrights should have sought to concoct an innovation whose freshness of treatment would have a wide appeal. They do not consider that this final major blood-transfusion in Elizabethan-Stuart drama was wholly bad for the patient. Though they may find the new blood thinner in quality than some of the old, they discover virtues in it, and even suspect that it helped to keep the patient relatively flourishing until 1642.

To complete, from this viewpoint, our re-examination of the Fletcher and Company achievement does not require an exhaustive analysis of the plays. Much of their craftsmanship has already been made manifest through the heterogeneous critical appraisals of the past. More of it has become apparent as we determined the influences which the milieu of our dramatists, and their early playwriting ventures, had upon them. There remains only such a probing into the complex of their theatre-craft as will synthesize our re-interpretation of Fletcher, Beaumont and

Company in the light of critical opinion about them from the seventeenth century to the present.

I

Since our playwrights were writing their tragicomedies and tragedies not for modern readers but for the playgoers of their own age, the testimony of the latter concerning the effect of these dramas on spectators should throw some light on their authors' craftsmanship. We have seen that the Blackfriars audience of 1608 had rejected *The Faithful Shepherdess* in spite of its vivid contrasts and parallels and its partial emotional patterning of its materials. Whatever later plays of our corpus were poorly received, such rejections did not long remain the norm.

To the nature of the impact which the more serious plays had on Stuart playgoers, the eulogies of the First Folio clearly testify. Francis Palmer of Christ's Church, Oxford, writes, as a theatregoer who had often witnessed the effect of these dramas upon an audience,

> But when Thy Tragicke Muse would please to rise
> In Majestie, and call Tribute from our Eyes;
> Like Scenes, we shifted Passions, and that so,
> Who only came to see, turn'd Actors too.
> How didst thou sway the Theatre! make us feele
> The Players wounds were true, and their swords, steele! . . .
> Frozen with griefe we could not stir away
> Until the Epilogue told us 'twas a Play.[7]

Thomas Stanley, minor poet and generous assister of needy literary men during the years of the Commonwealth, is somewhat more specific about the audiences' emotional responses to certain of "Fletcher's" plays:

> He to a Sympathie those soules betrai'd
> Whom Love or Beauty never could perswade;
> And in each mov'd spectatour could beget
> A reall passion by a Counterfeit:
> When first Bellario bled, what Lady there
> Did not for every drop let fall a teare?
> And when Aspatia wept, not any eye
> But seem'd to weare the same sad livery;
> By him inspir'd the feign'd Lucina drew
> More streams of melting sorrow then the true; . . .[8]

Stanley also appears to have sensed our playwrights' tendency to exaggeration in their handling of passions, but praises Fletcher for this:

> He Nature taught her passions to out-doe,
> How to refine the old, and create new;
> Which such a happy likenesse seem'd to beare,
> As if that Nature Art, Art Nature were.[9]

William Cartwright, too, was impressed by the power of the serious dramas to move the audience; Fletcher had

> . . . cloath'd affections in such native tires,
> And so describ'd them in their owne true fires;
> Such moving sighes, suc(h) undissembled teares,
> Such charms of language, such hopes mixt with feares,
> Such grants after denialls, such pursuits,
> After despaire, such amorous recruits,
> That some who sate spectators have confest
> Themselves transform'd to what they saw exprest,
> And felt such shafts steele through their captiv'd sence,
> As made them rise Parts, and goe Lovers thence.[10]

Here, indeed, was a direct effect of these dramas on life!

Jasper Maine likewise observed how completely the plays brought the audience into rapport with their own mimic world:

> Where e're you listed to be high and grave
> No Buskin shew'd more solem(n)e, no quill gave
> Such feeling objects to draw teares from eyes,
> Spectators sate part in your tragedies.[11]

Robert Herrick was impressed by the way in which Fletcher and Company could keep an audience marvelling at the turns of action and emotion:

> Here's words with lines, and line with Scenes consent
> To raise an Act to full astonishment; . . .

Nor should we forget that he found a "high designe" in *A King and No King*, and thought that "None writes lov's passion in the world, like Thee."[12]

Moreover, Cartwright, who had himself written dramas which were performed at Christ's Church, Oxford, praised the constructional ingenuity by which our playwrights kept their audiences happily perplexed about what was to come. He tells us that none can anticipate

> . . . the Fancy, and see through
> At the first opening; all stand wondring how
> The thing will be untill it is; which thence
> With fresh delight still cheats, still takes the sence; . . .

Furthermore, he considered the plays well constructed:

> The whole designe, the shadowes, the lights such
> That none can say he shewes or hides too much:
> Businesse growes up, ripened by just encrease,
> And by as just degrees againe doth cease,
> The heats and minutes of affaires are watcht,
> And the nice points of time are met, and snatcht;
> Nought later then it should, nought comes before: . . .[13]

These Caroline testimonies, and others like them, demonstrate that the serious plays of our corpus had a strong and affecting impact on the emotions of Stuart playgoers. They also indicate that these dramas, and the comedies as well, were so articulated as to baffle conjecture about their courses, and to delight spectators with their surprises and reversals. Such testimonies, as Mizener discovered,[14] are clues to the deliberate and deftly planned emotional patterning of the tragicomedies and tragedies —a patterning we have found foreshadowed in Fletcher's *The Faithful Shepherdess.*

It needs no demonstration that Elizabethan and Stuart playgoers, with their delight in dramatized story, had a lively zest for sensational incidents. Haworth comments that "all the dramatists of the age vied with one another in their efforts to excite rare emotions and exploit unheard-of crimes."[15] Hence, plays which sought to generate a cluster of more or less harmonious emotions by sets of scenes loosely bound as narrative were, as Mizener remarks,[16] not uncommon to Jacobean drama. Nonetheless, most of the plays which preceded *Philaster,* however sensational in incident and complication, were organized in terms of such narrative elements as character, and intrigue or event. These were the foundations from which emotional situations more or less logically resulted. There were, of course, some dramas controlled by their didactic intent, and others, after 1598, by a satirical scheme and purpose.

Fletcher and Beaumont, however—and the later collaborators—organized the materials of their dramas squarely around "the network of conflicting emotions"[17] which they had envisioned, and with which they wished to play upon the sensibilities of their audience. Plots were cunningly shaped, not to the end of a well wrought dramatic narrative as such, nor on the basis of probability, but in order to make a complex of varied passions sufficiently plausible to induce a "willing suspension of disbelief for the moment" in the tense spectators. Characters were contrived in such manner that, either in their central traits or in minor ones, they could be brought into sharp conflict with one another. Thus, the tragicomedies and tragedies of our corpus were ordered in terms of their emotional pattern or, as Mizener expresses it, their "emotional or psychological form."[18]

Precisely this was the main source of the irritation which neo-classical critics like Rymer felt towards the Fletcher and Company dramas. By Rymer's standards these plays, at every turn, violated probability and decorum, alike in plotting and in characterization. He studied their technique only to condemn it. Dryden accepted Rymer's criticisms of the construction of *A King and No King*, and yet found that the play moved him on the stage by "its lively touches of the passions." So he relaxed his own theories sufficiently, in this one instance, to argue that the tragi-comedy possessed "the best of their designs," and was a praiseworthy specimen of an "inferior sort of tragedies" that concluded with "a prosperous event."[19] But other neo-classical critics during the next hundred years, as we have discovered, expressed the opinion that our playwrights were devoid of skill in construction.

If the emotional patterning of our dramas was in conflict with the theories of dramatic structure held by Rymer, Dryden and other neo-classicists, the method itself was not generally understood by the romantic critics and their successors. For the plays were certainly not functional in terms of character and of dramatic poetry as these were conceived by nineteenth century critics. Coleridge, as a consequence, looked upon our dramas as "mere aggregations without unity." He was unable to perceive that the emotional form by which the plays were ordered gave them a unity not altogether mechanical.[20]

Other critics noted or deplored effects without penetrating to causes. Hazlitt thought that Fletcher and Beaumont "would have a catastrophe in every scene, so that you have none at last." He does not appear to have realized fully the power of their scenes in building, during a performance, to a climactic denouement. To Hazlitt, everything seemed merely to be "in a state of fermentation and effervescence."[21] In this respect, Swinburne was equally unperceptive. Fletcher found it sufficient, he thought, "to excite compassion [for meek women], as in the more masculine parts of his work it was enough for him to excite wonder, to sustain curiosity, to goad and stimulate by any vivid and violent means. . . ."[22]

In the twentieth century, Thorndike could still speak of our dramas as "collections of situations" giving "vivid momentary pictures of the passions." He did not observe any unity of design; he noted, instead, our playwrights' "concern with various, and often opposed, emotional impacts . . . rather than a concentration on a single emotion or character."[23] Miss Hatcher also recognized the absence of focus on "some powerful personal center," and accepted Coleridge's "mere aggregations" dictum.[24] Archer, applying the standard of realistic truth-to-life, found

many notable flaws in the plotting and motivation of *The Maid's Tragedy* and *Philaster*, and censured the latter drama as based entirely upon
"elements of unreason."[25]

Much more recently, Miss Bradbrook has failed to find structural unity
in our dramas. She holds that Fletcher wrote tragedies "against the
grain. . . . Character and narrative are not informed and unified by a
pressure of thought and feeling."[26] The only basis she can discover for
the tragedies and tragicomedies of our corpus is "an outrageous stimulation." She takes it for granted that it does not matter to our playwrights what their characters feel, or why, so long as they are "feeling
intensely all the time."[27] She condemns "the emotional egg-whisk" of
their "adjurations, addresses and tirades,"[28] and belabors the "offensive"
coarseness of Fletcher and Massinger.[29]

This persistent failure to recognize the unorthodox organization and
treatment which Fletcher, Beaumont and Company gave their plays has
thus tended, for some generations, to lead critics astray. They have found
the work of our playwrights defective according to neo-classical, romantic or realistic criteria. They have sometimes illuminated aspects of the
work, but they have usually not stopped to consider whether they understood what sort of play our dramatists were writing.

Even Miss Bradbrook, who has proved herself an able and often astute
student of the themes, conventions and stagecraft of Elizabethan tragedy,
appears largely to have followed the Coleridgean tradition in analyzing
the tragicomedies and tragedies of our corpus. Had she fully realized that
these dramas have an emotional form, and that their plotting, characterization, poetry and ethics are all bound up with this form, she would assuredly have judged their achievement more soundly, regardless of
whether or not she liked it. Mizener concludes that Miss Bradbrook's
critique is definite evidence of "something radically wrong with the usual
approach to Beaumont and Fletcher."[30] Her viewpoint would surely suggest the wisdom of following the clue afforded by the First Folio eulogists, and of recognizing that emotional patterning is the unifying and
determining element in our playwrights' tragicomedies and tragedies.

II

The more serious plays of Fletcher, Beaumont and Company, and
sometimes the comedies as well, have a deceptively solid appearance of
narrative structure. When the story element, however, is stripped down
to its bare skeleton, it will frequently be found that those events which
peg out the plots are fewer than might have been expected from all the

bustle and tensions, emotional conflicts and crises, which impress the playgoer or reader. The groundwork of the plotting has been deftly laid down and developed to intensify and to support the emotional contour of the play. The action gains concentration from a moderately close adherence to the unities of time and place. A smoothly devised, seemingly logical sequence of diverse and multiple emotional developments has been wrung out of the events. The sensibilities of the spectators are thereby variously played upon, and the audience gains the impression that the drama is elaborately constructed.

The "imposing pretense" of a "massive narrative structure," which Mizener soundly holds to be characteristic of our playwrights' work, was thus the result of treating narrative as a means of reinforcing the drama's emotional form.[31] Our playwrights were far more dexterous than Webster and most other Jacobean writers of serious drama in providing a neatly arranged plot foundation for exciting scenes and situations. It is doubtless this very skilfulness which has misled critics into thinking that the plot-structures of our plays are significant in themselves rather than as means to an end, and therefore sadly culpable for their improbabilities and exaggerations. But though plotting was important to our playwrights, it was chiefly so as the carefully dove-tailed framework upon which an elaborate emotional tapestry could be woven. From this standpoint, the narrative element of their plays proves to be, in most instances, smoothly contrived—except when a piece was too hastily improvised in collaboration, or was later given a clumsy revision.

Fletcher's tragedy, *Valentinian,* has sometimes been considered to afford a notable example of disunity of plot. Its structure has been thought to break in two upon the death of the title character. Because of Aëcius' divine rightist attitude, and because of the denouement, the drama has been stigmatised as teaching the moral of servility to tyrants. For these reasons, *Valentinian* serves particularly well to illustrate both the structural features of a typical play of our corpus, and the control of these features by the emotional form. In truth, this tragedy is an exception to the norm only in being one of the two plays in our corpus founded on a rape. It is also among the minority which have no element of romantic young love.

The central core of plot places *Valentinian* among the Jacobean tragedies of revenge. Maximus avenges the emperor's rape of his chaste wife, Lucina, by bringing to pass the death by poisoning of Valentinian. In turn, Eudoxia, wife of the emperor, causes Maximus' death by means of a poisoned wreath at his inaugural banquet as the new emperor. The two poisonings on which the plot-structure hinges are thus neatly counterpoised. This almost geometrical completeness of the overall pattern–

typical of other plays in our corpus as well—is one of the unifying elements in the drama.

In characteristic fashion Fletcher made revenge, though basic to the plot, only one of the motives in the varied emotional patterning elaborately contrived therefrom. True enough, all the emotional attitudes and fluctuations which could conceivably be derived from Maximus' pursuit of revenge upon Valentinian are fully exploited in a diversity of situations. But the testing of the close friendship of Maximus and Aëcius, Lucina's horror of unchastity, Aëcius' loyalty to the emperor even to the point of seeking his own death at the latter's command, and Captain Pontius' parallel faithfulness to Aëcius, are also fully developed. Furthermore, Maximus' ambition to be emperor is added in Act V. The only harrowing scene of vengeance, such as are endemic in revenge-tragedies, is the one (Act V, scene 2) wherein Valentinian, slowly and volubly dying in fiery torment, is taunted by the likewise perishing but gloating poisoner, Aretus. In contrast, there is only the barest hint of preparation for the surprise denouement of Maximus' death by poisoning, and attention is concentrated on the startling situation which his sudden demise produces rather than on the manner of his passing. So the central core of revenge plot, and its denouement, are not safe guides to the full meaning of the play.

As for the main events of the plot, these are set against the background of a corrupt Roman imperial court, and a demoralized Roman army. The luxurious, effeminate court is ruled by the sensualist and tyrant, Valentinian, and his favorite bawds and panders. The soldiery are idle, unpaid and discontented, Roman military glory tarnished. Resemblances to the Court of James I are not coincidental. The events themselves, as often in our plays, are fewer than might appear from all the excitement extracted from them. A number of them actually take place off-stage.

Valentinian, unable to procure Lucina as mistress through his panders and bawds, wins Maximus' ring in a dice game. With this ring the emperor's eunuch lures Lucina, believing that her husband has sent for her, to the palace, and there (off-stage) Valentinian rapes her. The dishonored Lucina, with her husband's hearty concurrence, goes home to commit suicide (off-stage). Maximus, finding Aëcius, general of the army and his bosom friend, intent on blocking vengeance on Valentinian, drops in the palace (off-stage) an anonymous letter to himself implying that Aëcius is fomenting rebellion among the soldiers. Valentinian unscrupulously reads the letter, sends for Aëcius and (off-stage) commands him to die. Captain Pontius, whom Aëcius has discharged from the army for speaking freely to the soldiers about their plight, is hired to kill him, but instead loyally sets him the example of suicide. Aëcius then dies by falling on his sword. His devoted follower, Aretus, prompted by Maximus, fatally poisons (off-stage) both Valentinian and himself. After their painful deaths, Maximus discards his plan to join Lucina and Aëcius among the shades of underground in favor of becoming emperor, and is elected to that office (off-stage) by the soldiers, only to die, poisoned by Eudoxia's wreath, at his inaugural banquet.

This train of events, thus baldly set down, obviously has narrative coherence. But it immediately raises questions of motivation. Lucina, after her arguments with Valentinian's bawds and panders, might well have been wary about her husband's ring. The emperor, it might be thought, should have been conscious of Aëcius' extreme divine rightism, and so have suspected a trap in Maximus' letter. Could the latter conceivably have plotted his bosom friend's death, even though Aëcius' loyalty to imperial authority made revenge on Valentinian difficult to achieve? The cast captain, Pontius, appears, by his suicide, to be as fantastically faithful to Aëcius as the latter is to the emperor. And Maximus' decision to seek the imperial throne is startling, to say the least.

The bare skeleton of the plot, though smoothly articulated, would seem to be somewhat rickety. It is clear that probability concerned Fletcher little in fabricating *Valentinian*. And so, judged by Aristotelean or even modern standards of self-consistency in structure, this drama does not belong to the highest order of tragedy: that which profoundly plumbs and illumines some tragic aspect of the human lot. The foundation is not solid enough for that, whatever may be thought of the superstructure. Relatively few tragedies, however, are of the highest order, and this one has no pretension to being so. It was concocted to afford moving entertainment. If we place too strong an emphasis on flaws of motivation, we may miss the point that the plot, as usual with our playwrights, was not the controlling factor in the drama's form.

Analysis of the narrative skeleton of *Valentinian* does not reveal how plausible and even convincing the tragedy must have appeared to Jacobean spectators. This is not merely a matter of "seeing is believing." It is, of course, a truism that an audience intent upon a persuasively acted performance of a drama is typically in a less critical mood than the solitary reader of its printed text. Of that Fletcher was well aware, and, as a consummate man of the theatre, he took full advantage of it. But he also blocked out, from his events, a well-ordered sequence of scenes, psychologically cumulative, in which the happenings gained conviction through his stress on the characters' dilemmas and passions, emotional oscillations and conflicts.

How well Fletcher distinguished what scenes would be most useful or effective for this purpose can be seen in the six events that he refrained from presenting on the stage—only one of which had, of necessity, to be so treated. The other five occurrences were wisely banished from sight because they had decidedly less power to move or surprise than the effects, actually dramatized, which they produced upon characters. For instance, Lucina's death on the stage would have been anti-climactic if presented after the moving scene in which Maximus, Aëcius and she have expressed their feelings about the rape, and about the suicide which would be a chaste Roman matron's approved reaction to it. The death, instead, is announced—and just when Maximus has been enlarging to Aëcius upon his suspicion that his wife may perhaps have been willing to become the emperor's mistress. The brief announcement thus comes with a piquant and arresting touch of tragic shock. This instance and, equally well, the other four afford a definite indication that it was not the train of events itself, but the particular emotional tensions which could be wrought from the events, which was the decisive factor in shaping *Valentinian's* "labyrinth of design."[32]

The multiplication of these tensions is the main cause for the misleading impression that *Valentinian* has a massive narrative structure. This can be more clearly realized by a somewhat detailed consideration of the sequence of scenes which Fletcher blocked out, in units of acts, so as to provide as rich a cumulative texture of affecting and even sensational scenes as possible. Each act was carefully ordered so as to complete one stage in the steadily intensifying grip on the playgoer's emotions. Each was so contrived as to contain one or more minor or major crises, and each except the final one, left the audience in increased suspense at its end. Viewed from this standpoint, Fletcher's craftsmanship is of a very high artistic order. Its only non-typical aspect is that as soon as Lucina's suicide is announced in Act III, the ending must clearly be tragic. Nonetheless, spectators characteristically cannot foresee the actual outcome at the end of Act IV, even if they are no longer in doubt about its kind.

Act I, though largely preparatory, is so laid down as to arouse some excitement in the spectators. Scene one provides necessary exposition in an interesting way through stressing the discouragement of Valentinian's panders about their inability to sway Lucina. The first desire of the audience is thus created: to see the chaste young Roman matron. It is immediately satisfied in the second scene, a livelier parallel to the first, in which two court bawds are shown trying to win Lucina over. This situation enables the latter to work up to a final speech railing at the bawds. The question has been raised: Can Lucina continue to elude Valentinian?

In the third scene, Lucina's husband and his bosom friend express their disgust at Valentinian's vile life and court, and at the demoralizing peace. Since Aëcius believes that the emperor's rule must be endured but

Maximus is doubtful, there develops a "debate" on divine right still more stirring to a Jacobean audience than anything that has gone before. Immediately thereafter, Aëcius daringly recounts to Valentinian all the soldiers' complaints about him. Valentinian's anger when the general mildly rebukes him precipitates the first crisis of the play. Feeling that he has gone too far, Aëcius passionately pleads that he may die a Roman. The tension is relaxed, however, when Valentinian finally calls Aëcius still his friend. Left alone, the emperor remarks that he could now repent, except that Lucina fires his blood. On this note of suspense, the skilfully ordered initial act ends. The audience has become alert to dangerous possibilities ahead.

Act II is chiefly devoted to increasing the suspense by means of those situations which are to result in the rape of Lucina. In the opening scene, Valentinian wins Maximus' highly prized ring in a dice game, then boasts he can now bring Lucina to the palace. The mystery thus created is solved in scene two when the emperor's eunuch tells Lucina that her husband, wishing to meet her at the palace, has sent the ring as token. When she comes to believe the messenger and agrees to go, the audience's lively expectation of trouble is heightened, especially as one of Lucina's maids suspects the trick.

The intrigue is now cannily held in temporary abeyance while Aëcius, in scene three, defends his dismissal of Captain Pontius from the service for complaining to the soldiers about their lot. The captain protests that he has uttered nothing disloyal to the emperor, and Maximus tries to defend him. A stirringly argumentative scene thereby underscores Aëcius' exaggerated notions of loyalty to the imperial crown, and also arouses expectations of later developments. The debate of Act I is thus paralleled, but with stronger emotional effect.

Scenes four and five—set in the palace with atmospheric use of love-songs and jewelry displays—might be described as tantalizing. The spectator sees the bustle of preparations for Lucina's arrival, and watches with mounting concern the sustained efforts of eunuchs, bawds and panders to tempt her. He suspects, with Lucina, that Maximus is not in the palace, and fears she will be led to Valentinian.

In scene six his fears are justified. Chastity confronts lust in the crisis of Act II, just as loyalty has confronted tyranny in that of Act I. Lucina movingly begs Valentinian, on her knees, not to ravish her. The emperor at length assures her that he has been urging himself on her to try her temper. But in a final aside he informs the spectator that this is merely not the right place in which to accomplish his desire. Thus, Act II, every scene of which has been chosen because, in some manner and degree, it can be made exciting, cleverly leaves the spectator, at its end, still not absolutely certain that Valentinian will succeed in his lustful aim, and concerned for the results of his attempt.

Act III is pivotal. As a unit, it turns upon the sufferings and suicide of the dishonored Lucina, and upon Maximus' emotional conflict about causing his bosom friend's death so that he may be free to inflict vengeance upon Valentinian. It opens just after the rape of Lucina has been accomplished, and closes with Maximus' decision. Between the two major scenes required for these developments is a minor one, relieving the tension of the first and at the same time subtly paralleling it, since it depicts the plight of the dismissed Captain Pontius who, like Maximus and Lucina, has suffered an injustice.

Scene one exploits every possible emotional effect which the rape of Lucina could provide. First, the frightened panders unhappily reveal that the outrage has been committed. Next Lucina, lamenting her situation, upbraids the unrepentant Valentinian, who offers her honors if she will be his mistress and warns her, with dramatic irony, that no one can avenge the deeds of an emperor. Left alone, Lucina bewails her dishonor in the eyes of the world. Then Aëcius and Maximus discover her in tears, and the latter, seeing his ring on her finger, recognizes what has happened. Stunned, he urges Lucina to commit suicide, while Aëcius— his loyalty to the emperor sorely strained—implores her to live a year to shame Valentinian out of his vices. Lucina desires only to die, and Maximus takes his final farewell of her. Aëcius, fearing that Maximus will seek revenge on Valentinian, seeks to restrain his friend's anger, and expresses his intention to keep close watch on him. Clearly, trouble may arise between the comrades. In the midst of Maximus' bewildered talk, the death of Lucina is reported in the manner already described. Upon this emotional climax—the turning point of the play—the scene ends.

It should now be obvious why, from the standpoint of emotional patterning, the second scene was pitched in a lower key. But the third brings to a crisis the conflict of loyalty and revenge, just as the final scenes of the previous acts have brought other oppositions to a head. The abstract and theoretical question of whether one should sacrifice his beloved friend to the gaining of revenge is thus given concrete and moving embodiment. First Maximus is shown, hesitant and in a deep quandary. Then Aëcius and he engage in a tense duel of dialogue in which the former is drawn into admitting that while he would stand by his friend, to the utmost, in battle and other extremities, he would oppose with all his powers any attempt on Valentinian's life. Finally, in a soliloquy, Maximus reaches his decision. Meanwhile, his emotional oscillations and his verbal fencing with Aëcius have tended to obscure any improbability which might be found in the decision, and the end of the act leaves spectators in a state of ardent curiosity about the following course of events.

Act IV presents the series of stirring and theatrically deft situations which culminate in the death of Aëcius. The first scene opens with Valentinian's passionate ravings about Lucina's suicide. The emperor, thus perturbed in spirit, is presented with a supposedly anonymous letter to Maximus, found in court. Its contents, which surprise the audience by urging Maximus to counsel Aëcius against leading a rebellion, recall to Valentinian the general's earlier frank account of the soldiers' grumblings. Learning that Aëcius is with the army now, the emperor's fears are confirmed, and he orders that the general be brought to him. That he fails to recall the latter's reputation for extravagant loyalty to himself is unobserved by the spectators, whose attention is soon diverted to Captain Pontius. Valentinian, inquiring about him from his friends, Aretus and Phidias, sends a pander to fetch him. The scene ends on the alarming expectation that the captain will be employed to murder Aëcius.

In the second scene, Maximus makes it clear that it was he who dropped the anonymous letter. When Aëcius enters, however, Maximus urges his betrayed friend not to go to Valentinian, and offers to use his sword in his friend's cause. This surprising reaction, really introduced for the sake of giving the scene emotional oscillation, could be made by an actor to appear to spring either from revulsion of feeling or from hypocrisy. Aëcius scouts the idea of danger, but stoutly asserts his determination to obey the will of the emperor, even if this should mean death. So Maximus embraces Aëcius in what he knows to be a last farewell, though his comrade does not. This emotionally piquant scene closes with Maximus' anguished assertion that if the emperor destroys his innocent friend, Valentinian's tragedy will begin in Aëcius' blood.

In scene three, which is less intense than the preceding one, Captain Pontius is engaged by one of the panders to kill Aëcius as a traitor. The captain agrees and, left alone, laments that in this corrupt court, Aëcius must die because he is honest. He creates mystery by his final remark that he will show the general a way to die truly.

Scene four, the climactic one of this act, contrasts cowardice and loyal courage. Aëcius now knows that he is doomed. Aretus and Phidias attempt unsuccessfully to persuade their beloved commander to lead a rebellion against Valentinian. But the general is determined to await death alone, his sword quietly drawn. The crisis, now at hand, is skilfully prolonged. Two panders are so hesitant and cowardly about killing Aëcius that finally, in angry disgust, he drives them away, killing one and wounding the other. In contrast, Captain Pontius, by whose soldierly hand Aëcius would welcome death, instead protests once more his innocence of any treason, and then loyally sets his commander the example of suicide. Aëcius is deeply moved. After some unimportant but lively stage bustle, the crisis is finally resolved when Aëcius makes his farewell speech, falls on his sword and dies.

The heroics now past, mourning and thoughts of revenge succeed. Aretus and Phidias lament Aëcius' death, and rail at Roman corruption. Maximus, also grieving, reminds the two men of their commander's many benefits to them, and hints that he will undertake vengeance himself. Thus prompted, Aretus and Phidias agree to avenge their leader, with Maximus' blessing. And so this variously exciting final scene of the fourth act ends with the audience hopefully expectant that Valentinian will receive his just deserts, but still blind to the actual outcome of the play.

Act V is so arranged that it will first thrill the spectators in the manner of revenge tragedy, and will then hold them in suspense by a surprising turn of events until the startling denouement and quick ending. The tension, which has been mounting act by act, will not be released until the finale.

In scene one, the audience discovers that Aretus has poisoned both Valentinian and himself. His companion, Phidias, has fatally stabbed himself. Aretus reveals that antidotes cannot affect the poison, and that the emperor has only four hours to live. He makes clear his intention to plague Valentinian, in spite of his own fiery pains.

Scene two, beginning with the beautiful, atmospheric lyric, "Care-charming Sleep," is the horror-climax of the play. The emperor, at last aware that he is merely human, complains in detail of his burning torments and distresses. Aretus, gloating over Valentinian's sufferings, strives to enhance them by telling of the pains still to be endured. When, finally, Aretus and then Valentinian die, the chilled spectators can relax somewhat over the terrors of the panders and bawds about their own fate—a terror increased by the report that the army is in tumult.

Scene three initiates the final sequence of events. Maximus, in a soliloquy, decides to postpone joining Lucina and Aëcius in death by seeking the imperial throne. This decision, however little motivated, has two theatrical virtues for the emotional pattern: it comes with a shock of surprise, and it immediately opens up further exciting possibilities. Scene four advances the new action. Afranius, a supporter of Valentinian, announces Maximus' election as emperor, and the latter, unexpectedly accompanied by Valentinian's widow, Eudoxia, promises the soldiers a reform of evils and the proscription of the bawds and panders.

Since Maximus has not committed suicide, as had been anticipated, but has waded through the blood of his dearest friend and of his reigning monarch to the throne, Jacobean spectators would scarcely expect that his prosperity could endure. About this issue, however, they are kept in suspense for three scenes. Two of these, affording mild comic relief, poke fun at a poet's "device" for the entertainment at the inaugural banquet. Sandwiched in between, the third displays Maximus wooing Eudoxia. Dissembling with her, Maximus invents a fiction which he himself knows to be clumsy: that, for Eudoxia's sake, he caused Lucina's rape in order to become emperor. Maximus' dishonest and vulgar scheming serves the purpose of sufficiently alienating from himself the audience's sympathy so that it will accept his death as just. Eudoxia, however, appears to be pleased by his explanation, and promises to make with her own hands the wreath of laurel with which he is to be crowned at the banquet.

Scene eight concludes the tragedy with a highly effective theatrical denouement. The inaugural banquet is elaborately staged, with all the spectacular effects of a masque: songs, set speeches, dancing, and the formal bestowal of Eudoxia's poisoned wreath on Maximus' head. Suddenly the new emperor slumps back in his seat, and it is discovered that he is not drunk but dead. This surprising turn of events produces confusion. Eudoxia admits poisoning Maximus, and is threatened, but Afranius succeeds in getting a hearing for her. When she narrates her own version of Maximus' deeds, including his rash lie about forwarding Lucina's rape, she is applauded, and the play ends swiftly on the promise of an immediate election of a worthy emperor. Revenge has come full circle.

In the light of this analysis of the emotional ordering of *Valentinian*, by act and by scene, Maximus' decision to become emperor gains in plausibility. If the decision is tested by the modern dogma that thoroughly consistent and tridimensional characterization is essential to tragedy, then it at once appears to be damagingly unmotivated. But since *Valentinian* is a romantic, rather than a realistic, tragedy fabricated to arouse emotional response, such a testing may be irrelevant. There is little likelihood that any sympathetic spectator of *Valentinian* ever felt that the play splits in two. Those Jacobean players who knew their *Astrée* recognized that, in this source likewise, Maximus decided to become emperor.[33] However cavalierly Fletcher treated his sources, he could not wisely eliminate so pivotal a fact, lest he undergo criticism from those theatregoers who had a good memory of D'Urfé's romance. For the other spectators, he typically decided upon the shock of surprise rather than upon a preparation which would create expectation.

The surprise, however, could not have affected Jacobean spectators quite as it has some more recent readers. No doubt the state of high emotional tension which the performance had previously built up is a partial explanation. But the audience had also noted that Maximus lacked such emotional stability as Aëcius displayed (except for his exaggerated notion of the emperor's rights). Maximus, however extreme his provocation, had engineered his friend's death; and a capacity for unwavering friendship stood high among Renaissance virtues—witness Book Four of *The Faerie Queene.* Captain Pontius' unswayed loyalty to Aëcius gave the measure of Maximus' reluctant disloyalty. Moreover, the latter had brought about the emperor's death. One has only to recall the horror which swept England when Charles I was beheaded in 1649 to recognize that Jacobean spectators of whatever political opinions would have had mixed feelings, by Act V, about Maximus.

It was for such reasons that they could accept Maximus' sudden and corrupt ambition as plausible, but sense that this unstable figure was doomed. Fletcher undoubtedly counted upon these reactions from his audience. The emotional patterning of the play demanded that the cycle of revenge be completed, and a change in Maximus' purpose which would not strain the credulity of the Stuart playgoer made this possible. Maximus' decision, however, would further alienate sympathy from him, and his unexpected death by poisoning must have seemed a providential and edifying fate. In terms of the emotional form, therefore, Fletcher was justified in his treatment of the final scenes of *Valentinian.* On that basis—the one that really concerned him—the tragedy does not break in two.

The critical aberration that the play justifies tyranny and the divine right of kings scarcely needs disproof. The "debate," significantly, comes in the scene which introduces us to Aëcius and Maximus. Interesting in itself at that point to the spectators, its more important function is to prepare for Maximus' and Aëcius' attitudes towards each other and the complications which ensue therefrom—including the death-scene heroics of Aëcius and Captain Pontius. The emotional form of the play would be a poor, shrunken thing without Aëcius and his extravagant loyalty. But the complications which he makes possible prove nothing about divine rightism except, possibly, that a believer in it can have heroic qualities in spite of his belief.

What the emotional form of the play does reveal about ideas is that Fletcher was unsympathetic to a corrupt, lascivious court and to a slothful peace. Here the evidence is conclusive. Valentinian, his bawds and panders, are all so unfavorably presented as to arouse the audience's antipathy. Playgoers would be, in most cases, thoroughly in accord with the attitudes towards the demoralizing peace and the woes of the army expressed variously by Maximus, Aëcius, Captain Pontius and other characters. They would perceive, as Fletcher intended, the partial parallel between the court of Valentinian and that of James the First. Many of them were denizens of the latter court.

The majority of the spectators—some of them military men—disliked James's pacifism, and his friendly relations with Spain, England's traditional enemy. They did not require any mention of Spain in the play to recognize points of resemblance in the plight of the Roman soldiery. If James did not lust for women, like Valentinian, he was generally felt to give scandalously too much power to handsome young male favorites. The drama, typically embedding its particular ideas in the emotional pattern of the play rather than in the plot-structure, was as daring about these ideas as it was safe to be in Jacobean years. But unless the modern reader seeks for them in the right place, they will not be apparent to him. Our playwrights, after *The Faithful Shepherdess,* normally avoided "whole meaning," that is, the full illustration of a theme in the structure and characterization of a play.

From the foregoing discussion of *Valentinian,* it should be crystal clear that Fletcher's main aim was variety of emotional impact on his audience. So it was with all our playwrights. Paul Elmer More, aware of this, made the comment that the dramas of our corpus shifted what he called the theme from the single dominant passion of earlier playwrights to a number of passions. Just here, in fact, is the major difference in treatment between *The Faithful Shepherdess,* dealing with the power of chastity, and *Valentinian.* In the latter drama we have found, as motifs which could be juxtaposed in sharp contrast or in parallelism, loyalty (to emperor, to commander), tyranny, chastity, lust, comradeship and the sacrifice of it, revenge, courage, cowardice, ambition. More, furthermore, considered none of the passions in a typical Fletcher and Company play to be central, and all to be loosely coordinated. Hence, he thought, unity was sacrificed to a less rigid structure and a freer play of emotions.[34]

Less rigid the structure of our plays clearly is than in many earlier dramas, and the emotions do have freer play. All that More failed to perceive was that the better tragedies and tragicomedies of our corpus have a well-wrought emotional form. None of the passions of *Valentinian,* strictly speaking, is central. Yet the tragedy is built upon the foundation of a double avenging, and the passions are all such as could be evoked with some plausibility by the structure raised thereupon. They are carefully rather than loosely coordinated. Fletcher selected the material for each of his scenes because of its contribution to the emotional acceleration of the play or to a temporary ebbing of tension. He gave each act unity, yet integrated it with those which followed, preceded, or both. The diverse emotional attitudes and passions are effectively and even, on occasion, sensationally employed in the psychologically right situations and order. The spectator gains an impression, thereby, of their harmonizing with one another. And it was this emotional unity which our playwrights valued, and attained to again and again, in their better plays, with considerable artistry.

It might fairly be objected that *Valentinian*, like any other tragedy or tragicomedy of our corpus, does not reveal in full every method used by our playwrights to give their dramas a complex emotional form. It is true, for instance, that Fletcher's *Bonduca* coordinates more threads of plot than *Valentinian*, has a more operatic quality, and employs a wider variety of emotional effects, ranging from those characteristic of farce through the pathetic to the tragic, in a curious and yet theatrically effective melange.[35] *The Knight of Malta*, a tragicomedy concocted by three playwrights—Fletcher, Field and Massinger—and, largely for this reason, mediocre in coordination, has a plot that comes to a dead pause at the end of Act II. Definitely inferior in structure to *Valentinian*, it is more spectacular as well as less plausible, and not so well sustained. Yet, in its concentration on playing upon the emotions of the audience, it has some unity of effect. The dexterous *Philaster*, in a measure because of Beaumont's collaboration but also because of its subject, is more lyrical in its emotional treatment than *Valentinian*, and maintains a somewhat higher, though not more spontaneous, poetic level. But in spite of such differences in individual dramas, *Valentinian* nonetheless lucidly demonstrates the basic nature of our playwrights' craftsmanship in plot-construction and emotional patterning.

Miss Bradbrook, looking at one feature of the latter, finds our dramatists' "complex manipulation of suspense . . . clever . . . but little more." She considers it to be "the kind of thing which can be learnt; the reward of competence."[36] This appears to be her estimate of their theatre-craft more generally. But if this were wholly true, why were other Stuart playwrights unable to employ their methods with equally successful total results? Fletcher and his collaborators were more than merely competent craftsmen.

Miss Ellis-Fermor is of the opinion that "much has been sacrificed to structure" in our plays. If structure is thought of as including emotional form, this is true enough. Miss Ellis-Fermor continues that it is therefore "fitting that that structure should be good. It is indeed superlatively good."[37] Fletcher, Beaumont and Company, at their best, have few peers among dramatists as purveyors of refined and even poetic sensationalism —of sophisticated melodrama which, if baroque, is aesthetically well-executed. Should they be denied excellence in their kind because the kind is theatrical rather than solidly dramatic?

III

In *The Summing Up,* Somerset Maugham asserts that "Only idolatry can refuse to see the great shortcomings . . . sometimes in the characterization of Shakespeare's plays; and this is very comprehensible since, as we know, he sacrificed everything to effective situation."[38] However true about Shakespeare this statement may be thought to be, it is much more so about Fletcher, Beaumont and Company. The characters in their dramas are wholly concocted in terms of the roles they are to play in the emotional pattern. And despite Gayley, this applies to Beaumont quite as much as to Fletcher and his other collaborators.

The characters of *The Faithful Shepherdess* had been contrived with an almost allegorical simplicity, reminiscent both of *The Faerie Queene* and of Jonson's satirical figures. This simplicity of conception was carried over into the later tragicomedies and tragedies of our corpus and, indeed, into the comedies as well. In his study of Fletcher's tragicomic characterizations, Waith demonstrates that this playwright gave his important figures, "in addition to their chief ethical characteristics, one or two other traits to be made use of on certain occasions."[39] Aëcius of *Valentinian* is a case in point. He is the typical blunt, honest, courageous soldier, but he has also been given, for use in certain emotional situations, that extravagant loyalty to the divine right of the emperor which is not altogether harmonious with his general good sense. To Maximus Fletcher added an inconsistent ambitiousness not displayed until after the deaths of Lucina and his friend.

The result is that the characters of all our playwrights are normally, though not always, sufficiently plausible so as not to over-strain credulity, and yet often consist, in Miss Ellis-Fermor's words, "of a series of imperfectly associated groups of responses to the stimulus of carefully prepared situations."[40] The grouping is determined by the functions which the characters must fulfill in the drama's complex of emotions. The plot is first blocked out and the emotional patterning devised; as these develop, the type characters are supplied with motives and with the necessary additional traits. In the better plays this is usually done thoughtfully and subtly enough to conceal the mechanism—and sometimes, especially in the comedies, the characters attain a good deal of consistency. But throughout the work of our playwrights, the events and emotional conflicts determine the treatment of the characters and, at many moments in the play, there is nothing inevitable in the behavior of the puppets.

And so the typical handling of characters in our body of drama can be sufficiently illustrated from individual situations.[41] Waith contends that "the pattern of the Fletcherian situation is an issue towards which two characters assume diametrically opposed attitudes."[42] While this is not true of all situations in any of our plays, it is the norm, especially in scenes of emotional crisis. Sometimes, of course, three or four characters will be importantly involved in a scene, and there will be shifting among them as to the pair in opposition at any particular point.[43]

In order to support this situation-pattern, protagonists who are not naturally antithetical in character will be given divergent minor traits; or else the particular situation will be so arranged that a temporary opposition can be extracted from it. For example, Aëcius and Captain Pontius are both honest, loyal soldiers, and neither would knowingly speak treason of the emperor. For this very reason, their contretemps about the captain's outspoken criticisms of the army's plight is the more striking.

Our playwrights' scenes, so treated, often have "an aesthetic perfection," deriving from "a symmetry of design"[44] and from a patterned oscillation of emotional responses. The audience accepts without cavil speeches which, when coldly examined, are found to be exaggerated in intensity, arranged for effect, and not precisely what the characters—realistically treated—would have said. And yet, in their particular place in the emotional curve of the situation, these speeches carry conviction to the audience. The characters' sequences of behavior-reactions will also be stylistically patterned rather than natural. They will appear to succeed one another in a psychologically sound order. But when that order is analyzed, it will be found to have been calculated in terms of an audience's probable series of responses. And perhaps the calculation has not even been fully conscious; Fletcher, in particular, seems to have soon acquired an almost effortless knack for the right arrangement of scenes for producing definite emotional effects.

As a result of such treatment, many situations have the quality, for some modern readers, of being, as Waith remarks, "hypothetical."[45] It is as though an extreme instance were being worked out, in emotional terms, with symbolic figures as pawns. Such a situation in *Valentinian* is that of Maximus' quandary—resolved through a fencing dialogue with Aëcius—about causing his comrade's death so that vengeance may be wrought on the emperor. But for Stuart spectators, the presence of a number of such situations in a drama must have had a somewhat different aspect than it does for modern readers. Playgoers would appear simply to have found themselves engrossed in a world of dilemmas more exciting than those of humdrum daily existence. Their actual world was much closer than ours to the mimic one of the plays.

The characteristic features of the Fletcher, Beaumont and Company treatment of situation and of character are brilliantly displayed in the famous "quarrel scene" between Amintor and Melantius in *The Maid's*

Tragedy.[46] Written by Beaumont, the scene is not quite so flamboyant and volatile as Fletcher might have made it. Otherwise, it typifies the best work of both in the handling of emotional crises.

Before the scene begins, Amintor has, at the king's command, broken his engagement to Aspatia and married Evadne, Melantius' sister and, secretly, whore to the king. On his wedding night Amintor, in a superbly theatrical scene, has learned the truth from his bride, and on the following morning has been trying to conceal his mortification by an over-acted joy. Melantius, having perceived that his close friend and new brother-in-law is behaving strangely, has determined to discover the reason for this.

There is, as one might expect, a sharp antithesis in one trait of the two friends, necessary for the effectiveness of this scene. Both are good swordsmen, brave, sensitive of their honor, and nobly aristocratic according to Jacobean standards. But while Amintor, like Aëcius, is a devout believer in the divine right of kings, Melantius resembles Maximus in lacking such convictions. Whereas the divinity that hedges a king renders Amintor impotent to right his wrongs, so that he appears almost spineless rather than, like Hamlet, vacillating, Melantius is akin to Laertes in his promptness to avenge any injury to his family from whatever quarter it comes. Both Amintor and Melantius have been equally dishonored by the king, since one is the husband and the other the brother of Evadne. Nonetheless, Melantius might be expected, at first, to resent a charge that his sister is a whore. Here are the similarities and the antitheses from which a contention could arise between the two comrades and brothers-in-law.

The pattern of the quarrel scene is symmetrically arranged. First Melantius, and then Amintor, becomes so impassioned that he challenges the other to a duel. In each case the fencing seems imminent, and yet is averted by the unwillingness of the challenged to fight and by a sudden reversal of attitude upon the part of the challenger. The conduct of Amintor and Melantius is given the appearance of springing from plausible emotional reactions. Actually, however, their behavior is attuned to the skilfully symmetrical arrangement of the scene. There results a pair of counterpointed emotional crises tense for an audience always thrilled by challenges to a duel.

Act III, scene 2, opens with threatened sword play—but between Melantius and the elderly Calianax, the father of the wronged Aspatia. After challenging Melantius to duel with him, Calianax confesses to the audience that he dares not fight and, on Melantius' re-iterated command to be gone, slinks away to beat his own servants instead. This comic counterpart of the more serious challengings yet to come not only prepares for them but suggests to Melantius that Amintor's "distracted carriage" may

derive from his wronging of Aspatia. The audience at once perceives that
he does not suspect the true cause.

The preparations for the quarrel scene thus completed, Amintor enters
and soliloquizes about his "grief hid from the world."[47] Melantius accost-
ing him, Amintor pretends gaiety. He replies to Melantius' charge that
his ridiculous jollity hides inward sadness by detailing all the joys of his
situation, concluding with

>   . . . Faith, marry too;
> And you will feel so unexpress'd a joy
> In chaste embraces, that you will indeed
> Appear another.[48]

Amintor's dissembling arouses Melantius' deep displeasure, and thus
precipitates the first emotional crisis of the scene. When coldly analyzed
out of context, Melantius' speech will be seen to be somewhat more impassioned than the occasion warrants. But in its context it plausibly
brings matters to a head:

>   . . . but 'tis not like a friend
> To hide your soul from me. 'Tis not your nature
> To be thus idle: I have seen you stand
> As you were blasted 'midst of all your mirth. . . .
>   World, what do I here? a friend
> Is nothing. Heaven, I would ha' told that man
> My secret sins! I'll search an unknown land,
> And there plant friendship; all is wither'd here.
> Come with a compliment! I would have fought,
> Or told my friend a' lied, ere sooth'd him so.
> Out of my bosom!
>   Amin.   But there is nothing.
>   Mel. Worse and worse! farewell:
> From this time have acquaintance, but no friend.[49]

This crisis, being both minor and the first, would edge over into the
ridiculous if further exploited; so Amintor tells Melantius he shall know
what his trouble is.

>   Mel. See, how you play'd with friendship! be advised
> How you give cause unto yourself to say
> You ha' lost a friend.
>
>   Amin.   Forgive what I ha' done;
> For I am so o'ergone with injuries
> Unheard of, that I lose consideration
> Of what I ought to do,—oh!—oh!
>
>   Mel. Do not weep. What is't?[50]

But the audience must be kept waiting for the answer. So Amintor tells Melantius that he has "held it most unfit For you to know,"[51] and the latter swears to don armor and cut through Amintor's foes—a good, round warrior's answer. A second "What is it?" almost brings a reply; but still the audience must wait:

> *Amin.* Why, 'tis this—it is too big
> To get out—let my tears make way a while.
> *Mel.* Punish me strangely, Heaven, if he scape
> Of life or fame, that brought the youth to this!
> *Amin.* Your sister—
> *Mel.* Well said.[52]

Now surely it must out; but no! A delaying bit of dramatic irony must come first:

> *Amin.* You'll wish't unknown, when you have heard it.
> *Mel.* No.[53]

At last, the audience having been wrought to a pitch of intensity concerning its effect on Melantius, the expected revelation is made:

> *Amin.* Is much to blame,
> And to the King has given her honour up,
> And lives in whoredom with him.[54]

Immediately comes the surprising but shrewdly calculated reversal of feeling in Melantius which leads to the first challenge to a duel. He has literally forced the confession out of his friend, and vowed to avenge him; but instead he proceeds to grow furious at Amintor's re-iterated charge. Twice he demands to know the latter's "griefs," and then projects the new crisis with an outburst of passion:

> What, am I tame?
> After mine actions, shall the name of friend
> Blot all our family, and stick the brand
> Of whore upon my sister, unrevenged?
> My shaking flesh, be thou a witness for me,
> With what unwillingness I go to scourge
> This railer, whom my folly hath call'd friend!—
> I will not take thee basely: thy sword
> Hangs near thy hand; draw it, that I may whip
> Thy rashness to repentence; draw thy sword![55]

A disenchanted reader, calmly thinking this passionate speech over, would perhaps question whether an actual Melantius would have behaved in quite this way. Melantius knows Amintor well enough to recognize when his friend is dissembling. Then should he not also suspect that Amintor, obviously upset, is now telling the truth? The reader might logically expect Melantius to seek confirmation of the charge instead of at once taking an attitude of offended honor. The spectator, however, has already had his own sympathies sufficiently played upon that he will respond to this speech with an excitement foreign to the armchair. He accepts it without reflection because it is so pitched emotionally as to create the illusion that it is a congruous outgrowth of the preceding tensions. The playwright characteristically makes the speech sufficiently colloquial, and holds it just enough in restraint, to prevent its toppling over into the absurd for an audience.

Such speeches as this are climactic because, in Mizener's words, they resolve "a complex sequence of emotional tones, the tension of which has become almost intolerable."[56] This is one way in which the dramatic poetry of our playwrights was made to serve the emotional patterning of the situations. The result is, of course, a somewhat artificial poetry—whose artifice, however, is entirely appropriate to its purposes. When viewed in this light, our playwrights' verses cannot fairly be considered, in T. S. Eliot's metaphor, merely cut flowers stuck in sand. They have roots in the emotional form of a scene. They are in harmony with the remainder of the theatrecraft and are, in this sense, integral.

Amintor, thus challenged by Melantius, at first will not draw his sword. But the latter's charges of baseness and cowardice, of uttering lies and of having a guilty cause, lead the tortured bridegroom to say:

> Thou pleasest me: for so much more like this
> Will raise my anger up above my griefs
> (Which is a passion easier to be borne). . . .[57]

Melantius taunts him further, ending with the threat that if Amintor will not fight,

> I'll make thy memory loath'd, and fix a scandal
> Upon thy name forever.
>   *Amin.*   Then I draw
> As justly as our magistrates their swords
> To cut offenders off.[58]

These speeches, to this point, are a clear instance of the use of "the narrative effect of suspense to support and enrich an emotional climax."[59] This purpose having been effected at sufficient length, Amintor now continues, with reproach and pathos:

>   I knew before
> 'Twould grate your ears; but it was base in you
> To urge a weighty secret from your friend
> And then rage at it. I shall be at ease
> If I be kill'd; and, if you fall by me,
> I shall not long outlive you.[60]

Amintor's softened tone must now be supposed to have accomplished for Melantius what common sense did not. Tension is broken by Melantius' "Stay a while." This is followed by a Renaissance platitude about friendship:

> The name of friend is more than family,
> Or all the world besides: I was a fool.[61]

Melantius is now in the toils of suffering, too, and turns elegiac:

> Thou searching human nature, that didst wake
> To do me wrong, thou art inquisitive
> And thrusts me upon questions that will take
> My sleep away. Would I had died, ere known
> This sad dishonour![62]

His desire to duel with Amintor has completely evaporated with his sudden conviction that the latter's charge is true. With heroic flourish, he asks for pardon:

> If thou wilt strike, here is a faithful heart;
> Pierce it, for I will never heave my hand
> To thine. Behold the power thou hast in me!
> I do believe my sister is a whore,
> A leprous one. Put up thy sword, young man.[63]

Now Melantius has been offered no fresh evidence that his sister is guilty; he is simply displaying a fluctuation in feelings typical of our playwrights' figures. Yet the tension has been so considerable, and the emotional attitudes have succeeded each other in so seemingly natural an order, that his new mood appears entirely plausible to a fascinated audience.

Such a relaxation of tension and such a low-pitched mood must not be long maintained. There is now to follow the balancing challenge by Amintor to Melantius. It will be handled in a manner parallel to the one that has just petered out. Amintor fears that his disgrace will lead him to commit suicide, and Melantius retorts that it would be better for half the land to be buried alive. The friends briefly debate about who has been the more wronged by the adulterous king, and from this debate the rapid rise to the new crisis begins, as Melantius orates:

> The credit of our house is thrown away.
> But from his iron den I'll waken Death,
> And hurl him on this king: my honesty
> Shall steel my sword, and on its horrid point
> I'll wear my cause, and shall amaze the eyes
> Of this proud man, and be too glittering
> For him to look upon.[64]

These heroics, intended to thrill spectators, rouse up the extravagant divine rightism of Amintor. His first remark, "I have quite undone my fame,"[65] is purposely rather cryptic. But when Melantius bids Amintor to dry "thy watery eyes," because he will never cease his vengeance until he finds his friend's heart at peace, Amintor exclaims, "It must not be so. Stay."[66] Once more spectators receive the shock of surprise at a reversal of attitude.

Amintor now demands with passion that his friend give him back the secret which he has wrung from him:

> Give it me again;
> For I will find it, wheresoe'er it lies,
> Hid in the mortal'st part: invent a way
> To give it back.
>   *Mel.*   Why would you have it back?
> I will to death pursue him with revenge.
>   *Amin.* Therefore I call it back from thee; for I know
> Thy blood so high, that thou wilt stir in this,
> And shame me to posterity. Take to thy weapon.[67]

The new crisis has been reached; once more a duel is in immediate prospect. Hence, this is a situation to prolong as long as possible.

> *Mel.* Hear thy friend, that bears more years than thou.
> *Amin.* I will not hear; but draw, or I—
> *Mel.* Amintor!
> *Amin.* Draw, then; for I am full as resolute
> As fame and honour can enforce me be:
> I cannot linger. Draw!
>   *Mel.*   I do. But. . . .[68]

There is a slight momentary relaxation of tension as Melantius queries if they will not equally share the credit, should he "stir." This introduces a new point for the friends to debate, with swords drawn and ready for use.

> *Amin.*   No; for it will be call'd
> Honour in thee to spill thy sister's blood,
> If she her birth abuse, and on the King
> A brave revenge; but on me, that have walk'd
> With patience in it, it will fix the name
> Of fearful cuckold. Oh, that word! Be quick.[69]

This speech doubtless reflects the anticipated sentiments of the audience rather than those of Amintor, since the latter has known of his disgrace only for a few hours, and has just come from almost defiantly knuckling under to the king. His next speech, in response to Melantius' "Then join with me," rings truer to his own divine rightism:

> *Amin.* I dare not do a sin, or else I would.
> Be speedy.
> *Mel.* Then, dare not fight with me, for that's a sin.—
> His grief distracts him.—Call thy thoughts again,
> And to thyself pronounce the name of friend,
> And see what that will work. I will not fight.
> *Amin.* You must.[70]

But the situation has now been prolonged sufficiently, and the audience's interest has been subtly shifted from expectation of fencing to the question of whether Melantius will prevail with Amintor. As with the earlier threatened duel, the time has come for a softening, pathetic speech which will produce a recoil of emotion—in this case, in Amintor.

> *Mel.* I will be kill'd first. Though my passions
> Offer'd the like to you, 'tis not this earth
> Shall buy my reason to it. Think awhile
> For you are (I must weep when I speak that)
> Almost beside yourself.[71]

These lines precipitate the reversal, with its sentimental touch and its half-surprise:

> *Amin.*   Oh, my soft temper!
> So many sweet words from thy sister's mouth,
> I am afraid would make me take her to
> Embrace, and pardon her. I am mad indeed,
> And know not what I do.[72]

And so he makes the concession, to Melantius, necessary to the narrative:

> Yet have a care
> Of me in what thou dost.[73]

The tensions of this scene are thus rounded out with an appeal to the spectators' tear-ducts. Although Amintor still disagrees with Melantius' desire to kill the king, he is too confused to argue further. Melantius promises to be tender of Amintor's honor, as he tries to counsel him to take his mirth about him again.

> *Amin.* Thy love (oh, wretched!) ay, thy love, Melantius;
> Why, I have nothing else.
> *Mel.*   Be merry, then. *(Exeunt)*[74]

But scene three does not end here. After this pathos, a further shock to arouse fuller expectations of disaster ahead is needed. Melantius quickly returns to the stage, and after explaining that he has sent Amintor away

from him smiling, "to counterfeit again," exclaims, "Sword, hold thine
edge; my heart will never fail me."[75]

Diphilus, his brother, whom he has sent for, enters in a merry mood, in
antithesis to what has gone before, and announces that there has been
"such laughing."

> *Mel.* Betwixt whom?
> *Diph.*   Why, our sister and the King;
> I thought their spleens would break; they laugh'd us all
> Out of the room.
> *Mel.* They must weep, Diphilus.[76]

The last line, so jarring, is the turning point of the play. Henceforth,
alert spectators will expect a tragic outcome. The preparation for and the
placing of Melantius' quiet but omnious four words are managed with
theatrical perfection. The remark is, in a sense, the climactic outgrowth
of the "quarrel scene." The remainder of scene three is devoted to making certain preparations with Diphilus for the avenging, and to beginning with Calianax the intrigue which will deliver the fort to the re-
vengers. It is fitting that scene three should end, as it began, in a duologue with Calianax, but this time on a more serious issue that strength-
ens dire expectations in the audience. The ending thus counterpoints the
beginning.

This full analysis of the scene should have revealed how carefully its
surprises, reversals, crises and emotional fluctuations were prepared, and
how symmetrically balanced are both the Melantius-Amintor duologue
and the complete scene. It should also have demonstrated that the characters are so manipulated as to behave, not naturally and consistently,
but in terms of the sequence of emotional effects desired. At the same
time, this sequence is so ordered that the successive attitudes and emotions of the characters, though in reality stylized, carry conviction to an
audience caught in the spell of the play. The poetry, too, is made to sub-
serve the emotional effects desired. From these standpoints, the scene
could hardly be bettered aesthetically—even though its framework, when
closely examined, is found to be of plaster-and-lath construction. This
scene is verily of the highest order of artistry in its own sensational kind.
Have we the right to demand, under these circumstances, that the characterization should be "natural," "realistic," or psychologically motivated?

The seduction scene of *The Knight of Malta* (Act III, scene 4),[77]
which is similar in treatment to others of its nature in our corpus,[78]
will further illustrate the subordination of characterization to the emotional
sequence of a symmetrically arranged situation. At the same time, it will

show how the problem of our playwrights' moral standards is, in good measure, bound up with their treatment of situation and character as elements in a drama's emotional form. In its particular kind, this scene is as well handled, from the theatrical standpoint, as any that Fletcher wrote.

The scene is not an obligatory one and, as regards the plot-structure, little would be lost if it were omitted from the play. It is founded on the none too plausible hypothesis that the stainless Miranda, the title character and a virgin, might be conceived of as testing the chastity of his recently acquired slave-girl, Lucinda. What makes the scene especially piquant is the fact that chastity was among the virtues whose practice was required of knights of Malta. Miranda, in training for membership in the order, has already proven his skill in battle, and in the fifth act will be received into the order in an impressive ceremony. The testing of Lucinda is arresting to an audience because of the danger that Miranda might succumb to temptation himself.

Colonna, Miranda's male-slave, betrothed to Lucinda in happier days but now in disguise, brings the girl to her first meeting with her master, and decides to observe the progress of the meeting from a place of concealment. Throughout the scene, he makes choral comments upon the main dialogue, expressing his hopes and fears for Lucinda. These add considerably to the theatrical effectiveness of the situation.

The scene is so arranged as to provide a breath-taking reversal. Miranda proceeds deliberately in his attempt to seduce Lucinda, getting her to sit beside him, then kissing her, then telling her with Jacobean frankness that he must lie with her, and suggesting the pleasures that would ensue. Lucinda parries him with agile and even witty replies. The audience, bemused by the situation of this virgin-knight apparently forgetting his vows, doubtless finds its own sexual emotions being stirred.

And then comes the reversal. Lucinda, after appealing in vain to Miranda's sense of honor about preserving his own chastity, fastens on his Maltese cross, catechizes him about its Christian significance and virtues, and then exclaims:

> Why are you sick then, sick to death with lust?
> In danger to be lost? no holy thought
> In all that heart, nothing but wandring frailties
> Wild as the wind, and blind as death or ignorance
> Inhabit there.[79]

This is the crisis, and Miranda marks it by replying, "Forgive me heaven, she says true."[80] Lucinda hammers her point home, only to have Miranda inform her, after her final climactic speech, that he has been all the while testing her chastity. This surprise releases the audience's tension. With a shower of praise, the virgin-warrior kisses Lucinda a harmless goodnight, while the eavesdropping Colonna rejoices.

Now this scene does not owe its being to any dramatic need to stress further Miranda's chastity—and it stresses this only in a curious fashion. Nor does it serve any genuine religious purpose, even though the play deals with a holy order of Christian knighthood, and though the pagan Lucinda appeals to the Christian symbolism of the Maltese cross. Fundamentally, the scene exists partly to titillate the audience and partly to dramatize, by contrast, the startling and effective rebuke of Miranda by the slave-girl.

Is the scene, then, immoral? If we were to judge *The Knight of Malta* as genuinely earnest drama, possibly. And so the play is sometimes judged. But since this tragicomedy is merely a highly sophisticated entertainment for a worldly audience, it is questionable whether deeply serious moral standards are applicable to it. Judged in terms of an adult audience's reactions, it is doubtful if the scene can fairly be charged with immorality.

It is true that an intrigue in which a virgin-knight—surprisingly knowing and in command of the situation for one so inexperienced—is engaged in a seeming attempt to seduce his slave-girl will have "sex appeal" to spectators. Doubtless, too, the appeal is heightened by the eavesdropping of Colonna, who is known to be in love with Lucinda. But then Fletcher brings the audience up sharply with Lucinda's rebukes, and so sets the moral value straight before the scene ends. Something deeper than sexual interest has been appealed to, and this makes the last and deepest impression on the audience. Miss Bradbrook, commenting on a quite different situation, has remarked that "The letter and not the spirit of the action was the important thing" to an Elizabethan audience.[81] "And to even a greater extent [a] Jacobean," adds Mizener.[82] The climactic emphasis given Lucinda's rebuke and Miranda's acknowledgement of its justness establishes the letter of the action, in this seduction scene, as being definitely moral rather than immoral in its effect on the spectators.

The scene is not, however, altogether decorous. Lucinda, a grateful slave, is an incarnation of chaste virginity. Miranda, aside from being a valorous knight, is also delineated as an almost abstract embodiment of chastity, although he contrasts with Lucinda in not being wholly immune to temptation. His testing of her therefore violates decorum, since his behavior in this scene is below the standard we should expect, dramatically, of such a figure. And yet his final confession to Lucinda that he has been testing her, and the praise he bestows on her, appear to right the balance, and to give his behavior a certain consistency in spite of its lack of decorum. Entirely to the point, in this instance, is Waith's remark,

"Some, though by no means all, of Fletcher's sins against decorum can be explained by a consideration of the underlying abstractions, the various aspects of which are brought out by means of various contrasts."[83]

It can be readily granted that the expressions of our playwrights, and of Fletcher in particular, are, by modern standards, often coarse. Some of the language of such scenes as that between Miranda and Lucinda; the frequent talk, in comic situations, of wenching and its physical consequences; some of the witty or commonplace phrases and words denoting physical functions of the body; all these contribute to the impression, often denounced, that Fletcher was pandering to his audience. But it is notable that in the private correspondence of respectable people and in the sermons of earnest Puritan preachers one frequently finds a similar downrightness of expression, jarring to some modern ears. Even so ethical a writer as Milton turns, in his prose pamphleteering, to vituperation often adjudged as deplorable.

We may not like the seventeenth century lack of reticence in speech and writing. But it is rather hard on a popular Jacobean entertainer to condemn him for reflecting the standard of propriety of his audience, even if it may not be ours, and even if we find it flippant and unpleasant. To a reader well acquainted with seventeenth century practices in this matter, Lovelace's commendation of Fletcher's relative decency will not seem absurd. Shakespeare can be just as vulgar as Fletcher when he chooses, and the moral Jonson possibly even more so.

When the moral quality of the plays of our corpus is considered from the standpoint of the emotional reactions they induce in spectators, it will generally be found that the dramas, despite their indecorums (painful to neo-classicists) and their license of speech, are neither corrupting nor subversive to morals. True, our playwrights do not take ethical questions with deep seriousness; the narrative element of their dramas, as Mizener remarks, lacks a "morally significant" pattern. Fletcher, Beaumont and Company, as popular dramatists, were more concerned with "providing the maximum number of exciting moments" than with the ethical meaning of characters and events.[84] Accordingly, they annoy those who persist in taking our body of drama too seriously. But none of our playwrights was concerned with turning accepted Jacobean moral principles and beliefs upside down, however much their plays may reflect the uninhibited speech and behavior of the social world of their day.

Indeed, when seen as Stuart spectators would view them, the dramas, in most instances, might understandably be given a clean bill of moral health. This, it will be recalled, was the attitude taken towards them by the eulogists of the First Folio. And not all these Caroline gentlemen were, by any means, moral libertines, nor even altogether concerned with countering Puritan objections. Some of the harsh moral condemnation which our body of plays has since incurred springs from a failure to recognize just what kind of drama these pieces are, and has had, at times, an almost pathological note.

One further aspect of our playwrights' treatment of character—their use of the convention of conversion—can be well illustrated by a portion of Act IV, scene 1, of *The Maid's Tragedy*.[85] In this scene, Melantius argues Evadne into repenting her liaison with the king, and convinces her that it is her duty to undertake her paramour's murder. When examined with coldly appraising eyes, Evadne's "conversion" appears to some critics inconsistent with the hard and calculating ambition she has previously demonstrated. Melantius' arguments are adjudged unconvincing, and he himself has even been criticized as a bully.

Now conversion, except under the most probable and well motivated circumstances, is a dangerous device for any modern playwright to use. But Elizabethans were less sceptical about this process. They had, for instance, a much stronger sense than we that Providence could always intervene in human affairs. Howard Baker points out that they "conceived of change in character as something that could happen for no tabulated reasons." Adding that this was "an inherited view," he warns that we must accept it as a convention. Otherwise we shall make little sense of such diverse characters as Shakespeare's "Cressida, Prince Hal, and Angelo," or such attitudes as Othello's belief that Desdemona could turn false, Leontes' sudden jealousy of Hermione, and Claudio's immediate acceptance of the charge against Hero.[86] Baker's assertions, of course, have a bearing on Maximus' decision in Act V of *Valentinian*.

There is also another element involved—one that has little relation to Maximus' change of plans, but much to "conversions" such as Evadne's. And that is the invincible Renaissance conviction of the persuasiveness of eloquence. The whole educational system was permeated with this conviction. The heart of university education was the disputation, which trained the student to argue convincingly; logic and rhetoric were intensely cultivated to this end. The clergyman, the lawyer, the statesman took it to be his business to bring his hearers over to his own point of view. This universal respect for the powers of eloquence was bound to be reflected in Elizabethan drama, which, indeed, is full of arguments intended to persuade. It was not merely in church that one might be converted by the right argumentative appeal.

It was therefore wholly credible to Jacobean playgoers that Evadne should be converted by the impassioned pleading, the railing and the threats of her brother. However hardened a sinner she was, it could be brought home to her by eloquence how thoroughly she had disgraced the honor of her aristocratic family. The alteration in her behavior which takes place because of her conviction of sin would therefore seem normal, and her perception of that sin through the force of her brother's plead-ing would seem natural. A Stuart audience would not find that incon-sistency in her character which later critics have found.

Nor would Melantius have appeared a bully. Under such extreme pro-vocation, Jacobean fathers and brothers would be forgiven the use of force and the threat of immediate death. The family honor was at stake. The audience would have been in sympathy with Melantius' behavior. And it would have been spellbound by the consummate theatrical skill with which Fletcher built up to the final collapse of Evadne under her brother's arguing and threats.

This scene, indeed, affords as able an example of the emotional use of the device of conversion as can be found in our body of drama. In terms of the play's emotional form and the attitudes of the time, the situation was soundly and even brilliantly handled. Nor does it strike all modern critics otherwise. But in instances where conversion seems less plausible, it might be well to bear in mind the general acceptance of this conven-tion before condemning it. Too many other playwrights, including Shakespeare, are likewise vulnerable.

Waith remarks that one must find one's enjoyment of Fletcher's tragi-comedies through "the appreciation of a series of emotions expressed by characters who are important only as elements in the design of each scene."[87] This would seem, in general, a sensible approach to the dramatis personae of all our playwrights. To this it should be added that one may frequently find his enjoyment also in the skilful emotional patterning—often counterpointed—of the situation, the scene, the act, and the entire play. Even the most hastily concocted pieces of our corpus will usually con-tain brilliantly devised individual scenes among the shale. As for the better dramas, what Waith remarks of Fletcher's tragicomedies might be said of them all: that their authors were justified in their methods of characteri-zation because these result "in plays of high artistic merit."[88] If that merit be baroque in kind, it nonetheless deserves its measure of acclaim.

IV

From the standpoint of synthesis, relatively little remains to be added to what has already been said—by previous critics and this one—about the practices and abilities of Fletcher in the lighter forms of drama. Beau-mont's gift for satire and burlesque has already been sufficiently discussed.

Massinger contributed relatively little to the comedy in our plays. Moreover, Fletcher and Beaumont both wrote comedy more naturally than Massinger, whose bent was genuinely graver than theirs—as well as more pedestrian.

Massinger's usual contributions as collaborator with Fletcher were to the more sober areas of a play. Employing in his scenes the technique perfected by the "twins," he was not so theatrically sure-handed and lively as they. Since he had somewhat more of the conventional interest in plotting and characterization, he has been often considered, with a certain amount of plausibility, a beneficent restraining influence on Fletcher's extravagance. His heroic first and last acts of *The False One,* for instance, have been thought to provide a fortunate stabilizing framework for Fletcher's more effervescent and theatrical middle ones.[89] That may be. But he lacked his partner's coruscating wit, sure command of racy, idiomatic, spontaneous dialogue and lyric pathos, and keen theatrical eye. His role was evidently either that of junior partner or else of later reviser, but not, unless in the instance of *Barnavelt,* that of the main designer of the play's structure. It is therefore natural that from Caroline times to the present he has figured little in Beaumont and Fletcher criticism. In fact, his individual gifts can be studied most satisfactorily in his own independent dramas.

Fletcher's main contribution to seventeenth century playwriting was the new tragicomedy (and tragedy) which he pioneered in *The Faithful Shepherdess,* and then perfected in cooperation with Beaumont in *Philaster, The Maid's Tragedy* and *A King and No King.* His best independent tragicomedies, such as *A Wife for a Month* and *The Loyal Subject,* are genuinely artistic achievements in their own baroque genre, and even *The Island Princess* has some merit. The power of his accomplishment in this admittedly artificial form has usually not been fully appreciated because his dramatic method in it has not been clearly understood.

And yet who will quarrel seriously with the long accepted opinion that Fletcher's major, or at least happiest, talent was on the whole for farce, and for comedies combining intrigue with manners or romance? Ever since the eulogists of the First Folio united in praising Fletcher for his sprightly wit, few have denied him this quality, though attention has often been drawn to his "witty obscenity." Since Dryden gave the verdict that this playwright understood the conversation of gentlemen better than Shakespeare, disagreement has largely centered on the question of whether the latter's better delineated gentlemen are not more genuinely so termed than Fletcher's "curled darlings." Coleridge, that one-eyed Polyphemus of dramatic criticism, found little enough to like in our corpus; but he did express enthusiasm for a few of the gayest pieces. The ebullient Swinburne waxed lyrical about Fletcher's special sunlit comic province, which no other playwright has occupied. Miss Hatcher, who did not understand Fletcher's aim in tragicomedy, condemned his theatrecraft in this kind. Yet she recognized not only his genuine and fluent poetic gift but also his excellence in light comedy, and she analyzed with acuteness his comic methods and their success. And these are only a few of those critics who have found virtues in Fletcher as purveyor of comedy.

Fletcher always leaned towards farce and rapid intrigue when writing in the lighter vein, just as he moved towards extravagant romance and refined melodrama in his more serious plays. These two tendencies are the natural complements of each other. Both mark the playwright more concerned with a constant and varied response from the audience than with consistency of characterization and action. Emotional patterning in the more serious plays, plots and scenes; patterning for variety of smiles, chuckles and laughter in the lighter ones: these are but two facets of the same approach.

It is no wonder, then, that Fletcher derived some of his dramatic technique from the comedies he had witnessed at Paul's, Blackfriars and the Globe, and used it in tragedy and tragicomedy as well as in its native genre. Nor is it remarkable that his chief innovation should have been Jacobean tragicomedy, which blended the moods of comedy and tragedy into something not precisely either. Likewise, it is understandable that it should sometimes be puzzling to decide just where one type of play shades into the next, and also that Fletcher should have succeeded in deftly combining tragicomedy with farce in such a capital entertainment as *The Humourous Lieutenant.*

It stands to reason that there would be some differences in materials and treatment between such a farce as the merry, high-spirited *The Chances* and the tragic *Valentinian*—however few and slight these might, on investigation, prove to be. Yet, as Miss Hatcher's analysis of Fletcher's dramatic method demonstrated,[90] the same basic ingredients of theatrecraft were used throughout his individual plays. The exact substance and proportions of any single mixture varied, however, according to the particular combination of tones and effects which were desired for that play, or which were suggested by its narrative base. This homogeneity of theatrecraft will be found in all the plays of our corpus in which Fletcher had any share.

Here, certainly, is a root-source of Miss Bradbrook's disturbance over our playwright's "blurring" of the tragic and the comic. And yet Mizener is on solid ground when he protests that, in their tragicomedies and tragedies, "comic contrasts are clearcut and carefully calculated."[91] For instance, a careful examination of the emotional patterning of *Bonduca,* whose farcical elements are distasteful to some modern readers, would nonetheless substantiate Mizener's opinion. But Miss Bradbrook does not appear to mean just this alone. She objects that the narrative of the more serious plays is itself often farcical. She cites the hastily jerry-built *Cupid's Revenge, The Bloody Brother* of hodge-podge authorship, and the Fletcher-Massinger melodrama, *Thierry and Theodoret,* as a group of tragedies "in which the rapid intrigue is of greater interest than the sensations of the characters."[92]

It is doubtful if that is the way these particular "tragedies" effected Jacobean spectators. The first two are among the weaker dramas, in workmanship, of our corpus; hence, their failings, when examined in terms of consistency of action and characterization, are especially evident. *Thierry and Theodoret,* though much better constructed, is a sensational melodrama of blood and revenge. It is true that these three plays are no more devoid of theatrecraft learned from comedy than other tragicomedies and tragedies of our corpus, and they may appear to have a larger infusion of such craftsmanship. But if the plays are examined from the standpoint of their emotional form, it will be found that, in spite of the inferiority of at least two of them, it was the web of passions and emotional tensions which controlled their planning, and not the narrative. And it was this web to which the audience responded.

Melodrama is akin to farce. Thousands have discovered, in recent years, how comic a melodrama of the past can appear to an audience no longer willing to take seriously the outworn dramatic attitudes and behavior of its characters. For there have been many successful attempts to convulse an audience with an arch or a deadly serious treatment of such plays— plays which caught our forefathers in their spell of enchantment. This instability of the attitudes which can be accepted, from generation to generation, in plays of melodramatic treatment appears to be the source of the modern opinion that the narrative of our three plays (and other serious dramas of our corpus as well) is farcical. The opinion is reinforced, of course, by the extravagance of the villains and villainy in these plays.

Granting that the other two tragedies are not really worth reviving, it would be interesting to watch a modern audience's reactions to a skilled performance of *Thierry and Theodoret.* It might well prove that the melodrama's emotional patterning would still have such a grip on the spectators that it would move them more nearly as its authors intended than to laughter at its extravagant "intrigue." All three plays, whatever the quality of their workmanship, were intended to have that grip.

Practicing playwrights know that the line between tragic and comic is a thin one. Many themes and plots can be given a light or a serious treatment, according to the emphasis a playwright wishes to place on his dramatic materials. There are numerous modern plays which cannot readily be classified as comic or tragic—although their treatment, in response to modern demands for realism, may be quite different from that of Fletcher and Company. Much modern drama is, in reality, of a mixed genre, combining farcical or comic with serious or even tragic elements.

It might therefore be argued, with some plausibility, that our playwrights, in their blending of elements hitherto considered the property of farce, satire or comedy with others similarly held peculiar to tragedy, were actually moving in the modern direction! Such an argument would make at least as much sense as the contention that they were decadent blurrers of the proper effects of tragedy and comedy.

That the theatrecraft of Fletcher's comedies resembles that of his more serious plays is excellently illustrated by his late farce-comedy, *Rule a Wife and Have a Wife,* long popular on the stage and still a promising vehicle for the right ensemble of comedians. The play has a double plot, neatly interwoven. The two plots are at once parallel and in antithesis. They are parallel in that, in each case, one character turns the table on another; they are antithetical in that, in one, the man (Leon) wins the victory over his wife (Margarita) while, in the other, the woman (Estefania) achieves the dominance over her husband (Michael Perez, the Copper Captain). The whole structure of the play has both that symmetry of design, and that employment of similarity and contrast, that we have come to look for in the body of our drama.

The main outlines of the double plotting are simplicity itself, and the actual events that peg out the plot are fewer than the play's complicated and lively bustle might lead one to suspect. As with *Valentinian,* not all the events are dramatized on stage, and when the play is analyzed by act and scene, it will be found that every situation was chosen for its "emotional" impingement—in the broad sense of that term—on an audience, tightening the comic tension, surprising with its reversals and arousing hilarious laughter. There are several crises of main importance, each skilfully placed; there are moves and countermoves, emotional oscillations, and many other of the theatrical devices we expect to find in Fletcher's work. The handling of dialogue, complications, scenes and, indeed, of the whole comic "emotional" form is, from an aesthetic viewpoint, excellent in its kind.

As with *Valentinian,* the characters of *Rule a Wife* are largely conceived in terms of the roles they must play in the various situations in which they become involved. And yet they will doubtless seem, on the whole, more "probable." For one thing, we tend to accept extravagance in the behavior of characters who have their being in a play verging towards farce more leniently than we do for those involved in the serious complications of tragedy. Moreover, the genial, witty and companionable playwright would himself be much in sympathy with such figures as the cleverly masterful Leon and the quick-witted, roguish Estefania. Then, too, such a play as *Rule a Wife* is moderately realistic rather than exotically romantic, and so extravagance in securing sharp character contrasts is more under limitation, except, perhaps, for such a farcical humour figure as Cacafogo. And yet, upon analysis, the characters will prove to have been constructed in much the same manner as those in *Valentinian*—that is, for their theatrically useful major and minor traits.

As this brief consideration of *Rule a Wife* indicates, the comedies of our corpus are best understood, like the serious plays, in terms of their emotional form—or, if one prefers, their patterning for variety and fullness of comic response. Often this patterning is deft indeed, as in *The Wild-Goose Chase,* wherein the moves of Oriana and her two gentlewoman friends to attract Mirabel and two gentleman friends are checkmated by the latter. The successive moves are made and countered rather in the manner in which a tennis ball is hit back and forth over the net, until finally the gentlemen are caught, and the chase of the "wild-goose," Mirabel, ends.

And so it is in the plays of mixed genres. In *Monsieur Thomas,* the delightful though racy pranks of the madcap title character—abetted by his charming if free-spoken sister, Dorothea—are loosely juxtaposed with the sentimental, essentially tragicomic story of Frank, Cellide and Valentine. This has been done not because, of inner necessity, these particular two plots had to be combined, but because their counterpointed moods afford a contrast which would appeal to a variety-loving audience. From that standpoint, the juxtaposition is justified, as it is with *The Spanish Curate,* however much more enjoyable some modern readers may find the uproariously farcical scenes of the latter play than its tragicomic element. So it is also with *The Custom of the Country,* that much impugned play, which blends with aesthetic skill three different strands of action, of different tones, yet harmonizing in the whole. As for the romantic *The Pilgrim* (based, like *The Wild-Goose Chase,* on the age-old comic motif of the chase), it is a cunning and inseparable mixture of tragicomic with farcical situations and moods—the farcical ones predominant, but providing by no means all the thrills and excitement.

If such plays as these and *The Chances, Wit Without Money* and *Women Pleased,* have less body than Shakespeare's romantic comedies, they have their own shallower charm. Their dialogue has doubtless lost something of the sparkle which it had when it was new coined, and standards of propriety in speech and behavior have changed. And yet it it still possible to recapture something of the Stuart enthusiasm for the comedy of our playwrights, which Cartwright expressed thus:

> When thou wouldst Comick be, each smiling birth
> In that kinde, came into the world all mirth,
> All point, all edge, all sharpnesse; we did sit
> Sometimes five Acts out in pure sprightfull wit,
> Which flowed in such true salt, that we did doubt
> In which Scene we laught most two shillings out.[93]

V

Miss Ellis-Fermor remarks, of Fletcher, Beaumont and Company, "irresponsibility . . . is an essential part of their attitude, the irresponsibility which creates fairy-tales. . . ."[94] Exactly; but it was fairy tales for Jacobean adults which they were creating. With their keen instinct for the theatre, they recognized, as Stoll has expressed it in speaking of Shakespeare, that "What is expected is what from life we do not get—enlargement, excitement, another world, not a copy of this."[95] And this expectation they fulfilled, content that their dramas should be plausible to spectators for the brief three hours' traffic of the playhouse. And so, in drama after drama, they proceeded "to set characters in a state of high commotion,"[96] and to keep them in that state by every theatrical device that could arouse sensations in their spectators.

In this they were not so very different from Shakespeare and other predecessors, from whom they learned their art, except that they placed their emphasis upon dramatic entertainment for the gentry, and had relatively little that they desired earnestly to say. And that little was, perhaps, of rather more interest to the gentlefolk of their own day than to us. Lacking Shakespeare's exceptional poetic gift and his often profound insight into the springs of action, they were content to skim the surfaces of Jacobean life. They belong among the accomplished playwrights rather than among the penetrating dramatists of the western world.

As sheer men of the theatre, however, who were also artists in their kind, the place of both Fletcher and Beaumont is high. Few playwrights have had more ready command of all the resources of their particular stage, or a more theatrically effective gift for the spectacular. Each had a selective and shaping power of a discriminating, though baroque, aesthetic quality; and each possessed a poetic talent of a more than common order, by means of which they could, when they chose, gracefully or stirringly bedeck their plays with ornament. The form of at least the better plays of our corpus is both coherent and, in terms of its emotional purpose, significant. If even the best of these dramas are "artificial" rather than "natural," they are not, by any means, mere mechanisms.

That reader who seeks greater truth to life and illumination of its problems than Fletcher, Beaumont and Company have to offer, would wisely leave them alone. They are not other Shakespeares, or even Jonsons. Yet their position in the seventeenth century triumvirate was inevitable, since they wrote exactly to the tastes of Jacobean and Caroline gentlefolk, and knew almost infallibly how to rouse them, whether to laughter or to tears. So, for the student of things human with a strong curiosity about seventeenth century life, they preserve some aspects of its color—exotically, it is true, but not the less interestingly for that.

And then Fletcher and Beaumont are, in a sense, playwrights' playwrights. Their technical proficiency was so marked, and within its limits so artistically displayed, that when once their dramatic method is understood, they will repay the study of those who aspire to write for the theatre. Nor that alone. Our playwrights will also refresh the student of English drama who—recognizing the nature of their work, and setting stern morality aside for the time as irrelevant— can recreate their better plays in his imagination as though they were being performed in a playhouse before his very eyes. He will then have entered their domain, and will then understand why even critics who deplore these dramas can yet sometimes be moved by their power. And he will have his reward, in enjoyment of our playwrights' baroque artistry and, perchance, of their poetry and their wit.

Si quid habent veri Vatum praesagia, vivam.[97]

Appendix

Notes

Bibliography

Appendix

A Brief Survey of the Stage Career of the Fletcher, Beaumont and Company Plays since 1700

Plays of Fletcher, Beaumont and Company were still holding the stage in the early years of the eighteenth century, though not in such numbers as formerly.[1] There was competition from Jonson's major comedies, from witty Restoration and sentimental Queen Anne and Georgian comedies, and from new farces, ballad-operas, burlesques and pantomimes. Despite this, the Fletcherian romances, farces and operatic adaptations held their own reasonably well for nearly half a century longer, whereas Shakespeare's romantic comedies still languished in the neglect which had befallen them in Restoration years.[2] Brome's *The Northern Lass* and *The Jovial Crew* appear to have offered the triumvirate almost the only competition from the older drama.

In more serious forms, however, the situation was grimmer for our playwrights. Shakespeare's rivals in tragedy were Restoration dramatists like Otway, Southerne and Lee.[3] The tragicomedies and tragedies of Beaumont and Fletcher, which even in Restoration days had not been so popular as their comedies, were now beginning to be played infrequently. In the first years of the century five tragicomedies were produced;[4] but two of these, *The Loyal Subject* and *Women Pleased,* quickly dropped from sight, and in some theatrical seasons none of the tragicomedies or tragedies were given.

Nicoll's data about the performances at the Drury Lane Theatre for the seasons of 1703-04 and 1704-05 sufficiently illustrate the new situation. In 1703-04, three comedies of our canon—two in revised versions—were presented for a total of ten nights: *The Pilgrim* (as an opera), *The Chances* and *Rule a Wife*. As against this, two alone of Shakespeare's comedies had a single performance each: *The Tempest* (as an opera) and *The Taming of the Shrew*. But in tragedy and tragicomedy the situation was reversed; seven tragedies of Shakespeare ran for 20 evenings, while Beaumont and Fletcher were not represented at all.[5]

Similar are the showings for 1704-05. Three comedies of our playwrights were given for the sum of five nights, *The Chances* and *Rule a Wife* being repeated, and *The Beggars' Bush* being new. Shakespeare's *The Taming of the Shrew* was played again, and *Henry the Fourth* for the first time, for a total of four performances. Ben Jonson was represented each year by three major comedies, a pace he would maintain quite steadily for half a century. But in the field of more serious drama, Beaumont and Fletcher were again absent from the stage, in stark contrast with 13 nights devoted to five tragedies of Shakespeare.[6] The Bard of Avon had been accepted by playgoers as the great tragic dramatist of the past.

When we move forward to the years 1707-10, we find the situation unchanged. According to Sprague's count, 14 plays of our group produced during Restoration years were again staged, and *Wit at Several Weapons* had its first performance since 1642. Of these, only five were tragedies or tragicomedies: *The Bloody Brother*, *The Humourous Lieutenant* (holding its own for its comic scenes), *A King and No King*, *The Maid's Tragedy*, and *Valentinian*. *The Island Princess*, as adapted, was operatic. This list balances nicely with 14 plays by Shakespeare, all but the three already mentioned being, however, tragedies or histories.[7] Since Shakespearean tragedies were receiving more performances than Fletcherian comedies, Shakespeare led in actual nights on the boards, and would continue to do so.

In 1718-19, according to Nicoll's lists, the Drury Lane Theatre played *The Chances, The Humourous Lieutenant, Rule a Wife* and *The Pilgrim* for a total of eight nights. Skipping forward to ten seasons later (1728-29), we find that the first three of these were again acted, and that *The Scornful Lady* and *Wit Without Money* were added, the five plays having eleven nights' run. Meanwhile, at the Lincoln's Inn Theatre, in 1718-19, our authors were represented by three operatic versions for seven nights: *The Island Princess, The Pilgrim* and *The Prophetess*. Ten seasons later these same three, plus *The Royal Merchant* (an adaptation by Henry Norris of *The Beggars' Bush*) ran nine nights. But in all four of these playlists the more serious dramas of our corpus are conspicuous by their absence, except for one performance of *The Maid's Tragedy* at the Drury Lane in the later season.[8] Among the ten plays here listed were all the comedies which Sprague found playing between the years 1707 to 1710. A definite majority of the plays of our authors had passed into acting obscuration.

These statistics, dry enough in themselves, lend a partial measure of support to the anonymous author of *Memoirs of Robert Wilks,* who stated that "Few of the Plays of Beaumont and Fletcher are now either prized or acted; the *Scornful Lady* and *Wit Without Money* are almost the only ones, which at this time of Day are capable of entertaining the Town."[9]

It was to Shakespeare's revived romantic comedies that the lighter pieces of Fletcher and Company succumbed. An opening skirmish in the unequal contest is amusingly hinted in Henry Fielding's satirical comedy, *The Historical Register for the Year 1736,* first acted at the Haymarket in May, 1737. In what amounts to the epilogue, Medley says, to "you, Ladies, whether you be Shakespeare's ladies, or Beaumont and Fletcher's ladies, I hope you will make allowances for a rehearsal, And kindly report us to the Town."[10] In 1737 the women playgoers were evidently warmly divided over the respective merits of these playwrights.

Nicoll's playlists for the season of 1738-39 show our dramatists still in the lead in comedy. Four old favorites ran, at Drury Lane and Covent Garden, for a sum of 20 performances, while five Shakespeare comedies could remain on the boards only 12. But the future was foreshadowed by the success this season of *Much Ado About Nothing,* first revived at Covent Garden on November 2, 1737.

The crest year for revivals of Shakespeare's romantic comedies was 1741. Prologued on December 20, 1740, by the reappearance of *As You Like It,* the next ten months brought to theatregoers of this generation *A Winter's Tale, The Merchant of Venice, All's Well that Ends Well,* and *The Comedy of Errors.*[11] It was the crucial season for Fletcher and Company comedies.

Although John Motley wrote, in 1747, that *The Chances* "still continues what they call a Stock-Play," and that *Rule a Wife* and *The Scornful Lady* "are still acted with applause,"[12] all we can find in Nicoll's list for the season of 1748-49 is *The Royal Merchant,* good for two performances, whereas seven comedies of Shakespeare ran for 45 nights at Drury Lane and Covent Garden! This is the more overwhelming when we note that there were 50 performances of Shakespearean tragedies in this same season—44 of them, under David Garrick's inspiration, at Drury Lane.[13]

It was two or three years later that Henry Fielding jotted down, in his *Covent Garden Journal,* under the date of March 7, 1752, what was merely a dissenter's opinion of this collapse in our authors' popularity, when he exclaimed, "What can we sometimes conceive of an Audience at a Play-House, where I have heard the dullest Chitchat between Gentlemen and Ladies called Humour . . . and the Little French Lawyer of Fletcher was hissed off the stage."[14] Even though the plays of our corpus would not completely vanish from the theatres for two or three generations more, Shakespeare's triumph was complete.[15]

And what, meanwhile, of Fletcher and Company plays in provincial theatres during this first half of the century? Miss Rosenfeld's research into surviving records of some provincial companies suggests that it parallels their career on the boards in London. Between 1700 and 1721 she found recorded performances of the operatic *Island Princess* at Greenwich, Richmond Hill and Newcastle; of *The Maid in the Mill* at Greenwich, of *The Prophetess* at Norwich. Then these three plays, as might have been expected, drop out of sight in the provinces.[16]

The records of the Norwich Company for 1721 to 1750 show five Beaumont and Fletcher stock-plays in their repertory: *The Maid's Tragedy* and four comedies, *The Chances, The Royal Merchant, Rule a Wife* and *The Scornful Lady.* This contrasts, on the one hand, with 14 dramas by Shakespeare and, on the other, with only two other pre-Restoration pieces.[17] During the same years *The Pilgrim* seems to have been popular in the provinces. It was performed at Canterbury (on the Kentish Circuit) in 1732 and 1739, by the Bristol Company in 1742, and was played about 1738 and revived in 1748 at Richmond Hill.[18] Records also survive of performances of *The Royal Merchant* at Bristol and *Rule a Wife* at Canterbury in these decades.[19]

Between 1751 and 1756, at Simpson's Theatre in Bath, the fashionable watering-place, there were at least four performances of Fletcher and Company plays: *Rule a Wife* in 1751, *The Chances* in the two successive seasons from 1754 to 1756, and *The Royal Merchant* in 1755-56. Since the two last seem to have been the only pieces of our playwrights to be presented in the latter season, while 18 performances of nine Shakespeare plays are recorded as given then, it is evident that Bath was simply echoing the taste of London.[20]

Although this evidence of our playwrights' career in the provinces is scanty, it is sufficient to indicate that the same plays which held the stage in London were carried into the countryside by the strolling players. It supplies some factual ground, also, for that passage in Oliver Goldsmith's *The Vicar of Wakefield* (1766), in which the genial Dr. Primrose is drawing out a provincial actor:

"I fancy, Sir," cried the Player, "few of our modern dramatists would think themselves much honoured by being compared to the writers you mention. Dryden and Rowe's manner, Sir, are quite out of fashion; our taste has gone back a whole century. Fletcher, Ben Johnson, and all the plays of Shakespear, are the only things that go down."—"How," cried I, "is it possible the present age can be pleased with that antiquated dialect, that obsolete humour, those overcharged characters, which abound in the works you mention?"—"Sir," returned my companion, "the public think nothing about dialect, or humour, or character; for that is none of their business, they only go to be amused, and find themselves happy when they can enjoy a pantomime, under the sanction of Johnson's or Shakespeare's name.[21]

However the provinces may have responded to Jonson and Fletcher, their plays were indeed acquiring the reputation of being antiquated and obsolete for the London Stage. In 1757, a critic, when giving advice to young actresses in *The Theatrical Examiner*, pointed out a serious difficulty they would encounter in acting the old plays: "The great ladies of Ben. Johnson, are north country chambermaids in point of breeding, Beaumont and Fletcher the same."[22] In 1761 the neo-classical Goldsmith commented, more mordantly than his vicar, "Old pieces are revived, and scarcely any new ones admitted . . . the public are again obliged to ruminate over those hashes of absurdity, which were disgusting to our ancestors even in an age of ignorance." The eighteenth century's self-complacency here expressed is merely an extension of that given voice by Dryden in Restoration years.

So far as Shakespeare is concerned, Goldsmith's attack was partly on adaptations which were still playing; yet he did find that dramatist "blind of one eye," and wished that "many of his scenes were forgotten."[23] No doubt "hashes of absurdity" sufficiently described the dramas of our corpus for Goldsmith, since Shakespeare and Jonson were the only playwrights mentioned by name.

The old plays still had their defenders. George Colman the Elder, later to be editor of the 1778 edition of the Beaumont and Fletcher corpus, challenged Garrick, in an essay prefixed to the 1761 edition of Massinger, to revive the dramas of Shakespeare's contemporaries at Drury Lane:

Shakespeare has been transmitted down to us with Successive Glories, and you, Sir, have continued, or rather increased, his Reputation. . . . But. . . . Has not the Contemplation of Shakespeares Excellencies almost dazzled and extinguished your Judgement, when directed to other Objects, and made you blind to the Merits of his Cotemporaries? Under your Dominion have not Beaumont and Fletcher, nay even Johnson, suffered a kind of theatrical Disgrace?[24]

Colman maintained that it was both pleasant and profitable to observe the manners of an older day in its plays. These would not seem obsolete if given the same kind of effective production as Garrick's *Every Man in His Humour*.[25]

Garrick, however, was unconvinced. As regards our body of plays, the *Drury Lane Calendar, 1747 to 1776*, will show why. In 1747 *The Scornful Lady* ran but a single evening, in 1749 *The Little French Lawyer* failed in two performances and *The Spanish Curate* in one, while in 1750-51 *The Pilgrim* managed to survive four presentations, and in 1757 and 1760 *The Tamer Tam'd (The Woman's Prize)* lasted three. All five plays disappeared from the stock-list after their ill success.[26] As against this record of failure, only two comedies continued to draw: *The Chances*, with 20 performances between 1754 and 1758, and *Rule a Wife*, which between 1756 and 1761 had been steadily produced from once to four times a year. The best complete record made by any play of our corpus during Garrick's three decades at Drury Lane was that of *Rule a Wife*, with 50 performances spread over 17 different seasons.[27] But set beside the 115 performances of *Hamlet* and the 80 of *Every Man in His Humour,* this was only a mediocre stockplay achievement.[28] Obviously, Garrick considered revivals of Fletcher and Company plays, even in revised versions, hazardous.

Since the great actor-manager remained obdurate, Colman altered Beaumont and Fletcher's *Philaster,* and produced it himself on October 8, 1763, while managing Drury Lane in Garrick's absence. William Powell, newest recruit in the star system, made his first appearance in this piece. According to Page, the production "was a great success. Powell's reputation was at once established, and the success of the theatre assured for the season."[29] Colman's version ran for 17 performances that season, and three the next.[30] It also spread to the provinces, for the York company gave it soon after its London premiere.[31] Thereafter there were occasional London performances, extending into the nineteenth century; but its success was essentially temporary.[32]

In the "advertisement" prefixed to his publication of this version, Colman resumed his pleading. "The pieces of Beaumont and Fletcher in particular," he contended, ". . . abound with beauties, so much of the same colour with those of Shakespeare, that it is almost unaccountable, that the very age that admires one, even to idolatry, should pay so little attention to the other." He added the significant statement, agreeing with *Drury Lane Calendar* records, that "the Spanish Curate, the Little French Lawyer, and the Scornful Lady of our authors, as well as the Silent Woman of Johnson, all favourite entertainments of our predecessors, have, within these few years, encountered the severity of the pit, and received sentence of condemnation." In order that the "uncommon" merit of *Philaster* might not endure a like fate, Colman thought it advisable to "clear it of ribaldry and obscenity."[33] He cut the play by one-third, eliminated Philaster's wounding of Arethusa and Bellario, but preserved, in the main, the language of Beaumont and Fletcher.[34]

Colman made one more attempt to resuscitate our playwrights with an adaptation—this time of Fletcher's *Bonduca,* a favorite of his. It ran for 12 performances at the Haymarket in the summer of 1778. In order to make it palatable to contemporary taste, Colman made many changes in the original. For once Garrick paid some honor to our authors: he wrote the prologue![35]

Although Colman was the only adapter doughtily to champion the "Beaumont and Fletcher" plays, he was by no means the only playwright of his century to draw on this body of theatrical entertainment. An age which thought the wit of Molière bettered in English dress[36] would have no scruples about pilfering from these rude barbarians of the ignorant past. Colley Cibber, making use of their "loose confed'rate Muse" for four of his plays, derived the first two acts of *Love Makes a Man* from *The Elder Brother,* and the last three from *The Custom of the Country!*[37] Nicoll mentions by name seven other adaptations in the first half-century, tells us that some of the earlier comedies were reduced to farces between 1730 and 1750, and adds that "we find a great number of types and of single situations taken over in more or less disguised forms."[38] He also names 13 other plays which, in the second half-century, drew on our corpus for themes or for actual adaptations.[39]

Yet, in spite of this evidence that a few dramatists were still finding these plays treasure trove for their own efforts, Colman was swimming against the tide in championing them. Davies, in his *Dramatic Miscellanies* (1784), said of them that "two only at present preserve their rank on the stage, the *Chances* and *Rule a Wife and have a Wife.*" A true child of his century, he pointed the moral: "No writers, sure, ever experienced such a reverse of fortune. To be tumbled from the highest exaltation of fame to neglect and oblivion is a mortifying lesson to all successful writers."[40]

In addition to reasons already noted for this reversal of fortune on the stage for Beaumont and Fletcher (and for Jonson as well) there was another one, not so immediately apparent. The "obsoleteness" of their plays was not alone due to the superiority of Shakespeare, changes in taste, and dislike of their "grossness." Developments in the structure of theatres and the conditions of staging plays, which trace back to the early years of the Restoration period, also contributed to this result.

We have observed a tendency in Dryden and others to look upon their ancestors as rude barbarians,—a view that gained strength in the Augustan age. As a matter of course, the new generations scorned the Elizabethan playhouses and their arrangements as outmoded, turned their backs on older traditions, and soon lapsed into contented ignorance about most of them.

The Restoration stages were not of a structural, multiple-stage construction, as even the indoor Blackfriars had been. They were rather the crude beginnings of the modern picture-frame stage, (with platform modified into huge apron), difficult to light, and making much use of scenery. These, as well as women in place of boys in feminine roles, were looked upon as great improvements. But this stage was not well adapted to plays written in terms of scenes, and many of them, in rapid succession—as the plays of the triumvirate had been. Here was one of the causes, and a practical one, for so many adaptations of the older dramas, however deplorable many of these new versions may have been.

As the theatres grew in size in the eighteenth century, they lost the intimacy of the small Elizabethan playhouses, and were far more clumsy tools than their structural ancestors. The unity of place, and the reduction in numbers of scenes, inevitably gained pertinence from the difficulties of scene-shifting. The immediacy of reaction in the Elizabethan theatre between spectator and actor, to which the old plays had been pitched, was much diminished in the larger and dimly lit auditoriums. That the old plays were thus given under greatly changed and unfavorable conditions, had no little to do with their waning on the boards.

Before the end of the century, some theatregoers were, in fact, finding even Shakespeare disappointing in this alien environment. Lamb was not expressing a novel conviction, in his charmingly paradoxical essay, *On the Tragedies of Shakespeare*,[41] that these dramas were better read than acted. Yet what scanty information still persisted about the Elizabethan playhouse created the hazy opinion that the Elizabethan stage was crude and bare!

Davies' estimate, in 1784, about the stage neglect of our playwrights was sound. By the turn of the century Fletcher, Beaumont and Company were still meagerly holding the boards, but revivals were growing rare. As for their hardiest stock-plays, Weber reported in 1812 that "except for the comedies of Rule a Wife and have a Wife and The Chances, none of our poets' dramas are performed."[42] Genest testified in 1832 that "latterly even the Chances has been laid aside."[43] Dyce (1843-46) explained why this had happened with the remark that more than twenty years before, *The Chances* had been "degraded into a flimsy opera." He never expected the play to appear again under the lamplights; but *Rule a Wife* was "still an attractive entertainment of the stage."[44] This late farce by Fletcher was the last stock-play to go.

Fletcher, Beaumont and Company have not totally vanished from the theatre. For instance, in 1883 Macaulay reported, in his study of Beaumont, that *The Maid's Tragedy* "still occasionally appears on the stage.[45] Both the Elizabethan Stage Society, since 1881, and The Phoenix Society, since 1918, have given, in London, some plays of our corpus as items in their programs devoted to dramas of the English past.[46] There have also been, from time to time, college or university productions,—most frequently of *The Knight of the Burning Pestle.*[47] But it is today a rare occasion when a lover of Elizabethan-Stuart drama is able to see one of the plays of the Beaumont and Fletcher canon come alive, even in a non-professional playhouse.

Notes to the Chapters and Appendix

NOTES TO CHAPTER ONE

1. Cf. Thomas Fuller: *The Histories of the Worthies of England,* 3 vols., London, (1662) 1840, vol. II, p. 513. Fuller was one of the first to compare Beaumont and Fletcher to "Castor and Pollux (most happy when in conjunction)"—a figure of speech which became conventional as applied to these playwrights.

2. Gerald Eades Bentley, in his *Shakespeare & Jonson: Their Reputations in the Seventeenth Century Compared,* 2 vols., Chicago, 1945, amasses a convincing weight of evidence to prove that Jonson's reputation, at least until about 1690, was definitely greater than Shakespeare's. It was in the eighteenth century that the latter clearly established his reputation as the supreme English dramatist.

3. Cf. *The Works of Francis Beaumont and John Fletcher,* 10 vols., edited by Arnold Glover and A. R. Waller, "Cambridge English Classics," Cambridge, England, 1905-12, vol. I, pp. xl and xli for the remarks of J. Berkenhead and William Cartwright, in their contributions to the "Commendatory Verses." These will be discussed later in this chapter. Hereafter this edition of the works of our playwrights will be referred to as *"Works of B. and F.,* Glover-Waller edition."

4. *Works of B. and F.,* Glover-Waller edition, vol. I, p. xxxiv. An almost contemporary sign of the confusion is Drummond's record of Jonson's remark about a play by Fletcher alone: "Flesher and Beaumont ten years since hath written the Faithful Shipheardesse a Tragi-comedie well done." Cf. Ben Jonson: *Conversations with William Drummond of Hawthornden, 1619,* Bodley Head Quartos no. 5, edited by G. B. Harrison, London and New York, 1923, pp. 10-11. Yet Jonson had written a tribute to Fletcher's play—to be quoted from later—scarcely ten years before!

5. See "Catalogue" in *Works of B. and F.,* Glover-Waller edition, vol. I, p. lvii. R. C. Bald: *Bibliographical Studies in the Beaumont and Fletcher Folio of 1647,* Oxford, 1935, pp. 8, 10, has lists of these plays as entered in "The Stationers' Register" on 4 September 1646 and 29 June 1660.

6. *The Beggars' Bush, The Custom of the Country, The Double Marriage, The False One, The Honest Man's Fortune* (with Field), *The Knight of Malta* (with Field), *The Little French Lawyer, The Lovers' Progress, The Prophetess, The Queen of Corinth* (with Field), *The Sea Voyage, The Spanish Curate.*

7. *The Coxcomb, The Fair Maid of the Inn.*

8. Alfred Harbage: *Annals of the English Drama, 975 to 1700,* London, 1940. Listings of all plays of the Beaumont and Fletcher corpus are on pp. 76-99.

9. E. H. C. Oliphant: *The Plays of Beaumont and Fletcher,* New Haven and

London, 1927, pp. 481 and 426. Oliphant's and Harbage's assignments of these 34 plays have been checked against each other throughout. They are sufficiently representative of modern opinion about authorship for our purposes. Also cf. U. M. Ellis-Fermor: *The Jacobean Drama*, London, 1936, pp. 325-27. Miss Ellis-Fermor's attributions vary somewhat from both Harbage's and Oliphant's, but chiefly regarding the more doubtful cases in the corpus.

10. E. H. C. Oliphant, *op. cit.*, p. 377. With this particular assignment by Oliphant I agree.

11. *The Captain, Love's Pilgrimage, Wit at Several Weapons.*

12. *The Beggar's Bush, The Nice Valour, The Noble Gentleman.*

13. *Four Plays in One, The Honest Man's Fortune, The Knight of Malta, The Queen of Corinth.*

14. E. H. C. Oliphant, *op. cit.*, pp. xii-xiii, lists them as follows: *Bonduca, The Chances, The Faithful Shepherdess, The Humourous Lieutenant, The Island Princess, The Loyal Subject, The Mad Lover, Monsieur Thomas, The Pilgrim, Rule a Wife and Have a Wife, Valentinian, A Wife for a Month, The Wild-Goose Chase, Wit Without Money, The Woman's Prize, Women Pleased.* To these might be added *The Night Walker*, except that this now exists only in a later Shirley revision.

15. Cf. Alfred Harbage, *op. cit.*, pp. 86-99.

16. An examination of the "Commendatory Verses" distributes the tributes as follows: to Beaumont alone, 4; to Beaumont and Fletcher, 6; to Fletcher alone, 25; to Massinger, o. Cf. *Works of B. and F.*, Glover-Waller edition, vol. I, pp. xv-lvi

17. Sir Aston Cockaine: *Small Poems of Divers Sorts*, London, 1658, p. 186.

18. R. C. Bald, *op. cit.*, pp. 3-6, gives an interesting account of this transaction.

19. *Works of B. and F.*, Glover-Waller edition, vol. I, pp. ix-x.

20. *Ibid.*, vol. I, p. xiv.

21. *Ibid.*, vol. I, p. xiii.

22. *The Poems of Abraham Cowley*, edited by A. R. Waller, Cambridge, England, 1905, "The Preface of the Author," p. 5.

23. *Works of B. and F.*, Glover-Waller edition, vol. I, pp. xix-xx.

24. Aston Cockaine, *op. cit.*, pp. 91 and 117. Both poems are quoted in Orie L. Hatcher: *John Fletcher: A Study in Dramatic Method*, Chicago, 1905, p. 10.

25. Gerard Langbaine: *An Account of the English Dramatick Poets*, Oxford, 1691, p. 217.

26. *Works of B. and F.*, Glover-Waller edition, vol. I, pp. xli-xlii.

27. *Ibid.*, vol. I, p. xxxv.

28. Cf. Orie L. Hatcher, *op. cit.*, chapter I, for a reasonably detailed historical account of the authorship problem to 1905. E. H. C. Oliphant, *op. cit.*, gives his own and others' views of the authorship of each of the plays of the whole corpus. Baldwin Maxwell: *Studies in Beaumont, Fletcher, and Massinger*, Chapel Hill, 1939, sheds much new light on this and other problems.

29. Thomas Rymer: "Preface to the Translation of Rapin's Reflections on Aristotle's Treatise of Poesie," London, 1674, in Joel E. Spingarn, editor, *Critical Essays of the Seventeenth Century*, 3 vols., Oxford, 1908, vol. II, p. 164.

30. Sir Philip Sidney: *The Defense of Poesy*, edited by Albert C. Cook, Boston, 1890, pp. 47-52.

31. In his *The Tragedies of the Last Age Consider'd*, London, 1678.

32. William Prynne: Histrio-Mastix (etc.), London, 1633, [1632]. H. J. C. Grierson: *Cross Currents in English Literature of the XVIIth Century*, London, 1929, pp. 69-84, has an interesting discussion of Puritan attacks on the drama, with a sound analysis of Prynne's diatribe.

33. "Essay of Dramatic Poesy," in W. P. Ker, editor: *The Essays of John Dryden*, 2 vols., Oxford, 1900, vol. I, p. 81.

34. John Tucker Murray: *English Dramatic Companies, 1558-1642*, 2 vols., Boston, 1910, vol. I, p. 174.

35. *Ibid.*, vol. I, pp. 174-176.

36. *Ibid.*, vol. I, p. 363.

37. Gerald Eades Bentley: *The Jacobean and Caroline Stage*, 2 vols., Oxford, 1941, vol. I, pp. 94-100.

38. *Ibid.*, vol. I, p. 29.

39. *The Lyric Poems of Beaumont and Fletcher*, edited by Ernest Rhys, London, 1897, "Introduction," p. xx.

40. *The Dramatic Records of Sir Henry Herbert, Master of the Revels, 1633-1673*, edited by Joseph Quincy Adams, "Cornell Studies in English," III, New Haven, 1917, p. 58.

41. Henry Glapthorne: *White-Hall (a Poem) Written in 1642*, London, 1643; quoted in Leslie Hotson: *The Commonwealth and Restoration Stage*, Cambridge, Mass., 1928, p. 11. Nine years later Samuel Sheppard informs us in the "Third Pastoral" of his volume, *Epigrams Theological, &c.*, London, 1651, p. 251, that

> Two happy wits, late brightly shone,
> The true sonnes of Hyperion,
> Fletcher, and Beaumont, who so wrot,
> Johnsons Fame was soon forgot,
> Shakespeare no glory was alow'd,
> His sun quite shrunk beneath a cloud.

Quoted in Gerald Eades Bentley: *Shakespeare & Jonson*, vol. II, p. 83.

42. Leslie Hotson: *op. cit.*, p. 16.

43. James Wright: *Historia Histrionica: A Dialogue of Plays and Players*, London, 1699, in Robert Dodsley: *A Select Collection of Old English Plays*, 15 vols., edited by W. C. Hazlitt, London, 1874, vol. XV, pp. 410-11, and *passim*.

44. Hyder E. Rollins, "A Contribution to the History of English Commonwealth Drama," *Studies in Philology*, XVIII (1921), pp. 267-333.

45. Leslie Hotson, *op. cit.*, p. 26. Exiled aristocrats were also interested in this play. Rollins mentions a plan of the gentlemen and maids of honor, in Holland, to perform the play at Whitsuntide, 1654, before the Princess Royal. Cf. Hyder E. Rollins: *op. cit.*, p. 313.

46. Leslie Hotson, *op. cit.*, p. 40.

47. *Ibid.*, p. 55.

48. *Ibid.*, pp. 24-25.

49. *Ibid.*, p. 34.

50. John James Elson, editor: *The Wits, or Sport Upon Sport*, "Cornell Studies in English," XVIII, Ithaca, N. Y., 1932, "Introduction," pp. 18-19.

51. *Ibid.*, p. 1.

52. *Ibid.*, "Contents," pp. xi-xii. The "B. and F." plays represented are: *The Beggar's Bush, The Bloody Brother, The Chances, Cupid's Revenge, The Custom of the Country, The Humourous Lieutenant, The Knight of the Burning Pestle,*

The Maid in the Mill, The Maid's Tragedy, Monsieur Thomas, Philaster, Rule a Wife and Have a Wife, The Scornful Lady, The Spanish Curate.

53. *The Dramatic Works of Ben Jonson, and Beaumont and Fletcher,* 4 vols., edited respectively by Peter Whalley and George Colman, London, 1811, vol. II, p. liv. Richard Brome, Jonson's servant and, later, Caroline playwright, tells us of Fletcher that

> Most knowing Johnson (proude to call him Sonne)
> In friendly envy swore, He had out-done
> His very selfe.

Brome's memory may be confused here. Jonson's poem to Beaumont says of the latter, not of Fletcher, "For writing better, I must envy thee." Cf. *Works of B. and F.*, Glover-Waller edition, vol. I, p. xl. Brome also indicates Fletcher's popularity in 1625 when he adds:

> I knew him till he dyed;
> And, at his dissolution, what a Tide
> Of Sorrow overwhelm'd the Stage; . . . *Ibid.*, p. lv.

54. *The Works of Mary and Charles Lamb,* 7 vols., edited by E. V. Lucas, London, 1904, vol. IV, "Dramatic Specimens and the Garrick Plays," pp. 533-34.

55. *Works of B. J. and B. and F.*, Whalley-Colman edition, vol. II, p. liv.

56. *The Complete Works of John Webster*, edited by F. L. Lucas, 4 vols., London, 1928, vol. I, pp. 107-08.

57. Thomas Heywood: *The Hierarchie of the Blessed Angells*, London, 1634, p. 206.

58. Owen Felltham: "To the Memory of Immortal Ben," in *Jonsonus Virbius, or The Memorie of Ben Jonson Revived,* London, 1638.

59. "His Mistres Shade," in "An Addition of Some Excellent Poems . . . by other Gentlemen," to *Poems: Written by Wil. Shake-speare*, London, 1640, sig. L6. Quoted in *The Jonson Allusion Book*, edited by Jesse F. Bradley and Joseph Q. Adams, New Haven, 1922, p. 263.

60. In so saying, I accord with Forsythe's views. Cf. Robert Forsythe: *The Relations of Shirley's Plays to the Elizabethan Drama*, New York, 1914, pp. 48-50.

61. *The Dramatic Works and Poems of James Shirley*, 6 vols., edited by Rev. Alexander Dyce, London, 1833, vol. V, p. 357.

62. Robert Anton: *The Philosophers Satyrs*, London, 1616. Quoted in *The Jonson Allusion Book*, p. 99.

63. Aubrey, for instance, asserts that Beaumont's "maine businesse was to correct the overflowings of Mr. Fletcher's witt." Cf. John Aubrey: *Brief Lives (etc.)*, 2 vols., edited by Andrew Clark, Oxford, 1898, vol. I, pp. 95-96.

64. The facts of this paragraph are based on R. C. Bald, *op. cit.*, pp. 1-10, who gives an excellently documented account of Moseley's activities. Cf. *Works of B. and F.,* Glover-Waller edition, vol. I, pp. xiii-xiv, "The Stationer to the Reader."

65. R. C. Bald, *op. cit.*, p. 1.

66. Cf. *Works of B. and F.*, Glover-Waller edition, vol. I, pp. ix-lvi.

67. *Ibid.*, p. x.

68. *Ibid.*, p. xi.

69. In 1641, while still flourishing, The King's Men had secured a warrant from the Lord Chamberlain restraining printers from publishing, without their consent, any of the 60 plays on an attached list, 27 of them from the workshop of Fletcher and Co. But now they must have been delighted to come to terms

with Moseley. Supporters of the King, they may have had the thought, more-over, that the appearance of this book might prove a comfort and encourage-ment to royalists. Cf. R. C. Bald, *op. cit.*, pp. 5-6.

70. *Works of B. and F.*, Glover-Waller edition, vol. I, p. xxv.

71. *Ibid.*, pp. xxviii-xxix.

72. *Ibid.*, p. xvii. In *The Works of Henry Vaughan*, 2 vols., edited by Leonard Cyril Martin, London, 1914, "Upon Mr. Fletchers Playes, published, 1647," vol. I, p. 55, Vaughan, too, questions whether the Presbyterian parliament will like the publication of the Folio:

> Will not the Eares assemble, and think't fit
> Their Synod fast, and pray, against thy wit? . . .
> Yet shall these Conquests of thy Bayes outlive
> Their Scotish zeale, and Compacts made to grieve
> The Peace of Spirits, and when such deeds fayle
> Of their foule ends, a faire name is thy Bayle.

73. *Works of B. and F.*, Glover-Waller edition, vol. I, p. xvii.

74. *Ibid.*, p. xxvii.

75. *Ibid.*, p. xxiv.

76. *Ibid.*, p. lvi.

77. *Ibid.*, p. xxx.

78. *Ibid.*, p. lvi.

79. *Ibid.*, pp. xlv, xx, lii, xxiv, xxxvii, xxvii, xlviii.

80. *Ibid.*, pp. xviii, xvi, xlix.

81. *Ibid.*, p. xxiii.

82. *Ibid.*, p. xxxviii.

83. *Ibid.*, p. xxxviii.

84. *Ibid.*, p. xlii.

85. *Ibid.*, p. xli.

86. *Ibid.*, pp. xxxix-xl: To these appraisals might be added Henry Vaughan's, in *The Works of Henry Vaughan*, vol. I, p. 55, in which the Silurist places Jonson first among English dramatists, Fletcher next, and does not mention Shakespeare:

> This, or that age may write, but never see
> A Wit that dares run Paralell with thee.
> True, Ben must live! but bate him, and thou hast
> Undone all future wits, and match'd the past.

87. *Works of B. and F.*, Glover-Waller edition, vol. I, p. xlix.

88. *Ibid.*, p. xii.

89. *Ibid.*, p. xxv.

90. *Ibid.*, p. xxxi.

91. *Ibid.*, p. xxi.

92. *Ibid.*, p. xlv. Richard Brome, who knew Fletcher well, assures us (*Ibid.*, p. lv) that Fletcher's comic vein was natural and spontaneous:

> He did not pumpe nor dredge,
> To beget Wit, or manage it; . . .
> You that have known him, know
> The common talk that from his Lips did flow,
> And run at waste, did savour more of Wit,
> Than any of his time, or since have writ,

(But few excepted) in the Stages way:
His Scenes were Acts, and every Act a Play.

93. The issue of the morality of the "Beaumont and Fletcher" plays will recur at many points in this book.

94. *Works of B. and F.*, Glover-Waller edition, vol. I, p. xxi.

95. *Ibid.*, p. xv.

96. *Ibid.*, pp. xxv-xxvi.

97. *Ibid.*, p. xliii.

98. *Ibid.*, p. xxxiv.

99. *Ibid.*, p. xxxiii.

100. *Ibid.*, p. xxv.

101. Jeremy Collier: *A Short View of the Immorality and Profaneness of the English Stage*, London, 1698 (third edition), p. 51.

102. *Ibid.*, pp. 52-53.

103. *Ibid.*, p. 155.

104. John Dryden: "Preface to the Fables," in W. P. Ker, editor, *op. cit.*, vol. I, p. 273.

105. *Works of B. and F.*, Glover-Waller edition, vol. I, p. xli.

106. *Ibid.*, p. liii.

107. *Ibid.*, "To the Reader," p. xii.

108. *Ibid.*, p. xxxi.

109. In Chapter VII.

110. *Works of B. and F.*, Glover-Waller edition, vol. I, pp. xxxvii, xxxviii.

111. Cf. *Ibid.*, pp. xix, xlvii, lv, xliii, xlix, *passim*; many other phrases could be culled to similar effect.

112. *Ibid.*, pp. xliv-xlv.

113. *Ibid.*, p. xlix.

114. *Ibid.*, pp. xlvii-xlviii.

115. I have known college students of little literary background to pass with relief, in a survey course in English literature, from a study of several plays by Shakespeare to *The Maid's Tragedy*. They found the latter easier to read and understand, and did not at first perceive why Shakespeare is the greater dramatist.

116. *Works of B. and F.*, Glover-Waller edition, vol. I, p. xxxiv.

117. *Ibid.*, p. lxiii.

118. *Ibid.*, p. li.

119. *Ibid.*, p. xxvi.

120. *Ibid.*, pp. li-lii.

121. *Ibid.*, p. xxvi.

122. John H. Wilson: *The Influence of Beaumont and Fletcher on the Restoration Stage*, Columbus, Ohio, 1928, p. vii. The book treats this influence interestingly, but should be supplemented by Kathleen M. Lynch: *The Social Mode of Restoration Comedy*, "University of Michigan Studies in Language and Literature," III, New York and London, 1926, and Alfred Harbage: *Cavalier Drama*, New York and London, 1936.

123. *The Dramatic Records of Sir Henry Herbert*: pp. 82 and 116-18.

124. John H. Wilson: *op. cit.*, p. 12.

125. John Dryden: "An Essay of Dramatick Poesy," in *The Essays of John Dryden*, edited by W. P. Ker, vol. I, p. 81.

126. Helen McAfee: *Pepys on the Restoration Stage*, New Haven, 1916, pp. 81-101. Pepys' views that follow are based on Miss McAfee's selections from his diary.

127. *Ibid.*, p. 27.

128. Arthur Colby Sprague: *Beaumont and Fletcher on the Restoration Stage*, Cambridge, Mass., 1926, p. 123. This book is a full and authoritative treatment of its subject.

129. *Ibid.*, p. 125.

130. *Ibid.*, p. 53, and *passim*.

131. Cf. *Works of B. and F.*, vol. I, pp. lix-lxii.

132. *A Little Ark, Containing Sundry Pieces of Seventeenth-Century Verse*, edited by G. Thorn-Drury, London, 1921, p. 48.

133. Arthur Colby Sprague: *op. cit.*, p. 53. He discusses in detail each adaptation made of the plays of our authors in Restoration years.

134. *Ibid.*, pp. 102-103. Readers who may wish further to investigate Fletcher, Beaumont and Company on the Restoration stage are referred to this book.

135. Alfred Harbage: *Cavalier Drama*. Cf. especially chapters II and III. Fletcher's relationship to Cavalier Drama is ably discussed on pp. 41-44.

136. It seems appropriate that *The Faithful Shepherdess*, which did have a neo-platonic element, was revived by the King's Men for a performance at Court to please Queen Henrietta and her literary cult. Sir Henry Herbert gave the following account of it: "On Monday night, the sixth of January [1634] Twelfe Night, was presented at Denmark-house, before the King and Queene, Fletchers pastorall called *The Faithfull Shepheardesse,* in the clothes the Queene had given Taylor [of the King's Men's Company] the year before of her owne pastorall." Herbert adds that Inigo Jones "made" the scenery. Cf. *The Dramatic Records of Sir Henry Herbert*, edited by Joseph Quincy Adams, p. 53.

137. Richard Flecknoe: *A Discourse of the English Stage*, prefaced to his play, *Love's Kingdom* (1664), in W. C. Hazlitt: *The English Drama and Stage*, London, 1869, p. 277.

138. John Dryden: "Of Heroick Plays, an Essay," in *The Essays of John Dryden*, edited by W. P. Ker, vol. I, pp. 149-50.

139. Kathleen M. Lynch: *op. cit.*, pp. 19, 23, 24. Cf., more generally, chapters II and V.

140. Edward Denby Lewis: *John Fletcher: His Distinctive Structural and Stylistic Contribution to English Drama*, Yale University Dissertation, unpublished, New Haven, 1941.

141. William Congreve: *The Way of the World*, acted in 1700. Ned Bliss Allen: *The Sources of Dryden's Comedies*, "University of Michigan Studies in Language and Literature," XVI, Ann Arbor, 1935, p. 28, expresses the opinion that some of Fletcher's rakes and witty ladies, in their sophisticated attitude towards sex and marriage and in their love of wit, gave "noteworthy hints" to dramatists of the Restoration who wrote comedies of manners.

142. *The Dramatic Works of Mr. Nathaniel Lee*, 3 vols., London, 1734, vol. II, pp. 7-8.

143. *The Island Princess: As it was Acted at the Theatre Royal, Reviv'd with Alterations*, London, 1687. Quoted in Arthur Colby Sprague: *op. cit.*, p. 139. Sprague deals in detail with 20 adaptations on pp. 129-267.

144. Allardyce Nicoll: *Dryden as an Adapter of Shakespeare*, London, 1922, p. 8.

145. Arthur Colby Sprague: *op. cit.*, p. 126.

146. John H. Wilson: *op. cit.*, p. 17.

147. In Joel E. Spingarn, editor: *op. cit.*, vol. II, p. 292.

148. "On Mr. Abraham Cowley his Death and Burial amongst the Ancient Poets," in *The Poetical Works of Sir John Denham*, edited by Theodore Howard Banks, Jr., New Haven, 1928, p. 150.

149. Gerard Langbaine: *op. cit.*, p. 370.

150. *Ibid.*, p. 428.

151. Richard Flecknoe: *op. cit.*, p. 278.

152. Edward Phillips: *Theatrum Poetarum*, 1675, p. 108. Quoted in *The Jonson Allusion Book*, p. 379.

153. William Winstanley: *Lives of the Most Famous English Poets*, London, 1687, p. 128; T. P. Blount: *De Re Poetica*, London, 1694, p. 22.

154. Richard Flecknoe: *op. cit.*, p. 278.

155. Richard Flecknoe: *Epigrams*, 1670, p. 71. Quoted in *The Jonson Allusion Book*, p. 359.

156. *The Works of John Dryden*, 18 vols., edited by Sir Walter Scott and George Saintsbury, London, 1892, vol. XV, pp. 378-392.

157. Robert Gale Noyes: *Ben Jonson on the English Stage, 1660-1776*, Cambridge, Mass., 1935, p. 25.

158. William Arrowsmith: *The Reformation: a Comedy*, 1673, Act IV, scene 1, pp. 46-47. Quoted in *The Jonson Allusion Book*, p. 374.

159. Edward Howard: "Preface" to *The Women's Conquest*. London, 1671.

160. Thomas Rymer: *The Tragedies of the Last Age Consider'd*, p. 143.

161. *Ibid.*, p. 11.

162. *Ibid.*, pp. 6-7.

163. *Ibid.*, cf., pp. 110, 37-38, 17, 47, 8-9, 140-41, 24, and *passim*.

164. *Ibid.*, p. 19.

165. *Ibid.*, p. 25.

166. *Ibid.*, p. 36.

167. *Ibid.*, p. 37.

168. *Ibid.*, pp. 38-47.

169. *Ibid.*, pp. 52-53.

170. *Ibid.*, p. 57.

171. *Ibid.*, p. 59.

172. *Ibid.*, pp. 58-59.

173. *Ibid.*, pp. 61-62.

174. *Ibid.*, pp. 67-69.

175. *Ibid.*, p. 64.

176. *Ibid.*, pp. 106-07.

177. *Ibid.*, p. 3.

178. *The Poetical Works of Samuel Butler*, edited by Richard Brimley Johnson, "The Aldine Edition of the Poets," 2 vols. London, 1895, vol. II, p. 175.

179. W. P. Ker, editor: *op. cit.*, vol. I, "Introduction," p. xv. Dryden was, however, to a considerable, though not slavish, extent under the influence of the neo-classical theories of his age.

180. Theophilus Cibber: *The Lives of the Poets,* London, 1753, pp. 159-60.

181. *The Works of John Dryden,* Scott-Saintsbury edition, vol. XV, pp. 378-80. (Editors' introduction to the *Heads*). They were published again, in altered form, by Dr. Samuel Johnson, who had them from Garrick.

182. For instance, he remarked that ". . . it is not enough that Aristotle has said so, for Aristotle drew his models from Sophocles and Euripedes; and if he had seen ours, might have changed his mind." *Ibid.,* p. 390.

183. *Ibid., Heads,* p. 388.

184. *Ibid.,* pp. 382-83.

185. *Ibid.,* p. 388.

186. *Ibid.,* pp. 384-85.

187. Cf. *Ibid.,* pp. 386-87, for the foregoing points.

188. *Ibid.,* p. 387.

189. Thomas Rymer: *A Short View of English Tragedy,* London, 1693, "Preface." This treatise provoked an answer by Charles Gildon: *Some Reflections on Mr. Rymer's Short View of Tragedy,* London, 1694, in which Rymer is dubbed a "hypercritic," and the cudgels are taken up in behalf of Shakespeare. Gildon did not, however, greatly admire our authors. Like Rymer, he had a strong neo-classical bent.

190. Gerald Eades Bentley: *Shakespeare & Jonson: Their Reputations in the Seventeenth Century Compared,* vol. I, pp. 101-02, and *passim,* makes it clear that this opinion of Dryden was not the characteristic one of the Restoration era, when it was Jonson's reputation that was dominant. Bentley adds, however, that Dryden's consistent championing of Shakespeare's supremacy was doubtless the most important single factor in that dramatist's rise to primacy among English playwrights, in the judgment of critics, during the eighteenth century.

191. W. P. Ker, editor: *op. cit.,* "An Essay of Dramatick Poesy," p. 79.

192. "Prologue" to *The Tempest; or The Enchanted Island,* by Dryden and Davenant, 1667, in *The Works of John Dryden,* Scott-Saintsbury edition, vol. III, p. 109.

193. John Dryden: *MacFlecknoe: A Satire against Thomas Shadwell,* London, 1682, in *The Works of John Dryden,* Scott-Saintsbury edition, vol. X, p. 448.

194. W. P. Ker, editor; *op. cit.,* vol. I, pp. 56-89.

195. *Ibid.,* p. 57. This was a usual neo-classical dislike.

196. *Ibid.,* p. 65.

197. *Ibid.,* p. 60.

198. *Idem.*

199. *Ibid.,* p. 66.

200. *Ibid.,* pp. 57-58.

201. *Ibid.,* p. 68.

202. *Ibid.,* pp. 77-79.

203. *Ibid.,* p. 73.

204. *Ibid.,* p. 81.

205. *Ibid.,* p. 72.

206. *Ibid.,* p. 81.

207. *Ibid.,* pp. 53-54.

208. *Ibid.,* pp. 141-42. This is the remark which caused Jeremy Collier to assert that he could cite examples of just punishment in Fletcher's comedies.

209. *Ibid.,* pp. 139-40.

210. *The Best Plays of John Dryden*, 2 vols., edited by George Saintsbury, "The Mermaid Series," London and New York, n.d., vol. I, p. 211.

211. George Villiers, Duke of Buckingham: *The Rehearsal*, London, 1672, Act II, Scene 1.

212. *The Best Plays of John Dryden*, edited by Saintsbury, vol. I, p. 37.

213. Cf. *Essays of John Dryden*, edited by W. P. Ker, vol. I, p. 172: " . . . he knows not when to give over. If he wakes in one scene, he commonly slumbers in another; and if he pleases you in the first three acts, he is frequently so tired with his labour, that he goes heavily in the fourth, and sinks under his burden in the fifth." Dryden's own ideals of plotting, of course, were largely neo-classical, as his concern about "decorum" indicates.

214. *Ibid.*, vol. I, p. 166.

215. *Ibid.*, p. 165.

216. *Ibid.*, p. 166.

217. *Ibid.*, pp. 174-75.

218. *Ibid.*, p. 166.

219. *Ibid.*, pp. 176-77.

220. *The Collected Works of John Wilmot, Earl of Rochester*, edited by John Haywood, London, 1926, p. 57.

221. W. P. Ker, editor: *op. cit.*, p. 211.

222. *Ibid.*, pp. 217, 220.

223. *Ibid.*, p. 212.

224. *Ibid.*, pp. 227-28.

225. Thomas Brown: *The Reasons of Mr. Bays Changing His Religion. Considered in a Dialogue between Crites, Eugenius, and Mr. Bays*, 1688. Quoted in *The Jonson Allusion Book*, p. 417.

226. Gerald Langbaine: *op. cit.*, pp. 133, 150. Langbaine also informs us, of Fletcher, that "no man ever understood or drew the Passions more lively than he and his brisk Raillery was so drest, that it rather pleased than disgusted the modest Part of his Audience." Cf. p. 203.

227. Charles Gildon: *Lives and Characters of the English Dramatick Poets*, London, 1699, p. 57.

228. Gerard Langbaine: *op. cit.*, p. 484.

229. James Drake: *The Antient and Modern Stages survey'd*, London, 1699, p. 201.

NOTES TO CHAPTER TWO

1. A fuller, though still brief, survey of the stage career of the Fletcher, Beaumont and Company plays will be found in the Appendix.

2. Robert Hamilton Ball: *The Amazing Career of Sir Giles Overreach*, Princeton, N. J., 1939, pp. 40-43, and ff., *passim*.

3. *The Critical Works of John Dennis*, 2 vols., edited by Edward Niles Hooker, Baltimore, 1939 and 1943, vol. II, "Introduction," p. cxxx.

4. *Ibid.*, pp. cxxxi and 409.

5. W. B. C. Watkins: *Johnson and English Poetry Before 1660*, pp. 4-5, 11, 65.

6. M. C. Bradbrook: *Elizabethan Stage Conditions,* Cambridge, England, 1932, p. 9.

7. August Ralli: *A History of Shakespearean Criticism,* 2 vols., Oxford, 1932, vol. I, p. 34, remarks that it was in this century that the foundations for the appreciation of Shakespeare were laid: "He is thought to be either unique, or at least equal to the ancients, as dramatist, poet, philosopher, portrayer of character." While some critics deplored his want of art, more discerning ones praised both his art and his imagination.

8. Clarence C. Green: *The Neo-Classic Theory of Tragedy in England During the Eighteenth Century,* Cambridge, Mass., 1934, p. 79.

9. W. B. C. Watkins: *op. cit.,* p. 64.

10. George Farquhar: "A Discourse Upon Comedy, in Reference to the English Stage," in *Critical Essays of the Eighteenth Century, 1700-1725,* edited by Willard Higley Durham, New Haven, 1915, p. 277.

11. George Henry Nettleton: *English Drama of The Restoration and Eighteenth Century,* New York, 1932, p. 137.

12. Charles Gildon: *The Life of Thomas Betterton,* London, 1710, pp. 171-72.

13. *Ibid.,* p. 173. Gildon, however, thought better of Shakespeare than he did of our playwrights, except in comedy.

14. In *The Spectator: No. 361* for Thursday, April 24, 1712, Addison did, however, use cat-calling at a performance of *The Humourous Lieutenant* as the basis for a whimsical dissertation on the cat-call. Apparently the audience did not like the play; it drowned this revival out with cat calls. Cf. *The Spectator,* 8 vols. in 4, Everyman's Library edition, London and New York, n.d., vol. V (3), p. 160.

15. Joseph Addison: *The Spectator: No. 40,* Monday, April 16, 1711, Everyman's Library edition, vol. I, pp. 147-48.

16. *Ibid., No. 409,* Thursday, June 19, 1712, Everyman's Library edition, vol. VI, pp. 48 ff.

17. Richard Steele: *The Tatler: No. 191,* Thursday, June 29, 1710, in *The Tatler,* 6 vols., London, 1786, vol. V, pp. 173-74.

18. Richard Steele: *The Spectator: No. 266,* Friday, January 4, 1712, Everyman's Library edition, vol. IV, pp. 58-59.

19. *Ibid., No. 270,* Wednesday, January 9, 1712, Everyman's Library edition, vol. IV, pp. 72-75.

20. *Ibid., No. 141,* Saturday, August 11, 1711, Everyman's Library edition, vol. II, p. 215.

21. Charles Harold Gray: *Theatrical Criticism in London to 1795,* New York, 1931, p. 59.

22. Margaret E. Cobb: "Pope's Lines on Atticus," *Modern Language Notes,* XXXVI (1921), pp. 350-51.

23. Austin Warren, in "Pope's Index to Beaumont and Fletcher," *Modern Language Notes,* XLVI (1931), pp. 515-17, conjectures that, probably at the time Pope was working on his edition of Shakespeare, he also had some intention of editing Beaumont and Fletcher as well. Among the Pope manuscripts in the British Museum are three sheets of an incomplete index to the Second Folio of 1679.

24. *The Poetical Works of Mr. Samuel Daniel,* 2 vols., London, 1718, vol. I, p. xx.

25. Giles Jacob: *The Poetical Register,* London, 1723, pp. 103-04.

26. *The Dramatic Works of Aaron Hill, Esq.*, 2 vols., London, 1760, vol. I, p. xv.

27. Charles Harold Gray: *op. cit.*, p. 93.

28. In *The Poems of William Collins*, edited by Christopher Stone, London, 1907, p. 23.

29. Arthur P. I. Samuels: *The Early Life Correspondence and Writings of the Rt. Hon. Edmund Burke*, Cambridge, England, 1923, "The Reformer, 4th Feb. 1748," p. 167.

30. *Biographia Britannica*, 2 vols., London, 1747, 1766, vol. I, pp. 623-27. W. R. Chetwood: *The British Theatre*, London, 1752, though it states that "the true Drama received Birth and Perfection from the creative Genius of Shakespear, Fletcher, and Johnson," is much worse as a handbook. It devotes two and one half pages (28 to 31) to our authors, is inaccurate in its biographical facts, and contains, as its single critical remark, the hackneyed comparison between Beaumont's judgment and Fletcher's wit. Shakespeare receives only ten pages.

31. Richard Foster Jones: *Lewis Theobald*, New York, 1919, p. 211.

32. *Robert Dodsley's Select Collection of Old English Plays*, edited by W. C. Hazlitt. Dodsley had remarked in his preface that "the true drama is ascribed only to the miraculous creative genius of Shakespeare, Fletcher, and Jonson." Cf. Chetwood's similar statement, above.

33. Richard Foster Jones: *op. cit.*, p. 175.

34. Cf. *Ibid.*, p. 224.

35. According to Richard Foster Jones: *op. cit.*, p. 214, these were: *The Maid's Tragedy, Philaster, A King and No King, The Scornful Lady, The Custom of the Country, The Elder Brother*, and the almost completed *The Spanish Curate* and *The Humourous Lieutenant.*

36. Orie Latham Hatcher: *John Fletcher*, p. 15, referring to Seward, comments that "the mutilations to which he and his colleague subjected the texts of the plays have earned for them ever since the anathemas of critics."

37. Richard Foster Jones: *op. cit.*, pp. 212-215, gives an excellent account of Theobald's labors, his collaboration with Seward and Sympson, and the virtues of Theobald's portion of the work. Cf. also pp. 244-45.

38. *The Dramatic Works of B. J., and B. and F.*, Whalley-Colman edition, vol. II, p. xx.

39. *Ibid.*, vol. II, p. xxi.

40. *Ibid.*, vol. II, p. xxii. Cf. Peter Whalley: *Ibid.*, vol. I, p. xi (1756): "Shakespeare, and Beaumont and Fletcher are the only contemporary writers that can be put in competition with [Jonson]; and as they have excellencies of genius superior to those of Jonson, they have weaknesses and defects that are proportionately greater. If they transcend him in the creative powers, and the astonishing flights of imagination, their judgment is much inferior to his; and if he doth not at any time rise so high, neither perhaps doth he sink so low as they have' done." Eight years earlier, in *An Inquiry into the Learning of Shakespeare*, Whalley had said that our playwrights had been supreme in a morally decadent time, but now Shakespeare held the primacy. Cf. Augustus Ralli: *op. cit.*, vol. I, p. 25.

41. *Ibid.*, vol. II, pp. xxii-xxiii.

42. *Ibid.*, vol. II, p. xxiv.

43. *Ibid.*, vol. II, pp. xxv-xxxiii.

44. *Ibid.*, vol. II, pp. xxxiii-xxxiv. Incidentally, he appears to have recognized the influence of Shakespeare's quarrel scene upon the Beaumont and Fletcher one.

45. *Ibid.*, vol. II, p. xliii. Three years later, Theophilus Cibber: *Lives of The Poets*, p. 158, footnote, was more downright, saying of our playwrights: "There is a coarseness of dialogue, even in their genteelest characters, in comedy, that appears now almost unpardonable . . . nor is the great Shakespeare entirely to be acquitted thereof." But he adds the bromide that their age was a "sufficient apology for their defects."

46. *Ibid.*, vol. II, pp. xliii-xliv.

47. *The Correspondence of Richard Hurd and William Mason*, edited by the Rev. Ernest Harold Pearce, Cambridge, England, 1932, p. 10. Evidently Hurd did not appreciate Garrick's natural or "character" acting, nor his insistence on ensemble playing. It is curious to find Hurd attacking Garrick for being what he was not. Perhaps Garrick's reforms in acting were too much for Hurd; possibly he was merely consoling his friend. It does seem from these criticisms, however, that he preferred the old-school ranting and declaiming.

48. *Hurd's Letters on Chivalry and Romance, with the Third Elizabethan Dialogue*, edited by Edith J. Morley, London, 1911, p. 70.

49. Hugh Blair: *Lectures on Rhetoric and Belles Lettres*, eighth American edition, New York, 1819, Lecture XLVII, p. 453.

50. Edward Young: *Conjectures on Original Composition*, 1759, edited by Edith J. Morley, in "Modern Language Texts, English Series," London, 1918.

51. The Plays of William Shakespeare, 15 vols., edited by Samuel Johnson and George Steevens, fourth edition, London, 1793, "Mr. Capell's Introduction," Vol. I, p. 268.

52. Quoted by Charles Harold Gray: *op. cit.*, p. 279.

53. Cf. Appendix, pp. 246-247, for Colman's other activities in behalf of Beaumont and Fletcher.

54. *The Dramatic Works of B. J., and B. and F.*, Whalley-Colman edition, vol. II, p. xcvi.

55. Eugene R. Page: *George Colman the Elder*, New York, 1935, pp. 252-53.

56. *The Dramatic Works of B. J., and B. and F.*, Whalley-Colman edition, vol. II, pp. xcv-xcvi.

57. *Ibid.*, vol. II, p. xcvii.

58. *Ibid.*, vol. II, p. cii.

59. Thomas Davies: *Dramatic Miscellanies*, 2 vols., London, 1784, p. 391.

60. *Ibid.*, p. 392.

61. *Ibid.*, p. 394.

62. *Ibid.*, pp. 392-93.

63. *Ibid.*, pp. 398-99.

64. John Ferriar, M. D.: "Essay on the Dramatic Writings of Massinger" (1786), printed in *The Plays of Philip Massinger*, 4 vols., edited by William Gifford, second edition, London, 1813, vol. I, p. cxliv.

65. *Ibid.*, pp. cxli, cxliii.

66. Philip Neve: *Cursory Remarks on Some of the Ancient English Poets*, London, 1789, pp. 31-38.

67. Edmond Malone: *The Plays and Poems of William Shakespeare*, 21 vols., London, 1821 edition, vol. I, pp. 248-50.

68. J. Monck Mason: *Comments on the Plays of Beaumont and Fletcher*, London, 1798, pp. iv-v. In 1779, Mason had been concerned that Dr. Johnson's dictionary did not quote Beaumont and Fletcher or Massinger. He considered that "they are more correct and grammatical than Shakespeare, and appear to have had a more competent knowledge of other languages, which gave them a more accurate idea of their own." Cf. *The Dramatic Works of J. Monck Mason*, London, 1779, "Preface."

69. Cf. Appendix, p. 248.

70. Allardyce Nicoll: *A History of Early Nineteenth Century Drama*, 2 vols., New York, 1930, vol. I, p. 61.

71. Samuel Taylor Coleridge: *Lectures and Notes on Shakespeare and Other English Poets*, collected by T. Ashe, Bohn's Standard Library, London, 1904, p. 179.

72. Charles Dibdin: *A Complete History of the Stage*, London, 1800, p. 204-05.

73. *Ibid.*, pp. 227-29.

74. *Ibid.*, pp. 208-219.

75. Cf. especially Felix E. Schelling: *Foreign Influences in Elizabethan Plays*, New York and London, 1923, pp. 117-121. It is most probable that any resemblances are due to two facts: that both the Spaniard and the Englishmen were writing sheer entertainment under similar conditions in the same age, and that Fletcher levied on Spanish fiction (not drama) for many of his plots. The *novellas*, however, were always accessible in French or English translations in the 17 instances that have been discovered.

76. Charles Dibdin: *op. cit.*, pp. 206, 229.

77. *Ibid.*, p. 229.

78. *Ibid.*, p. 231.

79. *The Plays of Philip Massinger*, Gifford edition, vol. I, pp. xlv and xcix.

80. *Ibid.*, vol. I, p. lxxix.

81. Roy Benjamin Clark: *William Gifford, Tory Satirist, Critic, and Editor*, New York, 1930, p. 131.

82. *The Works of Charles and Mary Lamb*, 7 vols., edited by E. V. Lucas, London, 1904, vol. IV: *Dramatic Specimens and the Garrick Plays*, "Introduction," p. v. All of Lamb's cullings are reproduced in this volume.

83. *Idem.*

84. *Idem.* The importance of Lamb's services can be graphically realized from a hasty examination of *Biographia Dramatica*, edited by David E. Baker (1764), Isaac Reed (1782), and Stephen Jones (1812), London, 1812. This new edition by Jones brought down upon its accounts of the English playwrights the following well-merited censure by a reviewer in *The Quarterly Review*, VII (June, 1812), p. 282: "a meagre account of their births and burials, with catalogues of their plays compiled from the most obvious and unauthenticated sources. Theatres not laying claim to an earlier origin than our own, are far more fortunate in the respect paid to their native playwrights, . . ." The account of Beaumont and Fletcher (vol. I, pp. 23-25) is inaccurate, and the slight amount of critical comment is jejune and conventional.

85. *Ibid.*, p. xi.

86. *Ibid.*, pp. xi-xii.

87. *Ibid.*, p. xii.

88. *Ibid.*, p. 285. The purchase of his folio copy of Beaumont and Fletcher,

now in the British Museum, was nonetheless an exciting event to Lamb when, one Saturday evening about the year 1800, he mustered up the determination to acquire it. His own account of the transaction will be familiar to readers of "Old China." [Cf. *The Essays of Elia,* edited by Alfred Ainger, London and New York, 1903, p. 329.]

89. *Ibid.,* p. 332.

90. *Ibid.,* p. 329. *Cymbeline,* at least, might be urged against Lamb here.

91. *Idem.*

92. *Ibid.,* p. 341.

93. *Ibid.,* p. 329. Lamb, who liked the wooing scene ("sweet, natural and unforced") in Act V, scene 4, of *Love's Pilgrimage,* thought that Massinger may have profited from studying it. (Cf. p. 319). Since this scene sounds to my ear like Fletcher's manner, revised and regularized in meter by Massinger—or perhaps Shirley—and since it would be congenial in spirit to Massinger, I consider Lamb's observation a sensitive one.

94. *Ibid.,* p. 312. Lamb also remarked (p. 293) on how extremely popular the character, Bellario, in *Philaster* must have been in her day. He was wrong, however, in thinking her the first of her type on the stage. The novelty with Bellario lay in concealing her feminine sex from the audience (as well as the characters) until the final scene of the play.

95. Samuel Taylor Coleridge: *Lectures and Notes on Shakespeare and other English Poets,* p. 425 ("Lectures and Notes of 1818").

96. *Ibid.,* p. 419.

97. *Coleridge's Shakespeare Criticism,* 2 vols., edited by Thomas Middleton Raysor, London, 1930, vol. I, p. 60 (Note on *Lear*).

98. Daniel Morley McKeithan: *The Debt to Shakespeare in the Beaumont-and-Fletcher Plays,* Austin, Texas, 1938, pp. 216, 223, and *passim.*

99. *Lectures and Notes on Shakspere,* p. 419.

100. Cf. *Coleridge's Shakespearean Criticism,* vol. I, pp. 219-24.

101. *Lectures and Notes on Shakspere,* p. 449.

102. Cf. *Coleridge's Shakespearean Criticism,* vol. I, p. 224.

103. *Lectures and Notes on Shakspere,* pp. 399-400.

104. *Coleridge's Shakespearean Criticism,* vol. II, p. 357.

105. *Lectures and Notes on Shakspere,* p. 400.

106. *Coleridge's Shakespearean Criticism,* vol. I, p. 59, and vol. II, p. 34. The example given, of *The Mad Lover's* literal treatment of his lady's desire to possess his heart, is basically no more improbable than the pound-of-flesh bond of *The Merchant of Venice,* though the treatment may be less plausible.

107. *Ibid.,* vol. I, p. 241. Having observed a great many student playwrights wrestling with ideas, and developing plays—good, bad, and indifferent—out of them, I am convinced that this objection is of no force. A surprisingly large number of plots can be given farcical or serious, comic or tragic, treatment, depending upon their manipulation. The question here is really one of congruity of treatment.

108. *Ibid.,* vol. I, p. 60. This, again, is a poet's rather than a dramatist's statement—though true enough in its way. Did Coleridge clearly realize that the action of a play, and the actors' interpretive stage business and delivery of their lines, make the phrase "a series of dramatic dialogues" inadequate?

109. *Lectures and Notes on Shakspere,* p. 40. This is pretty severe, even

granted that the characters are frequently stage-pieces, and puppets of their plots.

110. *Ibid.,* pp. 428-29.

111. *Ibid.,* p. 443.

112. *Ibid.,* p. 442.

113. *Coleridge's Shakespearean Criticism,* vol. I, p. 133.

114. *Ibid.,* vol. II, p. 34.

115. *Ibid.,* vol. II, p. 266.

116. *Ibid.,* vol. II, pp. 34-35. Dante, with greater moral health, placed sensualists just below Limbo, in the second circle of the Inferno.

117. *Lectures and Notes on Shakspere,* pp. 441-42.

118. *Coleridge's Shakespearean Criticism,* vol. II, p. 355.

119. *Ibid.,* vol. II, p. 268. It came hard with Coleridge to be obliged to admit that Shakespeare could ever be gross.

120. *Lectures and Notes on Shakspere,* p. 442.

121. *Ibid.,* pp. 429, 437, 405; *Coleridge's Shakespearean Criticism,* vol. I, pp. 136, 147, 151.

122. *Coleridge's Shakespearean Criticism,* vol. I, pp. 136, 151; *Lectures and Notes on Shakspere,* pp. 437, 405.

123. *Lectures and Notes on Shakspere,* pp. 437, 429; *Coleridge's Shakespearean Criticism,* vol. I, p. 136.

124. In Chapter V, section II.

125. *Lectures and Notes on Shakspere,* pp. 402, 428, 540.

126. *Ibid.,* p. 446. Modern critics are still echoing Coleridge's imagery. T. S. Eliot almost parodies it in his witty remark that "The blossoms of Beaumont and Fletcher's imagination draw no sustenance from the soil, but are cut and slightly withered flowers stuck into sand." Cf. T. S. Eliot: *Selected Essays,* 1917-1932, New York, 1932, p. 135.

127. *Lectures and Notes on Shakspere,* p. 432. Coleridge also considered Massinger (p. 401) "more perfect . . . in story and affecting incidents" than Fletcher and Beaumont. While Massinger did have more concern with conventional methods of plotting a play, the second point is dubious, to say the least.

128. *Ibid.,* p. 402.

129. *Coleridge's Shakespearean Criticism,* vol. II, p. 34.

130. *Lectures and Notes on Shakspere,* pp. 532, 445, 533.

131. *Coleridge's Shakespearean Criticism,* vol. II, p. 357.

132. *The Complete Works of William Hazlitt,* 21 vols., "Centenary Edition," edited by P. P. Howe, London and Toronto, 1931, vol. VI, "Lectures on the Age of Elizabeth," pp. 176 and 170. This is both the definitive edition of his work, and a splendid example of book-making. In Hazlitt's previous course at the Surrey Institution, *Lectures on the English Comic Writers* (1819), he had already devoted a lecture to Shakespeare and Jonson, with an appreciative paragraph at the end—later to be quoted from—on some of Fletcher's comedies.

133. *Ibid.,* vol. VI, "Lectures on the Age of Elizabeth," p. 248.

134. *Ibid.,* vol. VI, p. 249. Again that emphasis on poetry!

135. *Ibid.,* vol. VI, p. 248.

136. *Ibid.,* vol. VI, pp. 248-49.

137. *Ibid.,* vol. VI, p. 249.

138. *Ibid.,* vol. VI, p. 250.

139. *Ibid.*, vol. VI, p. 251.

140. *Ibid.*, vol. VI, p. 252.

141. *Ibid.*, vol. VI, p. 254.

142. *Ibid.*, vol. VI, pp. 254-56.

143. *Ibid.*, vol. VI, p. 262.

144. *Ibid.*, vol. VI, p. 261.

145. *Ibid.*, vol. V, "A Short View of the English Stage," p. 353.

146. *Ibid.*, vol. V, p. 234. Hazlitt had also liked Kean less well than Kemble in the rôle of Leon.

147. *Ibid.*, vol. VI, "Lectures on the Age of Elizabeth," p. 249.

148. *Ibid.*, vol. VI, "Lectures on the English Comic Writers," pp. 48-49.

149. *Ibid.*, vol. VI, "Lectures on the Age of Elizabeth," pp. 261-62.

150. Sir Walter Scott: *An Essay on the Drama*, in *The Prose Works of Sir Walter Scott*, 28 vols., Edinburgh, 1861, vol. VI, pp. 343-44. Since the article attempted a survey of all western drama from Greek to contemporary times, Scott apologetically gave brief treatment to the quadrumvirate, but suggested a wider acquaintance than Coleridge's with the Elizabethan-Stuart drama by mentioning Shirley, Ford, Webster and Dekker.

151. Leigh Hunt: *A Jar of Honey*, London, 1897, pp. 148-49. Curiously enough, Hunt thought these objections the reasons for the play's failure, when first produced about 1608. Such a misconception of the London audience of that day rather vitiates his attacks on our playwrights as panders to it.

152. Leigh Hunt: *Beaumont and Fletcher . . .* , second edition, London, 1862. The quotation is from p. xv of the preliminary "Remarks."

153. *Ibid.*, p. xxi. One copy of the second edition appropriately found lodging, in mid-Victorian times, in a New England female seminary.

154. *The Correspondence of Leigh Hunt*, 2 vols., edited by his own son [Thornton Hunt], London, 1862, vol. I, pp. 282-83.

155. Leigh Hunt: *Imagination and Fancy*, fourth edition, London, 1871, pp. 184-86.

156. Leigh Hunt: *Beaumont and Fletcher*, "Remarks," pp. vii-viii.

157. *Ibid.*, p. xviii.

158. *Ibid.*, p. xiii.

NOTES TO CHAPTER THREE

1. *The Dramatic Works of Ben Jonson, and Beaumont and Fletcher*, edited by Peter Whalley and George Colman respectively. The three Beaumont and Fletcher volumes (II-IV) could also be purchased separately.

2. *The Works of Beaumont and Fletcher*, 14 vols., edited by Henry Weber, Edinburgh and London, 1812. Hereafter referred to as *"Works of B. and F.,* Weber edition." This is, in format, still a pleasant edition to use, in spite of its somewhat unsatisfactory text.

3. Cf. Chapter II, p. 58.

4. *Works of B. and F.*, Weber edition, vol. I, *Introduction*, pp. lxvii-lxvii. On the following page (lxix) Weber quoted from vol. III, p. ii, of *The British Drama* (London, 1811) the following remarks, which demonstrate why he

thought some measure of defense of our playwrights' plotting to be necessary: "Fletcher, with the extremity of negligence, run his actors into a chaos of incident and bustle, without much attention to propriety, probability, or, indeed, anything more than throwing a comic light on each isolated scene. The whole was winded up with some extraordinary accident, some sudden change of mind and temper in a leading personage, or such other similar inartificial expedient, as no audience could admit to be fitting and natural, . . ."

5. *Ibid.*, pp. lxviii-lxix.

6. *Ibid.*, p. lxx.

7. *Ibid.*, p. i.

8. *Ibid.*, pp. xcv, xxxiii.

9. *Ibid.*, p. lxxiv.

10. *Ibid.*, p. xxxiii. Weber, of course, had no assured body of Beaumont's work on which to base these comparisons; but some of the plays which Fletcher wrote alone, and a few of those in which Beaumont had a hand, were already correctly attributed on the basis of evidence accrued.

11. *Ibid.*, p. lx.

12. *Ibid.*, pp. lxxv-lxxvii.

13. *Ibid.*, p. lxxviii.

14. *Ibid.*, pp. lxxviii-lxxix. Virolet of *The Double Marriage* came closer to resembling Hamlet, to his own disadvantage, than did Philaster, "a perfect original."

15. *Ibid.*, p. lxxx.

16. *Ibid.*, p. lxxxi.

17. *Ibid.*, pp. lxxxi-lxxxii. Weber's attitude towards our playwrights' "bad" and "good" women appears to have sprung from an idealizing tendency distinctly romantic in hue. Does it, perhaps, afford a clue as to why Jacobean and Caroline audiences responded warmly and even sentimentally to the virtuous women in love of our playwrights?

18. He questioned, however, the wisdom of applying the caricaturing "humour" technique to comparatively serious purposes, as with Arbaces, Memnon and Shamont—thereby "exceeding the bounds of nature" in characterizations of a soberer cast.

19. *Works of B. and F.*, Weber edition, pp. lxxxiv-lxxxv.

20. *Ibid.*, pp. xc-xci.

21. *Ibid.*, pp. lxxxv-lxxxvii.

22. *Ibid.*, p. lxxiii.

23. *Ibid.*, pp. xl-xli.

24. *Ibid.*, pp. xii-lvii. For particular praise he chose *The Maid's Tragedy;* three tragicomedies: *The Faithful Shepherdess, Philaster* and *Women Pleased;* and seven comedies: *The Chances, The Knight of the Burning Pestle, The Little French Lawyer, Rule a Wife, The Spanish Curate, The Wild-Goose Chase* and *Wit Without Money.* I should myself place all of these among the better plays of our corpus. Weber did not comment on some dramas at all, and considered others much "abated" by their defects.

25. *The Works of Beaumont and Fletcher*, 2 vols., with an introduction by George Darley, London, "new edition," 1883. Hereafter referred to as "*Works of B. and F.*, Darley edition." The first edition: London, 1839.

26. *Ibid.*, vol. I, p. lxiii.

27. Shakespeare was "far too high-souled for a gallant age but not at all a romantic,"—an age when "exalted imagination and profound enthusiasms were confined to the Puritans." *Ibid.*, p. xxiv.

28. *Ibid.*, pp. xxiii-xxiv.

29. *Ibid.*, pp. xxiv-xxv. Darley added that "Shakspeare knew what the stage required, Fletcher what the spectator"—a distinction which, however partially valid, Darley sought to drive home with a malignancy that rather reminds one of Rymer. Had Darley been reading Hazlitt, who also made this point, but less sourly?

30. *Ibid.*, p. xxvii. From remarks such as these and others, one wonders if Leigh Hunt read the Darley edition in preparing his book of selections. There is more than a little resemblance in some of their attitudes.

31. *Ibid.*, p. xxiv.

32. *Ibid.*, p. xl. For once Darley liked the characterization. In *The Knight of the Burning Pestle* "the characters are depicted forcibly and naturally, and consistently from first to last: none by Shakspeare are better sustained than those of the Citizen, and his Wife." This is high praise, coming as it does from a Shakespeare enthusiast.

33. *Ibid.*, p. xxi. *A King and No King* was another product of "their brightest phase." In these three plays and *The Knight of the Burning Pestle* Darley recognized Beaumont's hand as dominant, therefrom drawing the conclusion that he was a much abler dramatist than Fletcher. As for non-Beaumont serious plays: *Thierry and Theodoret* and *Valentinian* at least "much surpass their most select comic pieces."

34. *Ibid.*, pp. xxiv-xxv.

35. *Ibid.*, p. xxv.

36. *Ibid.*, p. xxvi. Darley, though a poet, does not display Hallam's degree of understanding of playcraft. He sounds more like Scott. He may, of course, be giving us his own feebler version of Coleridge's utterances about our playwrights' mechanical and unorganic structure.

37. *Ibid.*, pp. xxviii-xxix.

38. *Ibid.*, p. xxv.

39. Why caprices and fashions are not genuine to human nature is a puzzling conjecture.

40. *Works of B. and F.*, Darley edition, p. xxvi. This idea has a curiously neoclassical ring.

41. *Ibid.*, p. xliii. Victorian sentimentality about women is reflected in this remark, rather than "truth to nature."

42. *Ibid.*, p. xxix.

43. *Ibid.*, p. xxx. Darley was also horrified that the "sweetest domestic rite" of kissing should be so widespread in the plays—even though this was simply a social custom of the time.

44. *Ibid.*, pp. xxxv, xxxii.

45. *Ibid.*, pp. xxxix, xxxv.

46. *Ibid.*, p. xxxviii. Moreover, Fletcher volubly talked a deal of "skimble-skamble" stuff, and threw his words at thoughts in the hope of hitting them!

47. *Ibid.*, pp. xxxi.

48. *Ibid.*, p. xlii. This was not, however, a Beaumont and Fletcher play. Its

authorship is much in dispute; even Fletcher's presence has been doubted, though he is usually thought to have had a hand in the piece. Middleton and Rowley, whether as collaborators or revisers, are the other playwrights most often suspected of a connection with this inferior drama.

49. Cf. pp. 88-89 for discussion of Henry Hallam.

50. *The Works of Beaumont and Fletcher,* 2 vols., edited by Rev. Alexander Dyce, Boston and New York, 1854. Hereafter referred to as *"Works of B. and F.,* Dyce edition." The first edition, in eleven volumes, was published in London, 1843-46.

51. *Ibid.,* vol. I, pp. 1-46.

52. Quoted by Dyce from John Donne: *Poems,* London, 1633, p. 77: "To Sir H. Wotton."

53. *Works of B. and F.,* Dyce edition, vol. I, pp. 23-24.

54. *Ibid.,* vol. I, p. 24. Dyce quaintly added that even Addison, read aloud, might sometimes cause the family circle to blush.

55. *Ibid.,* vol. I, pp. 15-16, 32.

56. *Ibid.,* vol. I, pp. 30, 29, 14, 32-33, 40, 18.

57. *Ibid.,* vol. I, pp. 17-18, 14.

58. The reader will recall Lamb, and Hazlitt, as respectively the first to make the last two points.

59. *Works of B. and F.,* Dyce edition, vol. I, pp. 16-17.

60. *Ibid.,* vol. I, pp. 22, 33, 30, 31-32, 33, 34, 31.

61. *Ibid.,* vol. I, pp. 34, 40, 35-36, 37, 17.

62. *Ibid.,* vol. I, pp. 23, 22-23, 34, 36, 34, 41-42.

63. *Ibid.,* vol. I, pp. 20, 35, 14, 19.

64. *The Works of Francis Beaumont and John Fletcher, Variorum Edition,* 4 vols. completed, edited by A. H. Bullen, London, 1904-12, has useful factual introductions, (though they are now sometimes a little out of date) for each of the 20 plays included. *The Works of B. and F.,* Glover-Waller edition (1905-12), reprints the introductory materials of the First and Second Folios, with the text of the latter, collated with quartos and the First Folio.

65. Nathan Drake: *Shakespeare and His Times,* Paris, 1838. The 1819 edition was published in London. That Drake was well acquainted with Lamb's *Specimens* is evident from his quotations from that book.

66. S. A. Dunham: *Lives of the Most Eminent Literary and Scientific Men of Great Britain,* 3 vols., published as part of the *Cabinet Cyclopedia,* edited by Rev. Dionysius Lardner, London, 1837.

67. Nathan Drake: *op. cit.,* pp. 605-615.

68. Of the Pre-Shakespeareans, the bohemian Greene was allowed 27 pages, but Marlowe a modest ten. Kyd, Peele, Lyly and Nashe were also present.

69. Cf. Nathan Drake: *op. cit.,* p. 604. The Beaumont-Fletcher plays he named were: *Philaster, The Maid's Tragedy, A King and No King, The Knight of the Burning Pestle, The Scornful Lady, The Coxcomb, Cupid's Revenge* (Field rather than Beaumont?), *The Captain* (Beaumont very doubtful), *The Honest Man's Fortune* (Fletcher, Massinger, Field) and *The False One* (Fletcher, Massinger).

70. *Ibid.,* pp. 603-05.

71. S. A. Dunham: *op. cit.,* vol. II, pp. 207-50.

72. Henry Hallam: *Introduction to the Literature of Europe in the Fifteenth, Sixteenth, and Seventeenth Centuries,* 2 vols., New York, 1841. The first edition was published in London, 1837.

73. *Ibid.,* vol. II, chapter 6, pp. 210 (par. 73) and 213 (par. 84).

74. *Ibid.,* pp. 210 (par. 73) and 213 (par. 86).

75. *Ibid.,* p. 212 (par. 82).

76. *Ibid.,* p. 213 (par. 85). Like many others, before the matter was investigated by source-hunters, Hallam believed that the Spanish stage probably furnished subjects, and "perhaps many of the scenes," for Fletcher's comedies. He suggested the investigation of Lopez da Vega and other Spanish playwrights.

77. *Ibid.,* pp. 210 (par. 73) and 213 (pars. 84, 86).

78. *Ibid.,* pp. 213-14 (par. 87).

79. *Ibid.,* p. 212 (par. 82).

80. Hallam conjectured (p. 210, par. 74) that the moral intended by Fletcher, in his *Valentinian,* was "that the worst of tyrants was to be obeyed with unflinching submission."

81. *Ibid.,* p. 207 (par. 63).

82. *Ibid.,* p. 207 (par. 64).

83. *Ibid.,* p. 212 (par. 81).

84. *Ibid.,* p. 213 (par. 86).

85. *Ibid.,* pp. 212-13 (par. 83). Hallam also adjudged Fletcher's thoughts "noble, and tinged with the ideality of romance; his metaphors vivid, though sometimes forced; his versification . . . often rhythmical and sweet."

86. *Ibid.,* p. 214 (par. 87).

87. William Bodham Donne: *Essays on the Drama,* London, 1858, "Beaumont and Fletcher," pp. 34-36. The essay was reprinted from *Fraser's Magazine* for March, 1850.

88. *Ibid.,* pp. 50-51.

89. *Ibid.,* p. 66.

90. *Ibid.,* pp. 58-60.

91. *Ibid.,* pp. 55-56. The implications in the association of Beaumont and Fletcher with Montaigne and Voltaire in temper are interesting, if a bit puzzling. Probably Donne was not responsive to the intellectual scepticism of the French writers (as well as of Lucian). I am not inclined to think that many readers find Montaigne, at least, derisive.

92. *Idem.*

93. As evidence Donne mentioned the records of State Trials, and the denunciations by such Anglican clergymen as his namesake, John Donne, and Lancelot Andrewes.

94. William Bodham Donne: *op. cit.,* pp. 38-39.

95. *Ibid.,* pp. 60-62.

96. Cf. *The Captain, The Humourous Lieutenant,* and *The Custom of the Country* respectively.

97. William Bodham Donne: *op. cit.,* pp. 63-64.

98. Cf. *The Loyal Subject, The Bloody Brother, A Wife for a Month* and *The Beggars' Bush* respectively.

99. William Bodham Donne: *op. cit.,* pp. 57-58.

100. *Ibid.,* pp. 64-65.

101. George Gilfillan: *A Third Gallery of Portraits,* London, 1855, p. 186.

102. Edwin P. Whipple: *Essays and Reviews,* 2 vols., fifth edition, Boston, 1871, vol. II, p. 59.

103. Should the reader desire to pursue this matter further, he might begin with the following passages, whose temperance in moral pronouncement is various: George L. Craik: *A Compendious History of English Literature and the English Language,* 6 vols., New York, 1845, vol. III, p. 199. William Minto: *Characteristics of English Poets from Chaucer to Shirley,* 2nd edition, Edinburgh and London, 1855, pp. 352-53. Edwin P. Whipple: *The Literature of the Age of Elizabeth,* Boston, 1869, pp. 161, 165-66, 176-77. Charles Cowden Clarke: "On the Comic Writers of England," published in *The Gentleman's Magazine,* n. s., VII (1871), p. 48. Edmund Gosse: *The Jacobean Poets,* New York, 1894, p. 83. Cf. also C. Bathurst: *Remarks on Shakespeare's Versification,* London, 1857, which contains on p. 184, in addition to moral reproof, the curious theory that Fletcher's taste and temper may have been spoiled by the failure of his *Faithful Shepherdess* and *The Knight of the Burning Pestle.*

104. Thomas Babington Macauley: *The Comedy of the Restoration,* first published in *The Edinburgh Review* for July, 1841; conveniently reprinted in *Readings in English Prose of the Ninteenth Century,* edited by R. M. Alden, Boston, 1917, Part I, p. 292.

105. Samuel Taylor Coleridge: *Lectures and Notes on Shakspere,* p. 399.

106. George L. Craik: *op. cit.,* vol. III, p. 197.

107. If Dyce had not accepted the Langbaine tradition that Fletcher wrote Beaumont's *Woman-Hater,* he might have been more successful in his attempts to assign plays involving these two. Cf. Orie Latham Hatcher: *John Fletcher,* Chapter I, pp. 17-18.

108. Miss Hatcher's chapter, on which the foregoing paragraph is, in part, based, gives a useful and connected account of the history of the problems in authorship from the seventeenth century to 1905.

109. William Minto: *op. cit.,* pp. 349-50.

110. If Field wrote one or both of these short plays (as I am inclined to suspect), at any rate Field's and Beaumont's metrical characteristics have so much in common that they were hard to discriminate. Both playwrights belonged to the older order of metrists.

111. F. G. Fleay: "On Metrical Tests as Applied to Dramatic Poetry: Part II. Fletcher, Beaumont, Massinger." In *The New Shakspere Society's Transactions,* Series I, 1 (1874), London, pp. 51-72, with report of discussion following, on pp. 73-84.

112. F. G. Fleay: "On the Chronology of the Plays of Fletcher and Massinger," *Englische Studien,* IX (1886), pp. 12-35.

113. Samuel C. Chew: *Swinburne,* Boston, 1929, p. 249.

114. Charles Mills Gayley: *op. cit.,* pp. 8, 4. Swinburne's essay, "Beaumont and Fletcher," was published in his *Studies in Prose and Poetry,* London, 1894, pp. 53-83.

115. Algernon Charles Swinburne: *op. cit.,* p. 76.

116. *Ibid.,* p. 61.

117. *Ibid.,* pp. 62-63.

118. *Ibid.,* pp. 64-66.

119. *Ibid.,* p. 66.

120. *Ibid.,* pp. 70-71.

121. *Ibid.,* p. 72.
122. *Ibid.,* pp. 78-79.
123. *Ibid.,* pp. 68-69.
124. *Ibid.,* p. 76.
125. *Ibid.,* p. 79.
126. *Ibid.,* p. 81
127. *Ibid.,* pp. 82-83.
128. Robert Boyle's articles appeared in *Englische Studien,* as follows: V (1882), pp. 74-96; VII (1884), pp. 66-86; VIII (1885), pp. 39-61; IX (1886), pp. 209-39; X (1887), pp. 383-411.
129. E. H. C. Oliphant's articles also were published in *Englishe Studien,* as follows: XIV (1890), pp. 53-94; XV (1891), pp. 321-60; XVI (1892), pp. 180-200.
130. G. C. Macaulay: *Francis Beaumont,* London, 1883, pp. 42-45.
131. *Ibid.,* pp. 46-47.
132. *Ibid.,* pp. 45-46.
133. *Ibid.,* p. 48.
134. *Ibid.,* pp. 51, 48.
135. *Ibid.,* p. 52.
136. E. H. C. Oliphant tells us, on page 205 of *The Plays of Beaumont and Fletcher,* that Macaulay later admitted that perhaps Act V, scenes 3 and 4, and other scattering passages, were by Fletcher.
137. G. C. Macaulay: *op. cit.,* pp. 72-73. Beaumont used prose for "ordinary comic dialogue," but verse for "purposes of burlesque," one of his most characteristic tendencies. *Ibid.,* p. 103.
138. *Ibid.,* pp. 102-03.
139. *Ibid.,* p. 105.
140. Since the bulk of the writing in this play fell to Beaumont, however, Macaulay's choice was, perhaps, safer than Fleay's, for the first two playlets of *Four Plays in One* are increasingly claimed for Field—rightly, I believe—though the matter has not been conclusively settled.
141. G. C. Macaulay: *op. cit.,* pp. 52-53. So did Elizabethan and Jacobean audiences. As a matter of fact, more "extreme physical agony" can be proportionally found in playwrights like Kyd, Webster and Tourneur, not to mention any others. Nor is it absent from *King Lear* and other plays of Shakespeare.
142. *Ibid.,* pp. 103, 113.
143. *Ibid.,* p. 124. These characters appear in *The Coxcomb* and in *Four Plays in One (The Triumph of Love)* respectively. Violante was probably Field's creation.
144. *Ibid.,* pp. 125-26.
145. *Ibid.,* p. 54.
146. *Ibid.,* pp. 53-54.
147. Beaumont's concern for the stage effectiveness of his puppets was completely overlooked by Macaulay.
148. G. C. Macaulay: *op. cit.,* p. 117.
149. *Ibid.,* pp. 186-87.
150. *Ibid.,* pp. 187-88.
151. *Ibid.,* pp. 135-36. Macaulay granted Fletcher a single superiority over Beaumont: "in colloquial ease and . . . readiness of repartee." But even this he qualified. Beaumont was naturally grave, but "for wit he had humour, and

contributed to the common stock many of the most amusing scenes." (Cf. pp. 103-04). Macaulay also held the opinion that Fletcher was the spiritual father of Restoration comedy (Cf. p. 54).

152. Macaulay is also the author of the chapter on "Beaumont and Fletcher" in *Cambridge History of English Literature*, 14 vols., edited by A. W. Ward . . . and A. R. Waller . . . , Cambridge, England, 1907-16, vol. VI, chapter V. This chapter might well be rewritten today.

153. Adolphus William Ward: *A History of English Dramatic Literature to the Death of Queen Anne*, 3 vols., new and revised edition, London, 1899. The first edition—London, 1875—had appeared in two volumes.

154. *Ibid.*, vol. II, chap. VII, pp. 643-764.

155. Massinger is, however, treated separately in *Ibid.*, vol. III, chapter VIII, pp. 1-47.

156. *Ibid.*, vol. II, pp. 659-60.

157. *Ibid.*, p. 644. Ward would himself appear to have granted Ben Jonson second position. Cf. p. 298.

158. *Ibid.*, pp. 662-63.

159. *Ibid.*, pp. 757-58.

160. *Ibid.*, p. 758.

161. *Ibid.*, pp. 721, 732.

162. *Ibid.*, pp. 699, 689.

163. *Ibid.*, pp. 756-57.

164. *Ibid.*, pp. 748-51.

165. *Ibid.*, p. 759.

166. *Ibid.*, pp. 759-60.

167. *Ibid.*, pp. 760-61.

168. *Ibid.*, p. 640.

NOTES TO CHAPTER FOUR

1. Ashley H. Thorndike: *The Influence of Beaumont and Fletcher on Shakspere*, Worcester, Mass., 1901.

2. *Ibid.*, chapter VI. His omission of *Pericles* from this grouping is, however, questionable.

3. *Ibid.*, chapters III and IV; cf. also chapter II, *passim*.

4. *Ibid.*, chapter V.

5. These included the Beaumont-Fletcher *Philaster*, *The Maid's Tragedy*, and *A King and No King*, as well as *Four Plays in One*, *Thierry and Theodoret* and *Cupid's Revenge*, in which Beaumont is granted either no or a slight hand. The Shakespeare plays were *Cymbeline*, *The Winter's Tale* and *The Tempest*.

6. Ashley H. Thorndike: *op. cit.*, chapters VII and VIII.

7. *Ibid.*, chapter IX.

8. *Ibid.*, chapters X, XI and Appendix.

9. Cf. M. W. Sampson's review of Thorndike's book in *The Journal of Germanic Philology*, IV, no. 2 (1902), pp. 241-42.

10. Orie Latham Hatcher: *John Fletcher*, p. 32.

11. Charles Mill Gayley: *Beaumont the Dramatist*, p. 387.

12. *Ibid.*, pp. 387-90.

13. *Ibid.*, pp. 390-91.

14. *Ibid.*, p. 393. On pp. 344-45, Gayley had stated that *Pericles, Cymbeline, The Winter's Tale* and *The Tempest* were all "dramatic romances" on the theme of the loss and recovery of a wife or child, and that *Pericles* and *Cymbeline* both antedated *Philaster*.

15. *Ibid.*, p. 391.

16. *Ibid.*, p. 394.

17. *Idem.*

18. Middleton Murray: *Shakespeare*, New York, 1936, p. 319.

19. E. M. W. Tillyard: *Shakespeare's Last Plays*, London, 1938, pp. 5-12.

20. He also referred occasionally to *Four Plays in One* for its resemblances to the others, though he acknowledged that this hodge-podge was not properly a "romance."

21. This paragraph, and the preceding one, comprise a condensation of Ashley H. Thorndike: *op. cit.*, pp. 109-119.

22. Thorndike did not include Calianax of *The Maid's Tragedy* in this group, probably because this old courtier was not a scoundrel, though he shared in the cowardice of the group.

23. The foregoing three paragraphs summarize Ashley H. Thorndike: *op. cit.*, pp. 119-24.

24. *Ibid.*, pp. 124-30.

25. Cf. *The Maid's Tragedy*, Act I.

26. Ashley H. Thorndike: *op. cit.*, pp. 130-32.

27. Frank Humphrey Ristine: *English Tragicomedy*, p. xi.

28. The others were: Massinger's *Bashful Lover*, Shirley's *Young Admiral*, Carlell's *Deserving Favourite* and Davenant's *Love and Honour.*

29. Frank Humphrey Ristine: *op. cit.*, p. xiii. It is curious to note that practically this whole analysis could be applied with equal appropriateness to Sir Philip Sidney's *Arcadia*.

30. *Ibid.*, p. xiv. In the light of this condemnation, it is interesting to note that Ristine considered tragicomedy a natural outgrowth of the already mixed materials of Elizabethan romance—"its tragic complications, impending dangers, heroic exploits, suspended animation, averted tragedy, happy ending." Cf. p. 95.

31. *Ibid.*, p. 110. Ristine had also noted, on page 107, that Fletcher definitely drew on Guarini's theorizing when he wrote his own definition of tragicomedy in his "To the Reader," prefixed to the printed version of *The Faithful Shepherdess*. At least one collaborator was thinking about the nature of this form at approximately the time the new departure in *Philaster* was germinating.

32. *Ibid.*, p. 108.

33. *Ibid.*, p. 112. Perhaps Fletcher got this suggestion for this common pastoral incident from *Pastor Fido;* he used it first in *The Faithful Shepherdess*, Act IV, where Perigot wounds Amoret. Cf. *Works of B. and F.*, Glover-Waller edition, vol. II, p. 424.

34. *Ibid.*, p. 111.

35. *Ibid.*, pp. 113-14.

36. *Ibid.*, p. 117. This play, in Ristine's opinion, had a mishandled denouement, in which a tragic action was unethically wrenched into a happy outcome.

37. *Ibid.,* p. 122.
38. *Ibid.,* p. 124.
39. *Ibid.,* pp. 115-116.
40. *Ibid.,* p. 119.
41. *Ibid.,* pp. 116-17. Ristine also remarked that "In the distribution of the serious interest these plays range somewhat from a type where the climax is the culmination of one continuous succession of averted dangers, reverses, surprises, and scenes of violence, as in the 'Knight of Malta' and the 'Island Princess,' to such plays as 'A King and No King' and the 'Laws of Candy,' where the action moves ominously, but without disastrous interruption to one final tragic situation." It seems to me that the first treatment is more characteristic of Fletcher, who liked variety, whereas the second normally occurs when he is collaborating with Beaumont or Massinger, who cared more than he did for singleness of action.
42. *Ibid.,* pp. 117-18 and 123.
43. Orie Latham Hatcher: *op. cit.*
44. These she classified as follows: Tragicomedies—*The Loyal Subject, The Mad Lover, Women Pleased, The Island Princess, A Wife for a Month, The Humourous Lieutenant, Monsieur Thomas;* Tragedies—*Valentinian, Bonduca;* Comedies—*Wit Without Money, The Pilgrim, The Wild-Goose Chase, The Chances, Rule a Wife, The Woman's Prize.* Cf. *Ibid.,* pp. 29-30. In making this classification, she warned that it was not always easy to determine what "the prevailing spirit" of a play was intended to be, since Fletcher did not adhere to rigid dramatic forms. For the most part she set aside *The Faithful Shepherdess* and the final pair of *Four Plays in One* as less amenable to group treatment.
45. Curiously, she thought that "His business, as he conceived it, was to present life." Cf. p. 106. I am exceedingly doubtful that he so conceived it; to present an enthralling world of "escape" seems more likely to have been at the back of his mind.
46. Orie Latham Hatcher: *op. cit.,* pp. 55-57.
47. *Ibid.,* p. 112.
48. *Ibid.,* pp. 112-13 and 106.
49. *Ibid.,* pp. 112-13.
50. Carefree, lighthearted Spanish tales, romantic in temper, were closest of all to Fletcher's own sympathies. Italian *novelle* supplied him with intense romantic passions, situations and settings, but the over-tragic bent of these stories he always tempered. In history he sought mainly for effective stage situations, caring little for factual accuracy or historical atmosphere. Classical material had the least appeal of all to him. Cf. *Ibid.,* pp. 38-47.
51. *Ibid.,* p. 38. In passing, it might be noted that Fletcher's method of handling his sources was that of a true farceur and melodramatist.
52. *Ibid.,* p. 73.
53. *Ibid.,* p. 59. In view of this fact, Miss Hatcher thought that Beaumont's influence should be suspected in the bleak destinies of Aspatia, Evadne and Bellario, but not in the "unethical" evasion of tragic punishment for Arbaces.
54. *Ibid.,* p. 60.
55. *Ibid.,* pp. 81-82.
56. *Ibid.,* pp. 60-61 and 65-66.
57. *Ibid.,* pp. 61-62.

58. *Ibid.*, p. 63.

59. *Ibid.*, pp. 64, 65. Romantic love, discovery or recognition of "lost" persons, and domestic quarrels were other conventions of which he made much use.

60. *Ibid.*, pp. 67-70. When Fletcher adapted the "humour" figure to his purposes, he made it characteristically broader in scope, but treated it lightly and superficially. He also made much use of the principle of contrast in choice and treatment of characters.

61. *Ibid.*, p. 109.

62. *Ibid.*, p. 69.

63. Fletcher's favorite heroine. She was no passively lamenting Aspatia, but a resourceful young woman intelligently pursuing her ends, regardless of obstacles. Indeed, "Fletcher was more generous than either Shakspere or Beaumont in the intellectual endowment of his women."

64. Orie Latham Hatcher: *op. cit.*, pp. 72-73.

65. *Ibid.*, p. 83.

66. *Ibid.*, pp. 74-78.

67. *Ibid.*, pp. 78-81.

68. *Ibid.*, pp. 85-88. Miss Hatcher did admit that a few of his plays had an outer consistency of tone, but tended, in my opinion, to undervalue this. However, compare her attitude towards Fletcher's use of sources.

69. *Ibid.*, pp. 88-90. Miss Hatcher found this intensification of mood invariably unsuccessful in the serious plays, because it exaggerated unpleasantly a tension which remained overstrained and unbroken.

70. *Ibid.*, p. 88. To this particular attitude I shall later take exception.

71. *Ibid.*, pp. 90-91.

72. *Ibid.*, pp. 92-93.

73. *Ibid.*, pp. 93-94.

74. *Ibid.*, pp. 94-98. Miss Hatcher then presented analyses of the alternate moves of the opposed characters or groups of characters, in *The Woman's Prize*, *The Wild-Goose Chase* and *Rule a Wife*.

75. *Ibid.*, p. 105. But did he have this aim? Was he not rather bent on creating an entertaining "never never" land where anything might happen, serious and comic alike? His Stuart audiences do not seem to have been resentful, whatever may be the case of the modern reader.

76. *Ibid.*, pp. 33, 105.

77. *Ibid.*, p. 35.

78. *Ibid.*, p. 105.

79. *Ibid.*, p. 106.

80. *Ibid.*, p. 107.

81. *Ibid.*, pp. 110-11.

82. *Ibid.*, p. 106.

83. A. C. Swinburne: *Contemporaries of Shakespeare*, edited by Edmund Gosse and Thomas James Wise, London, 1919. The essay on "Beaumont and Fletcher" had, however, already appeared in *The English Review*, V (1910), pp. 202-16.

84. *Ibid.*, pp. 148-50. Comment on Arbaces from p. 153; on Ordella from p. 147. It is interesting to note that one comedy hero, the younger brother of *Wit Without Money*, won Swinburne's special approval. He considered that the figure

should prove that Fletcher was capable of presenting "a morally attractive and admirable young English hero." Cf. p. 163.

85. *Ibid.*, p. 164.

86. *Ibid.*, pp. 147-48.

87. *Ibid.*, p. 165.

88. *Idem.*

89. *Ibid.*, pp. 152-53.

90. *Ibid.*, p. 151.

91. *Ibid.*, pp. 163-64.

92. *Ibid.*, pp. 157-58. I confess that the sober Richardson's prudential morality does not seem to me, either, any improvement on Fletcher's light-hearted attitudes.

93. *Ibid.*, p. 151. He appears to have preferred Fletcher's "loveliest of all pastorals" to the "exquisite" but "academic" *Comus.*

94. Cf. Chapter I, p. 18.

95. A. C. Swinburne: *op. cit.*, pp. 145-46.

96. Rupert Brooke: *John Webster and the Elizabethan Drama*, London, 1916, pp. 70-75.

97. *Ibid.*, pp. 70-71. This estimate assuredly earns a place among the more sweeping condemnations of the past!

98. Note the irresponsibility and ill-will of this remark.

99. Rupert Brooke: *op. cit.*, pp. 72-75.

100. E. M. W. Tillyard: *op. cit.*, p. 6.

101. Charles Mills Gayley: *op. cit.*, p. 399. Likewise, in Webster's *White Devil*, contemporaneous with the Beaumont-Fletcher collaboration, there patently were "poisonous exhalations, . . . wildering of sympathy, disproportioned art."

102. *Ibid.*, p. 396.

103. This whole matter will receive further attention in Chapter V.

104. Charles Mills Gayley: *op. cit.*, p. 411.

105. *Ibid.*, p. 416.

106. *Ibid.*, p. 411.

107. *Ibid.*, pp. 400-01. Cf. Paul Elmer More: *With the Wits: Shelburne Essays, Tenth Series*, Boston and New York, 1919, pp. 31-32. Gayley had read the "Beaumont and Fletcher" essay, pp. 1-40, in its first form as three articles in *The Nation* for Nov. 12, 1912, April 24, 1913 and May 1, 1913.

108. Paul Elmer More: *op. cit.*, p. 31.

109. Charles Mills Gayley: *op. cit.*, pp. 401-03.

110. *Ibid.*, pp. 403-06. Cf. Paul Elmer More: *op. cit.*, p. 31. Also, cf. Eugene M. Waith: "Characterization in John Fletcher's Tragicomedies," *The Review of English Studies*, XIX (1943), pp. 155-62, for its penetrating analysis of Fletcher's methods of characterization in this play. It affords an antidote to Gayley's prejudiced treatment.

111. Cf. Charles Mills Gayley: *op. cit.*, p. 400.

112. *Ibid.*, pp. 414-15.

113. Cf. *Ibid.*, pp. 352-54 and 364-66.

114. *Ibid.*, pp. 389-99. Gayley agreed (p. 396) with More that the source of "decadence" in Elizabethan-Stuart tragedy was the shifting of the theme from a single passion to a number of them—none central and all loosely coordinated— resulting in a sacrifice of unity to a less rigid structure and a freer play of varied emotions. Cf. Paul Elmer More: *op. cit.*, pp. 4-5.

115. *Ibid.*, p. 413.

116. Cf. E. H. C. Oliphant: *The Plays of Beaumont and Fletcher*, pp. 31-45, 49-57 and *passim*. Oliphant's dislike of Fletcher appears to have been even stronger than Gayley's. Nor did the latter, like Oliphant, endeavor to find Beaumont a share in various plays in which his collaboration was, at best, dubious. He limited Beaumont to the whole or parts of eight plays. Cf. p. 378.

117. Cf. especially Charles Mills Gayley: *op. cit.*, pp. 211-16, on Fletcher's personality.

118. William Archer: *The Old Drama and the New*, Boston, 1923.

119. *Ibid.*, pp. 6-18.

120. *Ibid.*, pp. 19, 8. Archer commented acidly but shrewdly on the many "closet" dramatic poems in blank verse written by nineteenth century poets and poetasters in imitation of Shakespeare and his compeers.

121. *Ibid.*, p. 19.

122. *Ibid.*, pp. 48-49. When one recalls how often Fletcher has been blamed for trying to convert his blank verse into a more conversational medium, one smiles, a little wryly.

123. *Ibid.*, pp. 35-48.

124. *Ibid.*, pp. 53, 128.

125. *Ibid.*, p. 20.

126. *Ibid.*, Lecture III, pp. 50-77. The other three plays were *The Duchess of Malfi, The Broken Heart* and *The Revenger's Tragedy*.

127. *Ibid.*, p. 65. Cf. *Beaumont and Fletcher*, 2 vols., "The Mermaid Series," edited by J. St. Loe Strachey, London, 1887, vol. I, p. xxv.

128. *Ibid.*, pp. 65-66.

129. *Ibid.*, pp. 66-70.

130. There is, here, an interesting parallel, springing from different sources, in the viewpoint of Archer and of the neo-classicists in general, including Dryden.

131. M. C. Bradbrook: *Elizabethan Stage Conditions*, p. 126.

132. *The Plays of William Shakespeare*, edited by Samuel Johnson and George Steevens, vol. I, "Dr. Johnson's Preface," pp. 194-95.

133. *The Works of B. and F.*, Weber edition, vol. I, "Introduction," p. lxvii.

NOTES TO CHAPTER FIVE

1. This play, which had remained in manuscript for more than two centuries and a half, was first published by A. H. Bullen in his *Collection of Old English Plays*, London, 1883, vol. II, pp. 201-314. Cf. Wilhelmina P. Frijlinck: *The Tragedy of Sir John Van Olden Barnavelt*, Amsterdam, 1922, (distributed by the Oxford University Press), p. xi. Miss Frijlinck's edition has a sound and scholarly introduction, and a careful text.

2. John Cranford Adams: *The Globe Playhouse: Its Design and Equipment*, Cambridge, Mass., 1943.

3. Alfred Harbage: *Shakespeare's Audience*, New York, 1941.

4. William J. Lawrence: *Pre-Restoration Stage Studies*, Cambridge, Mass., 1927 p. 341, remarks, on this point, that "playwriting in Shakespeare's day was simply a trade, . . . plays were written wholly and solely to order, and . . . they were

never ordered until they were wanted." Doubtless, however, there were exceptions, from time to time, to this procedure.

5. Joseph Quincy Adams: *A Life of William Shakespeare*, Boston and New York, 1925, p. 21, makes this suggestion.

6. Charles Mills Gayley: *Beaumont the Dramatist*, p. 62. It is characteristic of the somewhat sketchy treatment he gave Fletcher that he did not mention the date of baptism, Dec. 20, which Dyce had discovered.

7. Joseph Quincy Adams: *op. cit.*, pp. 61 and 64-65.

8. Maurice Chelli: *Le Drame de Massinger*, Lyon, France, 1923, p. 39.

9. Joseph Quincy Adams: *op. cit.*, p. 79.

10. Charles Mills Gayley: *op. cit.*, p. 18.

11. Joseph Quincy Adams: *op. cit.*, pp. 90-96.

12. *Ibid.*, p. 125.

13. Charles Mills Gayley: *op. cit.*, pp. 62-63.

14. *Ibid.*, pp. 68-69.

15. *Ibid.*, p. 25.

16. Cf., for example, Joseph Quincy Adams: *op. cit.*, pp. 152-53.

17. *Ibid.*, p. 220.

18. Charles Mills Gayley: *op. cit.*, p. 29. Gayley does not give any source for this information. Unless there exists evidence to the contrary, it would seem more probable, according to Professor Dorothy Foster of Mount Holyoke College, that he took up residence at once in the Inner Temple, since he was a gentleman-commoner.

19. Maurice Chelli: *op. cit.*, pp. 41-42, and footnote 6, page 41.

20. Alfred Harbage: *op. cit.*, pp. 158-63, and *passim*.

21. Indeed, Fletcher, Massinger and Field appear to have begun their triple collaboration in 1613, with *The Honest Man's Fortune*.

22. Cf. Charles Mills Gayley: *op. cit.*, Chapter IV, "The Vaux Cousins and The Gunpowder Plot."

23. *Ibid.*, p. 64.

24. *Ibid.*, p. 67.

25. Maurice Chelli: *op. cit.*, p. 41, considered Massinger's upbringing in the Pembroke households only hypothetical. It seems to me that the probabilities are all in its favor, since Massinger's parents would most naturally reside at the Earl's estate. The father's position was one of great trust. A. H. Cruikshank: *Philip Massinger*, New York, n. d., [1920], p. 1., referred to him as the "house steward." Robert Hamilton Ball: *The Amazing Career of Sir Giles Overreach*, p. 12, said that Arthur Massinger held an honorable position with the Earls, and was sent on many confidential missions by them. Since he died in 1603, and William Herbert, Earl of Pembroke, "patronized" St. Alban's Hall, Oxford, which Philip Massinger attended, assistance from the Earl to the young student is quite possible.

26. Charles Mills Gayley: *op. cit.*, pp. 15-16.

27. James Edward Phillips, Jr.: *The State in Shakespeare's Greek and Roman Plays*, New York, 1940, *passim*.

28. Robert Hamilton Ball: *op. cit.*, p. 12. Ball also states, on this page, the fact that a large portion of the aristocracy did not approve of James' pacifistic and unparliamentary policies. It should be added that the well-to-do middle class patrons of Blackfriars, as well as those of lesser means, were, in still larger

numbers, hostile to these policies. Fletcher was, of course, well aware of the attitude of the majority of his spectators.

29. There is a succinct account in Frederick George Marcham: *A History of England*, New York, 1937, pp. 423-24, of some of the well-known facts assembled in the two foregoing paragraphs.

30. Cf. Chapter III, p. 102.

31. *The Tragedy of Sir John Van Olden Barnavelt*, edited by Wilhelmina P. Frijlinck, p. 83, lines 2981-2990. Words abbreviated in the text have been transcribed in full. The distress of modern critics that the two authors developed Barnavelt's character in different scenes with resultant inconsistencies should not blind us to the practical necessity of Fletcher's ending to the play.

32. Cf. Arthur Colby Sprague: *Beaumont and Fletcher on the Restoration Stage*, pp. 58-62, for a clear and detailed discussion of this baffling problem.

33. *Ibid.*, pp. 178-86, gives a useful analysis of these three versions.

34. See Chapter III, p. 89.

35. See Chapter III, pp. 91-92.

36. Oscar James Campbell: *Comicall Satyre and Shakespeare's Troilus and Cressida*, San Marino, Calif., 1938, and *Shakespeare's Satire*, London, New York and Toronto, 1943.

37. Joseph Quincy Adams: *Shakespearean Playhouses, A History of English Theatres from the Beginning to the Restoration*, Boston and New York, 1917, pp. 220-24.

38. *Works of B. and F.*, Glover-Waller edition, vol. IV, pp. 10-11.

39. *Ibid.*, vol. IV, pp. 13-16.

40. Malcolm MacKenzie Ross: *Milton's Royalism: A Study of the Conflict of Symbol and Idea in the Poems*, pp. 29-31, 34. It would be unjust to Mr. Ross to draw the inference that, because I disagree with him completely on the royalism of Fletcher, Beaumont and Company, I therefore do not think well of his able book as a whole. That is another matter.

41. *Ibid.*, pp. 29-30.

42. This play may be consulted in *Works of B. and F.*, Glover-Waller edition, vol. III, pp. 76-169.

43. *Ibid.*, pp. 126-28.

44. Benjamin Townley Spencer: "Philip Massinger," published in *Seventeenth Century Studies by Members of the Graduate School, University of Cincinnati*, edited by Robert Shafer, Princeton, N. J., 1933, pp. 3-119.

45. *Ibid.*, p. 112.

46. *Idem.*

47. *Idem.*

48. *Works of B. and F.*, Glover-Waller edition, vol. I, p. 74.

49. It is perhaps questionable whether Beaumont and Fletcher held as strong convictions as Massinger did against the assassination of tyrants. Lysippus, in *The Maid's Tragedy*, imposed no penalty on Melantius, the instigator of the king's murder. It was because Amintor—"my Sister, Father, Brother, Son; All that I had"—lay slain that Melantius vowed never to eat or drink again. In thus determining to follow his comrade into death, he was conforming to a romantic convention of friendship immediately grasped by Jacobean theatregoers. In somewhat similar fashion, the stoical Cleremont D'Ambois took his own life (in Chapman's *The Revenge of Bussy D'Ambois*, Act V, scene 5) upon hearing of the death of his intimate friend, the Duke of Guise.

50. Baldwin Maxwell: *Studies in Beaumont, Fletcher, and Massinger*, Chapter VIII, "The Attitude Towards the Duello in the Beaumont and Fletcher Plays."

51. Maurice Chelli: *op. cit.*, p. 42, note 3.

52. Cf. James Bass Mullinger: *The University of Cambridge from the Royal Injunctions of 1535 to the Accession of Charles I*, Cambridge, England, 1884, p. 394, and also Charles Edward Mallet: *A History of the University of Oxford*, 3 vols., New York, 1924, vol. II, p. 141.

53. *Works of B. and F.*, Glover-Waller ed., pp. 1-74; this situation begins to develop on pp. 15-16. The burlesque quality of this play is difficult for a modern reader to realize, because of changes of attitude towards love since Jacobean days.

54. Charles Mills Gayley: *op. cit.*, pp. 38-42.

55. Of course, Spenser was following, with exactness, a traditional pattern. By the same measure, however, much of the bawdiness and pornography of Elizabethan-Stuart drama had example from Ovid, the Roman satirists, the Renaissance tradition that comedy was licensed to coarse jesting, and so on. One wonders what some critics of our playwrights' moral standards would make of Spenser's very explicit tale of Paridell, the lascivious Dame Hellenore and the Satyrs in Book III, Canto X, of *The Faerie Queene*.

56. *The Works of Edmund Spenser, a Variorum Edition*, 6 vols. to date, edited by Greenlaw, Osgood, Padelford and others, Baltimore, 1932-   , vol. I, p. 167.

57. Charles Mills Gayley: *op. cit.*, pp. 42-44.

58. E. M. W. Tillyard: *Shakespeare's Last Plays*, pp. 11-12.

59. Joseph Quincy Adams: *Shakespearean Playhouses*, pp. 249, 235-36, 239.

60. *Ibid.*, pp. 267-69, 274-76.

61. Harold Newcome Hillebrand: *The Child Actors: A Chapter in Elizabethan Stage History*, published in the *University of Illinois Studies in Language and Literatures*, vol. XI, Urbana, Ill., 1926, p. 265.

62. Joseph Quincy Adams: *op. cit.*, p. 111.

63. *Ibid.*, pp. 201, 206, 183-84.

64. Cf. *ibid.*, p. 350.

65. *Ibid.*, p. 198.

66. *Ibid.*, pp. 198-200.

67. *Ibid.*, p. 201.

68. Cf. *ibid.*, pp. 195-97, for fuller treatment of these points.

69. John Cranford Adams: *op. cit.*, p. 90.

70. Charles William Wallace: *The Children of the Chapel at Blackfriars, 1597-1603*, Lincoln, Nebraska, 1908, p. 44. This book is one to be used with caution. Wallace thought that the Blackfriars stage went the width of the room, and that it was because of the "free" space at either end that gallants originally gained permission to sit on stools on this stage. One wonders, however, if Burbage would not have carried the galleries straight forward to the stage façade proper, as he was to do at the Globe. If so, the stage itself measured less than forty-six feet across.

71. For instance, in the "Commendatory Verses" prefixed to the first quarto of *The Faithful Shepherdess*, Nathan Field speaks of "the monster" that "clapped his thousand hands" and Beaumont of Fletcher's making "a thousand men in judgment sit" on this Blackfriars play. Cf. *Works of B. and F.*, Variorum edition, vol. III, pp. 10 and 11.

72. John Cranford Adams: *op. cit.*, "The Music Gallery," pp. 298-324. For *The Tempest*, see pp. 319-22; for *The Double Marriage*, see pp. 304-06. Adams

also makes this significant comment (p. 308): "The fact that *The Double Marriage, The Tempest,* and *The Roman Actor* were owned and produced by the King's Men suggests that the Blackfriars had a stage similarly located" to the music gallery of the Globe. Personally, I think it had—and likewise three galleries.

73. Cf. Joseph Quincy Adams, *op. cit.,* p. 197, who says: "The obvious advantage of artificial light for producing beautiful stage effects must have added not a little to the popularity of Blackfriars Playhouse."

74. J. Isaacs: *Production and Stage-Management at the Blackfriars Theatre,* pamphlet published for the Shakespeare Association, London, 1933. Though Mr. Isaac does not himself remark on the increase in spectacular effects, his data point to that conclusion.

75. *Ibid.,* p. 12; Joseph Quincy Adams: *op. cit.,* pp. 207-08.

76. Joseph Quincy Adams: *op. cit.,* pp. 203-04.

77. The increasing popularity of Jacobean masques was, it will be recalled, Thorndike's explanation.

78. Harold Newcomb Hillebrand: *op. cit.,* pp. 253-55, 266. It is, of course, true that plays were produced by boy actors at Paul's and elsewhere, especially in the 1570's and 1580's; and that schoolboys at the public schools often performed Latin comedies and sometimes plays in the vernacular.

79. *Ibid.,* pp. 260-62.

80. *Ibid.,* p. 264.

81. Joseph Quincy Adams: *op. cit.,* p. 114, points out that the boys of Paul's were suppressed near the end of 1590 because, with their playwright, Lyly, they became involved in the Martin Marprelate controversy. It may be that Lyly would otherwise have kept them longer afloat.

82. Harold Newcomb Hillebrand: *op. cit.,* p. 267.

83. Alfred Harbage: *Shakespeare's Audience,* p. 64, says on this point: "When the 'private' theatres opened and placed the minimum charge at 6 *d.,* no more effective means could have been devised for excluding utterly the great majority of the former audience." The purchasing power of sixpence would nearly equal two dollars as of 1945.

84. Oscar James Campbell: *Comicall Satyre and Shakespeare's Troilus and Cressida,* p. 155, makes this comment: "All the evidence shows that the patrons of the 'private theatres' took peculiar delight in social and ethical satire."

85. Joseph Quincy Adams: *op. cit.,* pp. 216-22, gives brief accounts of the difficulties over *Philotas, Eastward Ho!, The Isle of Guls,* and *The Conspiracy and Tragedy of Charles, Duke of Byron.*

86. Act II, scene 2, when Hamlet is first informed that a travelling company of players has reached Elsinore.

87. Oscar James Campbell: *op. cit.,* p. 1. Professor Campbell shows with clarity, in this book, how this restraining order caused the development of comical satire by Jonson and Marston, and thus brought about its practice by Shakespeare in *Troilus and Cressida.*

88. *Ibid.,* p. 135-36.

89. Henry W. Wells: *Elizabethan and Jacobean Playwrights,* New York, 1939, p. 296.

90. The dates of this and the preceding two paragraphs have been checked against those given in Alfred Harbage: *Annals of the English Drama, 975-1700.*

91. Oscar James Campbell: *Shakespeare's Satire*, pp. 99-100, succinctly discusses this point.

92. Cf. *The Works of John Marston*, 3 vols., edited by A. H. Bullen, London, 1887, vol. I, Webster's "Induction" for the King's Men, pp. 199-206, and especially p. 203, with its footnote. Chapman's *Bussy D'Ambois*, which was certainly constructed with the limitations of boy-actors in mind, also was later performed—and with success—by men's companies. Perhaps Nathan Field brought the play over with him at the time he joined the King's Men.

93. Cf., for instance, *Works of B. and F.*, Glover-Waller ed., vol. I, p. 88 (Philaster's description of Bellario) and p. 119 (Philaster's soliloquy).

94. Mina Kerr: *Influence of Ben Jonson on English Comedy, 1598-1642*, New York, 1912, p. 39.

95. *Ibid.*, pp. 39-42.

96. *Poetry of the English Renaissance, 1509-1660*, edited by J. William Hebel and Hoyt H. Hudson, New York, 1929, p. 540. Cf. also the following footnote.

97. *Works of B. and F.*, Dyce edition, Boston and New York, 1854 printing, vol. II, pp. 954-55 and 960. (Beaumont's verse-letter to Jonson will also be found on pp. 955-56).

98. *Poetry of the English Renaissance*, p. 540.

99. *Ben Jonson: The Man and His Work*, 2 vols., edited by C. H. Herford and Percy Simpson, Oxford, 1925, vol. I, p. 137.

100. Mina Kerr: *op. cit.*, p. 39.

101. Alfred Harbage: *op. cit.*, p. 80, dates both plays at 1609, while allowing *Philaster* the limits of 1608-10. This conforms to the existing evidence.

102. *Works of B. and F.*, Dyce edition, vol. II, p. 954.

103. *Ibid.*, vol. II, p. 960.

104. Cf. Chapter I, p. 39, and Chapter IV, p. 115.

105. Cf. Chapter IV, p. 115.

106. *Works of B. and F.*, Glover-Waller edition, vol. X, pp. 94-95, 107-08, 116-18, 134-35.

107. Mina Kerr: *op. cit.*, p. 39.

108. Cf. Chapter IV, p. 108.

109. It is not to be inferred, however, that the writers of satirical comedies originated the running commentary in Elizabethan plays, even though they exploited it fully for their satirical purposes. In Shakespeare's *Richard II*, for instance, other characters have much to say about the protagonist.

110. Mina Kerr: *op. cit.*, p. 39.

111. *Idem.*

112. Shakespeare's Falstaff, of course, is another figure who may have been in Beaumont's mind.

113. This clever series of complications can be studied in *The Works of John Marston*, Bullen edition, vol. II, pp. 367-74, 377-82, 397, 399-402, 415-16.

114. *The Plays and Poems of George Chapman: The Comedies*, edited by Thomas Marc Parrott, London and New York, 1914, p. 707.

115. Another play of Chapman's with fantastic situations is *Monsieur D'Olive*. In one of these a woman shuts herself up in her darkened home, and turns night into day, day into night, because she conceives that her honor has been insulted. In the other, a husband, inconsolable for his dead wife, keeps her body sitting in a chair as if alive, in order that he may gaze upon her. Of course, another

woman falls in love with his constancy! Both of these situations yield precedence, as the play progresses, to the humours of Monsieur D'Olive, though cures are wrought on each of the fantasts.

116. Cf. the Count's scornful dismissal of the intelligencers from the play, in *Works of B. and F.*, Glover-Waller edition, vol. X, p. 133.

117. Wilbur Daniel Dunkel: *The Dramatic Technique of Thomas Middleton in his Comedies of London Life*, Chicago, 1925, p. 12 and *passim*.

118. Act II, scenes 1, 2, 4, 5, 7. Another extravagant situation occurs in the comical satire, *The Phoenix*. This dramatizes a man's sale of his wife to a second man. Middleton's comedies afford many instances of farcical intrigue doing violence to probabilities.

119. Cf. Chapter IV, p. 115.

120. Cf. *The Works of Thomas Middleton*, 8 vols., edited by A. H. Bullen, London, 1885, vol. I, p. 255.

121. Miss Kerr: *op. cit.*, pp. 39-40.

122. *Ibid.*, p. 40.

123. Eugene M. Waith: "Characterization in John Fletcher's Tragicomedies," *Review of English Studies*, XIX, 1943, pp. 141-64. Students of Fletcher will find that this article well repays attentive reading.

124. Oscar James Campbell: *Comicall Satyre and Shakespeare's Troilus and Cressida*.

125. Eugene M. Waith: *op. cit.*, pp. 146-47, gives a fuller development of most of the foregoing points.

126. *Ibid.*, p. 147.

127. Cf. *ibid.*, pp. 144-51. Part of Waith's viewpoint will be developed in Chapter VI, in connection with *The Faithful Shepherdess*.

128. *Ibid.*, p. 39.

129. Not by name, however; she simply speaks (p. 39) of "a running comment in dialogue form within the play."

130. *Ibid.*, p. 41.

131. *Idem.*

132. *The Plays and Poems of George Chapman: The Comedies*, p. 736.

133. *Ibid.*, p. 761.

134. Charles Mills Gayley: *op. cit.*, pp. 390-91.

135. *Ibid.*, p. 392.

136. Daniel Morley McKeithan: *The Debt to Shakespeare in the Beaumont-and-Fletcher Plays*, pp. 32-42.

137. *Ibid.*, pp. 86-100. The use which Fletcher made of *A Midsummer Night's Dream* in planning and writing *The Faithful Shepherdess* will be discussed in Chapter VI. Interestingly enough, *Love's Labour's Lost* is one of the few Shakespeare plays for which McKeithan found not a trace of influence on the work of either Beaumont or Fletcher.

138. D'Urfé's *Astrée* might also be thought to have a claim. But although Fletcher later levied on it for plots, he avoided its "precious" treatment. If Beaumont and he knew this long-winded French romance at the time they were writing their collaborated plays, its main influence would simply have been to reinforce elements they had long since found in Sidney's *Arcadia* and other fiction of their youth.

139. Oscar James Campbell: *Shakespeare's Satire*, p. 64.

140. *Ibid.*, p. 124.

141. Frank Humphrey Ristine: *English Tragicomedy*, p. 100.

142. Hazelton Spencer: *The Art and Life of William Shakespeare*, New York, 1940, pp. 292-93.

143. Donald Joseph McGinn: *Shakespeare's Influence on the Drama of his Age, Studied in Hamlet*, New Brunswick, N. J., 1938, pp. 53-56, also demonstrates that King Claudius of *Hamlet* was the prototype of Lavall, villainous son of the Duke of Anjou, in Fletcher's miniature revenge tragedy, "The Triumph of Death," in *Four Plays or Moral Representations in One*. Evidently, *Hamlet* made a deep impression on our playwrights.

144. Cf. Donald Joseph McGinn: *op. cit.*, pp. 256-63, and Daniel Morley McKeithan: *op. cit.*, pp. 32-36.

145. Cf. Daniel Morley McKeithan: *op. cit.*, pp. 36-40.

146. Cf. Donald Joseph McGinn: *op. cit.*, pp. 63-64. The latter motivation was suggested, of course, by the line in *Hamlet* concerning the "divinity [that] doth hedge a king. . . ."

147. Cf. Daniel Morley McKeithan: *op. cit.*, pp. 44-48.

148. Cf. Donald Joseph McGinn: *op. cit.*, pp. 65-67.

149. *Ibid.*, pp. 64-65.

150. Daniel Morley McKeithan: *op. cit.*, pp. 43-44. Seward, who wrote the Introduction to the 1750 edition of our playwrights' works, commented, it will be recalled, on this resemblance.

151. Donald Joseph McGinn: *op. cit.*, pp. 117-18 and 147-48, cites a number of Marston's imitations of passages in *Hamlet*.

152. For instance, in *The Dutch Courtesan*, the title character bids Malheureux kill his young friend, young Freevil, and in turn Malheureux is almost trapped to death by her. But Marston's real aim appears to have been to answer the sentimental Dekker-Middleton treatment of a prostitute in *The Honest Whore* by opposing a realistic one. He treats his material much in the manner of a comical satire, and the tragicomic possibilities are not developed.

153. Thomas Marc Parrott and Robert Hamilton Ball: *A Short View of Elizabethan Drama*, New York, 1943, p. 98.

154. *Idem.*

155. Margaret's smearing of her face with poison, Vincentio's offer to marry her regardless, her generous refusal, and the restoring of her beauty are matched in the story of Argalus and Parthenia in *Arcadia*, Book I. The resemblance is so close that it seems probable Chapman borrowed these situations from Sidney's romance.

156. Thomas Marc Parrott and Robert Hamilton Ball: *op. cit.*, p. 98. I question whether this should be considered a hall-mark of our authors' plays, for banishment was a conventional enough punishment before they were ever written.

157. Gerald Eades Bentley: *Shakespeare & Jonson: Their Reputations in the Seventeenth Century Compared*, p. 109, adds a new bit of evidence as to its popularity in the seventeenth century. It stands seventh among the Shakespeare items in the composite list of "Allusions to Individual Works of Shakespeare and Jonson" with a score of 24 allusions. To the first Shakespeare item, *The Tempest*, there were but 16 more.

158. Hazelton Spencer: *op. cit.*, p. 357.

159. John Tucker Murray: *English Dramatic Companies, 1558-1642*, vol. I, p. 151.

160. Alfred Harbage: *op. cit.*, p. 78. He gives 1608-09 as the limits.
161. Ashley H. Thorndike: *The Influence of Beaumont and Fletcher on Shakespeare*, p. 176, and p. 173.
162. *Ibid.*, pp. 173-74. It may be that our playwrights were, in general, scornful of the loosely built sort of romance that *Pericles* is, as Thorndike suggests. This would not prevent their being influenced by this particular Globe play of Shakespeare, however.
163. Cf. William J. Lawrence: *Pre-Restoration Stage Studies*, p. 351: "The one thing the players were particular about, and had to be assured of, was a striking plot. The plot had to be ratified by them before the labour of composition began."
164. *Works of B. and F.*, Glover-Waller edition, vol. I, p. xxv.
165. Cf. Chapter II, p. 72.
166. Cf. Chapter III, p. 93.
167. *The Works of Thomas Middleton*, Bullen edition, vol. III, pp. 305-08,

NOTES TO CHAPTER SIX

1. E. H. C. Oliphant: *The Plays of Beaumont and Fletcher*, p. 116.
2. *Ibid.*, pp. 117, 115.
3. Alfred Harbage: *Annals of English Drama, 975-1700*, pp. 76-81.
4. These are: *The Woman-Hater, The Knight of the Burning Pestle, Philaster, The Coxcomb, The Maid's Tragedy, Cupid's Revenge, A King and No King,* and *The Scornful Lady.*
5. Charles Mills Gayley: *Beaumont the Dramatist*, p. 69.
6. A careful search in England among diplomatic and other papers—in particular, any in which the activities of Dr. Giles Fletcher could be traced—might possibly reveal a few facts which would light up some part of these dark years.
7. Cf. *Works of B. and F.*, Glover-Waller edition, vol. X, pp. 278-80.
8. *Works of B. and F.*, Bullen edition, vol. III, p. 17.
9. Despite vexing problems of revision or of multiple authorship which *Wit at Several Weapons* raises, that satirical comedy likewise could possibly be an early Fletcher play. Middleton's hand, as well as Fletcher's, has been suspected in it. It is not impossible that the two men might have worked together at the outset of Fletcher's career. It is, however, doubtful.
10. I incline to the opinion that Fletcher began his career as a playwright about 1606 or 1607, or approximately the time when Beaumont entered the lists. This is based on the foregoing speculations about Fletcher, and on some scepticism as to how some of the plays proposed as early will meet the tests I have outlined. It was not germane to the purposes of this book to make a thoroughgoing analysis of these plays with intent to show whether they were sound claimants or not. This is, however, a study which might well be made on the basis I have suggested in this paragraph.
11. John Tucker Murray: *English Dramatic Companies, 1558-1642*, vol. I, p. 363.

12. Cf. E. H. C. Oliphant: *op. cit.*, pp. 217-19, for discussion of this point. I am disposed to agree that Fletcher made insertions into two or three scenes with which his friend was not satisfied.

13. *The Knight of the Burning Pestle*, edited by Herbert S. Murch, p. 7.

14. The coffin scenes of *The Night-Walker, or The Little Thief*, for instance, afford an interesting comparison with those of *The Knight of the Burning Pestle*. Though Shirley revised *The Night-Walker*, there is a Fletcherian ring about these scenes. One might also compare the coffin scene of *The Mad Lover*, though the mood of this one is less like those of *The Knight of the Burning Pestle*.

15. *The Knight of the Burning Pestle*, edited by Herbert S. Murch, p. 7.

16. Moreover, the Jacobean playgoer knew that he was at a play, and he had a dual consciousness of the world of the play and the world of reality. He was not concerned that a drama should create in him an "illusion of reality," in any modern naturalistic sense. The matter-of-fact inability of the Grocer's Wife to distinguish between the play and reality—which amuses the modern reader—may very well, therefore, have annoyed him.

17. E. K. Chambers: *The Elizabethan Stage*, 4 vols., Oxford, 1923, vol. III, p. 276.

18. Milton's *Comus* should not be included among such plays for two reasons: it is a masque, and it is only in part truly pastoral.

19. W. J. Lawrence: *Pre-Restoration Stage Studies*, pp. 142-43, advances his reasons for thinking that the trouble came when the wooden shutters were on the Blackfriars Theatre windows during the nocturnal acts of the play. Discontent at sitting in the dark (except for the stage candles) at a play that balked the spectators' expectations might certainly account for the abrupt, premature ending of the presentation.

20. *Works of B. and F.*, Bullen edition, vol. III, p. 18.

21. The success of *The Faithful Shepherdess* when presented by the King's Men before Queen Henrietta and the court in 1634, in sumptuous costumes which the Queen made available, gave the right answer. This was the proper sort of setting for this play.

22. Cf. Alfred Harbage: *Shakespeare's Audience*, pp. 54-55, 80, and *passim*.

23. This does not mean that Beaumont and Fletcher did not continue writing with their eyes primarily on the gentry. Their failures apparently taught them that purely amusement-seeking courtiers were a large element among the gentry, on whose literary and dramatic sophistication they had counted too heavily. No longer able to assume cultivated tastes in their spectators, they quickly solved the problem of how to cater to the gentry, who set the tone at least at the private theatres if not at the Globe.

24. *Works of B. and F.*, Bullen edition, vol. III, p. 18.

25. *Ibid.*, pp. 11-12.

26. U. M. Ellis-Fermor: *The Jacobean Drama, an Interpretation*, pp. 201-02.

27. *Works of B. and F.*, Glover-Waller edition, vol. I, p. xi.

28. Daniel Morley McKeithan: *The Debt to Shakespeare in the Beaumont-and-Fletcher Plays*, Chapter V, pp. 83-103, gives a convenient summary of the varied findings, while making a special case for *A Midsummer Night's Dream*.

29. Cloe might also be considered an intriguer. But she does not, like Corisca and Amaryllis, set her heart on one man and intrigue to win him to her will.

Cloe is simply an over-ripe virgin lustful for sexual experience (a common enough human type), and any man will do to satisfy her longings.

30. Clorin's faithful attendance on the grave of her dead lover faintly suggests the absurd situation in Chapman's *Monsieur D'Olive* wherein a gentleman keeps his dead wife sitting in a chair, as in life, so that he may adore her. Thenot's infatuation for Clorin's constancy is also reminiscent of the love of the young woman of Chapman's play for the constant gentleman. Professor Dorothy Foster of Mount Holyoke College has suggested to me an interesting possible parallel between Clorin and the Sir Eglamour of Shakespeare's early *The Two Gentlemen of Verona*. Sir Eglamour was chosen by Sylvia as her escort when she escaped from Milan. She stated to this gentleman, as her reason for selecting him, that he was noted for his fidelity to his dead lover.

31. Fletcher likewise reverses the treatment of the Satyr. Whereas the one in Guarini's play is lustful, the one in Fletcher's is beneficent, symbolizing the purity of the creature close to nature and obeying her behests, or perhaps, the purity of nature's influences. This conception has probably rightly been traced to similar ones in *The Faerie Queene*. Fletcher transfers the lustful nature of Guarini's Satyr to his own Sullen Shepherd.

32. Daniel Morley McKeithan: *op. cit.*, pp. 91-98.

33. *Ibid.*, p. 88.

34. There appears to have been no exact prototype of Clorin in Book III of *The Faerie Queene*; but Fletcher was nonetheless influenced, in all probability, by Spenser's neo-Platonism in creating this character. Incidentally, Amoret's name came from Book III.

35. *Works of B. and F.*, Bullen edition, vol. III, p. 14.

36. Henry W. Wells: *Elizabethan and Jacobean Playwrights*, pp. 168-70. Wells' whole account of *The Faithful Shepherdess* is fresh and stimulating.

37. The status of the others, largely as characterized in Wells' words, is as follows: Amoret symbolizes "true love less pure and religious" than Clorin's; Perigot, true love, "yet frail with jealousy, passion and mistrust"; Amarillis, the Corsican intriguer, lust for a single individual (Perigot) but "capable of nobility"; Thenot, "infatuation without desire"; Daphnis, "bashfulness"; Alexis, "looseness in men"; Cloe, "looseness in" virgins.

38. W. W. Greg: *Pastoral Poetry and Pastoral Drama: A Literary Inquiry, with Special Reference to the Pre-Restoration Stage in England*, London, 1906, p. 268.

39. *Ibid.*, p. 266.

40. Although Wells thinks the lesson includes the idea that it is better not to love at all, the devotion of the almost holy Clorin to her dead lover casts doubt on this conclusion. Moreover, Perigot and Amoret, Alexis and Cloe, are matched at the end of the play, and it is assumed that Amarillis will meet her true love one day. The dishumouring, of course, suggests comical-satire influence.

41. *Works of B. and F.*, Bullen edition, vol. III, p. 9.

42. U. M. Ellis-Fermor: *op. cit.*, p. 211.

43. *Works of B. and F.*, Bullen edition, vol. III, p. 18.

44. Miss Ellis-Fermor speaks of the "middle mood" of our playwrights' tragicomedy as one "which lies, as Fletcher suggests, somewhere between the light heartedness of unshadowed comedy and the apprehension of shock and mystery which attend a tragic catastrophe." Cf. U. M. Ellis-Fermor: *op. cit.*, pp. 204-05.

45. Cf. Chapter IV, p. 109. Fletcher was the first English playwright to express a theory of the nature of tragicomedy. His doing so in connection with *The Faithful Shepherdess* is a circumstance which adds its bit of weight to the probability that this drama was the initial tragicomedy written by any of our playwrights.

46. *Works of B. and F.*, Bullen edition, vol. III, p. 26.

47. *Ibid.*, p. 27.

48. Cf. Chapter V, pp. 161-2.

49. *Works of B. and F.*, Bullen edition, vol. III, p. 28.

50. Cf. Eugene M. Waith: "Characterization in John Fletcher's Tragicomedies," p. 142, for his analysis of the same scene.

51. From the treatment which the love-sick maiden was normally given in Elizabethan literature, it is clear enough that Cloe's desperate efforts to ensnare a lover were intended to have at least a partially comic appeal. The usual prescription suggested for the cure of the virgin longing for sexual experience—whether fully conscious of her desire or not—was marriage.

52. Eugene M. Waith: *op. cit.,* p. 149. Analyses of situations: pp. 148-149.

53. *Ibid.*, p. 150.

54. *Ibid.*, pp. 150-51.

55. Eugene M. Waith: *op. cit.*, p. 142.

56. *Ibid.*, p. 143. This disguising reminds one slightly of the true and false Florimels of *The Faerie Queene.*

57. *Ibid.*, p. 144.

58. *Idem.*

59. *Works of B. and F.*, Glover-Waller edition, vol. I, p. xli.

60. Robert Herrick: *The Hesperides and Noble Numbers,* 2 vols., edited by Alfred Pollard, "The Muses' Library," London and New York, 1898, "An Ode for Him" [Jonson], vol. II, p. 110.

61. *Works of B. and F.*, Glover-Waller edition, vol. I, p. xiv.

62. *Ibid.*, vol. I, p. xxxviii.

63. Gayley supplies an interesting bit of testimony that supports such a conclusion. Applying Thorndike's "ye" (Fletcher) and "you" (Beaumont) test to a number of the collaborated plays, he concluded that the final writing was Beaumont's in *Philaster, The Maid's Tragedy* and *A King and No King*—and in *The Knight of the Burning Pestle* and *The Coxcomb* as well. Cf. Charles Mills Gayley: *op. cit.,* p. 273.

64. *Works of B. and F.*, Bullen edition, vol. I, pp. 123-32, 133, and 118.

65. *Ibid.*, p. 117.

66. John Tucker Murray: *op. cit.,* vol. I, p. 175.

67. W. J. Lawrence, in "The Riddle of Philaster," *Times Literary Supplement*, London, 1921, p. 751, expresses the theory that Fletcher, with the help of some dramatic hack, wrote *Philaster* for one of the companies of boy actors, and that, at the collapse of the company, the King's Men purchased the manuscript and called in Beaumont to rewrite it. I am sceptical of this theory; I see no reason, for instance, to think that *Philaster* preceded *The Faithful Shepherdess* or was written before March, 1608. But if, nonetheless, this was the truth of the matter, I am confident that Beaumont would have worked, in some measure, with Fletcher in the rewriting.

68. Beaumont also appears to have written alone an historical play, *Mador, King of Britain*, which was entered in the Stationers' Register in 1660, but which

is now lost, and probably was not printed. Alfred Harbage: *Annals of the English Drama*, 975-1700, p. 76, lists this play under date of 1606, but gives as limits "c. 1605-1616," and wisely puts a question-mark after Beaumont's name.

69. It could be argued, of course, that Beaumont's other obligations and activities prevented his giving a great deal of attention to playwriting. Even so, he could have been a playwright of relatively few original ideas, but an ideal collaborator. So far as his talents have been revealed by the plays which he wrote or collaborated on, his most native gift seems to have been for comedy of satirical intent.

70. Cf. Chapter IV, pp. 112 and 113.

71. Such, for instance, as the Fletcher-Beaumont *Cupid's Revenge* and the Fletcher-Massinger *The Prophetess*.

NOTES TO CHAPTER SEVEN

1. U. M. Ellis-Fermor: *The Jacobean Drama*, p. 202.
2. *Ibid.*, p. 205.
3. M. C. Bradbrook: *Themes and Conventions of Elizabethan Tragedy*, p. 240.
4. U. M. Ellis-Fermor: *op. cit.*, p. 225.
5. M. C. Bradbrook: *op. cit.*, pp. 240-50.
6. Louis B. Wright: *Middle-Class Culture in Elizabethan England*, Chapel Hill, North Carolina, 1935, p. 610, remarks, à propos of this, that "of all the public theatres, the Globe was the most favored by fashionable theatregoers and well-bred dandies. Attending a play at the Globe or Blackfriars was the smart thing for a social-climbing gallant. . . ."
7. *Works of B. and F.*, Glover-Waller edition, vol. I, p. xlviii.
8. *Ibid.*, vol. I, p. xxvii.
9. *Idem.*
10. *Works of B. and F.*, Glover-Waller edition, vol. I, p. xxxix.
11. *Ibid.*, vol. I, p. xxxvi.
12. *Ibid.*, vol. I, p. xli.
13. *Ibid.*, vol. I, pp. xxxvii-xxxviii.
14. Arthur Mizener: "The High Design of *A King and No King*," *Modern Philology*, XXXVIII (1940-41), pp. 133-54. I had made the same discovery some years before I read his article—which, like Waith's will repay study.
15. Peter Haworth: *An Elizabethan Story-Book: Famous Tales from the Palace of Pleasure*, London and New York, 1928, pp. xiv-xv.
16. Arthur Mizener: *op. cit.*, p. 135.
17. *Ibid.*, p. 135; quoted from *The Quarterly Review*, LXXXIII (1848), p. 349.
18. *Ibid.*, p. 135.
19. *The Essays of John Dryden*, edited by W. P. Ker, vol. I, p. 212. We have already noted, in Chapter I, p. 62, that Dryden considered Fletcher's plots to be "lame," because the latter did not understand correct plotting, nor the "decorum of the stage."
20. Cf. Chapter II, p. 65.
21. Cf. Chapter II, pp. 70-71.
22. Cf. Chapter III, p. 96.
23. Cf. Chapter IV, p. 108.

24. Cf. Chapter IV, p. 115.

25. Cf. Chapter IV, p. 123.

26. M. C. Bradbrook: *op. cit.*, p. 250.

27. *Ibid.*, p. 247.

28. *Ibid.*, p. 245.

29. *Ibid.*, pp. 242-43.

30. Arthur Mizener: *op. cit.*, pp. 153-54.

31. Arthur Mizener: *op. cit.*, p. 153. Since Mizener's article sufficiently analyzes *A King and No King*, I shall not draw upon this tragicomedy as a source of illustration in this chapter. No doubt "the charm of [the] ingenuity" of this apparently massive structure added, as Mizener says, to the excitement of spectators.

32. Dryden applied this phrase to *The Maid's Tragedy*. It is equally valid when transferred to *Valentinian*. Cf. Chapter I, p. 39.

33. Cf. *Works of B. and F.*, Bullen edition, vol. IV, pp. 210-11.

34. Paul Elmer More: "Beaumont and Fletcher," in *With the Wits*, pp. 210-11.

35. Arthur Mizener: *op. cit.*, p. 149, insists that our playwrights' "comic contrasts are clearcut and carefully calculated." If the comedy in *Bonduca* does not altogether appeal to modern taste, it at least measures up to the norm as regards comic contrasts, and was to the taste of many educated Jacobeans.

36. M. C. Bradbrook: *op. cit.*, p. 249.

37. U. M. Ellis-Fermor: *op. cit.*, p. 212.

38. Somerset Maugham: *The Summing Up*, New York, 1938, p. 160.

39. Eugene M. Waith: *op. cit.*, p. 154.

40. U. M. Ellis-Fermor: *op. cit.*, p. 208.

41. Readers who desire to have the handling of characters analyzed, for them, for the full length of a play should read the able treatment of *A Wife for a Month* by Eugene M. Waith: *op. cit.*, pp. 155-64.

42. *Ibid.*, p. 162.

43. Arthur Mizener: *op. cit.*, pp. 141-49, makes a full and able analysis of a scene of this ordering: Act III, scene 1 of *A King and No King*. The particular patterning of this scene is quite different from the one I have chosen to anatomize in *The Maid's Tragedy*, so that the two analyses might well be read together.

44. Eugene M. Waith: *op. cit.*, p. 163.

45. Cf. *ibid.*, p. 162.

46. Act III, scene 2; *Works of B. and F.*, Bullen edition, vol. I, pp. 62-69.

47. *Ibid.*, p. 62, ll. 47-48.

48. *Ibid.*, p. 63, ll. 83-86.

49. *Ibid.*, p. 64, ll. 88-101.

50. *Idem*, ll. 103-09.

51. *Idem*, ll. 112-13.

52. *Ibid.*, p. 65, ll. 120-25.

53. *Idem*, ll. 126-27.

54. *Idem*, ll. 127-29.

55. *Idem*, ll. 138-47.

56. Arthur Mizener: *op. cit.*, p. 144.

57. *Works of B. and F.*, Bullen edition, vol. I, p. 66, ll. 155-57.

58. *Idem*, ll. 163-66.

59. Arthur Mizener: *op. cit.*, p. 151.

60. *Works of B. and F.*, Bullen edition, vol. I, p. 66, ll. 166-71.

61. *Idem*, ll. 172-73.
62. *Idem*, ll. 174-78.
63. *Ibid.*, pp. 66-67, ll. 179-83.
64. *Ibid.*, p. 67, ll. 193-99.
65. *Idem*, l. 200.
66. *Idem*, l. 207.
67. *Ibid.*, pp. 67-68, ll. 213-20.
68. *Ibid.*, p. 68, ll. 221-25.
69. *Idem*, ll. 227-32.
70. *Idem*, ll. 233-40.
71. *Idem*, ll. 240-44.
72. *Ibid.*, pp. 68-69, ll. 244-48.
73. *Ibid.*, p. 69, ll. 248-49.
74. *Idem*, ll. 261-62.
75. *Idem*, ll. 266-67.
76. *Ibid.*, p. 70, ll. 269-72.
77. *Works of B. and F.*, Glover-Waller edition, vol. VII, pp. 130-34.
78. Eugene M. Waith: *op. cit.*, pp. 159-60, has dealt ably with the wedding-night scene of *A Wife for a Month*, which has much the quality of a seduction scene, though it has other aspects as well.
79. *Works of B. and F.*, Glover-Waller edition, vol. VII, p. 133.
80. *Idem*.
81. M. C. Bradbrook: *op. cit.*, p. 60.
82. Arthur Mizener: *op. cit.*, p. 137.
83. Eugene M. Waith: *op. cit.*, p. 156.
84. Arthur Mizener: *op. cit.*, pp. 140, 143.
85. *Works of B. and F.*, Bullen edition, vol. I, pp. 73-79.
86. Howard Baker: *Induction to Tragedy: A Study in a Development of Form in Gorbuduc, The Spanish Tragedy and Titus Andronicus*, University, Louisiana, 1939, p. 167.
87. Eugene M. Waith: *op. cit.*, pp. 163-64.
88. *Ibid.*, p. 164.
89. Cf. Thomas Marc Parrott and Robert Hamilton Ball: *A Short View of Elizabethan Drama*, pp. 196-97. Incidentally, my hearty disagreement with their statement that the structure of *Valentinian* was wrecked by indulgence of sensation will be obvious. Massinger might have toned down the play, as they suggest, but I believe he might also have spoiled the emotional patterning of this baroque tragedy. I agree that the respective shares of *The False One* were wisely assigned.
90. Cf. Chapter IV, pp. 112-116.
91. Arthur Mizener: *op. cit.*, p. 149.
92. M. C. Bradbrook: *op. cit.*, p. 248.
93. *Works of B. and F.*, Glover-Waller edition, vol. I, p. xxxix.
94. U. M. Ellis-Fermor: *op. cit.*, p. 206.
95. Elmer Edgar Stoll: "Source and Motive in *Macbeth* and *Othello*," *The Review of English Studies*, XIX (1943), p. 31.
96. *Idem*, p. 32.
97. This is the motto printed on the title page of the First Folio of 1647. Translated, its meaning is this: "If the prophesies of the poets are true, I shall

live." For three hundred years now the poet-soothsayers have been borne out in their predictions—at least in some measure. The motto can be found in *Works of B. and F.*, Glover-Waller edition, vol. I, p. iii.

NOTES TO APPENDIX

1. Cf. Chapter I, section IV, for an account of the stage history of the plays during the Restoration era.

2. Gerald Eades Bentley, in his *Shakespeare & Jonson*, vol. I, pp. 117-18, points out that the low estimation in which Shakespeare's romantic comedies were held in the seventeenth century "is too conspicuous to ignore." Apparently it was not until these were successfully revived on the stage in the later 1730s that they finally came into their own.

3. George Henry Nettleton: *English Drama of the Restoration and Eighteenth Century*, New York, 1932, p. 173.

4. Frank Humphrey Ristine: *English Tragicomedy*, New York, 1910, p. 189.

5. Allardyce Nicoll: *A History of Early Eighteenth Century Drama, 1700-1750*, Cambridge, England, 1925, pp. 108-09 and 55-56.

6. *Ibid.*, pp. 109 and 56.

7. Arthur Colby Sprague: *Beaumont and Fletcher on the Restoration Stage*, pp. 20-21.

8. Allardyce Nicoll: *op. cit.*, pp. 133-34, 137-38, and 58.

9. Quoted by Arthur Colby Sprague: *op. cit.*, p. 124.

10. *The Complete Works of Henry Fielding*, 16 vols., edited by William Ernest Henley, "Edition deluxe," New York, 1903, vol. XI, p. 268.

11. Allardyce Nicoll: *op. cit.*, pp. 135-36 and 140-41.

12. John Motley: *A List of All the Dramatic Authors, with Some Account of their Lives*, affixed to Thomas Whincop: *Scanderbeg: or, Love and Liberty*, London, 1747.

13. Allardyce Nicoll: *op. cit.*, pp. 137-38 and 59.

14. Henry Fielding: *The Covent Garden Journal*, 2 vols., edited by Gerard Edward Jensen, New Haven, 1915, p. 249. Fielding probably referred to the revival of this play at Drury Lane on October 7 and 10, 1749, after which Garrick never produced it again. Cf. *Drury Lane Calendar, 1747-1776*, compiled by Dougald MacMillan, Oxford, 1938, p. 272. In *The Covent Garden Journal* for February 22, 1752, p. 230, Fielding had satirically remarked that "Beaumont and Fletcher often contented themselves with two Scenes of Wit, and filled the rest with Dullness," because of the "Puerile" and "Vapid" state of their "Grub Street" audience.

15. Theophilus Cibber, in his *Lives of the Poets*, London, 1753, pp. 158-59, confirms this situation, saying that though two plays of our ensemble might have been presented for one of Shakespeare "when Dryden writ, the case is now reversed, for Beaumont and Fletcher's plays are not acted above once a season, while one of Shakespeare's is represented almost every third night."

16. Sybil Rosenfeld: *Strolling Players and Dramas in the Provinces, 1660-1765*, Cambridge, England, 1939, pp. 270, 279, 111.

17. *Ibid.*, p. 71.

18. *Ibid.*, pp. 232, 214, 294.

19. *Ibid.*, pp. 207, 238.

20. *Ibid.*, pp. 187, 201, 203.

21. Oliver Goldsmith: *The Vicar of Wakefield*, London, 1766, chapter XVIII.

22. p. 78; quoted in Robert Gale Noyes: *Ben Jonson on the English Stage, 1660-1776*, p. 31.

23. Oliver Goldsmith: *An Inquiry into the Present State of Polite Learning in Europe*, in *The Works of Oliver Goldsmith*, 12 vols., edited by Peter Cunningham, Boston and New York, n.d., vol. III, chapter XI, pp. 67-68.

24. George Colman: "Critical Reflections on the Old English Dramatic Writers," in *The Dramatic Works of Philip Massinger*, 4 vols., edited by Thomas Coxeter, London, 1761, vol. I, and in George Colman: *Prose on Several Occasions*, 2 vols., London, 1787, vol. II.

25. *Idem.*

26. *Drury Lane Calendar, 1747-1776*, pp. 322, 272, 324, 304, 329.

27. *Ibid.*, pp. 217-18, 319-20.

28. *Ibid.*, pp. 253-56, 242-43.

29. Eugene R. Page: *George Colman the Elder*, New York, 1935, pp. 90-91.

30. *Drury Lane Calendar*, pp. 303-04.

31. Sybil Rosenfeld: *op. cit.*, p. 161.

32. Frank Humphrey Ristine: *op. cit.*, p. 189.

33. *The Dramatic Works of George Colman*, 4 vols., London, 1777, sigs. B2, B3.

34. Eugene R. Page: *op. cit.*, pp. 91-92. He confirms my own examination of the alteration.

35. *Ibid.*, pp. 253-54.

36. Allardyce Nicoll: *Dryden as an Adapter of Shakespeare*, p. 7.

37. Richard H. Barker: *Mr. Cibber of Drury Lane*, New York, 1939, pp. 33, 45, 108, 130-31.

38. Allardyce Nicoll: *A History of Early Eighteenth Century Drama, 1700-1750*, pp. 139-40.

39. Allardyce Nicoll: *A History of Late Eighteenth Century Drama, 1750-1800*, Cambridge, England, 1927, pp. 112-13.

40. Thomas Davies: *Dramatic Miscellanies*, 2 vols., London, 1784, vol. II, p. 386. Charles Harold Gray: *Theatrical Criticism in London to 1795*, New York, 1931, tells us, on p. 219, of an anonymous critic of strong moralistic tendencies who wrote in *The General Evening Post* (season of 1772-73) about his sense of shock at "the immorality as well as silliness" of *Rule a Wife*. Although this particular comedy still had much life in its old bones for the stage, the critic's attitude may well be indicative of why other plays of our ensemble fell by the wayside.

41. Charles Lamb: "On the Tragedies of Shakespeare, Considered with Reference to their Fitness for Stage Representation," in *The Dramatic Essays of Charles Lamb*, edited by Brander Matthews, New York, 1891, pp. 163-196. Samuel Johnson had maintained that "Many of Shakespeare's plays are the worse for being acted: Macbeth, for instance." Cf. Joseph Wood Krutch: *Samuel Johnson*, New York, 1944, p. 277.

42. *The Works of Beaumont and Fletcher*, 14 vols., edited by Henry Weber, Edinburgh and London, 1812, vol. I, "Introduction," p. ci.

43. John Genest: *Some Account of the English Stage, 1660-1830,* 10 vols., Bath, 1832, vol. VI, p. 41.

44. *The Works of Beaumont and Fletcher,* 2 vols., edited by Rev. Alexander Dyce, Boston and New York, 1854, vol. I, pp. 34, 37. The first edition, in 11 volumes, was published in London, 1843-46.

45. G. C. Macaulay: *Francis Beaumont,* London, 1883, p. 127.

46. Anna Irene Miller: *The Independent Theatre in Europe, 1887 to the Present,* New York, 1931, pp. 183-88.

47. Herbert S. Murch, in his edition of *The Knight of the Burning Pestle,* New York, 1908, pp. xvi-xx, shows that this burlesque, unsuccessful at its premiere (in 1607), had some popularity with the Caroline gentry about 1635-40, and that it was given in Restoration days, before 1671, with the glamourous Nell Gwyn acting in it. Then it vanished for good from the professional theatre.

Bibliography

This bibliography does not aim at completeness; it simply lists, in alphabetical order, the books and articles referred to in the text and notes. Readers desiring further bibliographical information about Fletcher, Beaumont and Company should consult Samuel A. Tannenbaum: Beaumont and Fletcher (A Concise Bibliography), "Elizabethan Bibliographies Number 3," and Philip Massinger (A Concise Bibliography), "Elizabethan Bibliographies Number 4," New York, 1938. The listing that follows, however, contains a number of items not included in the Tannenbaum bibliographies, and so may usefully supplement them.

Adams, John Cranford: The Globe Playhouse: Its Design and Equipment. Cambridge, Mass., 1943.
Adams, Joseph Quincy: A Life of William Shakespeare. Boston and New York, 1925.
——Shakespearean Playhouses, A History of English Theatres from the Beginnings to the Restoration. Boston and New York, 1917.
Addison, Joseph and Steele, Richard: The Spectator. 8 vols., in 4, Everyman's Library Edition, London and New York, n.d.
Allen, Ned Bliss: The Sources of Dryden's Comedies. "University of Michigan Studies in Language and Literature," XVI, Ann Arbor, 1935.
Archer, William: The Old Drama and the New. Boston, 1923.
Aubrey, John: Brief Lives (etc.), edited by Andrew Clark. 2 vols., Oxford, 1898.
Baker, Howard: Induction to Tragedy: A Study in a Development of Form in Gorbuduc, The Spanish Tragedy and Titus Andronicus. University, Louisiana, 1939.
Bald, R. C.: Bibliographical Studies in the Beaumont and Fletcher Folio of 1647. Oxford, 1938.
Ball, Robert Hamilton: The Amazing Career of Sir Giles Overreach. Princeton, N. J., and London, 1939.
Barker, Richard H.: Mr. Cibber of Drury Lane. New York, 1939.
Bathurst, C.: Remarks on Shakespeare's Versification. London, 1857.
Beaumont and Fletcher: The Best Plays of Beaumont and Fletcher, edited by J. St. Loe Strachey. "The Mermaid Series," 2 vols., London, 1887.
——The Dramatic Works of Ben Jonson, and of Beaumont and Fletcher, edited respectively by Peter Whalley and George Colman. 4 vols., London, 1811. Vols. II to IV are devoted to Beaumont and Fletcher.

——The Knight of the Burning Pestle by Beaumont and Fletcher, edited by Herbert S. Murch. New York, 1908.
—— The Lyric Poems of Beaumont and Fletcher, edited by Ernest Rhys. London, 1897.
—— The Works of Francis Beaumont and John Fletcher, edited by A. H. Bullen. Variorum Edition, 4 vols., London, 1904-12.
—— The Works of Beaumont and Fletcher, with an introduction by George Darley. 2 vols., London, 1883 ("new edition"). (First edition: London, 1839).
—— The Works of Beaumont and Fletcher, edited by Rev. Alexander Dyce. 2 vols., Boston and New York, 1854. (First edition: 11 vols., London, 1843-46).
—— The Works of Francis Beaumont and John Fletcher, edited by Arnold Glover and A. R. Waller. 10 vols., "Cambridge English Classics," Cambridge, England, 1905-12.
—— The Works of Beaumont and Fletcher, edited by Henry Weber. 14 vols., Edinburgh and London, 1812.
Bentley, Gerald Eades: The Jacobean and Caroline Stage. 2 vols., Oxford, 1941.
—— Shakespeare & Jonson: Their Reputations in the Seventeenth Century Compared. 2 vols., Chicago, 1945.
Biographia Britannica. 2 vols., London, 1747, 1766.
Biographia Dramatica, edited by David E. Baker (1764), Isaac Reed (1782), and Stephen Jones (1812). Jones edition, London, 1812.
——, reviewed in *The Quarterly Review*, VII (June, 1812), p. 282.
Blair, Hugh: Lectures on Rhetoric and Belles Lettres. Eighth American edition, New York, 1819. (First published in 1759).
Blount, T. P.: De Re Poetica. London, 1694.
Boyle, Robert: Articles on the authorship of "Beaumont and Fletcher" plays. *Englische Studien,* as follows: V (1882), 74-96; VII (1884), 66-86; VIII (1885), 39-61; IX (1886), 209-39; X (1887), 383-411.
Bradbrook, M. C.: Elizabethan Stage Conditions. Cambridge, England, 1932.
Brooke, Rupert: John Webster and the Elizabethan Drama. London, 1916.
Butler, Samuel: The Poetical Works of Samuel Butler, edited by Richard Brimley Johnson. "The Aldine Edition of the Poets," 2 vols., London, 1895.
Campbell, Oscar James: Comicall Satyre and Shakespeare's Troilus and Cressida. San Marino, Calif., 1938.
—— Shakespeare's Satire. London, New York and Toronto, 1943.
Chambers, E. K.: The Elizabethan Stage. 4 vols., Oxford, 1923.
Chapman, George: The Plays and Poems of George Chapman: The Comedies, edited by Thomas Marc Parrott. London and New York, 1914.
Chelli, Maurice: Le Drame de Massinger. Lyon, France, 1923.
Chetwood, W. R.: The British Theatre. London, 1652.
Chew, Samuel C.: Swinburne. Boston, 1929.
Cibber, Theophilus: The Lives of the Poets. London, 1753.
Clark, Ray Benjamin: William Gifford, Tory Satirist, Critic, and Editor. New York, 1930.
Clarke, Charles Cowden: "On the Comic Writers of England," *The Gentleman's Magazine*, n.s., VII (1871), p. 48.
Cobb, Margaret E.: "Pope's Lines on Atticus." *Modern Language Notes*, XXXVI (1921), 350-351.

Cockaine, Sir Aston: Small Poems of Divers Sorts. London, 1658.

Coleridge, Samuel Taylor: Coleridge's Shakespeare Criticism, edited by Thomas Middleton Raysor. 2 vols., London, 1930.

———— Lectures and Notes on Shakspere and Other English Poets, collected by T. Ashe. Bohn's Standard Library, London, 1904.

Collier, Jeremy: A Short View of the Immorality and Profaneness of the English Stage. London, 1698. (Third edition).

Collins, William: The Poetry of William Collins, edited by Christopher Stone. London, 1907.

Colman, George: Critical Reflections on the Old English Writers, in The Dramatic Works of Philip Massinger, edited by Thomas Coxeter, vol. I. 4 vols., London, 1761.

———— The Dramatic Works of George Colman. 4 vols., London, 1777.

———— Prose on Several Occasions. 2 vols., London, 1761.

Cowley, Abraham: The Poems of Abraham Cowley, edited by A. R. Waller. Cambridge, England, 1905.

Craik, George L.: A Compendious History of English Literature and the English Language. 6 vols., New York, 1845.

Critical Essays of the Eighteenth Century, 1700-1725, edited by William Higley Durham. New Haven, 1915.

Cruikshank, A. H.: Philip Massinger. New York, n.d. [1920].

Daniel, Samuel: The Poetical Works of Mr. Samuel Daniel. 2 vols., London, 1718.

Davies, Thomas: Dramatic Miscellanies. 2 vols., London, 1784.

Denham, Sir John: The Poetical Works of Sir John Denham, edited by Theodore Howard Banks, Jr. New Haven, 1928.

Dennis, John: The Critical Works of John Dennis, edited by Edward Niles Hooker. 2 vols., Baltimore, Md., 1939 and 1943.

Dibdin, Charles: A Complete History of the Stage. London, 1800.

Dodsley, Robert: A Select Collection of Old English Plays, edited by W. C. Hazlitt. 15 vols., London, 1874.

Donne, William Bodham: Essays on the Drama. London, 1858. The essay on Beaumont and Fletcher was reprinted from *Fraser's Magazine* for March, 1850.

Drake, James: The Antient and Modern Stages survey'd. London, 1699.

Drake, Nathan: Shakespeare and His Times. Paris, 1838. (First edition: London, 1819).

Drury Lane Calendar, 1747-1776, compiled by Dougald MacMillan. Oxford, 1938.

Dryden, John: The Best Plays of John Dryden, edited by George Saintsbury. "The Mermaid Series," 2 vols., London and New York, n.d.

———— The Essays of John Dryden, edited by W. P. Ker. 2 vols., Oxford, 1900.

———— The Works of John Dryden, edited by Sir Walter Scott and George Saintsbury. 18 vols., London, 1892.

Dunham, S. A.: Lives of the Most Eminent Literary and Scientific Men of Great Britain, in The Cabinet Cyclopedia, edited by Rev. Dionysius Lardner. 3 vols., London, 1837.

Dunkel, Wilbur Daniel: The Dramatic Technique of Thomas Middleton in his Comedies of London Life. Chicago, 1925. University of Chicago dissertation.

Eliot, T. S.: Selected Essays, 1917-1932. New York, 1932.

Ellis-Fermor, U. M.: The Jacobean Drama: An Interpretation. London, 1936.

Ferriar, John, M. D.: Essay on the Dramatic Writings of Massinger (1786), in The Plays of Philip Massinger, edited by William Gifford, vol. I. Second edition, 4 vols., London, 1813.

Fielding, Henry: The Complete Works of Henry Fielding, edited by William Ernest Henley. "Edition de Luxe," 16 vols., New York, 1903.

———The Covent Garden Journal, edited by Gerard Edward Jensen. 2 vols., New Haven, 1915.

Fleay, F. G.: "On Metrical Tests as Applied to Dramatic Poetry: Part II. Fletcher, Beaumont, Massinger." The New Shakspere Society Transactions, Series I, 1 (1874), London.

——— "On the Chronology of the Plays of Fletcher and Massinger." Englische Studien, IX (1886), pp. 12-35.

Flecknoe, Richard: A Discourse of the English Stage (1664). In W. C. Hazlitt: The English Drama and Stage. London, 1869.

Fletcher, John, Massinger, Philip, and Field, Nathan: The Knight of Malta, edited with introduction and notes by Marianne Brock. Bryn Mawr, Pennsylvania, 1944. Bryn Mawr College Dissertation.

Fletcher and Massinger: The Tragedy of Sir John Van Olden Barnavelt, edited by Wilhelmina P. Frijlinck. Amsterdam, Holland, 1922. (Distrbuted by the Oxford University Press).

Forsythe, Robert: The Relations of Shirley's Plays to the Elizabethan Drama. New York, 1914.

Fuller, Thomas: The Histories of the Worthies of England. 3 vols., London, (1662) 1840.

Gayley, Charles Mills: Beaumont the Dramatist. New York, 1914.

Genest, John: Some Account of the English Stage, 1660-1830. 10 vols., Bath, 1832.

Gildon, Charles: The Life of Thomas Betterton. London, 1710.

——— Lives and Characters of the English Dramatick Poets. London, 1699.

——— Some Reflections on Mr. Rymer's Short View of Tragedy. London, 1694.

Gilfillan, George: A Third Gallery of Portraits. London, 1855.

Goldsmith, Oliver: An Inquiry into the Present State of Polite Learning in Europe. In The Works of Oliver Goldsmith, edited by Peter Cunningham. 12 vols., Boston and New York, n.d.

——— The Vicar of Wakefield. London, 1766.

Gosse, Edmund: The Jacobean Poets. New York, 1894.

Gray, Charles Harold: Theatrical Criticism in London to 1795. New York, 1931.

Green, Clarence C.: The Neo-Classic Theory of Tragedy in England During the Eighteenth Century. Cambridge, Mass., 1934.

Greg, W. W.: Pastoral Poetry and Pastoral Drama: A Literary Inquiry, with Special Reference to the Pre-Restoration Stage in England. London, 1906.

Grierson, H. J. C.: Cross Currents in English Literature of the XVIIth Century. London, 1929.

Hallam, Henry: Introduction to the Literature of Europe in the Fifteenth, Sixteenth, and Seventeenth Centuries. 2 vols., New York, 1841. (First edition: London, 1837).

Harbage, Alfred: Annals of the English Drama, 975 to 1700. London, 1940.

——— Cavalier Drama: An Historical and Critical Supplement to the Study of the Elizabethan and Restoration Stage. New York and London, 1936.

────── Shakespeare's Audience. New York, 1941.

Hatcher, Orie Latham: John Fletcher: A Study in Dramatic Method. Chicago, 1905. University of Chicago dissertation.

Haworth, Peter: An Elizabethan Story-Book: Famous Tales from The Palace of Pleasure. London and New York, 1928.

Hazlitt, William: The Complete Works of William Hazlitt, edited by P. P. Howe. Centenary Edition, 21 vols., London and Toronto, 1931. Especially, vol. VI: Lectures on the Age of Elizabeth, and on the English Comic Writers.

Herbert, Sir Henry: The Dramatic Records of Sir Herbert Henry, Master of the Revels, edited by Joseph Quincy Adams. "Cornell Studies in English," III, New Haven, 1917.

Herrick, Robert: The Hesperides and Noble Numbers, edited by Alfred Pollard. "The Muses' Library," 2 vols., London and New York, 1898.

Heywood, Thomas: The Hierarchie of the Blessed Angells. London, 1634.

Hill, Aaron: The Dramatic Works of Aaron Hill, Esq., London, 1760.

Hillebrand, Harold Newcomb: The Child Actors: A Chapter in Elizabethan Stage History. "University of Illinois Studies in Language and Literature," XI, Urbana, Ill., 1926.

Hotson, Leslie: The Commonwealth and Restoration Stage. Cambridge, Mass., 1928.

Howard, Edward: The Women's Conquest. London, 1671.

Hunt, Leigh: Beaumont and Fletcher; or, The Finest Scenes, Lyrics, and other Beauties of these two Poets, Now first Selected from the Whole of their Works, To the Exclusion of whatever is Morally Objectionable. London, 1862.

────── The Correspondence of Leigh Hunt, edited by his own son [Thornton Hunt]. 2 vols., London, 1862.

────── Imagination and Fancy. Fourth edition, London, 1871.

────── A Jar of Honey. London, 1897.

Hurd, Richard: Hurd's Letters on Chivalry and Romance, with the third Elizabethan Dialogue, edited by Edith J. Morley. London, 1911.

────── The Correspondence of Richard Hurd and William Mason, edited by the Rev. Ernest Harold Pearce. Cambridge, England, 1932.

Isaacs, J.: Production and Stage-Management at the Blackfriars theatre. Pamphlet published for The Shakespeare Association, London, 1933.

Jacob, Giles: The Poetical Register. London, 1723.

Jones, Richard Foster: Lewis Theobald. New York, 1919.

Jonson, Ben: Ben Jonson: The Man and His Work, edited by C. H. Herford and Percy Simpson. 2 vols., Oxford, 1925.

────── Conversations with William Drummond of Hawthornden, 1619, edited by G. B. Harrison. Bodley Head Quartos no. 5, London and New York, 1923.

The Jonson Allusion Book, edited by Jesse F. Bradley and Joseph Q. Adams. New Haven, 1922.

Jonsonus Virbius, or The Memorie of Ben Jonson Revived. London, 1638.

Kerr, Mina: Influence of Ben Jonson on English Comedy, 1598-1642. New York, 1912.

Krutch, Joseph Wood: Samuel Johnson. New York, 1944.

Lamb, Charles: The Dramatic Essays of Charles Lamb, edited by Brander Mathews. New York, 1891.

────── The Essays of Elia, edited by Alfred Ainger. London and New York, 1903.

────── The Works of Charles and Mary Lamb, edited by E. V. Lucas. 7 vols., London, 1904. Especially, vol. IV: Dramatic Specimens and The Garrick Plays.

Langbaine, Gerald: An Account of the English Dramatick Poets. Oxford, 1691.

Lawrence, William J.: Pre-Restoration Stage Studies. Cambridge, Mass., 1927.

────── "The Riddle of Philaster." *Times Literary Supplement*, London, 1921, p. 751.

Lee, Nathaniel: The Dramatic Works of Mr. Nathaniel Lee. 3 vols., London, 1734.

Lewis, Edward Danby: John Fletcher: His Distinctive Structural and Stylistic Contribution to English Drama. Unpublished dissertation, Yale University.

A Little Ark, Containing Sundry Pieces of Seventeenth-Century Verse, edited by G. Thorn-Drury. London, 1921.

Lynch, Kathleen M.: The Social Mode of Restoration Comedy. "University of Michigan Studies in Language and Literature," III, New York and London, 1926.

Macaulay, G. C.: Chapter on Beaumont and Fletcher (vol. VI, chap. 5), in Cambridge History of English Literature, edited by A. W. Ward . . . and A. R. Waller . . . 14 vols., Cambridge, England, 1907-16.

────── Francis Beaumont. London, 1883.

Macaulay, Thomas Babington: "The Comedy of the Restoration," reprinted in Readings in English Prose of the Nineteenth Century, edited by R. M. Alden. Boston, 1917.

McAfee, Helen: Pepys on the Restoration Stage. New Haven, 1916.

McGinn, Donald Joseph: Shakespeare's Influence on the Drama of his Age, Studied in Hamlet. New Brunswick, N. J., 1938.

McKeithan, Daniel Morley: The Debt to Shakespeare in the Beaumont-and-Fletcher Plays. Austin, Texas, 1938.

Mallet, Charles Edward: A History of Oxford University. 3 vols., New York, 1924.

Malone, Edmond: The Plays and Poems of William Shakespeare. 21 vols., London, 1821 edition.

Marcham, George Frederick: A History of England. New York, 1937.

Marston, John: The Works of John Marston, edited by A. H. Bullen. 3 vols., London, 1887.

Mason, J. Monck: The Dramatic Works of J. Monck Mason. London, 1779.

────── Comments on the Plays of Beaumont and Fletcher. London, 1798. (First edition: 1797).

Massinger, Philip: The Plays of Philip Massinger, edited by William Gifford. Second edition, 4 vols., London, 1813.

Maugham, Somerset: The Summing Up. New York, 1938.

Maxwell, Baldwin: Studies in Beaumont, Fletcher, and Massinger. Chapel Hill, North Carolina, 1939.

Middleton, Thomas: The Works of Thomas Middleton, edited by A. H. Bullen. 8 vols., London, 1885.

Miller, Anna Irene: The Independent Theatre in Europe, 1887 to the Present. New York, 1931.

Minto, William: Characteristics of English Poets from Chaucer to Shirley. 2nd edition, Edinburgh and London, 1855.

Mizener, Arthur: "The High Design of *A King and No King.*" *Modern Philology,* XXXVIII (1940-41), pp. 133-154.

More, Paul Elmer: With the Wits, "Beaumont and Fletcher," pp. 1-40. Shelburne Essays, Tenth Series, Boston and New York, 1919.

Motley, John: A List of All Dramatic Authors, with some Account of Their Lives. Affixed to Whincop, Thomas: Scanderbeg: or, Love and Liberty. London, 1747.

Mullinger, James Bass: The University of Cambridge from the Royal Injunctions of 1535 to The Accession of Charles I. Cambridge, England, 1884.

Murray, John Tucker: English Dramatic Companies, 1558-1642. 2 vols., Boston, 1910.

Murray, Middleton: Shakespeare. New York, 1936.

Nettleton, George Henry: English Drama of the Restoration and Eighteenth Century. New York, 1932.

Neve, Philip: Cursory Remarks on Some of the Ancient English Poets. London, 1789.

Nicoll, Allardyce: Dryden as an Adapter of Shakespeare. London, 1922.

―――― A History of Early Eighteenth Century Drama, 1700-1750. Cambridge, England, 1925.

―――― A History of Late Eighteenth Century Drama, 1750-1800. Cambridge, England, 1927.

―――― A History of Early Nineteenth Century Drama. 2 vols., New York, 1930.

Noyes, Robert Gale: Ben Jonson on the English Stage, 1660-1776. Cambridge, Mass., 1935.

Oliphant, E. H. C.: Articles on the authorship of "Beaumont and Fletcher" plays. *Englische Studien,* as follows: XIV (1890), 53-94; XV (1891), 321-60; XVI (1892), 180-200.

―――― The Plays of Beaumont and Fletcher: An Attempt to Determine Their Respective Shares and the Shares of Others. New Haven and London, 1927.

Page, Eugene R.: George Colman the Elder. New York, 1935.

Parrott, Thomas Marc, and Ball, Robert Hamilton: A Short View of Elizabethan Drama. New York, 1943.

Phillips, James Edward, Jr.: The State in Shakespeare's Greek and Roman Plays. New York, 1940.

Poetry of the English Renaissance, 1509-1660, edited by J. William Hebel and Hoyt H. Hudson. New York, 1929.

Prynne, William: Histrio-Mastix (etc.). London, 1633 [1632].

Ralli, August: A History of Shakespearian Criticism. 2 vols., Oxford, 1932.

Ristine, Frank Humphrey: English Tragicomedy: Its Origin and History. New York, 1910.

Rollins, Hyder E.: "A Contribution to the History of English Commonwealth Drama." *Studies in Philology,* XVIII (1921), 267-333.

Rosenfeld, Sybil: Strolling Players and Dramas in the Provinces, 1660-1765. Cambridge, England, 1939.

Ross, Malcolm MacKenzie: Milton's Royalism: A Study of the Conflict of Symbol and Idea in the Poems. "Cornell University Studies in English," XXXIV, Ithaca, N. Y., 1943.

Rymer, Thomas: A Short View of English Tragedy. London, 1693.

—— The Tragedies of the last Age Considered. London, 1678.

Sampson, M. W.: Review of Thorndike, Ashley H.: The Influence of Beaumont and Fletcher on Shakspere. *The Journal of Germanic Philology*, IV, no. 2 (1902), pp. 241-42.

Samuels, Arthur P. I.: The Early Life Correspondence and Writings of the Rt. Hon. Edmund Burke. Cambridge, England, 1923.

Schelling, Felix E.: Foreign Influences in Elizabethan Plays. New York and London, 1923.

Scott, Sir Walter: An Essay on the Drama. In The Prose Works of Sir Walter Scott, vol. VI. 28 vols., Edinburgh, 1861.

Shakespeare, William: The Plays of William Shakespeare, edited by Samuel Johnson and George Steevens. Fourth edition, 15 vols., London, 1793.

Shirley, James: The Dramatic Works and Poems of James Shirley, edited by Rev. Alexander Dyce. 6 vols., London, 1833.

Sidney, Sir Philip: The Defense of Poesy, edited by Albert C. Cook. Boston, 1890.

Spencer, Benjamin Townley: "Philip Massinger." Published in Seventeenth Century Studies by Members of the Graduate School, University of Cincinnati, edited by Robert Shafer. Princeton, N. J., 1933.

Spencer, Hazelton: The Art and Life of William Shakespeare. New York, 1940.

Spenser, Edmund: The Works of Edmund Spenser, a Variorum Edition, edited by Greenlaw, Osgood, Padelford and others. 7 vols. to date, Baltimore, Md., 1932—.

Spingarn, Joel E., editor: Critical Essays of the Seventeenth Century. 3 vols., Oxford, 1908.

Sprague, Arthur Colby: Beaumont and Fletcher on the Restoration Stage. Cambridge, Mass., 1926.

Steele, Richard: The Tatler. 6 vols., London, 1786.

Stoll, Elmer Edgar: "Source and Motive in *Macbeth* and *Othello.*" *The Review of English Studies*, XIX (1943), pp. 25-32.

Swinburne, A. C.: Contemporaries of Shakespeare, edited by Edmund Gosse and Thomas James Wise. London, 1919. The essay on Beaumont and Fletcher also appears in *The English Review*, V (1910), pp. 202-16.

—— Studies in Prose and Poetry. London, 1894.

Tillyard, E. M. W.: Shakespeare's Last Plays. London, 1938.

Thorndike,. Ashley H.: The Influence of Beaumont and Fletcher on Shakspere. Worcester, Mass., 1901.

Vaughan, Henry: The Works of Henry Vaughan, edited by Leonard Cyril Martin. 2 vols., London, 1914.

Villiers, George, Duke of Buckingham: The Rehearsal. London, 1672.

Waith, Eugene M.: "Characterization in John Fletcher's Tragicomedies." *The Review of English Studies*, XIX (1943), pp. 141-64.

Wallace, Charles William: The Children of the Chapel at Blackfriars, 1597-1603. Lincoln, Nebraska, 1908.

Ward, Adolphus William: A History of English Dramatic Literature to the Death of Queen Anne. 3 vols., new and revised edition, London, 1899. (First edition: 2 vols., London, 1875).

Warren, Austin: "Pope's Index to Beaumont and Fletcher." *Modern Language Notes,* XLVI (1931), 515-517.

Watkins, W. B. C.: Johnson and English Poetry Before 1660. Princeton, N. J., 1936.

Webster, John: The Complete Works of John Webster, edited by F. L. Lucas. 4 vols., London, 1928.

Wells, Henry W.: Elizabethan and Jacobean Playwrights. New York, 1939.

Whipple, Edwin P.: Essays and Reviews. Fifth edition, 2 vols., Boston, 1871.

────── The Literature of the Age of Elizabeth. Boston, 1869.

Wilmot, John: The Collected Works of John Wilmot, Earl of Rochester, edited by John Haywood. London, 1926.

Wilson, John H.: The Influence of Beaumont and Fletcher on the Restoration Stage. Columbus, Ohio, 1928.

Winstanley, William: Lives of the Most Famous English Poets. London, 1687.

The Wits, or Sport Upon Sport, edited by John James Elson. "Cornell Studies in English," XVIII, Ithaca, N. Y., 1932.

Wright, James: Historia Histrionica: A Dialogue of Plays and Players. London, 1699. In Robert Dodsley: A Select Collection of Old English Plays, vol. 15.

Wright, Louis B.: Middle-Class Culture in Elizabethan England. Chapel Hill, North Carolina, 1935.

Young, Edward: Conjectures on Original Composition, 1759, edited by Edith J. Morley. "Modern Language Texts, English Series," London, 1918.

Index

(Prepared with the painstaking and generous assistance of Barrett and Elizabeth Davis, and my wife.)